Wealth of Persons

VERITAS
Series Introduction

". . . the truth will set you free" (John 8:32)

In much contemporary discourse, Pilate's question has been taken to mark the absolute boundary of human thought. Beyond this boundary, it is often suggested, is an intellectual hinterland into which we must not venture. This terrain is an agnosticism of thought: because truth cannot be possessed, it must not be spoken. Thus, it is argued that the defenders of "truth" in our day are often traffickers in ideology, merchants of counterfeits, or anti-liberal. They are, because it is somewhat taken for granted that Nietzsche's word is final: truth is the domain of tyranny.

Is this indeed the case, or might another vision of truth offer itself? The ancient Greeks named the love of wisdom as *philia*, or friendship. The one who would become wise, they argued, would be a "friend of truth." For both philosophy and theology might be conceived as schools in the friendship of truth, as a kind of relation. For like friendship, truth is as much discovered as it is made. If truth is then so elusive, if its domain is *terra incognita*, perhaps this is because it arrives to us—unannounced—as gift, as a person, and not some thing.

The aim of the Veritas book series is to publish incisive and original current scholarly work that inhabits "the between" and "the beyond" of theology and philosophy. These volumes will all share a common aspiration to transcend the institutional divorce in which these two disciplines often find themselves, and to engage questions of pressing concern to both philosophers and theologians in such a way as to reinvigorate both disciplines with a kind of interdisciplinary desire, often so absent in contemporary academe. In a word, these volumes represent collective efforts in the befriending of truth, doing so beyond the simulacra of pretend tolerance, the violent, yet insipid reasoning of liberalism that asks with Pilate, "What is truth?"—expecting a consensus of non-commitment; one that encourages the commodification of the mind, now sedated by the civil service of career, ministered by the frightened patrons of position.

The series will therefore consist of two "wings": (1) original monographs; and (2) essay collections on a range of topics in theology and philosophy. The latter will principally be the products of the annual conferences of the Centre of Theology and Philosophy (www.theologyphilosophycentre .co.uk).

Conor Cunningham and Eric Austin Lee, *Series editors*

Wealth of Persons

Economics with a Human Face

JOHN McNERNEY

Foreword by David Walsh

CASCADE *Books* · Eugene, Oregon

WEALTH OF PERSONS
Economics with a Human Face

Veritas

Cascade Books
An Imprint of Wipf and Stock Publishers
199 W. 8th Ave., Suite 3
Eugene, OR 97401

www.wipfandstock.com

PAPERBACK ISBN: 978-1-4982-2993-7
HARDCOVER ISBN: 978-1-4982-2995-1
EBOOK ISBN: 978-1-4982-2994-4

Cataloguing-in-Publication data:

Names: McNerney, John. | Walsh, David, foreword.

Title: Wealth of persons : economics with a human face / John McNerney ; foreword by David Walsh.

Description: Eugene, OR: Cascade Books, 2016 | Veritas | Includes bibliographical
references and index.

Identifiers: ISBN 978-1-4982-2993-7 (paperback) | ISBN 978-1-4982-2995-1 (hard-
cover) | ISBN 978-1-4982-2994-4 (ebook)

Subjects: LCSH: Capitalism—Moral and ethical aspects. | Christianity and poli-
tics–Catholic Church. | Global Financial Crisis, 2008–2009. | Economics—So-
ciological aspects. | Capitalism—Social aspects.

Classification: HB523 .M40 2016 (print) | HB523 .M40 (ebook)

Manufactured in the U.S.A.   AUGUST 29, 2016

For Ashley Donohoe, Olivia Burke, Eoghan Culligan, Lorcán Miller, Eimear Walsh, and Niccolai Schuster, who died in the Berkeley tragedy in California, and for those who were injured.

For Tom O'Gorman, whose life unfolded for me the wealth, beauty, and truth of what it means to be a human person.

And for Michéal Mannion. Ar dheis Dé go raibh a anam.

How does someone judge which is his right and which his left hand? How do I know that my judgment will agree with someone else's? How do I know that this colour is blue? If I don't trust *myself* here, why should I trust anyone else's judgment? Is there a why? Must I not begin to trust somewhere? That is to say: somewhere I must begin with not-doubting; and that is not, so to speak, hasty but excusable: it is part of judging.

—LUDWIG WITTGENSTEIN

Contents

Foreword

JOHN MCNERNEY'S *WEALTH OF Persons* is a highly readable and innovative contribution to a much wider debate on economics and the economy. The Great Recession, whose long aftereffects we are still enduring, has occasioned considerable soul-searching among professional economists, policymakers, and the broader public. Have the assumptions that had underpinned the long period of real economic growth since the Second World War lost their salience? Awareness of growing inequalities within contemporary capitalist societies have shaken the consensus on which decades of harmony has been based. The attention paid to Thomas Piketty's bestselling indictment of the failure of economics and economies is reflective of the social mood. It is into this setting that John McNerney offers a very different approach, one informed by a philosophical and Christian understanding of the person that challenges the very terms of the debate. Rarely have the times been so ripe for a work that opens up an alternative perspective to what has prevailed in the mainstream.

Without proposing a revision in economic theory, McNerney has succeeded in enlarging the horizon within which such questions are addressed. He suggests that economics is not about material prosperity and participation in its benefits, but is primarily about persons. He challenges the materialist model that even today paralyzes our thinking about economic issues. Yet he does not jettison the profit motive as irrelevant, nor does he engage in utopian dreaming about social transformation. Instead, McNerney simply reminds us of the abstraction that is contemporary economic thought and policy. He shows that although tangible returns may be an important motivator, they are not the motivation for human activity. Rarely do we think of ourselves as profit-maximizers, for we are continually balancing rewards against myriad other factors that are more important to us. We want to lead full human lives and spend time with friends and family, even when it means that we make less money. All of this is known at a common-sense level. What McNerney has done is demonstrate how this also explains economic activity.

He shows how the labor theory of value of the classical economists, from Smith to Ricardo and Marx, has been superseded by the more concrete analysis of the Austrian School. Von Mises and Hayek, and eventually Schumpeter, understood that economic decisions must be understood in human terms rather than pseudo-objective abstractions. Everything turns on what individual human beings are thinking when they engage, not just in transactions, but in economic planning. Price and its incentives are quite important in this context but only as a way of aggregating the different perspectives in a market. It is always up to individuals, producers and consumers, to make their own responses. This is the setting in which human creativity comes to the fore. In a very valuable central section of the work, McNerney reviews the analysis of entrepreneurship, the factor that is so crucial and yet so often overlooked. This is where his analysis really shines because, unlike standard approaches, McNerney understands well the centrality of the person in social events. To reduce it to the crass calculation of returns utterly misses the essential aspects, for it is in creativity that the real enlargement of the person occurs. The entrepreneur is the one who is able to step outside of his or her circumstances and visualize something quite different. The hardships and risks the entrepreneur is willing to bear are often out of all proportion to the likelihood of reward. As Warren Buffett remarked, his was the kind of job that he would do even if no one paid him for it. The excitement of creation far outweighs anything purely material. Economics is thus at its core a spiritual activity, and McNerney gives us an intriguing case study of Agnes Morrogh-Bernard, who founded Foxford Mills in Mayo more than a hundred years ago. Contrary to the image of the church as primarily concerned with sharing wealth, it turns out that it can also venture into the heart of its creation.

This may not be a common self-understanding among Christians but it is not far from what they are about, if only they can see their way toward it. *Wealth of Persons* provides just such a direction. It takes its stand firmly on the priority of the person over all social and economic processes, but can do so without apology because it also grasps the centrality of the person within those processes. An economy is ultimately an inner apprehension within its most forward-looking participants. By putting the entrepreneur at the center, McNerney has put the person at the heart of it. In this way he can expand the concluding chapter of the book into a wider consideration of personalist philosophy. This is what Catholic social teaching has been calling for over many decades but without any very concrete sense of what it entailed. Now we see that the wealth of nations is ultimately the wealth of persons who create and sustain them. Mere monetary value recedes in significance in light of the incalculable value of persons. This is a powerful and eloquent analysis, quite unlike anything else in the raucous inequality debates that occupy the airwaves. Persons both transcend such narrow frameworks and compel us to transcend them. It is not inequality that demands a response, but the fundamental equality of persons who cannot be valued in purely economic terms.

Professor David Walsh
The Catholic University of America
Washington, DC

Preface

THE EPIGRAPH IN THIS book is taken from Ludwig Wittgenstein's *On Certainty*. He outlines how *trust* is essential for human beings to *know* since "if I don't trust *myself*" how can I begin to make judgments at all? Indeed, "why should I trust anyone else's judgment?"[1] In *Wealth of Persons*, I likewise seek to show how economics is ultimately based upon fundamental anthropological characteristics and moreover that these cannot be just assumed. Indeed, such anthropological truths like "human trust," which are essential to an understanding of the working of the free market, can simply disappear down the sinkhole of economic analysis or in praxis. In fact, we can suffer from what I call a type of "anthropological anorexia" when it comes to an adequate theoretical reflection in economics and in our understanding of doing the "business of business."

Historically, even if we go back to the economic collapse experienced during the Weimar Republic in the 1920s we can see this anthropological atrophy quite distinctly. Adam Fergusson in *When Money Dies* surveys the vast array of literature, economic and otherwise, on the defeat of the Central Powers during the First World War. One point that emerges is that the various analyses have by and large "ignored the human element to the whole story." He notes how the German people "did not understand how it happened to them, and who the foe was who had defeated them." He explains how in economic terms "money is no more than a medium of exchange" that has value only when "acknowledged by more than one person"; because the Germans did not acknowledge its value, their paper money suddenly "had no value or use—save for papering walls or making darts." The discovery that shattered their society was, in fact, that there "was no means left of measuring the worth of anything. For many, life became an obsessional search for *Sachwerte*, things of 'real,' constant value." This insight was not just economic. When, in fact, the radiating light of the human element was extinguished from the operation

1. Wittgenstein, *On Certainty*, 150.

of the economy "man's values became animal values." Fergusson outlines how the experience was far from salutary because they were left in the "unknown known" of the question of the "value" of "value." In such an economic situation of hyperinflation "a kilo of potatoes was worth, to some, more than the family silver . . . A prostitute in the family was better than an infant corpse."[2] This has not just economic meaning but immeasurable human significance. Thus, economic sense cannot be merely reduced to the pecuniary because it also has ultimate implications.

Actually, when we turn to the contemporary situation a diagnosis of the contributory factors leading to the creation of the Great Recession beginning in 2008 would be in terms of a "breakdown of trust, integrity, and responsible freedom."[3] In *Wealth of Persons* I contend that economic theory is never necessarily neutral from the anthropological perspective even if the truth of the human person has been ejected from the particular model used. In other words, the free economy and economists' reflections on it are after all "case sensitive" when it comes to its fundamental anthropological roots. Thomas Piketty's *Capital in the Twenty-First Century* has undoubtedly reawakened public debate not only about economic issues but also about the nature of the economy itself. But if one understands in the first place the "personcentric" dimensions at the heart of the market economy, it will be no real surprise to realize that if even one of these essential elements, like *trust*, is pulverized out of the bedrock of the process, we are left with a mutant reality. The way toward an adequate retrieval of true reality is to return to the human origins of the economic process.

Although many schools of economic thought do not clearly outline an economic anthropology, the purpose of *Wealth of Persons* is to recapture the "emergent" philosophy of the human person nascent in some economists' writings but never adequately articulated. In terms of an apposite methodology there's a need for "collaborative creativity"[4] in our approach. A certain intellectual humility is necessary to recognize that we've created a kind of Tower of Babel in the human sciences and this happens when it comes to economic reflection, too. When we operate only within our own narrow horizons we can be involved in what Bernard Lonergan calls "breakdowns."[5] It is often the case that challenges are more

2. Fergusson, *When Money Dies*, ix, 255–56.

3. Sirico, *Defending the Free Market*, 3.

4. Lonergan, *Method in Theology*, xi.

5. Ibid., 243–44.

acute in the human sciences when "reductionists extend the methods of natural sciences to the study" of the human person. He observes, "their results, accordingly, are valid only in so far as man resembles a robot or a rat and, while such resemblance does exist, exclusive attention to it gives a grossly mutilated and distorted view."[6] There's therefore a need for an about-face in method, a "conversion" that is at least on the intellectual level but may also entail moral or spiritual dimensions.[7] A "collaborative creativity" is, I suggest, consequently needed to "restore harmony among and within dissociated disciplines" and especially in economic reflection in order to develop an adequate "integralist" view of the human person in economic action.[8] That's why throughout this book we apply insights and analyses taken from many different scholars, various disciplines, and charismatic entrepreneurs like Thomas Aquinas, Alexis de Tocqueville, Karl Marx, Agnes Morrogh-Bernard, Joseph Schumpeter, Alfred Schutz, Wilhelm Röpke, Ludwig von Mises, János Kornai, David Walsh, Luigino Bruni, and many others. In the economic system we've produced in the last century, there is something clearly wrong, but at the same time new anthropological horizons are emerging or can be recaptured by a collaborative approach. Perhaps, as economist Luigino Bruni argues, it is the case that we need "resurrection eyes"[9] to be able to see it, but certain new approaches and business models are an attempt to measure up to the multidimensional reality and truth about the human person. *Wealth of Persons* is a contribution to the whole debate and hopefully will unfold for the reader new horizons of meaning in an enhanced understanding of the human face of the free economy.

6. Ibid., 248.
7. Ibid., 238.
8. Raymaker, "Theory-Praxis of Social Ethics," 347.
9. Bruni, "Economic Crisis and the Eyes of the Resurrection."

Acknowledgments

IN WRITING THIS BOOK I'm especially grateful to Dr. Brendan Purcell, who knows every line of this book and could even read it backwards, such is his attention to detail. I'm deeply indebted to him for helping me unearth the philosophical splendor, beauty, and truth of the human person in the economic horizon. Professor David Walsh was inspirational in his insights into the area I was attempting to investigate. He enabled me to trace the luminosity of the philosophical roots of an existential revolution in economic thought. Dr. Joseph McCarroll was a continuous bright light of optimism and acted as a human catalyst for further philosophical thought.

I'm also grateful to Professor Gerard Casey and Dr. Timothy Mooney of the School of Philosophy at University College Dublin for their kind academic support, which helped me in the articulation of this material at its very early stages. I'd like to include the very gracious students from the UCD Lochlann Quinn School of Business and the UCD Michael Smurfit Graduate Business School who listened to lectures based on this material with open hearts and minds. Professor Raymond Kinsella and Dr. Cormac MacFhionnlaoich happily engaged with me in the communication of the material through various seminars to students on International Banking and Finance courses. Many thanks to all my dear friends in the Business school who always welcomed me—Evelyn Corrigan, Deirdre Linehan-O'Brien, Orlaith McGourty, Margaret Maher, Jessica Tuohy, Áine Ní Rian, Esther Sanz, Madeline Molyneaux, Anita Blake, Paulina Martyniak, Elaine Tyrrell, Claire Kingston, Áine Doherty, and my office neighbors, Aoife Doherty and Robert Reed.

A group of UCD students evoke warm affection in me because of our weekly Friday meetings in the university—Laura Cullen, Padraig Bermingham, Mark Soye, Camille Vianin, Sofia Noguera, Silvia Pititto, and Harry Fitzgerald—you were all inspirational in your sharing and your challenging questions over lunch. You helped me realize the "why" worth living for in life. My great colleague and student adviser, Jacqueline

Levine, was a constant encouragement through it all, showing great academic insight and always cheering me on to the finish line! Brona Kavanagh was a tower of strength in our conversations and in helping me explain the unexplainable in "ladybird" version, as she says! The UCD student advisers were also a great support.

I cannot forget Anne Tynan, who worked with me closely in the chaplaincy. I will always remember her personal support shown to me and to all students. She could write a book! Caroline Brady worked with me too in student support services. She showed immense kindness to students and to us all involved in helping difficult cases. To you, Anne and Caroline, thanks for the joy in the midst of our always trying to help the "other."

I want to mention in a special way my colleagues Leon Ó'Giolláin, John Callanan, and Gillian Kingston, who worked with me (and suffered no doubt) on the university chaplaincy team. They had the discernment to freely admire and love the gifts and the differences of the "other," leading to a beautiful experience of our unity as one family. Frances Jegbfume always made a home for us all at St. Stephen's. And then "my boss" in UCD Dominic O'Keeffe, Director of Student Services, was always looking forward to the book launch date. He was and is a great "encourager" and would always ask "why not?" when a new idea was proposed. The members of the Irish Commission for the Economy of Communion who I work with have always been interested in the project, encouraged me and even listened to me speak at various meetings! I thank Donal Lawlor, Patricia Brandon, Lia Sala, Lorna Gold, Paul Connolly, Fran Maher, Andrew Basquille, Eugene Murphy, and Roisin Lynch.

I have to mention other friends, too, like Eddie Carroll, who read the manuscript at various stages and then like a Socratic muse entered into dialogue with me. It usually ended up in me realizing that I didn't know that I didn't know. Dr. Marie Murray, former Director of Student Counseling at the university, always gave personal support to me and was involved in various collaborative seminars with me. My other friends too, Pat, Michael, Peter, Fergus, and Hugh, who always knew of "the book," helped me along the way. Indeed, it was along with them and other friends in the Focolare like Lorna Gold that I got in contact with the Economy of Communion and the Bologna School. There was also the "road trip" taken to Foxford Woolen Mills with Sr. Bernadette Duffy of the Religious Sisters of Charity and our friend Anne Delaney. It was an unforgettable experience seeing the river Moy that Morrogh-Bernard harnessed to reveal the "wealth of persons" at the heart of her entrepreneurial project. My mum and dad cannot be forgotten since they lived a real *oikonomia* of the Trinity with us all at home. To Eamonn, my twin brother, whose life ever inspires me as he always puts me first, so much does he love me; and then to Michael, Geradene, and family, who have always been there for me, I express a profound gratitude.

Finally, I wish to acknowledge the assistance of the publisher, Wipf and Stock, and all the editorial staff involved. Dr. Conor Cunningham of the University of Nottingham read the initial manuscript and was instrumental in the recommendation for its publication. I'm all the more grateful to him as he was in the midst of his own research but found the time for what I've called "collaborative creativity" in reading the text. Thankfully, he saw in the reflections of the "other" a contribution to academic multidimensionality. It is sometimes difficult to see in the "other" an "otherness" that is new, but he did.

1

The Great Recession Points Us to the *Crisis* of Economics

I. Introduction

THIS BOOK CAN BE best described as a quest, a search to find a way of unearthing and understanding something which, I believe, frequently lies hidden beneath the workings of the free market economic process. This is the centrality and true wealth of the acting human person who is at the kernel of the proper workings of the free economy. I remember during a trip to the University of California, Berkeley in the United States, I spent the first few days attempting to get my geographical bearings. I was working in the Haas Business School on research connected to my doctoral studies. But like any first-time visitor to San Francisco, I was also keen to catch a glimpse of the different sights, like the Golden Gate Bridge and the Pacific Ocean. One particular morning, I went down to the Berkeley marina near where I was staying, hoping to see across the bay. Unfortunately, the fog restricted visibility. My trip was seemingly made in vain. Just then, I asked a resident if she could point out to me the direction of the famous landmarks, so that I could try to make them out in the haze. She genially did so but also advised me that the best vantage point to see the famous bridge was up from the surrounding hills. I was directed to drive to the Grizzly Peak area in the Tilden Regional Park to get a better panorama. I took the woman's advice and sure enough the view was breathtaking and well worth the effort. In order to gain a view of the broader vista it is often necessary to travel away from the particular spot and so look back upon the object of interest from a different perspective. This is true equally in the field of any kind of research and while the remit of our study is primarily a philosophical investigation into human action, we will focus on how this intersects with and applies to the economic drama of human life. Indeed, scholars repeatedly refer to the need for a multidisciplinary approach since we are dealing with a multidimensional reality when we come to study the human person. In a research paper the Nobel Prize–winning economist Daniel McFadden notes how the models economists use need considerable enhancement. He says, in fact, the typical "*Homo economicus*" model economists deal with is "a rare species." So, he claims economics "should draw much more heavily on fields such as psychology, neuroscience and anthropology."[1]

Earlier on, I spoke of the need to change my geographical location because the climatic conditions in the East Bay region prevented me from seeing the famous sights from the Berkeley marina. Apparently, just like in Ireland, the weather conditions are always a topic of conversation in the Bay Area. Mark Twain is alleged to have remarked, "The coldest winter I ever spent was a summer in San Francisco." Berkeley is situated northeast of the city of San Francisco, so it is possible from there to catch glimpses of the city and its sights through what the Californians call the "high fog." I use this example of shifting our horizons in order to see things more clearly because philosophy can offer a specific perspective and make a thought-provoking contribution to the investigation of what I call the truth and wealth of a "personcentric" economy. This is so even if in the Great Recession the human person became derailed from the prevailing economic paradigm.

There is always a tendency to "pass the parcel" and simply blame others for financial and economic implosions. But there is a concomitant need for a development in our understanding of human economic action. For instance, an all too common approach today is to say that the "free market economy" is a fundamentally flawed system because it is just about "greed." This is somewhat simplistic because avarice, or what I would call "Gekkoism" (that is, the "Greed is good" mantra of Gordon Gekko, the main character of *Wall Street*), is part but not the totality of what caused the financial crash and subsequent recession. The usual perception is to say it happened because "unregulated laissez-faire capitalism was allowed to let rip and the greed of bankers . . . led them

---

1. *The Economist*, "Debt to Pleasure," 27 April 2013, 64.

to an unprecedented degree of risk taking."[2] From this perspective, free-market economics created a monster machine of Frankensteinian proportions and we are the victims of what Saul Bellow calls "addition and subtraction."[3]

Indeed, Thomas Piketty clearly sets out a case in *Capital in the Twenty-First Century*, which considers that free markets have built within them a "deep structure of inequality."[4] Therefore, there must be direct intervention by governments to intervene on behalf of the majority to address capitalism's propensity to concentrate wealth in the hands of the few and so also fundamentally corrupting the democratic process. Piketty outlines how, if capitalist economies are simply left untethered, returns to capital will inevitably grow more rapidly than the economy as a whole. But he sees that "there are ways democracy can regain control over capitalism and ensure that the general interest takes precedence over private interests." In his analysis he outlines how "the dynamics of wealth distribution reveal powerful mechanisms pushing alternatively toward convergence and divergence. Furthermore, there is no natural spontaneous process to prevent destabilizing, inegalitarian forces from prevailing permanently." Piketty sees the intrinsic inequality of capital ownership arising from the "principle of accumulation" as being "difficult to accept and peacefully maintain within a single national community." The conventional wisdom that economic growth is a "marvelous instrument for revealing individual talents and aptitudes" is mere subterfuge often used to "justify inequalities of all sorts" and results in "gracing the winners in the new industrial economy with every imaginable virtue." Piketty maintains that we cannot "rely solely on market forces or technological progress" if we want to satisfy an economic system that is based on "democratic and meritocratic hope." He foresees the rise of a new form of "patrimonial capitalism" based on the tendency in capitalism to develop into a concentration of wealth among the few. The remedy he advocates is a global tax of 2 to 5 percent on the "super-wealthy."[5]

There is no doubt that Piketty's book has provoked worldwide interest not just about the Great Recession but also about the nature of

2. Gregg and James, *Natural Law*, 227.

3. Bellow, *Dangling Man*, 45.

4. Piketty, *Capital in the Twenty-First Century*, 2. See also his *Economics of Inequality*.

5. Piketty, *Capital in the Twenty-First Century*, 1, 7–11, 21, 70–71, 85, 96, 154, 515–39.

economics itself. In fact, a "Piketty bubble" exploded in terms of reviews and reactions to his work. When some writers in the *Financial Times* critiqued the work, Paul Krugman retorted, "inequality denial persists. There are powerful groups with strong interest in rejecting the facts, or at least in creating a fog of doubt."[6] I cannot go into a comprehensive analysis of Piketty's contribution to the debate. But his fundamental solution to the conglomeration of wealth problem is addressed in terms of a "distributive approach" which, while being legitimate insofar as it goes, does not adequately deal with the actual importance role of "wealth creators" and wealth creation in the free economy. Piketty is strong on the description of income and wealth distribution but actually weak when it comes to a balanced explanation of the essential characteristics of the free market process.[7] "Distribution" in itself does not sufficiently explain *how* wealth is created or the importance of its formation for the whole of society. In my view this is because Piketty does not wrestle with the "anthropological question" (see my reference in the preface to the preponderance of "anthropological anorexia" in the debate among economists) which helps explain the importance of "wealth-creation" and of the role of its "creators" in the free market process. This is to be understood not just in monetary terms but also in how the human "creativity" involved helps unfold the reality of the human person acting in economic life. Piketty contends that the differential returns on capital versus labor are the driving force of the free economy but this is, in fact, "a partial and misleading view" because the central human "driving force of the capitalist system is relentless innovation that improves productivity and raises living standards."[8]

The political philosopher John Tomasi published a stimulating study just before Piketty's titled *Free Market Fairness*. In it he explains how a false dichotomy can often be set up between two approaches in terms of tackling the question of economic inequality said to be inherent in the free market process; one is that of "distributive justice" (and we can see this approach in terms of Piketty's methodology) and is opposed to those who favor total economic liberty and are called "libertarians." He outlines how John Rawl's *Theory of Justice* set out the requirements of social justice on the one side and with on the other Friedrich Hayek's defense of

6. Krugman, "Rich Getting Wealthier but Inequality Denial Persists."
7. See Kelly, "How the Rich Got Richer."
8. Piereson, "Thomas Piketty's 'Le Capital.'"

the free market in *The Mirage of Social Justice* in which he denounced the whole idea of social justice. But Tomasi argues that it is not simply a case of "either-or," that is, a "fettered" or "unfettered" free economy. There is, he suggests, an alternative economic perspective which he calls "market democracy." Actually, Michael Novak and Bernard Lonergan used similar terms.[9] Tomasi says that the antinomies "property rights *or* distributive justice. Limited government *or* deliberative democracy. Free markets *or* fairness" are not necessarily contradictory. Actually, from the perspective of "democratic economics" wealth is understood as important for anthropological reasons because "it increases the worth of the rights and liberties of the most poor." Thus, economic growth and material wealth are not bad things because for people "who are secure holders of liberal rights, wealth empowers them to become authors of lives thoroughly their own." In this way "free market fairness interprets the distributive requirements of social justice in ways that honor those citizens, whatever life script each choose to compose."[10] Furthermore, Tomasi outlines how we are increasingly moving "to a world where the individual, autonomous person is central—to the *personalized economy.*" He gives examples of new emerging cultures in workplaces like those of "high-technology enterprises such as Apple Inc. and flying start-ups such as Google" where the old "accumulatory" form of capitalism is being supplanted by a more decentralized model. It is in this new type of economy that we understand that "increases in value tend to be the result of innovation driven primarily by creative individuals and teams, rather than simply by the product of machines and unskilled workers backed by massed capital. The result is a reunification of personal and economic progress."[11] Tomasi understands that fundamental to uniting the clearly limited approaches of high liberals (who basically believe that social justice often demands direct intervention) and that of libertarians and classical liberals (who hold that interference is inimical to understanding the whole economic process) is the central need to strive towards "the most appropriate conception of personhood."[12]

---

9. Novak used the term "democratic capitalism" in *The Spirit of Democratic Capitalism.* Lonergan spoke of a "democratic economics" in *For a New Political Economy*, 3–5, 26, 37, 110.

10. Tomasi, *Free Market Fairness*, 267, 269.

11. Ibid., 64–65.

12. Ibid., 102.

Thus, *Wealth of Persons* is hopefully a contribution to a more enhanced explanation of the "personcentric" roots of the free economy and a development of the whole debate initiated by Piketty and others.[13] It outlines how "wealth-creation" is not necessarily inimical to what it means to be a human being but is essentially constitutive of human flourishing. Throughout this book I would like the reader to try to keep in mind one fundamental insight, that the "free-market economy" is not nor need not be, in fact, a soulless machine; when it functions correctly it is an economic *process* where human action and decisions are central. But during the Great Recession it is essentially this human dimension which was eclipsed from the market's operation and left us dangling over the precipice of disaster. The economist Paul Dembinski points this out very well in his study called *Finance: Servant or Deceiver?*, when he observes how "over the last quarter-century the West has experienced an inversion of ends and means. There also has been a shift away from relationships (as a mode of human social and economic reaction) towards transactions (which allow relationships to be unilaterally and abruptly terminated)."[14]

In other words, the Great Recession points us to the *crisis* of economics, that is, the continuing danger of the eclipse of the reality of the human person in the whole process. Speaking to a group of young people, Pope Francis remarked how

> the whole world at this time is in a moment of crisis. And the crisis . . . is not something bad. It's true that the crisis makes us suffer, but we must—and you young people especially—must be able to read the crisis. What does this crisis mean? What must I do to help to come out of the crisis? The crisis that we are living at this time is a human crisis. They say: but, it's an economic crisis, it's a crisis of work. Yes, it's true, but why? Because the problem of work, the problem of the economy, is a consequence of the great human problem. What is in crisis is the value of the human person, and we must defend the human person . . . I once read an account of a Medieval Rabbi of the year 1200. This Rabbi explained to the Jews of that time the story of the Tower

13. See Anthony B. Atkinson's *Inequality: What Can Be Done?*, which examines how to understand the meaning of inequality and how it can be influenced. Atkinson does not accept that rising inequality is inevitable; he says that "it is not solely the product of forces outside our control" (*Inequality*, 302). See also Robert D. Putnam's *Our Kids: The American Dream in Crisis* and Philip McShane's *Piketty's Plight and the Global Future*.

14. Dembinski, *Finance*, 2.

of Babel. It wasn't easy to build the Tower of Babel: bricks had to be made; and how is a brick made? One must find the clay, the straw; mix them, put them in the oven: it was enormous work. And after this work, a brick became a real treasure! Then they would take the bricks to the top to build the Tower of Babel. But if a brick fell, it was a tragedy, the worker who dropped it was punished; it was a tragedy! However, if a man fell, nothing happened! This is the crisis we are going through today: it's the crisis of the person.[15]

Financial journalists and economic commentators also refer in their analyses to what I call the "anthropological" missing link when it comes to an adequate understanding of human economic action. Gillian Tett in *Fool's Gold* mentions how people in the financial world had made the assumption that "it was perfectly valid to discuss money in abstract, mathematical, ultra-complex terms, without any reference to tangible human beings."[16] Larry McDonald, author of the book *A Colossal Failure of Common Sense*, about the Lehman Brothers collapse, concluded his reflections on the financial crash by saying,

It changed me. It stripped away all the careless glances at stock charts I have lived with all my life. The ramifications of those charts have a different meaning now. Where once I stared at the zigzagging lines, and just thought, *Up, down, win, lose, profit, crash, problem, solution, long, short, buy, sell*, now I see mostly people. Because every movement, up or down, has a meaning. I see it because I've been there. Every fraction of every inch of those financial graphs represents hope or fear, confidence or dread, triumph or ruin, celebration or sorrow. There's nothing quite like a total calamity to focus the mind . . . And, I say again, it never should have happened.[17]

II. An Exploration: Toward Recovering the Truth and Wealth of a "Personcentric" Economy

If we want to move toward an adequate understanding of human action in the economic drama of human life, there is a need to step outside the

---

15. See "Pope's Q-and-A with Students of Jesuit Schools," http://www.zenit.org/en/articles/pope-s-q-and-a-with-students-of-jesuit-schools.

16. Tett, *Fool's Gold*, xii–xiii.

17. McDonald and Robinson, *Colossal Failure of Common Sense*, 339.

box of our own specialized disciplines because none of them is sufficient in itself. Just as in the other sciences, economics also produces many questions that are beyond the scope of its own methods. This requires a certain type of "methodological humility," which leads to what I call "reciprocal knowledge." So, I suggest throughout this book the need for an enlargement of our human perspective when it comes to the appropriation of an ample insight into human economic action. John Henry Newman also often spoke about the necessity for the enlargement of the human mind and heart in the journey towards any adequate personal acquisition of universal human knowledge.[18] He acknowledges the need for specialization in the sciences and how, for instance, the division of labor is "an undisputed maxim in Political Economy." But while "greater skill and quickness" for the individual results in a larger "accumulation of national wealth" there is equally the problem of over-specialization in that the person's "mental powers and habits become contracted, and he resembles a subordinate part of some powerful machinery, useful in its place, but insignificant and worthless out of it." So, Newman concludes we must augment such an approach, "by bringing into action other principles, which may serve as a check and counterpoise to the main force."[19] In his *Oxford University Sermons* he builds towards the reciprocity of knowledge paradigm I have referred to when he observes that

> knowledge itself, though a condition of the mind's enlargement, yet, whatever be its range, is not that very thing which enlarges it. Rather the foregoing instances show that this enlargement consists in the comparison of the subjects of knowledge one with another. We feel ourselves to be ranging freely, when we not only learn something, but when we also refer it to what we knew before. It is not the mere addition to our knowledge which is the enlargement, but the change of place, the movement onwards, of that moral centre, to which what we know and what we have been acquiring, the whole mass of our knowledge, as it were, gravitates. And therefore a philosophical cast of thought, or a comprehensive mind, or wisdom in conduct or policy, implies a connected view of the old with the new; an insight into the bearing and influence of each part upon every other; without which there is no whole, and could be no centre. It is the knowledge,

18. See Crosby, *The Personalism of John Henry Newman*.
19. See Newman, *Idea of a University*, 167–68.

THE GREAT RECESSION AND THE *CRISIS* OF ECONOMICS 9

not only of things, but of their mutual relations. It is organized, and therefore living knowledge.[20]

It is my hope in this study to develop a corresponding "philosophical cast of thought, or a comprehensive"[21] approach and apply it in terms of achieving an "enlargement" of our understanding of the "acting person" in the economic drama of human life. In this regard, I find it thought-provoking to note a certain equivalence between Newman's philosophical perspective and that of the Canadian philosopher Bernard Lonergan.[22] In his analysis of the act of human insight as a way towards the recovery of our understanding into understanding, Lonergan speaks about the importance of the emergence of a "universal viewpoint." He explains how the "hallmark of scientific explanation . . . is that it rises, in its viewpoint, beyond a relativity [or bias] to a particular individual or group."[23] Nothing can or should be understood simply in terms of itself; just as, I will argue, it is impossible to completely comprehend the free market process solely as an "economic-centric" reality. In fact, there is a parallel penetrating insight in the popular viewpoint expressed when people say, "I want to live not just in an economy but in a society." Thus, Lonergan's philosophical perspective can be understood more clearly when he says that there is always a need of a higher viewpoint and indeed of "successive higher viewpoints" if we want to adequately investigate into a particular reality.[24] He outlines this gradual development towards a universal viewpoint but firstly gives an example of the need for "higher viewpoints" in his analysis of the nature of mathematics, which he gives in the seminal study *Insight: A Study of Human Understanding*. If we penetrate "deeply into the nature of mathematics,"[25] he claims, it even "makes the notion of insight more precise."[26] He moves through the critical insights involved in the mathematical operations of addition, multiplication, subtraction, division and

20. Sermon 14, "Wisdom, as Contrasted with Faith and with Bigotry," no. 21. See http://www.newmanreader.org/works/oxford/sermon14.html.

21. Ibid.

22. There is no doubt about Lonergan's indebtedness to Newman in the articulation of his own inquiry into human understanding. See Lonergan, *Caring about Meaning*, 13, 20; Kerr et al., *Cambridge Companion to John Henry Newman*, 80, 262–64, 268–69; Dulles, *John Henry Newman*, 45; and Mathews, *Lonergan's Quest*, 44–47.

23. See Mathews, *Lonergan's Quest*, 413.

24. See Lonergan, *Insight*, 40–42.

25. Ibid., 41.

26. Ibid., 18.

roots. The movement between arithmetic and algebraic understanding, for example, is not just one of internal logical expansion. Algebra cannot just be logically deduced from within the viewpoint of arithmetic and the same is true when you move on to "group theory." The link between them is not logically deduced but is actually "cognitional."[27] Lonergan explains:

> At each stage of the process there exists a set of rules that govern operations which result in numbers. To each stage there corresponds a symbolic image of doing arithmetic, doing algebra, doing calculus. In each successive image there is the potentiality of grasping by insight a higher set of rules that will govern the operations and by them elicit the numbers or symbols of the next stage. Only insofar as a man makes his slow progress up that escalator [which leads to successive insights and a movement from elementary to higher mathematics] does he become a technically competent mathematician. Without it he may acquire a rough idea of what mathematics is about, but he will never be a master, perfectly aware of the precise meaning and the exact implications of every symbol and operation.[28]

But this mathematical analysis need not occupy us here because what his notion of the universal viewpoint contributes to the question of how to acquire an insight into the workings of the free market process is that the interpreter needs to have the capacity to grasp multidimensional meanings.[29] The meanings I have in mind in regard to the appropriation of an adequate understanding of the market economy are the "anthropological" or "personcentric" principles upon which it is fundamentally based. The notion of a "universal viewpoint" is, as I have already said, comparable to Newman's concept of the "enlargement of mind," which he held was essential for the development of human knowing. Lonergan says of the "universal viewpoint" that "it would open his [the interpreter's] mind to ideas that do not lie on the surface and to views that diverge enormously from his own; it would enable him to find clues where otherwise he might look but would fail to see; it would equip him with a capacity to transport his thinking to the level and texture of another culture."[30]

27. For this whole explanation, see Mathews, *Lonergan's Quest*, 228.

28. Lonergan, *Insight*, 42.

29. Ibid., 588.

30. Ibid.

According to Lonergan the "universal viewpoint" has a "genetic" and "dialectic" nature to it.[31] If we apply this to the area of economic analysis there follows the possibility of a genetic sequence of studies on a particular economist or subject and then there is the emergence of different schools of economic thought. I have in mind here a book like Joseph Schumpeter's *Ten Great Economists: From Marx to Keynes.* Another useful work for consultation in terms of the "genetic" approach is *History of Economic Thought,* by Harry Landreth and David Colander. It lists some of the important writings in economics starting from c. 700 BC by author and date, and then situates the individual authors thematically. But Schumpeter's *History of Economic Analysis* is an example of the development of the "dialectic" dimension in economic understanding. In Schumpeter's *magnum opus* there is economic analysis with contributions from areas of history, philosophy, sociology, and psychology. He cites the writings of Plato, Aristotle up through to the time of Adam Smith, including the medieval Scholastics and natural law philosophers. He covers the works of Malthus, Mill, Ricardo, Marx, and other important European economists. We can speak of a "dialectical relationship"[32] because economics, or in the case of the subject matter of this book, the "free economy," can be understood from the perspective of various contributions that philosophers, psychologists, and sociologists can bring to the question.

Our investigation titled *Wealth of Persons: Economics with a Human Face* is primarily a philosophical contribution to a "universal viewpoint" on understanding economic life by going beneath the surface of the workings of the free market process. In this way we are "transporting our thinking" to a "higher viewpoint" in an attempt to recapture the deep anthropological roots of the economic reality we live in. Lonergan, speaking about the "historiographer himself," marvels at "his ability to envisage the protean possibilities of the notion of being."[33] So, too, in this book we can hopefully contemplate the richness of the human face, which emerges when we apply a philosopher's understanding to the free economy.

Which economic order we live within actually does matter. Václav Havel, who was founder of Charter 77 and served as Czech president until 2003, once wrote,

31. Ibid., 587–88.

32. See Mathews, *Lonergan's Quest,* 413.

33. Lonergan, *Insight,* 588.

> I have always known that the only economic system that works
> is a market economy, in which everything belongs to some-
> one—which means that someone is responsible for everything.
> It is a system in which complete independence and plurality of
> economic entities exist within a legal framework, and its work-
> ings are guided chiefly by the laws of the marketplace. This is
> the only natural economy, the only kind that makes sense, the
> only one that can lead to prosperity, because it is the only one
> that reflects the nature of life itself . . . Our recent great experi-
> ence, an experience none of the western democracies has ever
> undergone, was Communism. Often we ourselves are unable to
> appreciate fully the existential dimension of this bitter experi-
> ence and all its consequences, including those that are entirely
> metaphysical. It is up to us alone to determine what value we
> place on that particular capital.[34]

It is clear here that the capital Havel has in mind is not limited to a purely
pecuniary notion but goes beyond ordinary economic dimensions (Piketty, on the other hand, has in my view a somewhat reductive or economizing definition of capital).[35] There is no denying the fact that the free
market system has and still is undergoing an epochal transformative
experience and the outcome still remains uncertain. It is for this reason
that this philosophical study seems opportune.

In 1988 the Austrian economist Friedrich Hayek, a Nobel Prize winner, wrote a book called *The Fatal Conceit: The Errors of Socialism*. He and
some other economists like Ludwig von Mises and Wilhelm Röpke sought
to outline how the free market economy was not so much a *mechanism*
as a *process of human discovery*.[36] Fundamental to this process are the *human elements* that make up the reality of economic action. Hayek wrote
that it was with the emergence of the Austrian school of economics that
"the whole market process . . . became understood as a process of transfer
of information enabling men to use, and put to work, much more information and skill than they would have access to individually."[37] He sees
the *epistemic* challenge as being therefore fundamental to understanding
how an economy works. Socialism solves this "knowledge problem" by

34. Havel, *Summer Meditations*, 62, 126.

35. Piketty defines capital as "the sum total of nonhuman assets that can be owned
and exchanged on some market" (*Capital in the Twenty-First Century*, 46).

36. See Mises, *Human Action*; Röpke, *A Humane Economy*; Röpke, *The Social
Framework of the Free Market*.

37. Hayek, *Fatal Conceit*, 97.

centrist planning policies. The state or the *politburo* "decides" and solves the problematic. But Hayek stressed our fallible human nature and the uncertainty of human knowledge. He observed, "The economic problem is a problem of the utilization of knowledge which is not given to anyone in its totality."[38] Hayek's diagnosis about the fall of communism is ultimately due to what I would call the phenomenon and problem of "big-headedness" (thinking that we know more than we actually know or indeed can know) that can underpin some economic theories. The fatal conceit of classical socialism was to think all knowledge could be collected in one mind only. The mortal flaw of such an economic system is not just based upon a question of its economic inefficiency; it has rather a mistaken concept of the human person. It is built upon an "anthropological fault line" that collapses under the pressure of human reality.

Such faults are not just a part of socialism; they can be equally seen when it comes to an analysis and the actual praxis of the free economy. Economists often understand the economic agent here as a *purely self-maximizing agent*. But this perspective is an eclipse of the reality of who we are as human persons and it is not actually how the free market can optimally operate. In fact, Wilhelm Röpke states how such a view of the human person as "*Homo sapiens consumens* loses sight of everything that goes to make up human happiness apart from money income and its transformation into goods."[39] This perspective is, he says, "a false anthropology, one that lacks wisdom, [and] misunderstands man."[40] Are we then just to give in to the interpretation of the market economy as being based upon the "icy water of egotistical calculation," which lets people gain the world but lose their souls?[41] Some members of the Austrian school of economics and the newly emerging Bologna school of economics I refer to in this book believe not.

The Bologna school of economics are an emerging group of economists whose writings are mostly in Italian but some of them have studied in England under economists like Professor Robert Sugden. The school attempts to develop an adequate understanding of the "acting person" within the free market process. In these writers, I have discovered that certain anthropological principles like human alertness, insight, choice,

38. Hayek, *Individualism and Economic Order*, 78.

39. Röpke, *Humane Economy*, 120.

40. Ibid.

41. Ibid., 113.

initiative, and innovation (all associated as we will see in our analysis with entrepreneurial action) can be found, and these characteristics emerge as of central importance for an adequate philosophical understanding of the free economy. Luigino Bruni, a professor of economics at the University of Milano-Bicocca, and Stefano Zamagni, professor of economics at the University of Bologna, are central protagonists in the Bologna School.

In fact, Wilhelm Röpke called for a "new humanism" and argued that we should "adopt a philosophy which, while rendering unto the market the things that belong to the market, also renders unto the spirit what belongs to it."[42] Pope Francis in an address to the Centesimus Annus Foundation[43] alluded to the significance of the workings of the human spirit in the economy when he said, "The current crisis is not only economic and financial but it is rooted in an ethical and anthropological crisis." He remarked how it is continually forgotten that over and above business and "the logic and parameters of the market, [there] is the human being" and that there is something due to the human person *qua* person by virtue of their own innate dignity. He suggests a need to "return to the centrality of the human being, to a more ethical vision of human actions and relationships without the fear of losing something."[44]

Therefore, in *Wealth of Persons* we will investigate primarily the philosophical anthropological dimensions that emerge within economic thinking with particular reference to the Austrian School's contribution. But we will also make reference to the Bologna school of economics in the concluding sections of this study. This is because their approach contributes significantly to developing a "universal viewpoint" in regard to grasping an adequate understanding of the "multidimensional" reality of the human person acting in the free market process. So, I will outline in due course the Austrian approach to economic reflection. Suffice it here to say, their "methodology ('praxeology')" sticks close in its axioms to universally realistic common insights into the essence of human

42. Ibid., 116.

43. Pope John Paul II established this foundation in 1993. The organization is composed of businesspeople, academics, and professionals who reflect on the social teachings of the Church and the promotion of the thoughts contained within John Paul's social encyclical titled *Centesimus Annus* (1991). See Rousseau, *Human Dignity and the Common Good: The Great Papal Social Encyclicals from Leo XIII to John Paul II.*

44. See Pope Francis, "Discorso del Santo Padre Francesco alla Fondazione 'Centesimus Annus Pro Pontifice,'" http://www.vatican.va/holy_father/francesco/speeches/2013/may/documents/papa-francesco_20130525_centesimus-annus-pro-pontifice_it.html. Translation mine.

action."[45] Accordingly, three essential Austrian insights developed in this exploration, are the importance of the *human person, human action*, and the *habit of enterprise or human economic creativity* in the free market process.[46] It sometimes happens that these actual anthropological roots are covered over or eclipsed out of consideration in economic thought. We can be left with the husk of the theory in economics but without the existential kernel that constitutes economics' essence and praxis.

I have referred to different traditions of reflection because just as in the field of psychology there are different schools of thought within economics. There is a rich literature on the history of economic thought but this is not our concern here.[47] Suffice it is to say that during the twentieth century there emerged two prominent economic protagonists in John Maynard Keynes and Friedrich Hayek. Keynes's ideas gave rise to the "Keynesian" and Hayek's to the "Hayekian" schools of economic thought, respectively. "We are all Keynesians now" was a phrase coined by Milton Friedman and attributed to U.S. President Richard Nixon.[48] The differences between the two schools of thought are difficult to explain. But to put it succinctly, Keynes understood that inherent in the capitalist development was "a stationary state that constantly threatens to break down."[49] His "breakdown theory" is not unlike Karl Marx's in that the economic collapse is produced by endogenous causes, which are "inherent to working of the economic machine."[50] The only "parameter of action" and way to obviate this economic failure was "monetary

---

45. Rothbard, *Classical Economics*, 79.

46. See the writings of Gregory M. A. Gronbacher where he speaks of the need for "economic personalism": "The Wedding of Three Philosophical Traditions"; *Economic Personalism*; "The Need for Economic Personalism"; and "The Humane Economy."

47. Readers can consult Schumpeter's *Ten Great Economists* and *History of Economic Analysis*, as well as the following works: Landreth and Colander, *History of Economic Thought*; Screpanti and Zamagni, *An Outline of the History of Economic Thought*; Blaug, *Economic Theory in Retrospect*; Medema and Samuels, *The History of Economic Thought*; Spiegel, *The Growth of Economic Thought*; Rothbard, *An Austrian Perspective on the History of Economic Thought* (2 vols.); Vaggi and Groenewegen, *A Concise History of Economic Thought*; Kincaid and Ross, *The Oxford Handbook of Philosophy of Economics*; Tsoulfidis, *Competing Schools of Economic Thought*; Alvey, *A Short History of Ethics and Economics*; and White, *The Clash of Economic Ideas*.

48. See *Time*, 31 December 1965, for the Friedman article. See *New York Times*, 4 January 1971, where Nixon is reported as saying, "I am now a Keynesian in economics."

49. See Schumpeter, *Ten Great Economists*, 283–84.

50. Ibid., 284.

management."[51] Keynes claimed that economic recessions (and he wrote during the 1930s Depression) are the result of insufficient aggregate demand. One of his fundamental insights was that "the level of economic activity was determined by what he called 'effective demand' for goods and services."[52] He proposed that "if people were to spend more, the result would be higher production and, paradoxically, higher incomes. The result was that rises in government spending or tax cuts (which increase private spending) would raise production and reduce unemployment."[53]

As I have previously mentioned Hayek proposed something entirely different, as did those who belonged to what is called the Austrian school of economics.[54] He understood the economic breakdown as being the result "of imbalance between an economy's ability to sustain development of longer capital productive processes and its ability to produce immediate consumer goods."[55] As I have said, in the "breakdown" economic situation Keynes suggested the solution was to increase demand. You can do this by "spending" so that consumption of consumer goods increases. In such cases governments should increase expenditure. But for Hayek this was fundamentally a mistaken understanding of the economic process of discovery because "buying a consumer good" in those circumstances actually "prevents the longer capital processes from being completed,"[56] which results in waste.[57] In an interview with Nadim Shehadi, Hayek outlines his fundamental differences with Keynes when he says,

51. Ibid., 275.

52. See Backhouse and Bateman, *Capitalist Revolutionary*, 6. Keynes's three best-known books on monetary economics are *A Tract on Monetary Reform* (1923), *A Treatise on Money* (1930), and *The General Theory of Employment, Interest and Money* (1936). Robert Skidelsky has written a three-volume biography of Keynes, which is available in a one-volume version; see *John Maynard Keynes, 1883–1946: Economist, Philosopher, Statesman*. See also Peter Clarke's *Keynes*.

53. See Backhouse and Bateman, *Capitalist Revolutionary*, 6–7.

54. This school of economics began in the 1870s with the work of Carl Menger. Economists Eugen Böhm von Bawerk, Ludwig von Mises, and Murray Rothbard developed the Mengerian tradition. Other economists connected to this approach are Joseph Schumpeter, F. A. Hayek, Wilhelm Röpke, and Israel Kirzner. A lot of European intellectuals like Mises, Hayek, and the philosopher Eric Voegelin had to flee to the United States because of the rise of Nazism. Today, there are many adherents of the Austrian School in the United States and indeed throughout the world.

55. See Ebenstein, *Friedrich Hayek*, 54.

56. Ibid.

57. Ibid.

I never believed or came to believe that there is a simple function between aggregate [demand] and employment. I insist that if you take the whole production stream, the earlier parts of the stream can move to a great extent independently of what happens at the mouth of the stream. And on one occasion I almost got him [Keynes] to understand what I mean when I tried to explain to him that in certain circumstances an increase of the final demand will discourage investment because it became important to produce quickly even at a higher cost, while a low demand will force investment to reduce costs. So the relation may be a decrease in demand stimulating investment and an increase in demand discouraging investment. For the moment he [Keynes] was very interested, and then he said, "But that would be contrary to the axiom that employment depends on final demand. . . ." Because this was so much an axiom in his life that there was a positive correlation between final demand and total employment, anything which conflicted with it was dismissed as absurd.[58]

The intervention into the market that Keynes seems to suggest is actually for Hayek a decommissioning of the whole free market economic process. Hayek maintained that the verb "to compete" means "*enterprise, leadership, judgment, price-cutting,* and *innovation.*" In his famous essay "The Meaning of Competition," Hayek concludes,

Competition is essentially a process of the formation of opinion: by spreading information, it creates that unity and coherence of the economic system which we presuppose when we think of the market. It creates the views people have about what is best and cheapest, and it is because of it that people know at least as much about possibilities and opportunities as they in fact do. It is thus a process which involves continuous change in the data and whose significance must therefore be completely missed by any theory which treats these data as constant.[59]

It is not my intention in this book to enter into the economic debate between the Keynesians and the Austrian economists like Hayek because this is properly a task for economists. I want rather to focus on the actual absence of debate between Keynes and Hayek on what I have called the

---

58. Ibid., 53–54.

59. See Hayek, *Individualism and Economic Order*, 106. See also Hayek, *Prices and Production and Other Works*.

"missing link,"[60] that is, the grasping of an adequate understanding of the centrality of the role of the human person involved in the free market process. There is an essential link between theory and practice and this lies in the responsibility of measuring any economic theory against its openness to the claims of the reality of the mystery of the human person.[61] This somewhat like the proverbial elephant present in the room but which in all the debates between various economic theorists is seemingly left invisible and repeatedly fails to be considered. This is the reason the focus in this book is on what I call the role of "the wealth of persons" in the economic process which properly results in an understanding that economics has a human face.

Adam Smith wrote his famous study *An Inquiry into the Nature and Causes of the Wealth of Nations* in 1776. In one sense, Smith set out on an impossible mission, and indeed economists prior to him and subsequently tried to account for the creation of human wealth, some with greater success than others. Indeed, there has been a continuous struggle in economic literature to articulate that the ultimate cause of wealth, the efficient cause of economic activity, is the *"acting person."* Actually, Edmund Phelps, the 2006 Nobel Laureate in economics, indicates the continuing need for a whole heuristic process of discovery within economics when he writes, "We economists are just beginning to understand the subject. Prosperity and the development of the human spirit are linked in the dynamism of the economy."[62] This is why in his book *Mass Flourishing* he describes how there is a need for a cross-disciplinary approach in economics. His study is illustrative of the "methodical humility" I have argued for in the opening sections of *Wealth of Persons*. Phelps sets the understanding of the free economy in the context of "human creativity," though not creativity for its own sake but in terms of the "good." I would add that that "good" has to be seen in terms of the "good" of the "human person." Phelps uses the Aristotelian concept of "flourishing" to develop his perspective. He argues that "the flourishing that is the quintessential product of the modern economy resonates with the ancient concept of

60. Jürgen Habermas speaks of creating "an awareness of what is missing." See Habermas et al., *Awareness of What Is Missing*, 15.

61. I am indebted to Professor David Walsh for bringing to my attention the work of Ralph C. Hancock in this regard. See Hancock, *The Responsibility of Reason: Theory and Practice in a Liberal-Democratic Age*. See also David Walsh's own review of Hancock's book: Walsh, "Theory and Practice as Responsibility."

62. Phelps, "Economic Justice," 30.

the good life . . . The good life requires the intellectual growth that comes from *creating* and *exploring* in the face of great uncertainty." The unique contribution and insights of the humanities is that they help us understand "how an enterprising and innovative economy began to sprout up." Phelps stresses that if "political economy does not learn what the humanities have to teach, it will be the poorer for that: It will continue to be unequipped to deliver the winning argument in the re-emerging debate over the modern economy."[63]

To conclude: *Wealth of Persons* is a philosophical inquiry and reflection in which it emerges that it is "the wealth of human persons" and their actions that are the keystone of the free economy and its understanding. Economics actually concerns matters more than just an economic order where the allocation of resources is determined by the supply and demand created by diverse purposive individuals who are free to act without external constraint. It is also about the relationship of human persons to the natural world and their interaction with other human beings in the transformation of natural and humanly made things in order to "make a living" for the good of persons. The fundamental focus of this book is on the "acting person" who is to be understood as the efficient cause within the free market economic process. The propulsive factor in the economic free economy is attributed to the essential role of the entrepreneur, who perceives market opportunities and therefore combines the various factors of production together so as to exploit them in a business. The study presents an in-depth analysis of the function of the entrepreneur in the free market economy. Methodologically, this is attempted by "X-raying" human entrepreneurial action in order to capture the dynamic anthropological constituents involved in the economic process of creative discovery.

This opening chapter of *Wealth of Persons* examined the Great Recession that occurred in the free economy and how a whole legitimation crisis within economic and societal thinking emerged from it. The great crisis of the Great Recession points us to the real *crisis* of economics, that is, the challenge in recovering the truth and wealth of a "personcentric economy." The philosophical investigation undertaken in the book, by going beneath the surface of the workings of the free economy attempts to recapture the human dimension of this reality. The second chapter looks more specifically at the legitimation-clarification problematic in

63. See Phelps, *Mass Flourishing*, xi, 271. My emphases.

terms of the free economy. It seeks to clarify our economic vision and look honestly at the discontents within the process and asks if it is "still fit for purpose." The third chapter attempts a retrieval of the essential meaning of human economic action and outlines a philosophy of economic order based upon this understanding. The fourth chapter focuses upon the crucial role of the entrepreneur in economic action. It discusses the primacy of "person-centered" creativity in the free market process with special reference to the Austrian economist Joseph Schumpeter, whom I consider "a prophet of creative anthropology." Following on from the specific presentation on Schumpeter's contribution in chapter 4, I proceed to present an overall philosophical reflection on the role of the entrepreneur in human economic action in chapter 5. Chapter 6 examines how it is necessary to move toward a "higher anthropological viewpoint'" if we are to develop an adequate and more comprehensive vision of the reality of the acting person in economic life. Chapter 7 with the subtitle "Eastern Awakenings and Western Alertness" examines the writings of the Hungarian economist János Kornai and his discovery of the "human-centeredness" of economic action. There is also a presentation of Israel Kirzner's investigation into the role of human alertness in the free economy as a contribution toward a more comprehensive vision of the acting person.

Chapter 8 with the title "The Real Wellspring of Human Wealth Revealed" is a philosophical meditation on an Irish entrepreneur named Agnes Morrogh-Bernard, who in the shadowlands of post-famine Ireland founded the Providence Woollen Mills in Foxford, County Mayo, in 1892, still in production to this day. In this reflection, I attempt to show just as she harnessed the forces of the river Moy for her entrepreneurial project, so too she unfolded and recaptured the truth of the "creative" reality of the human person in economic action. The penultimate chapter moves towards a fuller articulation of a philosophical anthropology of the free economy, recapturing the human wealth of its "person-centered" roots. In doing this we present evidence of an "existential shift" within economic thinking which points to an enhancement in its understanding of the human person. Furthermore, I argue that if we really want to study the reality of all human action, there is also the need to go beyond the initial demarcating boundary set by the Austrian school of economics. This is because any adequate account of human action must measure up to the truth of the reality of the acting person, taking cognizance too of their "self-transcending" nature.

In chapter 10 I survey how some philosophers and theologians have made significant contributions in their investigations into "human action" by broadening its context and recognizing that human existence is defined by the free choice of individuals, who may, in fact, act on the basis of a "Trinitarian anthropology." The Trinitarian model is presented here as a paradigm for the integration of economic life. It is here that I make specific mention of the contributions of the economists involved in the Bologna school of economics.

Throughout the study the reader will be made aware of the challenge involved in developing an enhanced anthropology that will in some way be up to the level of what philosopher David Walsh describes as the notoriously difficult notion of the human person.[64] The human person has the capacity to step outside the realm of pure self-interest to the point where concern for the other transcends concern for oneself. This is why my study concludes with reference to the Bologna school of economics, because these theoreticians essentially take up this theme of the need for a higher anthropological viewpoint, which explains how human actions can go beyond purely economizing behavior even within the economic drama. So, in this book there is an attempt to philosophically articulate an adequate phenomenology of human economic action and thereby move beyond mere description to a "wealth of persons" explanation of the economic reality we call the free market economy. The philosophical analysis attempts to unveil the critical insight that the entrepreneurial function cannot be understood solely in terms of monetary motivations. A central argument is that entrepreneurial action is actually revelatory of person-centered principles like human alertness, the capacity to innovate and provide insights into creative initiatives that are for the good order of society at the economic level.

The Italian economist Luigino Bruni who belongs to the Bologna school of economics writes that the "first rule of the economy today is called participation"[65] and this is in my view key to understanding that economic action is a part of human action, without exhausting that reality because we are participants in a human drama that goes beyond us. In writing this book, I can only claim to have begun to discover that there is "more to economics than to consume and avoid risk."[66] Innovation and

64. See Walsh, *Guarded by Mystery*, 26. He writes, "Human beings are notoriously difficult to study."

65. See Baggio et al., *La crisi economica*, 51. Translation mine.

66. Phelps, "Economic Justice," 28.

entrepreneurial action are not the totality of the free market process because along with "creativity, there must be judgment—the judgment that
comes from insight and experience."[67] As I understand it, the Austrian
economic viewpoint at least begins with an emphasis on human action,
viewing economics as concerning the study of action in "every field of
endeavour" including the realities of "human nature, human aspiration, and human values" which are outlined in this study.[68] This is why
economics is never anthropologically neutral because its ongoing challenge is to adapt to the nature of the human person and not *vice versa*.
Wolfgang Münchau in a discussion on the financial crisis wrote that any
serious discussion about the proper "crisis resolution mechanism"[69] must
firstly "start with a more precise definition"[70] as to what the crisis is. As
stated already, it is my belief that the intellectual meltdown in regard to
an adequate elaboration of the anthropological dimensions underlying
the free economy actually blocks us from a thoroughgoing resolution of
the current crisis. It is my hope that *Wealth of Persons* contributes to a recapturing the reality of the wealth of the person-centered roots of the free
market process, which envisages the economy as not necessarily inimical
to human well-being but constitutive of its actual flourishing.

67. Ibid., 31.

68. Ibid., 28.

69. "Europe Planning to Solve the Wrong Crisis," *Financial Times*, 7 February 2011, http://www.ft.com/cms/s/0/ef5a3cea-322a-11e0-a820-00144feabdc0.
html#axzz411froJbn.

70. Ibid.

2

The Free Economy at the Crossroads:
Still Fit for Purpose?

I. Introduction: Clarifying Our Economic "Vision"

WE ARE PROPOSING IN this book to investigate the philosophical anthropological dimensions that emerge within economic thinking and to look at the particular contribution that the Austrian perspective in economics offers. But it is important to keep in mind that this particular school "of economics is not monolithic."[1] There are, in fact, various strands and groupings in the contemporary Austrian school. Despite the divergences within this tradition, they basically see the task of economics and the economist as twofold, that is, firstly, "the economist must render economic phenomena intelligible in terms of purposive action; and secondly, the economist must trace the unintended consequences of those actions."[2] There are three corresponding methodological principles associated with this approach. They are firstly, methodological individualism; secondly, methodological subjectivism and thirdly, the principle that theoretical attention should be on processes rather than equilibrium states.[3]

I have mentioned how the anthropological realities that are at the root of the free market economy are sometimes covered over or eclipsed

---

1. See Boettke, *Elgar Companion to Austrian Economics*, 1.
2. Ibid., 3–4.
3. Ibid., 4.

from economic thought and contemporary commentary. When this occurs we are really only left with the outside shell of a particular economic
theory without the essential substance that constitutes its essence. The
philosopher Alfred Schutz,[4] writing on the methodology of the social sciences, makes a similar point when he observes that "[the social scientists]
. . . have to deal with human conduct and its common-sense interpretation in the social reality . . . Such an analysis refers by necessity to the
subjective point of view, namely, to the interpretation of the action and its
settings in terms of the actor." However, when we come to economics, the
methodology seems to be otherwise. Schutz, in my view, perspicuously
asks,

> Is it not the "behavior of prices" rather than the behavior of
> men in the market situation which is studied . . . , the "shape of
> the demand curves" rather than the anticipations of economic
> subjects symbolized by such curves? . . . Closer investigation,
> however, reveals that this abstract conceptual scheme is nothing
> else but a kind of intellectual shorthand and that the underly-
> ing subjective elements of human actions involved are taken for
> granted or deemed to be irrelevant with respect to the scientific
> purpose at hand . . . Correctly understood, the postulate of sub-
> jective interpretation as applied to economics as well as to all
> the other social sciences means merely that we always *can*—and
> for certain purposes *must*—refer to the activities of the subjects
> within the social world and their interpretation by the actors
> in terms of systems of projects, available means, motives, rel-
> evances, and so on.[5]

In other words, a coherent economic theory generally presupposes
that there are participating human subjects and that their anthropological identity is constitutive of the overall hypothesis. In this regard Schutz
interestingly makes reference to the works of Austrian economists like
Ludwig von Mises and Friedrich A. Hayek.[6] Schutz underlines the fact
that Mises actually entitled his *magnum opus Human Action: A Treatise
on Economics.* The emphasis is upon human action, which is by definition dissimilar to other types of action as in "vegetative existence," for in-

4. Schutz belonged to the same *Geistkreis* in the University of Vienna that Eric
Voegelin was involved in. Schutz was a philosopher but also a banker. See references
to this in Voegelin, *Autobiographical Reflections*, 5–6.

5. See Schutz, *Collected Papers*, 1:34–35.

6. Ibid., 35.

stance.[7] In part one of his work Mises distinguished deliberately between "purposeful action and animal reaction."[8] In other words, economic thinking is based upon a philosophical anthropology that has at its basis fundamental characteristics that pertain to human agency. The abstract theory of an economic model is a reflection of a particular philosophy of the human actor. Schutz also refers to Hayek's book *The Counter Revolution of Science: Studies on the Abuse of Reason*. Analogous to Mises's approach, Hayek argued against any kind of *scientism* in regard to economic theory.[9] The focus of attention for the social sciences according to Hayek is "to explain the unintended or undesigned results of the actions of many men."[10]

He gives the example of the creation of a footpath through a forest that may be helpful to us here. Different people make individual choices in negotiating their way through the woods. A definite pattern eventually emerges and this we call a pathway or trail. It is unplanned; yet it is the result of deliberative actions by various people. Hayek then concludes

> it is not the observation of the actual growth of any particular track, and still less of many, from which this explanation derives its cogency, but from our general knowledge of how we and other people behave in the kind of situation in which successive people find themselves . . . It is the elements of the complex events which are familiar to us from everyday experience, but it is only by a deliberate effort of directed thought that we come to see the necessary effects of the combination of such actions by many people. We "understand" the way in which the result we observe can be produced, although we may never be in a position to watch the whole process or to predict its precise course and result.[11]

In short, the economist or social scientist can seek an explanation of how the pattern or order emerges because he has applied "directed thought" (understanding) to deliberative human actions. Still we keep in mind that a theory is an intellectual explanation; it is not the reality in

7. Ibid., 29.

8. Ibid., 11.

9. He would contend that "scientism involves a prejudice because, before even considering the nature of the subject area, it presumes to know the best way to study it." See Caldwell, *Hayek's Challenge*, 242.

10. See Hayek, *Counter-Revolution of Science*, 41.

11. Ibid., 71.

itself. The priority pertains to the *acting person* within the economic horizon and not vice versa. Otherwise, we risk our own *scientism* assuming we have a special knowledge that gives us the "power to refashion [order] in any way we desire."[12] Because, I believe, what's central is a "person-centered" order in the economic or social dimension in which we *act*.

Therefore, when it comes to economic theory, there is always the need and challenge to decipher what Schutz calls the "intellectual shorthand" and failure to do so runs the risk of decommissioning the whole basis of the theoretical reflection. That's why we try to recapture the reality of the wealth of human persons at the centre of the economic drama of humanity by means of various diagnostic and therapeutic philosophical methods at our disposal. The character Doris, Dr. More's wife in the Walker Percy's novel *Love in the Ruins*, seeks in vain to break out of the commonplace rut her life has fallen into when she claims that "we simply follow rules and habit like poor beasts on a treadmill."[13] Similarly, I would argue that there is a need to break away from the trap of any type of "treadmill" in respect of economic thought because there is a clear danger in just leaving analysis to the experts and pundits. Hayek, in the introduction to his study entitled *The Constitution of Liberty*, reflected on the fact that in his particular project, that is, the philosophical articulation of the reasons why "liberty is . . . the source and condition of most moral values" that he was leaving the strictly economic arena *per se* but actually "we are much too ready to leave the decision to the expert or to accept uncritically his opinion about a problem of which he knows intimately only one little aspect."[14] There is, therefore, the concomitant need to reflect upon the philosophical basis of the free economy and not just take a system for granted. Indeed, Alasdair MacIntyre reminds us of the philosophical nature of most of our human interactions when he comments that

> our everyday activities, including our political [and economic] activities, often presuppose and give expression to beliefs which already have an evidently philosophical character . . . [Indeed] the very language that we cannot avoid speaking, our everyday vocabulary and idiom, is itself not philosophically innocent, but to a significant degree inherited from and still informed by past

12. Ibid., 148.
13. See Percy, *Love in the Ruins*, 67.
14. See Hayek, *Constitution of Liberty*, 4, 6.

philosophical theories whose presence in our modes of speech, belief and action is no longer recognized.[15]

Evident within contemporary economic literature and commentaries is the substantive question about the "vision" within economic thought. In *Compassionate Conservatism: What It Is, Why We Need It*, Jesse Norman and Janan Ganesh argued that in the context in which they were writing—the situation in the United Kingdom in 2006—a new vision of society was needed. They called for a humane, principled, and long-term intellectual basis for our social renewal.[16] There is always a need for each generation to explicate the grounds for the endurance of particular structures and intermediary frameworks that advance the human person's well-being. The world of economics and business recoils at times from such investigations; but it does so at its own peril. Bernard Lonergan, in a chapter titled "Why? What? How?," refers to the objection made by John Maynard Keynes in his study *The General Theory of Employment*, where he points to the problems arising when only the more intelligent type of expert is able to understand the highly abstract theorems of modern economics.[17] Keynes considers politicians, bakers and industrialists as "practical men." Nonetheless, if they do not understand *how* the economy works; then without doubt they will be excluded, but, Lonergan adds, "so shall we, for they are our leaders."[18] Lonergan is an optimist in terms of human understanding and he holds that the "intervention of intelligence" is recurrent within humanity. He observes that

> the concrete realization of the succession of new practical ideas does not take place without human cooperation. It demands a division of labor, and at the same time it defines the lines along which labor is divisible. It invites men to specialize in the skilful use of particular tools and the expeditious performance of particular tasks. It calls forth some economic system, some procedure that sets the balance between the production of consumer goods and new capital formation, some method that settles what quantities of what goods and services are to be supplied,

---

15. See MacIntyre, *Edith Stein*, 3.

16. Norman and Ganesh, *Compassionate Conservatism*. See also Norman, *Compassionate Economics: The Social Foundations of Economic Prosperity*.

17. Lonergan, *For a New Political Economy*, 3.

18. Ibid.

some device for assigning tasks to individuals and for distributing among them the common product.[19]

Indeed, if you survey the history of economic thought there is clear
evidence of how minds differ greatly but at the same time the challenge
always is that "new insights have to be communicated" and a new "enthusiasm has to be roused."[20] And this applies equally to economic theory
and especially in regard to its fundamental anthropological dimensions.
As I have previously said the economic paradigm or system we live in is
critical and indeed human history attests to this fact. Václav Havel was
keenly aware of the unique social experiment and its cataclysmic failure
that he and millions experienced on the European continent. Notwithstanding all of this there is clearly, I believe, still evidence of a certain type
of "*scotosis*" in our understanding when it comes to the whole area of
the philosophical anthropological principles upon which the free market
is based. Lonergan describes "*scotosis*" as an "aberration of understanding" and it could be equally applied to the current miscomprehension in
terms of issues pertaining to the economy and its actual foundations.[21]
Lonergan interestingly describes a type of "flight from understanding"
when he says that

> just as insight can be desired, so too it can be unwanted. Besides
> the love of light, there can be love of darkness . . . To exclude
> an insight is also to exclude the further questions that would
> arise from it and the complementary insights that would carry
> it towards a rounded and balanced viewpoint. To lack that fuller
> view results in behaviour that generates misunderstanding both
> in ourselves and in others. To suffer such incomprehension fa-
> vours a withdrawal from the outer drama of human living into
> an inner drama of phantasy.[22]

A considerable number of philosophers and economists alike have
also referred to the ongoing challenge and responsibility of understanding the economic drama we live in. I mention here, for example, the
works of Edward Fullbrook, who presents the contributions of what's
often called the "post-autistic economics movement."[23] One of his books

19. Lonergan, *Insight*, 233–34.
20. Ibid.
21. See ibid., 191.
22. Ibid.
23. See also Ormerod, *The Death of Economics*, and Keen, *Debunking Economics*.

is called *The Crisis in Economics: The Post-autistic Economics Movement; The First 600 Days*, and another is *A Guide to What's Wrong with Economics*. In an essay in the later work, "Economics as Ideology and the Need for Pluralism," Peter Söderbaum remarks that "in neoclassical theory, only a market context is taken into account . . . But the individual is at the same time part of a number of 'we-contexts,'" and so he suggests that concern for others is a normal feature of economic life.[24] Sociologist Amitai Etzioni in a similar context proposed the importance of an "'I & We Paradigm' within social and economic models where egoistic tendencies and concern for others are combined rather than mutually exclusive."[25]

Fullbrook and many others involved in the so-called post-autistic movement hold that economics has become divorced from human reality and that there is a subsequent failure to account for personal and social "reciprocity." The Irish philosopher Philip McShane somewhat analogously speaks of the retreat of economics from the philosophy of "common sense." He uses the metaphor of driving a car and draws parallels between it and the economy. Controlling a car as such is not a matter for debate in parliament. He observes that an automobile "has norms of driving built into it: there are rhythms in which you press the accelerator, use the clutch, change gear, brake. If you go against these norms of driving, then you will fail to drive the car properly; indeed, you may damage the engine. The parallel emerges in the claim that the economy has norms of 'driving' built into it."[26] McShane argues that economics is democratic not just in terms of its powers of co-ordination of resources but also in regard to the insight into its workings. He says, "Economics is democratic, [and therefore] for everyone."[27] Robert Dahl in *A Preface to Economic Democracy* argues that democratic principles should be extended to the economic order, although it seems to me that Dahl has a "workplace democracy" more in mind here than McShane's actual concept of "democratic insight."[28]

There are certain norms for driving the economy just as there are for motoring from A to B. If the distance between A and B is 200 kilometers and the roadway is excellent but a driver insists on driving

24. Fulbrook, *Guide to What's Wrong with Economics*, 163.

25. Ibid.

26. See McShane, *Economics for Everyone*, 8–9.

27. Ibid.

28. See also Novak, "The Future of Democratic Capitalism." I have already referred to Tomasi's concept of "market democracy" in his *Free Market Fairness*.

continuously in first gear, we can adjudge the said driver to be driving his
car badly since his method of driving will possibly result in damaging the
gear mechanism or even the engine of the vehicle. When we transpose
McShane's image of driving a car to that of the economy we can begin
perhaps to understand the importance of trying to articulate and develop
the anthropology that underlies the market economy. Because as I argue
throughout this book, it is the human person who is the "wealth dynamic"
at the heart of the process. In arguing for "democratic responsibility" in
economics McShane points out that he is simply "not talking about some
blind acceptance of a bank-rate." Rather, he says, "I am talking about a
common view of proper economic driving that is prior to bank rates or
taxation policies. I am talking about a general democracy of minding
the economy."[29] Otherwise, we risk becoming "sleepers" at the wheel of
economic life. In other words, before we come to obvious concerns like
economic policy there is a need to clarify *how* the free market process
actually works and what are the central philosophical and anthropological foundations it is based on in the first place. It is my contention that
the process is actually person-based but that this has a history of being
eclipsed from our human understanding, and this is true too within economic reflection. As Havel reminds us in his *Summer Meditations*, the
real challenge is to become true participants in the drama of humanity
including its economic aspect and the corresponding responsibility that
confers upon us.[30]

II. The Free Economy and Its Discontents[31]

The cultural landscape we inhabit exhibits strong signs of discontent on
the personal, intellectual and social levels. In Europe, for example, we
have the "*post-Mauer*" generation who in turn forget the "*ante-Mauer*"
social and political context. The cry that "*die Mauer ist weg*" and the
collapse of the communist system behind that wall, seemed to usher in
a new springtime and openness to the advancement of the free market
economy. We must never forget the *historical* and *existential* magnitude

29. See McShane, *Economics for Everyone*, 9.

30. Havel, *Summer Meditations*, 62, 126. See Pontuso, "Free Markets and Civil Society: Citizen in the Global Economy."

31. It was Sigmund Freud in the 1930s who used the second part of this phrase in
his book *Civilization and Its Discontents*. Various authors have subsequently used it.
See Stiglitz, *Globalization and Its Discontents*.

of the revolutions of 1989 and the subsequent collapse of the Soviet Union in 1991. Professor Vladmir Tismaneanu adjudges that these revolutions were "the endpoint of the historical era ruled by utopia."[32] He points out how "the Soviet bloc's efforts to create the City of God here and now, the search for the perfect society, turned out to be an abysmal failure. The record sheet of these regimes was one of absolute failure, economically, politically, and morally."[33]

Indeed, the opening up of the archives in different Eastern bloc countries finally opens up the possibility of settling "the crucial issue of intentionality and criminal culpability" in regard to these regimes. Anne Applebaum's *Gulag: A History* outlines how the concentration camps in the Soviet Union were created as "the final stage in a long process of dehumanization" in which people were arrested not just for what they'd done but "for who they were" as human persons.[34] Applebaum also published *Iron Curtain: The Crushing of Eastern Europe, 1944–1956* where using the newly opened archives, she focuses on the totalitarian regimes in Hungary, East Germany and Poland. Such systems developed an all-embracing conception of the State such that "outside of it no human or spiritual values can exist, much less have value." Indeed, she notes how Friedrich Hayek's *Road to Serfdom* was a philosophical response to this dystopian vision.[35] The historian Timothy Snyder asserts that one of the often-ignored realities in any adequate historical analysis of totalitarian ideologies like the Soviet one, is the economic dimension. He observes that

> what is crucial is that the ideology that legitimated mass death was also *a vision of economic development*. In a world of scarcity, particularly food supplies, both regimes [Nazism and Communism] integrated mass murder with economic planning . . . If there is a general political lesson of the history of mass killing, it is the need to be wary of what might be called *privileged development*: attempts by states to realise a form of economic expansion that designates victims, that *motivates prosperity by mortality*. The possibility cannot be excluded that the murder of one group can benefit another, or at least be seen to do so. The only sufficient answer is an *ethical commitment to the individual, such that*

32. See Tismaneanu, *Devil in History*, 45.
33. Ibid., 27.
34. Applebaum, *Gulag*, xxxvi.
35. Applebaum, *Iron Curtain*, xxiii.

the individual counts in life rather than in death, and schemes of
this sort become unthinkable.[36]

In fact, among some economists a famous debate called the "socialist calculation debate" had gone on. Thinkers like Ludwig von Mises and
Friedrich A. Hayek had made the claims that "centrally planned economies were doomed to failure." Randall Holcombe remarks that

> the socialist calculation debate that so tarnished Austrian eco-
> nomics because Mises and Hayek refused to concede, became
> one of the crowning achievements of Austrian economics once
> the Berlin Wall came down in 1989, followed by the collapse
> of the Soviet Union in 1991. Mises was right, it turned out
> . . . Economists who at one time had dismissed the Austrian
> School wanted to discover what insights had led Mises and only
> a handful of others to be so certain of their ideas, despite the
> almost unanimous disapproval of academic and professional
> economists.[37]

Notwithstanding the collapse of communism in the Eastern European countries and the Soviet Union, the world at large is tending toward
increasing fragmentation as a result of the spectre of terrorism and other
political and economic tensions. World leaders cannot remain impervi-
ous to the anti-globalization protests and the civil unrest they give rise
to. Those who gathered at the G8 summit in Genoa back in 2001, for
instance, were shocked at the magnitude of the anti-globalization riots
and violence. It made uncomfortable reading for their national and international spectators. Global events—like Live-8[38] and the associated
debt relief campaign in order to "make poverty history," along with the
corporate scandals and the subsequent ushering in of the Sarbanes-Oxley
legislation in the United States and Basel II[39] in Europe—provide credible

36. See Snyder, "Holocaust: The Ignored Reality." All emphases mine. See also Syn-
der's *Bloodlands: Europe between Hitler and Stalin.*

37. See Holcombe, *15 Great Austrian Economists*, ix, xi.

38. The Live-8 event was organized on 2 July 2005 by the Irish rock star Bob
Geldolf. It globally linked up ten international rock concerts, with venues stretching
from Philadelphia to Moscow. The purpose was to lobby the world leaders of the G8
countries who were about to meet at Gleneagles in Scotland for their annual summit.
The goal was to urge them to combat poverty in Africa by debt relief and to remove
unfair trade laws, etc.

39. The Sarbanes-Oxley Act, signed into law in July 2002 in the United States, was
enacted in response to a series of corporate failings centered on deceptive financial
reporting in publicly owned companies. The legislation is geared toward protecting

evidence of the causal influence of public opinion and financial climatic changes upon politicians, businesses, economists and intellectuals alike. This all occurs in the milieu of an ever-increasing global economic perspective. The self-immolation of the street vendor Mohammed Bouazizi in protest against the confiscation of his wares and the humiliation inflicted on him by a civil official became a catalyst for the Tunisian Revolution and the subsequent Arab Spring.

In this field there is a plethora of literature both popular and academic on the issue of globalization, its problems, and the ensuing challenges it sets for the economic and political agenda. Some theoreticians and anti-globalization activists see the spread of a global economics as the diffusion of a more predatory form of capitalism which as such should be opposed at all costs. On the other hand, within the post-Great Recession context and the uncertainty of the Arab Spring there is in the commercial world the clear recognition of the need for change, while the development of concepts like "corporate social responsibility," "corporate governance," and a whole debate about "shareholder value theory"[40] are proof of this transformation of economic perspective. It is unlikely that these changes would have come about save for the mobilization of public opinion and the fallout effect of corporate corruption upon the current situation.[41]

Indeed, if you survey financial journals and literature you will observe in some of them a deep sense of foreboding at the present state of human economic activity. There is no doubt the attack on the Twin Towers of the World Trade Center on September 11, 2001, sent shock waves throughout financial centers and set in train a whole questioning of the economic system we work in. Edwin Heathcote of the *Financial Times* wrote that from a certain perspective "the World Trade Center was not a random target. It was destroyed as a representation of Babylon, an

---

investors and employees; the law addresses a wide range of accounting and financial issues. In the European context corporate governance matters are covered by the regulation titled the Basel Capital Accords, also referred to as Basel I, II, and III, respectively (cf. http://www.bis.org/publ/bcbs107.htm). In the global context all such legislation affects the world of business no matter where the economic concern is based.

40. See the following articles on "shareholder value theory" by *Financial Times* columnist Michael Skapinker: "It Is Time to Knock Shareholder Value off Its Pedestal" (23 February 2005) and "Measures of Success Must Go beyond Financial Results" (2 March 2005).

41. See Kinsella and McNerney, "Corporate Sickness and Corporate Health."

insolent attempt by (occidental) man to reach the heavens."[42] *The Economist*, for example, in a post-9/11 2002 issue, led with the cover story "American Capitalism Takes a Beating."[43] There is nothing particularly new in these kinds of headlines. Back in 1917 G. K. Chesterton wrote a piece titled "The Capitalist Is in the Dock," where he said

> if we were to say that it could by any possibility be represented as being the negro's fault that he was at that moment in America and not in Africa, we should be saying what frankly is unreasonable. It is every bit as unreasonable to say the mere supineness of the English workmen has put them in the capitalist slave-yard. The capitalist has put them in the capitalist slave-yard; and very cunning smiths have hammered the chains. It is just this creative criminality in the authors of the system that we must not allow to be slurred over. The capitalist is in the dock today; and so far as I at least can prevent him, he shall not get out of it.[44]

In regard to the various corporate scandals that have emerged in the past and we can see this even up to today, Geoffrey Owen of the *Sunday Telegraph* wrote that "the collapse of Enron at the end of 2001, and the other scandals which followed, revealed an extraordinary picture of greed . . . Senior managers, aided and abetted by supposedly upright auditors, had been speculating with shareholders' money on a grand scale, enriching themselves in the process."[45] In a special report in the *Financial Times* it was observed that "the sight of executives being led away in handcuffs before the world's gleeful cameras will be remembered as the defining image of 2002. Five of the top 10 bankruptcies that have ever taken place occurred in that single year, while no less a figure than the chairman of the Federal Reserve [Alan Greenspan] has mourned the 'infectious greed' eroding the legitimacy of wealth creation."[46] More recently we've had the Libor rigging scandal and then the revelations of the HSBC's tax avoidance schemes at its Swiss subsidiary.[47] It is insightful to read Governor of the Bank of England Mark Carney's speech "Inclusive Capitalism: Creating a Sense of the Systemic" in light of the Libor scandal and the

42. See Heathcote, "Moral Angle," 21.

43. *The Economist*, 13–19 July, 2002, 11–12.

44. See *Utopia of Usurers*, 59.

45. "Unfair Shares All Around," review of *Infectious Greed*, by Frank Portnoy, *The Sunday Telegraph*, 13 April 2003.

46. *Financial Times*, 24 February 2003.

47. See Roberts and Kynaston, *The Lion Wakes: A Modern History of HSBC*.

subsequent trial. The former trader Tom Hayes stood on trial in London on rate rigging charges. Hayes claimed he didn't realize that what he was doing was wrong. In an interview transcript read out to the court he said, "The practice was tried and tested, it was so endemic within the bank [UBS], I just thought . . . this can't be a big issue because everybody knows about it . . . [it was] such an open secret."[48] The Governor of the Bank of England remarked how "the combination of unbridled faith in financial markets prior to the crisis and the recent demonstrations of corruption in some of these markets has eroded social capital. When combined with the longer-term pressures of globalisation and technology on the basic social contract, an unstable dynamic of declining trust in the financial system and growing exclusivity of capitalism threatens."

Carney argues that it is vital to "recognise the importance of values and beliefs in economic life" and that "economic and political philosophers from Adam Smith (1759) to Hayek (19060) have long recognised that beliefs are part of inherited social capital, which provides the social framework for the free market." The values and beliefs at the foundations of inclusive capitalism are, according to the Governor, *dynamism, long-termism, fairness, trust* and an *engaged citizenship*. He outlines how "unchecked market fundamentalism" can devour these essential characteristics and we can move, as Michael Sandel suggests, from "a market economy to a market society." There is a need, Carney says, to rebuild a sense of vocation and responsibility. He concludes that the "reductionist view of the human condition" exposed in the corruption scandals "is a poor foundation for ethical financial institutions." The run-up to the crisis saw banking "become about banks not business; transactions, not relations; counterparties not clients." He outlines how it is important to recognize that "financial capitalism is not an end in itself, but a means to promote investment, innovation, growth and prosperity" in which the human person can individually and collectively flourish.[49]

It is within this scenario that fundamental questions are being asked about the whole basis of human actions in the economic arena. The debate is not just left to the street protestors; scholars have also joined in the discussion. Raghurman Rajan, professor of finance at the University

48. "Trader Tom Hayes 'Put Libor Wishlist on Facebook,'" *The Telegraph*, 13 July 2015.

49. Carney, "Inclusive Capitalism: Creating a Sense of the Systemic," 27 May 2014. For a transcript of the speech, see http://www.bankofengland.co.uk/publications/Documents/speeches/2014/speech731.pdf.

of Chicago Booth School of Business, argues, for example, that the global financial crisis cannot be blamed on a few greedy bankers who took irrational risks.[50] A key to understanding the Great Recession is to realize that the economic system is really built upon certain anthropological principles which can indeed become fault lines if the principles are not respected or properly understood. Rajan comments that

> the key then to understanding the recent crisis is to see why markets offered inordinate rewards for poor and risky decisions. Irrational exuberance played a part, but perhaps more important were the political forces distorting the markets. The tsunami of money directed by a US Congress, worried about growing income inequality, towards expanding low income housing, joined with the flood of foreign capital inflows to remove any discipline on home loans. And the willingness of the Fed to stay on hold until jobs came back, and indeed to infuse plentiful liquidity if ever the system got into trouble, eliminated any perceived cost to having an illiquid balance sheet.[51]

Rajan points out that most people do not have money as their sole motivation and the banker is necessarily no different. Indeed, a "primary motivation for many is the knowledge that their work makes the world a better place."[52] But it is important to keep in mind that a financier's role is also different and Rajan gives the following example to illustrate the point. He explains that "a broker who sells bonds issued by an electric power project is merely a cog in a gigantic machine, who never sees the plant she helped build. Second[ly], the most direct measure of her contribution is the money she makes for her firm. This is where both the merits of the arm's length financial system and its costs arise."[53] Indeed, the philosopher-theologian and former Chief Rabbi Jonathan Sacks' comments are insightful when he says that "no system—not scientific or political or economic—is self-justifying, worthy of endorsement just because it happens to be what it is."[54] So, it is actually a characteristic of the economic system we live in that there is almost always a lively discussion on the contents or "discontents" of the free economy. The Great Crash of

50. See Rajan, *Fault Lines: How Hidden Fractures Still Threaten the World Economy*.

51. Rajan, "Bankers Have Been Sold Short by Market Distortions," *Financial Times*, 3 June 2010.

52. Ibid.

53. Ibid.

54. See Sacks, *Dignity of Difference*, 89.

1929, for example, saw the greatest cycle of speculative boom and bust in modern times. John Kenneth Galbraith wrote his classic study on that disaster. He reminded his readers that "there is merit in keeping alive the memory of those days [the Great Crash]. For it is neither public regulation nor the improving moral tone of corporate promoters, brokers, customer's men, market operators, bankers, and mutual fund managers which prevents these recurrent outbreaks and their aftermath. It is the recollection of how, on some past occasion, illusion replaced reality and people got rimmed."

Galbraith points out how the great debacle of 1929 eventually resulted in the US Congress establishing legislation like the Securities Exchange Act of 1934. But it was not so much the promulgation of positive law that kept minds focused as "the memory of what happened to so many in 1929." Time does not stand still, however, and memories of even the most disruptive events fade. In a new edition of his classic book *The Great Crash, 1929* he points out how by the 1960s recollections of the tragedy had dimmed. He describes how

> almost everything described in this book had reappeared, sometimes in only a slightly different guise. Instead of the investment trusts there were now mutual funds . . . The admiration for skill in deployment of corporate capital that was once lavished on Samuel Insull and Howard Hopson settled now on the men who were parlaying smaller firms into big conglomerates. There were glamour stocks in both periods; in both periods glamour was a substitute for substance . . . Wall Street houses in the sixties were markedly more incompetent in their management than in the twenties and expanded much more recklessly. The consequences when the collapse came were far more troublesome than in 1929.

Galbraith discusses how the stock market crash in 1970

> was disagreeable—and the magnitude of the market decline was not so different from that in the autumn months of 1929. But it did not become cumulative . . . Yet the lesson is evident. The story of the boom and crash of 1929 is worth telling for its own sake. Great drama joined in those months with a luminous insanity. But there is the more somber purpose. As a protection against financial illusion or insanity, memory is far better than law. When the memory of the 1929 disaster failed, law and regulation no longer sufficed. For protecting people from the cupidity of others and their own, history is highly utilitarian.

> It sustains memory and memory serves the same purpose as
> the S.E.C. [Securities and Exchange Commission] and, on the
> record, is far more effective.[55]

Galbraith's summation here on the importance of "*memory*" read
from the perspective of philosophical anthropology is suggestive, I believe, of Plato's concept of *anamnesis*.[56] Suffice to say that in the area of
business and economic activity, the cycles of prosperity and decline involved in the process imply a constant need to keep in abeyance what
Paul Ricoeur calls "being stymied by a fruitless aporia"[57] when it comes
to the inner nature of the market economy. Ricoeur emphasizes that
anamnesis is a "recollection [which] consists in an active search."[58] In
our case we are speaking of an adequate philosophical understanding
of human economic activity within the parameters of the free economy.
Indeed, Ricoeur outlines his own path of study as moving "from 'What?'
to 'Who?' passing by way of 'How?'"[59]

Likewise, throughout the following chapters of the book we will
philosophically examine the "human action" which lies at the heart of
the economic drama of humanity in the free economy. We'll explore
what is involved, who is concerned in the economic activity, and how
the whole process has important anthropological significance. We can be
said to have here a "common-sense" approach to our field of enquiry.[60]
Indeed, Bernard Lonergan endorses this approach when he observes how
"the practicality of common sense engenders and maintains enormous
structures of technology, economics, politics, and culture, that not only
separate man from nature but also add a series of new levels or dimensions in the network of human relationships . . . In the drama of human
living, human intelligence is not only artistic but also practical."[61]

---

55. See Galbraith, *Great Crash*, 9–11.

56. "A philosophy of order is the process through which we find the order of our
existence as human beings in the order of consciousness. Plato let this philosophy be
dominated by the symbol of 'Anamnesis,' remembrance. Remembered, however, will
be what has been forgotten; and we remember the forgotten—sometimes with considerable travail—because it should not remain forgotten." Voegelin, *Anamnesis*, 36–37.

57. See Ricoeur, *Memory, History, Forgetting*, 3.

58. Ibid., 17.

59. Ibid., 4.

60. See Lonergan, *Insight*, 232.

61. Ibid., 234–35.

I find Lonergan's reflections insightful because in his own philosophical writings on economics, he always sought to use philosophical
and human understanding to try to articulate the reasons for the cycles
of growth and disintegration within economic activity he and others observed. William A. Mathews confirms this when he remarks that Lonergan always sought to address the following question:

> Does humanity progress? For he can agree with neither unquali-
> fied affirmations nor rejections of the idea of progress, seeing
> a need to distinguish between the principle and the cause of
> both progress and decline . . . he attempts to sketch the lines
> of decline that are based on the falsification of the intellect to
> be found in rationalism (Descartes to Kant), naturalism (Rous-
> seau and modern education, democratic government by public
> opinion), communism (Marx, Lenin, and Stalin), and racialism
> and the Nazis. The lines of both progress and decline are not
> separate tracks, but mixed and interacting forces . . . we should
> read . . . [Lonergan's] work on economics . . . within the context
> of the problem of progress and decline within a philosophy of
> history.[62]

In *Caring about Meaning* Lonergan further develops the point for us
when he explains that

> there is a problem in explaining the [trade cycles of boom and
> slump] but at least you have a datum there, something to ex-
> plain. When my father spoke about "the hard times in 1890,"
> people wanted to refer to earlier hard times. But they didn't talk
> about a cycle . . . The point is that you are not understanding
> your economy until you understand the cycles. It's the whole of
> economics, but it is the sort of thing that sticks out like a sore
> thumb.[63]

When Lonergan refers here to his father's experience and says that "they
didn't talk about a cycle," I am reminded of his opening comments in his
investigation of human understanding in *Insight*, when he uses the metaphor of "the ideal detective story" because this could be useful to us. All
the clues may be thrillingly and beautifully marshaled out in narration by
the author of a detective novel but this is just "seeing" the facts. They do
not necessarily lead one on to ascertain the identity of the perpetrator or
the reasons for the perpetration of the crime. There is a need for what he

---

62. Mathews, *Lonergan's Quest*, 111–12.

63. Lonergan, *Caring about Meaning*, 183–84.

calls "the supervening act of understanding" which constitutes "insight," and the same is true when it comes to the economic life.[64] The "un-un-derstandable" is what needs to be understood when it comes to the free market process. In Lonergan's estimation the question that remained to be answered was this: is the "sore thumb" of the free economy (that is, the sequence of boom and bust) due to some imponderable law of nature or to human negligence and/or a fundamental misunderstanding about the system? It was during the period between 1942 and 1943 that Lonergan wrote a series of essays now collected in his work *For a New Political Economy*.[65] In these economic writings the context and understanding of human economic activity that Lonergan underscores is *heuristic*. This essentially means that human understanding is fundamentally an ongoing learning process and this would apply equally to Lonergan's perspective on the nature of economics. He explains that

> "Heuristic" is from the Greek word *heurisko*: I find . . . a heuristic is a principle of discovering . . . The pursuit of knowledge is the pursuit of the unknown . . . The heuristic element in our knowing is quite explicit in Aristotle. He speaks of the *to ti estin* and the *to ti ę̃ einai*. In medieval philosophy there is the concern with *quidditas* . . . just as in [an] algebraic problem, by studying certain properties of . . . x . . . we . . . find out what . . . x is, so by making explicit our talk of the "nature of . . ." we will be on our way to discovering what the nature is.[66]

I suggest that we can trace here a possible connection between Lonergan's approach and that of the Austrian school of economics who also perceive the free economy as a "process" rather than a "mechanism." But this will be referred to at a later stage in this investigation when we focus on "human action" in the economy. In any discussion on "the free market and its discontents" and the Irish historical context we are, of course, ever aware of the "sore thumb" or the "discontents" contained within the nature of a rugged capitalism that, as Lonergan remarked, led British policymakers to the belief that they were actually morally obliged to apply the "necessary and ironclad laws" of the market process to the

---

64. Lonergan, *Insight*, 3.

65. Lonergan's writings in this field are contained in the companion volumes *Macroeconomic Dynamics: An Essay in Circulation Analysis* and *For a New Political Economy*. Lonergan revised his material as late as 1983, and this has been published in *Macroeconomic Dynamics*.

66. See Lonergan, *Understanding and Being*, 63–65.

THE FREE ECONOMY AT THE CROSSROADS 41

tragedy of the mid-nineteenth century Irish famine. Lonergan describes how his professor of economics had "published a book . . . on *Capitalism and Morality* at a time when 'the laws of economics were *iron*—not just necessary but iron. 'It would have been sinful to interfere with the Irish famine; that was supply and demand!'"[67]

III. The Austrian School's Approach to Economics

So, it is easy enough in the contemporary economic context to identify with Lonergan's questions and concerns. They are analogous to McShane's already mentioned call for a "democratic economics" in respect of the need to understand and clearly explicate the economic and anthropological principles that are at the foundation of human economic action.[68] The "iron-clad" notion of economic laws that Lonergan adverts to in his reference to the Irish Famine raises fundamental methodological questions as to the nature of economic science. Are economic principles necessarily "true," that is, is their basis fundamentally *a priori*? Posterity has termed this issue within economics "the Battle of Methods [*Methodenstreit*]." This dispute occurred between the "theoretical and historical economists."[69] As a controversy it created much smoke with really little fire. Schumpeter's summation is cautious and considered. Many of the arguments were based upon mutual misunderstandings, and the various theorists ended up somewhat like Cervantes' Don Quixote de la Mancha attacking windmills (Quixote) mistakenly took to be giants. Don Quixote says to his friend Sancho Panza,

> Fortune is directing our affairs even better than we could have wished: for you can see over there . . . a place where stand thirty or more monstrous giants with whom I intend to fight a battle and whose lives I intend to take . . .
> "What giants?" said Sancho Panza.
> "Those giants that you can see over there," replied his master, "with long arms: there are giants with arms almost six miles long."

---

67. See Mathews, *Lonergan's Quest*, 43. I refer readers to Cormac Ó Gráda's recent *Eating People Is Wrong*, which examines the role of market forces and market failure in the Irish Famine and in others.

68. See McShane, *Economics for Everyone*, 9.

69. See Schumpeter, *History of Economic Analysis*, 814.

"Look you here," Sancho retorted, "those over there aren't giants, they're windmills and what look like arms are sails— when the wind turns them they make the millstones go round."[70]

It is after all methodology that often explains the differences among economists and philosophers but methodology actually presupposes a particular anthropological viewpoint. I will not develop this theme, as it is not my main concern in the book. But it is nonetheless important to briefly mention the Austrian perspective on the study of economics.

Carl Menger (1840–1921)[71] wrote his famous book on methodology, *Investigations into the Method of the Social Sciences*, back in 1883.[72] He explains how during that period academic studies had not progressed to the level of a true methodology of the science of economics. Thinkers were more concerned with the parameters of the subject and its subdivisions. The time had come, he argued, for a more adequate articulation of the methods of economic science. It would be necessary therefore to clarify the answer to the following question: when economists say that they "know" something, what are they, in fact, saying when they assert that they "know" that they know? In this regard Menger and his successors in the Austrian school would, for instance, set out what I would call a more "personalistic" or "humanistic" account when it comes to an adequate theory of value in economic life. The emphasis given by Menger and his followers is to a *"subjective" theory* of value and I suggest that this can be conceivably interpreted as an attempt to recapture the original roots of the reality of the wealth of the human person as *Homo agens* who is at the heart of the free economic process. That is why in trying to elaborate an adequate economic anthropology I refer in this study to the Austrian school's perspective in economics, because notwithstanding their limitations they pay special attention to the *acting person* in economic action. In a sense the Austrian contribution is to put economic reflection back on track in terms of its "originary" anthropological foundations which philosophers and economists already recognized. It should not be forgotten, for instance, that Jean-Baptiste Say, who is often neglected by the

70. See Cervantes Saavedra, *Don Quixote*, 63–64, 419, 421.

71. It is interesting that between 1871 and 1874 three economists all published works that focused on the proper methodology for economics. W. S. Jevons wrote *Theory of Political Economy* (1871), Carl Menger, *Principles of Economics* (1871), and Léon Walras, *Elements of Pure Economics* (1874).

72. The original German title of the book is *Untersuchungen über die Methode der Sozialwissenschaften und der politischen Oekonomie insbesondere*.

Austrians, already understood the human being as the efficient cause in the economic process.

Indeed, Menger underscores something similar, when he explains that he wants to avoid any one-sided or mistaken account of economics. He observes that

> if nonetheless a number of writers on economic matters imagine they are concerned with economics, whereas in truth they are occupied with historical studies in the field of economy, it is truly worth the effort to inquire about the explanation of such an extraordinarily conspicuous error . . . The goal of scholarly research is not only the *cognition*, but also the *understanding* of phenomena. We understand it when we have recognized the reason for its existence and for its characteristic quality (the reason for its *being* and for its *being as it is*).[73]

Thus, Menger seeks to encourage economic theoreticians to recognize the lacunae in their own science and to reach in the philosopher Ortega y Gasset's words "to the level of one's time"[74] in order to explain the economic order of the free market adequately. This is comparable in a certain sense to the task that Lonergan sets himself and the reader in *Insight*. As we have mentioned previously he describes how

> in the ideal detective story the reader is given all the clues yet fails to spot the criminal. He may advert to each clue as it arises. He needs no further clue to solve the mystery. Yet he can remain in the dark for the simple reason that reaching the solution is not the mere apprehension of any clue, not the mere memory of all, but a quite distinct activity of organizing intelligence that places the full set of clues in a unique explanatory perspective.
>
> By insight, then, is meant not any act of attention or advertence or memory but the supervening act of understanding . . . The aim of the work is to convey an insight into insight. Mathematicians seek insight into sets of elements. Scientists seek insight into ranges of phenomena.[75]

So, it is in this philosophical context that Carl Menger's overall critique along with the other Austrians of the "Historical School" in economics can be best understood. In the last analysis the Historical School's fundamental failure in economic thought was that it did not achieve any

73. See Menger, *Investigations*, 9.

74. See Longergan, *Lonergan Reader*, 34.

75. See *Insight*, 3–4.

worthwhile human apperception of what *"insight into insight"* means in the economic perspective. It left us with if you like the husk of the "froth and bubble of the stream of history" but not with essential core of what economic life is fundamentally about, that is, as I will show, the unfolding of the creative capacities of the human person.

IV. An "Anthropological Surd" Giving Rise to Discontent within the Free Market Process

It is the wealth of the human person's creative capacities that reveal the human face of the economic drama. Lonergan when speaking of his own lifelong interest in economics enquires more specifically

> how can you get economic moral precepts that are based on the economy itself? That was my question. The needs of the family is an extrinsic base and *de facto* the family wage doesn't work. (Catholic moralists said the family wage is owed in charity but not in justice; you don't have to make restitution if you don't pay it.) So I had that concern. When I came back to Canada in 1930, the rich were poor and the poor were out of work. The rich were trying to get money selling apples in the street. Many theories were floating around. I was interested in Social Credit; I knew it would be inflationary if the banks dished out twenty-five dollars to everyone in the country every payday. Still, what was wrong with their argument? You had to understand the dynamic of events.

In other words, simplistic solutions based upon mistaken economic or philosophic principles can result in compounding the very issue that seeks resolution. It is interesting to note while Lonergan was back in Canada reflecting on these questions; the German economist Wilhelm Röpke (1899–1966) was being forced out of his own country and job as professor in early 1933 by the Nazis. Initially, on his return home from the First World War Röpke was drawn to socialism as an alternative. But reading the Austrian economist Ludwig von Mises's work changed his whole outlook. Röpke was part of an emerging "Ordoliberal" school of economics which gave rise to the German "economic miracle" after World War II. His ideas were grounded firmly in the Austrian tradition but he saw the inherent limitations of their approach. The "Ordoliberal" tradition "operated on the basic principle that the spiritual dimension of human life cannot be ignored and therefore neither can the transcendent dignity of each person."[76] In 1937 Röpke wrote a book titled *Die Lehre von der Wirtschaft*. It was translated into English as *Economics of a Free Society* in 1961. In it he comments on the enigmatic nature of economics. He says,

> once we have *become aware of the element of the mysterious in the economic process*, we are alerted as well to the enigmatic aspects of all the individual parts of the process. Once we have begun to ask questions and have sloughed off the naïve unconcern of the unphilosophical man who regards all things as "given," our intellectual curiosity pushes us ever deeper into the thickets of economics.[77]

Lonergan actually gives a philosophical underpinning to Röpke's approach when he explains that

> in so far as people are intelligent, reasonable, and responsible, there is progress. If they make mistakes they will notice them and correct them, so you have developing understanding. In so far as they are unobservant, unintelligent, unreasonable and irresponsible—any one of the four—you get the *social surd*, and society becomes a dump. Nothing fits together. The only thing you can do in this situation is to go back to correct all the mistakes that have been made . . . However, there is a second level in which people appeal to the facts: "You've got to live." (The dialectic is all these different things . . .) No moral precept will work in that situation. And what doesn't work is obviously absurd; why bother trying to do it? So you get an acceleration of the decline and false principles coming in.[78]

So, I argue here that Lonergan's notion of the "social surd" can be applied analogously, like an interpretative key to explaining the disjunction between anthropological theory and the "practical" or economic facts (which give rise to "discontent" with the reality) often occurring in economic reasoning. Some of the great dissatisfaction expressed in contemporary literature with respect to the free market process is due to the emergence of this phenomenon, which I call the *"anthropological surd."* Lonergan explains "why a surd is a surd," outlining that the "answer consists in showing that a surd cannot possess the intelligibility

76. See Zięba, *Papal Economics*, 122.

77. Röpke, *Economics of a Free Society*, 5.

78. See Lonergan, *Caring about Meaning*, 30–32, 87–88, my emphasis.

one would expect it to have."[79] What I mean by an application of the same Lonerganian concept here is that when it comes to understanding the free economy and its roots in the human person, that is, the anthropological reality, there seems to be a basic lack of intelligibility shown in the matter by economists and commentators alike. Indeed, as we will see later, the eclipse of the anthropological dimensions at the core of the free market process is clearly evidenced in the failure to comprehend the vital importance of "entrepreneurial action" in the whole dynamic economic process. Indeed, it was the Austrian economists who recaptured this aspect or returned to its roots and I hold that it was people like Joseph Schumpeter and others who made a considerable contribution in this regard. I will devote considerable discussion to this later. It is true that one crucial factor that needs consideration is the diagnostic moment of recognizing when the anthropological roots of the market economy are eclipsed from any economic analysis. But even so there is another significant element to understand: when the anthropological foundations are detected and recaptured the actual reality of the anthropological dimension remains "ungraspable." This is because human beings and their actions "are notoriously difficult to study."[80] The nature of the human person almost exhausts any ontological contents. The anthropological dimension is therefore surrounded by 'mystery' and is therefore part of what Röpke calls the "enigmas of economics."[81]

Contrary to the person-centered principles and perspectives that are at the basis of the free market economic process there is a type of "anthropological anorexia" in vogue in much modern economic literature, which is subsequently used to interpret and analyze the Great Recession. There is no doubt that progressive consumerism, commercialization and financial scandals are corrosive of the person-centered roots that are at the core of the economic system. Interestingly, an article in *The Economist* titled "Milton Friedman Goes on Tour" points to a survey carried out by an American firm called Edelman which indicates this. The article reports that Edelman "asked members of the 'informed public'—broadly, people with university degrees who are in the top quarter of wage-earners in their particular age groups and countries—what they think of Milton

---

79. See *Insight*, 45.
80. See Walsh, *Guarded by Mystery*, 6.
81. Röpke, *Economics of the Free Society*, 5.

Friedman's famous assertion that 'the social responsibility of business is to increase profits.'"[82]

The findings give a good overview of the attitude to so-called free market economics. Apparently, the world's most Friedman-friendly country is the United Arab Emirates, "with 84% agreeing with his dictum."[83] The second place goes to Japan, "a country normally associated with stakeholder capitalism, but which may have tired of its model after two decades of stagnation."[84] In Sweden 60 percent of people agreed with the Friedman principle. But *The Economist* writer observes, "Perhaps people feel little need for CSR [corporate social responsibility] when the government cares for them from the cradle to the grave."[85] The United States, Britain, and Ireland show lower signs of approval with ratings of 56 percent for the US and 43 percent for the Anglo-Irish area. The nations that are striving to gain in economic momentum to lift their populations from poverty seemingly disdain CSR. Among the top ten "Friedmanite" countries, which are included in the emerging markets category, are India, Indonesia, Mexico, and Poland. It should be noted that economists like Röpke and other Austrians were particularly mindful of the possibility of free market economic distortions. This is why Röpke remarked,

> Who can be at ease in the presence of the growing concentration in economic life . . . Who can fail to see that our civilization is being destroyed by the progressive commercialization of things that are beyond economics, by the obsessive business spirit that confuses ends and means and forgets that man does not live in order to work, but works in order to live, and this perverts all human values.[86]

It is important to keep in mind that market activity is constituted by "human action," and we cannot just apportion blame for the Great Recession and financial collapse to the escape of some kind of Frankensteinian monster from the lower ground floors of Wall Street. It is the total excision of the anthropological reality presupposed by the free economy that has led in some part to the economic impasse. We've to remember after

---

82. See "Milton Friedman Goes on Tour: A Survey of Attitudes to Business Turns Up Some Intriguing National Differences," *The Economist*, 27 January 2011.

83. Ibid.

84. Ibid.

85. Ibid.

86. Röpke, *Against the Tide*, 27.

all that it is in the free market economy that "we have a freedom of moral choice, and no one is *forced* to be a scoundrel."[87] The enigma of economics is its human basis but it is an understandable conundrum if we allow for the truth and unfolding of its reality. The Austrian economists at least catch a glimpse of the anthropological dimensions that embody and presuppose any free economic process. And these are principles like the "truths about human nature and human economy, about how men work and why they work, and how they cooperate most effectively to maximize the common good."[88]

I have spoken of the development of the phenomenon of the "*anthropological surd*" in certain economic reflections. It refers to the fact that when it comes to an adequate articulation of the role of the human person in the economic process there seem to be lacunae in some of the economic literature. It is important to stress here that markets do not by themselves generate anthropological principles, rather they actually presume them. This is something that not all economists take proper cognizance of. It is interesting that this was, for example, Röpke's central criticism of the economist John Maynard Keynes. In a sense Keynes debunked the human dimension in his overall analysis of the economic system. Röpke explains that for Keynes

> economics was a part of a mathematical-mechanical universe . . . economy and society were the result of mechanical *quanta* subject to precise measurement and direction by an omincompetent technical human intelligence . . . [In Keynes] we find a man who has forgotten those mysterious powers of the human soul and of human society which cannot be expressed in mathematical equations, nor confined within an assemblage of statistics or the rubrics of economic planning.[89]

So, Keynes and his followers analyzed economic action as being the product of quantifiable aggregates, like consumption and investment, and in so doing ran the risk of overshadowing the essential anthropological dimension. But economic activity is instead the result of actions by individual human persons. The Spanish philosopher Ortega y Gasset "once wrote of the expulsion of man from art,"[90] similarly there is the danger

---

87. Röpke, *A Humane Economy*, 121.

88. Zmirak, *Wilhelm Röpke*, 53.

89. Röpke, *Economics of a Free Society*, 224, 227.

90. Röpke, *Humane Economy*, xi.

of the "expulsion of man from economics."[91] The Austrian perspective within economics actually initiates a recovery of the forgotten dimension recognizing that "economics does not stand alone but forms part of a broader understanding of the human person."[92]

It is important to say, however, that "the market economy is not everything. It must find its place in a higher order of things which is not ruled by supply and demand, free prices and competition."[93] Then again it is something else to say that it is inherently evil. According to the second viewpoint, the ostensible "discontents" of the market economy can be understood solely as a result of the dynamics of the system itself. This is why there is an urgent need for an ongoing self-appropriation and understanding on the part of the "human person" (*Homo agens*) in the economic drama of life. Hopefully, a central part of the philosophical investigation contained in this book will lead to a disentanglement of the "*anthropological surd*" contained within some economic writings. The free market economy is based upon certain fundamental anthropological principles. Indeed, any economic structure grounds itself upon a particular philosophy of the human person. It is for this reason that an economic theory is never freestanding or anomic but is "embedded" into the philosophical and social fabric of a civilization and is therefore cognizant of the "sociality of the economic system."[94] There is always a presupposed worldview and an understanding of the human person. Philosophy and economics are not therefore as popular opinion would suggest "uncommon bedfellows." Indeed, Adam Smith saw their positive connection when he once wrote that "philosophy, by representing the invisible chains which bind together all these disjointed objects, endeavours to introduce order into this chaos of jarring and discordant appearances, to allay this tumult of the imagination."[95]

V. A Legitimation-Clarification Question

The German philosopher Jürgen Habermas wrote a work in the 1970s titled *Legitimationsprobleme im Spätkapitalismus* where he wrote about

91. Ibid., xii.
92. Ibid.
93. Ibid., 91.
94. See Milberg, "Robert Heilbroner Problem," 238.
95. See Heilbroner, *Essential Adam Smith*, 16.

the "crisis tendencies" in what he termed "advanced capitalism."[96] He contended that we are confronted in the contemporary world with a type of "legitimation crisis" and this is on all levels. Habermas in his overall work is primarily concerned with the legitimacy of a particular social or political order. It is in Part Two of *Legitimationsprobleme im Spätkapitalismus* that he analyzes "crisis tendencies" within developed capitalism.[97] By advanced capitalism he intends "organized or state-regulated capitalism." This, he asserts, refers to two phenomena, that is, "to the process of economic concentration—the rise of national and, subsequently, of multinational corporations—and to the organization of markets for goods, capital, and labor. On the other hand, it refers to the fact that the state intervenes in the market as functional gaps develop [through actions of the Welfare State]."[98] In terms of the phenomenon of "economic concentration" similar themes are developed by Piketty and I have made reference to this in the first chapter.

It is not my intention here to enter into the specific details of the Habermasian investigation. Suffice to say that he discerns within this particular "social formation" (advanced capitalism) a colonization of the *lebenswelt* that results in what he considers to be a reification of the concept of rationality. Just as, for Thomas Hobbes, man is a wolf to man, Habermas sees men and women in developed capitalism becoming commodities for one another, trapped in the nexus of apparently objective and increasingly instrumental relations and the concomitant form of rationality.[99] Habermas outlines a whole series of what he terms "crisis tendencies" or contradictions. He discusses and studies the following types: economic (state acting as planning agent of monopoly capital), rationality (erosion of rational powers to administer the system because of opposed interests of individuals), legitimation (side effects of the politicization of the system), and motivation (erosion of traditions important for continued

---

96. See *Legitimation Crisis*, 33. Habermas continues his analysis in *The Theory of Communicative Action*. There is a rich literature by other writers on similar themes— for example, Claus Offe and Johannes Berger. See Offe, *Contradictions of the Welfare State* and *Disorganized Capitalism*, and Berger, "Changing Crisis-Types in Western Societies." See also John Plender's *Going off the Rails: Global Capital and the Crisis of Legitimacy.*

97. See Habermas, *Legitimation Crisis*, 33–94.

98. Ibid., 33.

99. See *Theory of Communicative Action*, 1:359.

existence of the system) crises.[100] The philosopher, Thomas McCarthy, gives a salient summation of the Habermasian argument, when he writes that for Habermas "the crisis tendencies . . . are no longer located immediately in the economic sphere but in the sociocultural sphere; they do not directly concern the reproduction of the material conditions of life but the reproduction of reliable structures of intersubjectivity. Habermas thus attempts to make the case for the likelihood of a legitimation crisis, not an economic crisis."[101]

My own argument is to some extent comparable to this point but it is made for different reasons. It is my contention that legitimacy questions concerning the free economy model more often arise due to a failure to account for an adequate anthropological dimension within the economic process. Thus, a "crisis" is a growth point for development and decision; it is not necessarily just indicative of reversal or catastrophe. Originally, the word "crisis" comes from the Greek term *krisis*, from *krīnein*, that is, meaning to separate, judge. The Latin form as a noun is *discrimen* and means dividing line, or crisis. Therefore, the solely negative connotation that we often see in contemporary literature with respect to the debate about the crisis within capitalism is possibly an interpretative judgment in itself. There is no doubt that the economic meltdown and the Great Recession put the free market process into a "legitimation-clarification" moment. There have been differing interpretations of what happened, and the patient, Mr. Market, no matter which viewpoint you take, ends up somewhat like T. S. Eliot's patient, "etherized upon the table." The commentator Samir Amin, for example, gives perhaps the most strained interpretation, when he likens the global diffusion of the market economy to a liberal virus akin to the human AIDS threat.[102] Thomas Woods on the other hand would claim that if you want to be honest "in seeking out the culprit" you would find at the end of any enquiry that "it's not

100. See *Legitimation Crisis*, 50.

101. See McCarthy, *Critical Theory of Jürgen Habermas*, 358–59.

102. See *The Liberal Virus: Permanent War and the Americanization of the World*. Rather like the "Piketty bubble" there has been a mini-boom in literature seeking to explain the economic crisis. See George Cooper's *The Origin of Financial Crises: Central Banks, Credit Bubbles and the Efficient Market Fallacy*. Ray Kinsella, professor emeritus at the UCD Michael Smurfit Graduate Business School, wrote in the *Irish Times*, "The Paulson package takes the Fed where it did not want to go. It socialises the worst excesses of a cult that has turned banking and free markets inside out. Worse still it perpetuates the myth that this crisis can be resolved through regulation." See *Irish Times*, Opinion, 26 September 2008.

'capitalism.' It's not 'greed.' It's not 'deregulation.' It's an institution created by the government itself."[103] The institution Woods is referring to here is the central bank, which in the United States is called the Federal Reserve. Woods observes that "the economist F. A. Hayek won the Nobel Prize in economics in 1974 for a theory of the business cycle that holds great explanatory power—especially in light of the 2008 financial crisis, which so many economists have been at a loss to explain. Hayek's work, which builds on a theory developed by economist Ludwig von Mises, finds that the root of the boom-bust cycle is the central bank."[104]

It is interesting that in the midst of the plethora of publications on the economic crisis and the subsequent Great Recession, one book is of particular significance in describing the human dimension or face of the economy. I mentioned it in the preface to *Wealth of Persons*. It is Adam Fergusson's *When Money Dies*, which recounts the period in 1923 when the Weimar Republic was all but reduced to a barter economy. Fergusson's book was originally published in 1975 but it was republished again in 2010. It is useful to recall Fergusson's insight here. He finds that if you survey the vast array of literature on the defeat of the Central Powers during the First World War, one point that will emerge is that the various analyses have by and large "ignored the human element"[105] to the whole story. They did not understand how it happened to them, and who the foe was who had defeated them."[106] The Germans did not understand what had happened to them. But the result was apocalyptic and Fergusson recalls the consequences of the expulsion of the person-centered dimension from economic reality. He describes how the "discovery that shattered their society was that the traditional repository of purchasing power had disappeared, and that there was no means left of measuring the worth of anything. For many, life became an obsessive search for *Sachwerte*, things of 'real,' constant value . . . Man's values became animal values."[107] Fergusson explains it is in this context that there is the rediscovery that "what is precious is that which sustains life."[108] It is when life is secure that society "acknowledges the value of luxuries . . . without which life can proceed

103. Woods, *Meltdown*, 64.

104. Ibid., 65–66.

105. Fergusson, *When Money Dies*, ix.

106. Ibid., xi.

107. Ibid., 255–56.

108. Ibid., 256.

perfectly well."[109] But it is when life "is insecure, or conditions are harsh, values change."[110] The lesson here surely is that almost by "inverse insight" one can grasp that there is no real measurement of value if the human dimension is eclipsed from the reality. In a chilling conclusion, echoing Brecht,[111] Fergusson explains, "In war, boots; in flight, a place in a boat or a seat in a lorry may be the most vital thing in the world . . . In hyperinflation, a kilo of potatoes was worth, to some, more than the family silver . . . A prostitute in the family was better than an infant corpse; theft was preferable to starvation, warmth was finer than honour, clothing more essential than democracy, food more needed than freedom."[112]

VI. Conclusion

In conclusion, the word "crisis" is used frequently to describe economic situations like the Great Crash of 1929 or the more recent Great Recession. It is interesting that we could usefully refer to ancient Greek drama and the great tragedies and not just to the modern-day economic drama in Greece in order to recover a proper sense of the significance of the concept "*crisis*" and subsequently apply it to the various economic situations.[113] It was after all the *theatron* (literally "viewing space") that gave the opportunity for the Greeks to witness the drama of the *krisis* performed so that all could participate in the unfolding play. Lonergan explains, for instance, how Aeschylus depicts just one thing in *The Suppliants*, and that is "*a decision.*" In the play the daughters of Danaus are fleeing from the Egyptian youths. They seek asylum on an island where Pelasgos is king. Lonergan observes,

> [T]he whole play is the decision of the king to risk war with the Egyptians by giving asylum to the maidens. In other words, the play consists in objectifying, in setting before one's eyes as a spectacle, the inner process of deciding, of making a choice.

109. Ibid.

110. Ibid.

111. "Erst kommt das Fressen, dann kommt die Moral" (Grub first, then morality). From Bertolt Brecht's 1928 *Die Dreigroschenoper*, 67.

112. Fergusson, *When Money Dies*, 256.

113. Aeschylus (524–455) wrote *The Oresteia*, *The Persians*, *The Suppliants*, and *Seven Against Thebes*. Sophocles is best known for *Oedipus the King*, *Antigone*, and *Oedipus at Colonus*. Euripides (485–406) is best known for his plays like *Electra*, *Medea*, and *Hecabe* depicting women coming to violent decisions because of their suffering.

> Free will is a property of man, but it is one thing to have free
> will, and it is another to be able to think about one's own free
> will as one does about any other object. To take that step was an
> achievement of Greek tragedy.[114]

The spectators in Greek drama are classically presented with (1) the
dilemma, (2) the decision, and (3) the courage needed to implement the
judgment. The dilemma is often a tragic dislocation on individual, social,
and cosmic levels. Nonetheless, the unfolding drama leads to a resolution of this disorder. The blind prophet Teiresias, for example, reminds
Creon in Sophocles' play *Antigone*, "Now you are balanced on a razor's
edge . . . Why has this sickness struck against the state? Through your
decision . . . All men may err but error once committed, he's no fool nor
yet unfortunate, who gives up his stiffness and cures the trouble he has
fallen in. Stubbornness and stupidity are twins."[115] All the participants
within the drama are moved as subjects toward an existential judgment
and this pertains not just to the *dramatis personae* of Greek tragedy but
can also be applied to the economic drama of life. This is why I speak here
of a "meaningful crisis" with regard to the contemporary debate about
the legitimacy or otherwise of the free economy. If there are, as I have as
described, Attic precedents to the concept of a "crisis" on an individual
and social level, there are also instances of such inquiring in recent history into the raison d'être for the existence of the free economy. The Austrian perspective within economics offers the possibility to re-examine
the economic dilemma and to reflect on the nature of human action, and
it provides important anthropological insights into the nature of the free
market process. In Greek tragedy there was always the principle of *pathei
mathos*, that is, the fact that real wisdom often comes through suffering. This is important too in terms of understanding economic crises,
as there is no doubt the Great Recession has brought immense suffering
to people and families. Indeed, one reason for writing this book is that
in the case of the economic reality we are in, there is a need for a critical
anthropological reflection (and this can be painful) whereby the spectator is moved beyond pity, fear, and/or condemnation of others, to the
point of gaining the insight that the question of order or disorder on the
individual, social, and economic levels is also our individual responsibility—in other words, *tua res agitur* (this is your business). In the words of

114. See Lonergan, *Philosophical and Theological Papers, 1958–1964*, 246.
115. Sophocles, *Antigone*, 192–93.

King Pelasgus and applying them to the task of the "self-appropriation" involved in gaining an adequate understanding of the free market, "there is need of deep and saving counsel, like a diver's, descending to the depth, with keen eye and not too much perturbed, to make the end without disaster for us and for the city."[116]

So, when Habermas and other commentators speak of "crisis tendencies" within capitalism, I think that it is useful to keep in mind a much broader concept than just a negative judgment on the issue. Habermas, of course, does not necessarily have a negative appraisal in mind, but if you read some modern reflections on the free economy there is ample evidence of critique and rejection when it comes to a diagnosis of the state and nature of the theory that underlies it. There is therefore certainly a need for a "clearing up" or a "clarification" about the foundations of the free market process. There are evidently issues to be confronted when it comes to an adequate explanation of the free market as an economic system. Anti-globalizationists, for example, often critique globalization for its spreading of a kind of "turbocapitalism" that results in the supremacy of the "market."[117] Globalizationists, on the other hand, frequently view the fall of the Berlin Wall and the economic system upholding it as the final end of the historical conflict between communism and capitalism.[118] The collapse of communism saw in the late 1980s the publication of such works as Francis Fukuyama's *The End of History and the Last Man*. Fukuyama writes that his argument then was that

> a remarkable consensus concerning the legitimacy of liberal democracy as a system of government [and the economic system pertaining to it] had emerged throughout the world over the past few years, as it conquered rival ideologies like hereditary monarchy, fascism, and most recently communism. More than that, however, I argued that liberal democracy may constitute the "end point of mankind's ideological evolution" and the "final form of human government," and as such constituted the "end of history."[119]

116. See Aeschylus, *Suppliants*, 66c/407.

117. See Keane, *Global Civil Society?*, xi.

118. See also Huntington, *The Clash of Civilizations and the Remaking of World Order*.

119. Fukuyama, *End of History*, xi.

The jury of history is surely still out in terms of this assessment and in any case Fukuyama subsequently qualified his comments.[120] The very concept of an "end point" in history is controversial but not uncommon, as evidenced in Hegelian and Marxian analysis. He acknowledged clearly in his afterword that the "End of History" line of reasoning is the Achilles' heel of his investigation and that it was this that subsequently led to various misinterpretations and drove people away, he claims, from his original meaning. A solely economic interpretation of historical change is evident, for example, in the viewpoint he expresses when he says,

> liberal democracy remains the only coherent political aspiration that spans different regions and cultures around the globe. In addition, liberal principles in economics—the "free market"—have spread, and have succeeded in producing unprecedented levels of material prosperity, both in industrially developed countries and in countries that had been, at the close of World War II, part of the impoverished Third World.[121]

This could indeed be interpreted as a capitalist variant of the Marxian analysis of history. In the long run it seems to me that Fukuyama's overall analysis uses questionable premises in order to establish a reasonable viewpoint as to the causes for the diffusion of liberal democracy and the "free market." Nonetheless, in such a "historicist view of human development,"[122] and these are Fukuyama's own words, there is the danger that the multidimensional nature of human reality ends up being obscured and reduced. Indeed, Ludwig von Mises clearly points out that

> a dogma supported by many historicists asserts that tendencies of social and economic evolution as manifested in the past, and especially in the recent past, will prevail in the future too. Study of the past, they conclude, discloses therefore the shape of things to come . . . [But] we have only to realize that trends can change, have changed in the past, and will change in the future too. The historicist does not know when the next change will occur. What he can announce about trends refers only to the past, never to the future.[123]

120. See the afterword to the second paperback edition, in ibid., 341–54.

121. Ibid., xiii.

122. Although Fukuyama describes himself here as a "weak determinist" unlike the strong determinism of Marxism (ibid., 354).

123. See *Theory and History*, 204.

In his *Autobiographical Reflections* Eric Voegelin similarly points to the dangers of reductive approaches in understanding the drama of humanity. He gives, for example, an explanation of how in attempting to write his *History of Ideas* he slowly realized that

> a history of ideas was a senseless undertaking, incompatible with the present state of science. Ideas turned out to be a secondary conceptual development . . . Ideas transform symbols, which express experiences, into concepts—which are assumed to refer to a reality other than the reality experienced. And this reality other than the reality experienced does not exist. Hence, ideas are liable to deform the truth of the experiences and their symbolization . . . .I had to give up "ideas" as objects of a history and establish the experience of reality—personal, social, historical, cosmic—as the reality to be explored historically.[124]

There is a necessity in a sense to "unmask" the priority of the "theoretical" within economic reflection and return to what Voegelin calls "the reality experienced" and this will perhaps help us see and discover anew *how* the free economy can still be "fit for purpose."[125] The challenge in the next chapter is to develop a philosophical exploration of the function of economic order in society and so try to put into context the whole Austrian focus on *human action* in the explanation of the free market process. At the same time it is important to keep in mind that the analysis in my study is not primarily economic but philosophical. Joseph Schumpeter reminds us that at times many of the ideas about economics are "quenched in smoke"[126] and many of the principles are misunderstood. He argues that even in terms of "scientific analysis" there is no "straight-line fashion."[127] He comments, "It is not simply [the] progressive discovery of an objective reality—as is, for example, discovery in the basin of the Congo. Rather, it is an incessant struggle with creations of our own and our predecessors' minds and it 'progresses,' if at all, in a criss-cross fashion."[128]

Chapter three in its description of a philosophy of economic order will hopefully unearth further for the reader some of the anthropological

124. See *Autobiographical Reflections*, 79–80.

125. In a later chapter I will speak about the "existential shift" within modern economic thought.

126. Schumpeter, *History of Economic Analysis*, 3.

127. Ibid., 4.

128. Ibid., 3.

principles that shape the free economy. It is important to try to clarify the person-centered "vision" that is the "raw material" for the whole economic order we live in. It is for this very reason Schumpeter admonishes that "vision of this kind not only must precede historically the emergence of analytic effort in any field but also may re-enter the history of every established science each time somebody teaches us to *see* things in a light of which the source is not to be found in the facts, methods, and results of the pre-existing science."[129] Therefore, a "crisis," even if it is an economic one, is perhaps after all an opportune occasion to move toward the articulation of an economic anthropology that views the human person as the source of the "wealth" of any nation.

129. Ibid., 41.

3

Toward a Philosophy of Economic Order:
Retrieving the Human Meaning of the
Free Economy

When the Stranger says: "What is the meaning of this city?
Do you huddle close together because you love each other?"
What will you answer? "We all dwell together
to make money from each other"? or "This is a community"?
And the Stranger will depart and return to the desert.
O my soul, be prepared for the coming of the Stranger,
Be prepared for him who knows how to ask questions.

—T. S. Eliot, *Choruses from "The Rock"*[1]

I. Introduction

We are specifically concerned here with the free economy and the meaning of human action in this context. The focus is therefore upon the meaning of human economic activity. I have already referred to Alfred Schutz's remark regarding the core issue in economics, when he asked whether it is not the "behavior of prices" rather than the behavior of men in the market situation which is studied within economics.[2] This chapter focuses on how we can gain an understanding of the necessity of a

---

1. Eliot, *Complete Poems & Plays*, 155.
2. See Schutz, *Collected Papers*, 1:34–35.

particular social, political or economic order in terms of a philosophy of the human person and its meaning. Ludwig von Mises argued strongly for such an understanding of economics in his treatise on *Human Action* when he wrote, "economics must not be relegated to classrooms and statistical offices and must not be left to the esoteric circles. It is the philosophy of human life and action and concerns everybody and everything. It is the pith of civilization and of man's human existence."[3]

An adequate articulation of a philosophy of economic order in terms of economic systems and the human persons who participate in them involves us in "a common mode of understanding, a common measure of judgment and a common consent."[4] The adequacy and legitimacy of a particular economic process can be understood in terms of the dimension of meaning that a specific economic order possesses. When it comes to the free economy its legitimacy, as an economic order, is not based solely on questions of economic efficiency in terms of the allocation of scarce resources. In any case, efficiency would not be enough to legitimate an economic system because an economic order is ultimately grounded on the reality of the human person which enables their *"flourishing"* as such. In fact, central to understanding market exchanges are the human persons, human choices and human acts involved in the process. Careful reflection on the meaning of these factors as constitutive of economic order can contribute toward a greater understanding of the economic system we live in. In chapter two I remarked how in Lonergan's estimation the question that remained to be answered was: is the "sore thumb" of the free economy (that is, the sequence of boom and bust) due to some imponderable law of nature or is it due to human negligence or a fundamental misunderstanding about the system? We could reasonably say that the failure within economic theory to grasp the "sore thumb" is due to the eclipse of the anthropological dimensions at the core of the free market process.

Even Alexis de Tocqueville opened up the wider dimension of the meaning involved in the commercial order when he observed in *Democracy in America* that "the science of association" is the mother of all knowledge and progress.[5] He understood "association" as a powerful anthropological principle of free human action. He notes how "the

---

3. See Mises, *Human Action*, 878.

4. See Lonergan, *Collection*, 254.

5. Tocqueville, *Democracy in America*, 600.

most democratic country in the world is that in which men have in our time perfected the art of pursuing in concert the aim of their common desires and have applied this new technique to the greatest number of objectives." He pertinently asks, "Has this just resulted from an accident or is there in reality a necessary connection between associations and equality?"[6] Tocqueville opened up the horizons of meaning about economic life when he observed that "commerce is a natural opponent of all violent passions. It likes moderation, delights in compromise, carefully avoids angry outbursts. It is patient, flexible, subtle, and has recourse to extreme measures only when necessity obliges it to do so. Commerce . . . inclines . . . [men] to liberty but draws them away from revolutions."[7]

But as we've seen in economic crises and the ensuing critical debates there is always the risk in any analysis of actually derailing the fundamental anthropological basis and meaning of the free market economy. This is why there is a need for a rearticulation of the philosophical understanding that is at the kernel of the free economy. Professor John Kay clearly explained in his Wincott lecture, albeit on a pragmatic level, the danger of a lack of coherence about the nature and meaning of the market economy. Kay commented that

> the critique of the market economy today is, as it has been since the end of socialism, largely incoherent—an incoherence nicely captured in the demonstrator's slogan "capitalism should be replaced by something nicer." The defence of the market economy is often little more coherent. Supporters often do no more than point to the wealth of countries that have adopted the market economy—and to their own personal wealth. This isn't a necessarily bad argument. But it looks tarnished today. When the people who are the largest beneficiaries in terms of their own personal wealth have done substantial damage to the wealth of other people, such an argument becomes difficult to sustain.[8]

I argue here that in any given political, legal or economic mediating structure we can discern a common meaning and community that actually grounds and is the source of the value of that system. The basis of the free economy is essentially *person-centered*. The economic order we live in is not simply a response to the problem of the allocation of

6. Ibid., 596.

7. Ibid., 740.

8. "The Future of Markets," The Wincott Annual Lecture, 20 October 2009. See http://www.johnkay.com/2009/10/20/the-future-of-markets.

limited resources among competing ends. It involves us also in the drama of the application of knowledge in the unfolding story of human survival and flourishing. It is about the *"good of order"* in society and not only the *"good of desire."* This distinction which Lonergan makes between the good that is the *"object of desire"* and the *"good of order"* illustrates well, I believe, what we are involved in when it comes to differentiating the anthropological basis of a particular economic system.[9] The differentiation between the two orders is that they're contrasting the satisfaction of a specific concrete need (*"good of desire"*) and the systematic provision for continuously dealing with that need (*"good of order"*) which leads to the creation of a specific economic system. The free economy is fundamentally based on the *good of order* which also resolves the question of the satisfaction of various human needs but does not remain at that level alone. We might know of the ancient Chinese adages "Give me a fish and you feed me for a day; teach me *how* to fish and you feed me forever"; "Better to make a net than yearn for fish at the edge of the pond"; and "Do not climb a tree to look for a fish." These proverbs clearly contain seeds of economic truth and human wisdom. Evidently, the mere satisfaction of my current single desires will not change my given circumstances. The economic aspect enters in at the second level, that is, when I apply human insight to a given situation or circumstances, resulting in deliberative human actions which in turn create an order leading to my good and the good of others on the personal, political or economic levels. It is my contention that an essential aspect of the reality of the free economy is to understand that it is based upon a "good of order." I will return to this point later in the chapter.

Economic collapse or decay cannot just be reduced to questions of efficiency or failures in terms of the production of objects to satisfy desires. This is why Lonergan's analysis of the concept of the economic system as concerning the *"good of order"* is useful here. He notes how economic failures "are the breakdown and decay of the *good of order*, the failure of schemes of recurrence to function. Man's practical intelligence devises arrangements for human living; and in the measure that such arrangements are understood and accepted, there necessarily results the intelligible pattern of relationships that we have named the *good of order*."[10]

---

9. Lonergan, *Insight*, 238.
10. Ibid., 239, my emphases.

Actually, the failure to articulate the dimension of *meaning* within the discipline of economics has significant consequences. If you survey, for example, some of the basic undergraduate university textbooks in the area of economics there is a dearth in terms of a discussion of the whys and wherefores of a particular economic order. Philip McShane, for instance, makes critical reference to this absence of reflection on the "constitutive" meaning of economics in his study *Beyond Establishment Economics: No Thank-You Mankiw*. He explains that one of the difficulties in the discipline is "you are not used to being invited to push for understanding: the guinea-pig view of people pervades the realm of the first year text books. What are you used to? This is, in fact, a profound axial question. There are millennia of Empires and Orthodoxies gut-wrenching you towards stupefaction."[11] But none of these "axial questions" are, he claims, reflected on in the economic textbooks. McShane's reference to "axial questions" is interesting because it is comparable to the German philosopher Karl Jaspers' concept, when he identified an "axis-time" as occurring within history. This took place, he claims, "in China and India, in Iran, Israel, and Hellas, between 800 and 200 B.C., with a concentration around 500 B.C when Confucius, Laotse, the Buddha, Deutero-Isaiah, Pythagoras, and Heraclitus were members of the same generation." Jaspers sees this time as pivotal because it is in this epoch "man becomes conscious of the universe, himself, and his limitations . . . He asks radical questions." It was during this "axis-time" that "the fundamental categories we think to this day" were created.[12] Similarly, McShane suggests we should not simply remain "sleepwalkers" when it comes to an adequate anthropological understanding of the economic order we live in. In Heraclitus, for example, we see the emergence of "the basis for a critical, philosophical anthropology."[13] He does not attempt to explore "Being" by merely logical explanation and "human wisdom is a not a completed possession but a process."[14] Heraclitus's work is expressed only in fragments, but one of his most famous sentences is his observing how as humans we experience a world of flux, noting that "you cannot step twice into the same river" (B91.) So, the human drama occurs within the tension of participating "in the flux." Heraclitus un-

11. See Anderson and McShane, *Beyond Establishment Economics*, 3.
12. See Voegelin, *World of the Polis*, 86–87.
13. Ibid., 296.
14. Ibid., 297–98.

derstands that equilibrium "can be reached only through participation in the war of existence."[15] Actually, his insights could be equally applied to understanding the economic order we live in. Ludwig von Mises, for example, also wrote: "in life everything is continually in flux."[16] Applied to the economic drama of human life this means we have to embrace uncertainty and change and "we must innovate"[17] in order to participate in such an economic reality.

In terms of the retrieval of the human meaning of the free economy Mises argued that

> whoever neglects to examine to the best of his abilities all the problems involved voluntarily surrenders his birthright to a self-appointed elite of supermen. In such vital matters blind reliance upon "experts" and uncritical acceptance of popular catchwords and prejudices is tantamount to the abandonment of self-determination and to yielding to other people's domination . . . [A]ll reasonable men are called upon to familiarise themselves with the teachings of economics . . . Whether we like it or not, it is a fact that economics cannot remain an esoteric branch of knowledge accessible only to small groups of scholars and specialists. Economics deals with society's fundamental problems; it concerns everyone and belongs to all. It is the main and proper study of every citizen.[18]

Failure to give due regard to an adequate philosophical understanding of the "*good of order*" constitutive of the meaning of the free economy is, in the words of Lonergan, an "oversight." He describes the situations where besides "insights" "there are the contrary dynamic contexts of the flight from understanding in which oversights occur regularly and one might also say systematically. Hence, if insight into insight is not to be an oversight of oversights, it must include an insight into the principal devices of the flight from understanding."[19] Lonergan also describes the

---

15. Ibid., 308–10.

16. Mises, *Epistemological Problems of Economics*, 117.

17. See "The Shrink & The Sage: Should We Embrace Change?" by psychotherapist Antonia Macaro and philosopher Julian Baggini in *FT Weekend Magazine*, 16–17 November 2013, 51. The contributors refer to the Greek philosophers and to Heraclitus in particular.

18. Mises, *Human Action*, 878–79.

19. See Lonergan, *Insight*, 5.

cumulative advancement of such a decline and this can, I believe, be equally applied to the field of economics. He writes,

> the flight from understanding blocks the insights that concrete situations demand. There follow unintelligent policies and inept courses of action. The situation deteriorates to demand still further insights, and as they are blocked, policies become more unintelligent and action more inept. What is worse, the deteriorating situation seems to provide the uncritical, biased mind with factual evidence in which the bias is claimed to be verified. So in ever increasing measure intelligence comes to be regarded as irrelevant to practical living. Human activity settles down to a decadent routine, and initiative becomes the privilege of violence.[20]

This is why the focus in this chapter is on the question of the essential meaning of an economic system or order and its underlying philosophical basis. The relevance of the discussion can be understood in view of the fact that there is a crisis of vision or overall meaning in terms of modern economic thought and the current paradigm operated in the business world. Any omission in addressing this issue and outlining the specific meaning of an economic order would be a fundamental oversight.

II. The Meaning of Meaning and the Free Market Process

When it comes to an adequate understanding of human agency within the market process we have the empirical data (humans with specific desires and needs) but there is also a need to possess the insight into why the system works as it does and what it is doing when it works. When I ask the question, what is the free market process? I can explain this in terms of economics—how it is composed of individuals who are "personal-maximizers" in terms of their needs—and then explain the coordination and satisfaction of those desires by the intersection of demand and supply in a free market process. But this is a purely economic interpretation. It does not answer fully my query which must refer to a more universal viewpoint in order to adequately account for human action. A philosophical approach will attempt not just to "describe" the economic

20. Ibid., 8.

agent, that is, the human person, but also to "explain" the context of the human action. Thus, we do not want to simply reduce economic acts to economic events. We would like to capture the meaning of these acts and their full anthropological significance. In *John Paul II: Poet and Philosopher*, I observed how philosophy and phenomenology in particular,

> allows us to pause at the irreducible in human experience but metaphysics helps us understand the contents of the experience [in this case the human agent acting within the free market system] in terms of the whole of reality. As [the philosopher Rocco] Buttiglione describes, it is not a matter of showing phenomenologically that man is a person, but applying phenomenology to see *"in which way man is a person"* [in the economic *Weltanschauung*].[21]

In light of the Great Recession and the economic meltdown the terms "meaning" and "economic action" could be seen as opposed to each other. But, drawing on Milton Friedman's famous remark "the business of business is business," I believe that we can profitably ask, what is the business of business? Why does the human person engage in economic activity? It is Friedman's contention that "there is one and only one social [ethical] responsibility of business—to use its resources and engage in activities designed to increase its profits."[22] In fact, a lot of writers fail to quote Friedman in his entirety, in that he goes on to say in the same sentence that the profit motive must stay within what he calls the rules of the game, that is, "to engage in open and free competition, without deception or fraud,"[23] which means that economic activity occurs within a given moral framework or human perspective. In fact, on the occasion of the one hundredth anniversary of the birth of Friedman, Kevin Williamson's observations are insightful when he says,

> Friedman's libertarianism was based on an economics of love: for real human beings leading real human lives with real human needs and real human challenges . . . He loved human freedom . . . because it allowed for human flourishing on all levels . . . He didn't argue for capitalism in order to make the world safe for the Fortune 500, but to open up a world of possibilities for those who are most in need of them. The real subject of economics isn't simply supply and demand, but people, and to love liberty

21. McNerney, *John Paul II*, 149–50.
22. Friedman, *Capitalism and Freedom*, 133.
23. Ibid.

is to love people and all that is best in them. And it is something that can only be done when we are free to choose.[24]

In regard to the retrieval of the anthropological "meaning" of the economic order we live in we can say, "the meaning of meaning is meaning."[25] This might seem a tautology. There are, of course, diverse functions of meaning. I will outline here at least four such purposes and suggest how these can be applied to the economic order we live and thereby adequately recapture the anthropological significance of the economic dynamic we inhabit. I draw here on Lonergan's categories in *Method in Theology* to explore the dimension of meaning of an economic order. According to Lonergan, meaning is (a) *cognitive*, (b) *efficient*, (c) *constitutive*, and finally, (d) *communicative*. We must keep in mind that our interest is in the meaning of a specific economic structure. If it is stated that an economic system (the free economy) has a meaning, a reason for its existence, our main concern is to articulate the meaning of that meaning.

So, meaning is firstly *cognitive*. In other words at first I can experience the world just in terms of pure immediacy. I can see, touch, grasp and hear. I experience pain, hunger and thirst, eat and drink and so on. But as I develop in the use of language, I can begin to articulate and express in words "not only what is factual but also the possible, the ideal, the normative."[26] Lonergan explains how this cognitive function grows, when he writes that

> words express not merely what we have found out for ourselves, but also all we care to learn from the memories of other men, from the common sense of the community . . . from the investigations of scientists . . . from the meditations of philosophers. This larger world, mediated by meaning, does not lie within anyone's immediate experience . . . For meaning is an *act* that does not merely repeat but goes beyond experiencing. For what is meant, is what is intended in questioning and is determined not only by experience but also by understanding and, commonly, by judgment as well. This addition of *understanding and judgment* is what makes possible the world mediated by meaning,

24. Williamson, "Milton Friedman: An Economics of Love," *National Review Online*, 30 July 2012, http://www.nationalreview.com/exchequer/312703/milton-friedman-economics-love.

25. See Lonergan, *Philosophical and Theological Papers, 1958–1964*, 184.

26. Lonergan, *Method in Theology*, 76–78.

what gives its structure and unity, what arranges it in an orderly whole . . . In this larger world we live our lives.[27]

Just as the *cognitive* function of meaning grows and develops so too with the application of "*understanding* and *judgment*" to the economic order we live in, we should be able to articulate what gives the economic structure its fundamental significance.

A second purpose of meaning is that it is *efficient*. This means that as human persons our actions are purposeful and not merely gratuitous. The Austrian school of economics, for example, highlighted the human agent and in particular the entrepreneur as the efficient cause of economic activity. As previously mentioned, Alexis de Tocqueville is famous for his study *Democracy in America*. But it is in his relatively unknown work *Memoir on Pauperism* that he debunks any purely philanthropic approach (namely, "public charity") to poverty because it decommissions a central characteristic that pertains to human nature, and that is "human creativity." He argues that a social order based on "public charity" (handouts) merely traps the human person in an iron cage of idleness. He asks,

> What can be expected from a man whose position cannot improve, since he has lost the respect of his fellow men which is the precondition of all progress . . . What course of action is left to the conscience or to human activity in a being so limited, who lives without hope and without fear? He looks to the future as an animal does. Absorbed in the present and the ignoble transient pleasures it affords, his brutalized nature is unaware of the determinants of its destiny.[28]

So, *creativity* is in essence a unique distinguishing mark of the human person. The human being is an *efficient* cause in the economic drama and not just a cog in an anodyne, meaningless machine. He or she is a *chooser* and a *creator* independently and along with others. Lonergan describes this efficient sense of meaning as follows:

> Men work . . . From the beginning to the end of the process, we are engaged in acts of meaning . . . The pioneers on this continent [North America] found shore and heartland, mountains and plains, but they have covered it with cities, laced it with roads, exploited it with industries, till the world man has made stands between us and nature. The whole of that added,

27. Ibid., 77, my emphases.
28. Tocqueville, *Memoir on Pauperism*, 61.

man-made, artificial world is the cumulative, now planned, now chaotic, product of human acts of meaning.[29]

But if a human action is "inefficient" from the perspective of meaning it is therefore deprived of its fundamental significance. And this is the point I am making here regarding the *efficient* understanding of meaning. It was Karl Marx, of course, who gave one particular analysis of "inefficiency" of meaning in terms of worker "alienation." The French philosopher Jacques Maritain interestingly remarks that we should guard against any simplistic readings of Marx. Maritain writes that Marx, in fact,

> saw more deeply into things, and just as we may speak of a first "spiritual" impulse in him (his indignation at the condition imposed on man oppressed by things born of himself and his work, and himself made a thing), so we must say that in spite of certain formulas he always believed in a reciprocal action between economic and other factors, economics taken alone was not in his view the one and only source of history.[30]

The French philosopher Simone Weil also gave a phenomenological description of the *alienation* experienced by factory workers during the 1930s when their own human agency and efficiency was anaesthetized within highly industrial mechanized systems. This was, of course, a premonition of how conditions would develop in a National Socialist Europe that became one enormous factory whose raison d'être was the decommissioning and destruction of undesirable persons. Franco Fortini, in a postscript to an Italian translation of Weil's writings titled *Simone Weil: La condizione operaia*, reminds us that "the working conditions endured by Simone Weil, towards the end of 1934 and the following year, were similar to those of the rest of humanity . . . The same humanity who without social boundaries, would experience a little while later the complete loss of self, in the immense factory of slavery and violence into which Europe would be transformed."[31]

29. See *Method in Theology*, 77–78.

30. See Evans and Ward, "The Roots of Soviet Atheism," in *Social and Political Philosophy of Jacques Maritain*, 252.

31. See Weil, *La condizione operaia*, 297. Franco Fortini, the translator of this book on Weil, wrote, "la condizione operaia fu allora per Simone Weil, tra la fine del 1934 e l'estate dell'anno seguente, senza'altro la condizione umana . . . Quella stessa umanità che di lì a poco sarebbe costretta, senza più confine sociali, allo smarrimento totale di sé, nell'immensa fabbrica di schiavitù e di violenza in cui l'Europa sarebbe stata

Weil describes clearly the horror experienced if human activity is divested of its *effective* meaning. Of course, the cataclysmic experience of National Socialism in Europe was the apotheosis of such a "divestation" of human meaning. Weil observes that there are also dangers within a capitalism in which the human person ends up going "to work in order to eat, to eat in order to work . . . A squirrel turning in its cage . . . The great hardship in manual work is that we are compelled to expend our efforts for such long hours simply in order to exist. The slave is he to whom no good is proposed as the object of his labour except mere existence."[32] A necessary corollary to this function of meaning, its inherent efficiency, is that the order of society and the economy is not wholly random but is, as we will see, "person-centered." Indeed, it is philosophers like Weil and Karol Wojtyła who advanced a similar line of reasoning. Wojtyła, for instance, noted,

> The present age . . . is a time of great controversy, controversy about the very meaning of existence, and thus the nature and significance of the human being . . . This aptly describes the situation in Poland today with respect to the whole political reality that has arisen out of Marxism, out of dialectical materialism . . . The truth about the human being, in turn, has a distinctly privileged place in this whole process, it has become clear that at the centre of this debate is not cosmology or philosophy of nature but philosophical anthropology and ethics: the great and fundamental controversy about the human being.[33]

Weil equally observed how Marx had intuited that social dislocation was the result of how societies were deliberatively organized. She attests how "Marx showed clearly that the true reason for the exploitation of the workers is not any desire on the part of the capitalists to enjoy and consume, but the need to expand the undertaking as rapidly as possible so as to make it more powerful than its rivals." She argued that

> a methodological improvement in society in social organization presupposes a detailed study of the method of production, in order to try to find out on the one hand what we may expect from it, in the immediate or distant future, from the point of view of output, and on the other hand what forms of social and cultural

---

trasformata."

32. See Weil, *Gravity and Grace*, 158–59.
33. See Wojtyła, *Person and Community*, 220.

organization are compatible with it, [and are thereby efficient in meaning] and finally, how it may itself be transformed.[34]

This is the second function of meaning, that is, it is *efficient*, and human action is deconstructed without this essential characteristic.

The third role of meaning is that it is *constitutive*. Language, for example, has specific contents. It contains sound and meaning. Lonergan explains *constitutive* meaning when he explains how

> social institutions and human cultures have meanings as intrinsic components. Religions and art-forms, languages and literatures, sciences, philosophies, histories, all are inextricably involved in acts of meaning. What is true of cultural achievements, no less is true of social institutions. The family, the state, the law, *the economy* are not fixed and immutable entities.[35]

My point here in terms of the *constitutive* meaning of the economic order, is to say that it implies certain anthropological dimensions or horizons of meaning which are an essential part of its meaning. The history of economics is in itself illustrative of the fact that theoretical viewpoints adapt to different circumstances. Theorists can gain new insights into human economic action. The economic order functions also in virtue of a meaning attributed to the system and its organization. Social orders like the economy or state can change by revolutionary or democratic means. But in either case this implies in itself a modification of purpose and meaning and so it involves a diverse judgment or appraisal. Thus, the meaning of meaning has a *constitutive* function, that is, meaning is "*meaningful*" or else it is "*unmeaningful*" in terms of its contents. This is equally true when applying the concept of the *constitutive* dimension of meaning to the discipline of economics. We can show this briefly if you take the example of economists like the American Irving Fisher (1867–1947) and the Swede Knut Wicksell (1851–1926). Fisher developed a theory of interest that broke in some ways with Eugen von Böhm-Bawerk's (1851–1914) approach.[36] Fisher wrote and completed his work in 1930 and titled it *The*

---

34. See Weil, *Oppression and Liberty*, 40, 45–46.

35. See Lonergan, *Method in Theology*, 78, my emphases.

36. Böhm-Bawerk was a disciple of Menger; his opus magnum was *Kapital und Kapitalzins* (1884). English translations appeared as *Capital and Interest* and *Positive Theory and Capital*. He also wrote *Zum Abschluss des Marxschen Systems* (1896), translated as *Karl Marx and the Close of His System* (1898). Schumpeter calls Böhm-Bawerk "the bourgeois Marx" in *History of Economic Analysis*, 846.

Theory of Interest, while Wicksell wrote *Geldzins und Güterpreise* in 1898 with an English translation appearing as *Interest and Prices* in 1936. The specifics of the issues involved don't concern us here. But Axel Leijon-hufvud, in a chapter called "Episodes in a Century of Macroeconomics," points to the importance of the essential *constitutive* contents within meaning that economists attach to different theories when he observes that

> one hundred years ago, economists had some quantitative infor-mation on money, interest and prices, and on very little else. So the story begins with monetary theory and the two great names of Irving Fisher and Knut Wicksell. Fisher and Wicksell shared a passionate concern for *distributive justice* . . . Their shared conviction that changes in the price level had arbitrary and unfair distributive effects motivated their work on monetary theory. The objective was to learn how the price level could be stabilized.[37]

An observer could argue that the reality, in this case the economic facts about "money, interest and prices" are far more important than meaning because meanings can be diverse. It could be maintained that if we are looking for a common meaning in economics then inevitably we will end up disappointed. Lonergan discusses the same point when he says, "then to all appearances, it is quite correct to say that reality comes first and meaning is quite secondary."[38] But this is, in fact, an oversight. Human actuality is actually constituted "in large measure . . . through acts of meaning."[39] But an economist might suggest letting the economists get on with economic theorizing and allow others worry about the meaning of things. Or they might at least say: meaning as such does not concern us. Actually, with regard to "meaning" economists might identify with Ludwig Wittgenstein's dictum in the *Tractatus*: "Wovon man nicht spre-chen kann, darüber muß man schweigen," that is, "Whereof one cannot speak, thereof one must be silent."

But my point is that it is really a big "oversight" to think that mean-ing has no "*constitutive*" function in economics. Fisher and Wicksell were very concerned about "distributive justice" and their analysis of the quantitative data on money interest and prices was because of the

---

37. See Colander, *Post-Walrasian Macroeconomics*, 27, my emphasis.

38. See Lonergan, *Collection*, 232.

39. Ibid.

meaning they understood their work to be contributing toward. Present-day debates among economic theorists and students are evidence enough, I think, of the *constitutive* horizon. The contemporary direction and continued development of research in the economic, sociological, and philosophical fields on happiness, human well-being, interpersonal relations, and reciprocity illustrates well the need for critical reflection on the *constitutive* role of meaning.[40] In terms of an economic order that leads to overall human happiness as being constitutive of human well-being, the economists Bruno Frey and Alois Stuzer state that

> economists have shied away from dealing with happiness. They have long considered it to be an "unscientific" concept. Instead they have based their microeconomic theory on utility that has no material content but that allows the successful analysis of human behaviour. In the past few years the situation has changed: a number of economists see an advantage in measuring subjective well-being as expressed by the individuals themselves.[41]

One of the first present-day economists to study the empirical data on happiness was Richard Easterlin.[42] Professor Ruut Veenhoven has created a whole multidisciplinary database on the concept of "happiness" in nations; it is based in the department of Sociology at the Erasmus University of Rotterdam. The philosophy of this perspective is explained as follows:

> Happiness is a highly valued matter . . . Though not everybody accepts the utilitarian axiom that happiness is ultimately the only value . . . The aim of creating greater happiness for a greater number requires understanding of happiness. First of all it demands that we grasp the main determinants of happiness; not only *what* makes people happy, but also *why* . . . Happiness was a major issue in early Greek philosophy and several later philosophical schools. Currently the subject gains attention in the social sciences.[43]

Tocqueville, in a comparison between the New World (the democratic world) and the Old World (with its mercantilist approach), also

40. See Bruni, *Civil Happiness: Economics and Human Flourishing in Historical Perspective*; Bruni and Porta, *Economics and Happiness: Framing the Analysis*.

41. Frey and Stutzer, *Happiness and Economics*, vii.

42. See Easterlin, "Does Economic Growth Improve the Human Lot?," 89–125.

43. See R. Veenhoven, World Database of Happiness, http://worlddatabaseofhappiness.eur.nl/.

noted a difference in the "contents" that were, he claimed, constitutive of both worlds. He wrote, for example,

> When one moves from a free country into another which is not so, one is struck by a most extraordinary sight: there all is activity and bustle, here all is calm and stillness. In the former, improvement and progress are all that matter; in the latter, society appears to have obtained every blessing and simply longs for the leisure to enjoy them. However, the country which suffers so much turmoil to be happy is usually wealthier and more prosperous than the one that appears satisfied with its lot. And considering them one by one, it is hard to imagine how so many fresh needs are daily discovered in the one, while so few are experienced in the other . . . [I]f it seems useful to you to divert man's intellectual and moral activity upon the necessities of physical life and use it to foster prosperity . . . if, instead of moving through a brilliant society, you are satisfied to live in a prosperous one; if, finally, in your view, the main objective for a government is not to give the whole nation as much strength or glory as possible but to obtain for each of the individuals who make it up as much wellbeing as possible, while avoiding as much suffering as one can, then make social conditions equal and set up a democratic government.[44]

The philosophers John Locke and Adam Smith similarly referred to a clear "restlessness of desire" within the human heart for "meaning." They had the strong intuition that the human person is capable of self-creation and self-determination in terms of the act of meaning. Lonergan explains that besides the "transformation of nature" when meaning is "efficient" and "directive" there is also "man's transformation of man himself; and in this second transformation the role of meaning is not merely directive but also constitutive."[45] There is, I would contend, a correlation between this philosophical distinction and the one made in a paper presented at the University of Milan in 1977 by the philosopher Cardinal Karol Wojtyła in which he emphasized that his own reflections on human praxis were "intimately linked to an understanding of the human being as a person: a self-determining subject." He proceeded to present a view of human action as being "simultaneously *transitive* and *intransitive*. It is transitive as it tends *beyond the subject*, seeks an expression and effect in the external world, and is objectified in some product. It is intransitive,

44. Tocqueville, *Democracy in America*, 282–82, 286–87.
45. See Lonergan, *Collection*, 255.

on the other hand, insofar as it *remains in the subject,* determines the subjects essentially human *fieri.* In acting, we not only perform actions, but we also become ourselves through those actions—we fulfill ourselves in them."[46]

I want to suggest here a parallel between the Wojtylian use of the word "*intransitive*" as applied to the philosophical investigation of the notion of work and the Lonerganian analysis of the "*constitutive*" function of meaning. This can lead toward a philosophical understanding of human agency in the economic sphere as being, in fact, self-constitutive of the human subject. Our study will bring this out more fully as it develops. But this is why it is important in this chapter to give proper consideration to the importance of the retrieval of the role of the meaning of the free market economic order. Its importance is not solely economic but it has anthropological significance, namely, it also fulfills and unfolds who we are as creative human beings. Indeed, as I have mentioned already, Ludwig von Mises argued in his treatise on *Human Action* that "economics must not be relegated to classrooms and statistical offices and must not be left to the esoteric circles. It is the philosophy of human life and action and concerns everybody and everything. It is the pith of civilization and of man's human existence."[47]

In other words we can only grasp an understanding of the necessity of a particular social, political or economic order within the context of comprehending that it has a meaning in the first place. That is what is *constitutive* of meaning, which involves as we've remarked "a common mode of understanding, a common measure of judgment and a common consent"[48] about the economic order we operate in. We can discern in any given political, legal or economic system a common meaning and community that actually grounds and is the source for that structure. The failure to articulate this aspect of meaning within the discipline of economics has significant consequences.

When we reflect on the question of the essential meaning of an economic system or order it can indeed be argued that there is a crisis of vision or of overall meaning in terms of modern economic thought and the current paradigm operated within the business world. The economists Robert Heilbroner and William Milberg's evaluations on the crisis are

46. See Wojtyła, "The Problem of the Constitution of Culture through Human Praxis," in *Person and Community,* 265.

47. See Mises, *Human Action,* 878.

48. See Lonergan, *Collection,* 254.

provocative. They argue that it is a feature of modern day economics to be indifferent to the connection between theory and reality. They maintain that "analysis has thus become the jewel in the crown of economics. To this we have no objection. The problem is that analysis has gradually become the crown itself, overshadowing the baser material in which the jewel is set. To this we do indeed object, for without the setting there would be no crown."[49] Heilbroner and Milberg point to evidence in the history of economic theory of an "inward turn," of a turning in on itself and the failure to come up with a new paradigm that is strong enough to replace the existing model. The case in point that they refer to is the unraveling of the "Keynesian consensus." They use the example of Copernicus as illustrated by Gregory Mankiw[50] to explain their point. Mankiw observes, "Copernicus had a vision not only of what was wrong with the prevailing paradigm [geocentric system of Ptolemy], but also of what a new paradigm would look like. In the past decade, macroeconomists have taken only the first step in this process; there remains much disagreement on how to take the second step."[51] We are, I believe, conceivably at a stage similar to the time of transition between the Ptolemaic and Copernican systems in terms of anthropological developments toward a person-centered philosophy of economics. And in the words of Mankiw, some of our observations may seem irrelevant, but "ultimately they [may] point the way to a deeper understanding."[52] The decommissioning of one particular paradigm never really changes a culture; only an alternative that is better for the human person as a whole will bring this about.

That there is a crisis in terms of reflection and vision in the economic world is indisputable. The state of affairs in which humanity finds itself with respect to the world issues of terrorism, globalization and the various corporate scandals in the Western world, poses deep human and philosophical questions. The globalization debate, in particular, brings into relief the differing perspectives on the economic systems that we operate in. The Nobel Prize–winning economist Joseph Stiglitz observes that

> while economists may agree about the tools to be employed, there is no agreement about the basic economic model describing the

49. Heilbroner and Milberg, *Crisis of Vision*, 5.
50. Mankiw, "A Quick Refresher Course in Macroeconomics," 1645–60.
51. Ibid., 1658.
52. Ibid.

economy; while in many circles, the competitive model, with perfectly informed agents, rational consumers and value maximizing firms, is believed to provide the foundations for understanding both the aggregative behaviour of the economy and its components, in other circles, that model is viewed with some circumspection. Evidently, the tools are not strong enough to discriminate among fundamentally different hypotheses, or at least not strong enough to overcome differences in prior beliefs, beliefs which are often influenced by ideological concerns.[53]

There is a deafening silence in some basic economic reflections when it comes to the articulation of *how* and *why* a particular economic market process actually works. Descriptive accounts are often utilized by economists, but when it comes to "explanatory" systems there is what we can describe as "the noiseless noise." The point is that an economic order is *for* something but the pertinent question is what is it there for? An interesting and somewhat "rehabilitatory" university text in regard to these constitutive questions about meaning is called *Understanding Capitalism: Competition, Command, and Change*. The authors explain that their "three-dimensional approach" to economics is motivated by economists like Amartya Sen, Ronald Coase, George Akerlof, Joseph Stiglitz, Robert Fogel, Douglas North, Daniel Kahneman, Vernon Smith, John Nash, and others. They explain how

> during the last half of the 20th century, economics . . . became a unified but increasingly narrow field of study strongly influenced by Adam Smith's "invisible hand" metaphor and, to a lesser extent, by the work of John Maynard Keynes. In economics courses, students rarely encountered the ideas of Joseph Schumpeter . . . [T]he workings of markets became the main focus of economics. The "creative destruction" occasioned by technical change and economic progress . . . were thought to be of little interest. Of the three dimensions of what we term three-dimensional economics—competition, command, and change—only the first was seriously studied. Command and change were relegated to political science, history, or other disciplines. The "one-dimensional" approach, described . . . as *neoclassical economics*, eclipsed its rivals, except in the Communist countries, where a crude version of Marxian economics ("bastard economics") dominated the curriculum.[54]

53. Stiglitz, "Another Century of Economic Science," 134.
54. See Bowles et al., *Understanding Capitalism*, 83.

It is when the *constitutive* sense of meaning is applied in the economic sphere it becomes evident how many anthropological horizons and themes open up. Indeed, Lonergan explains that it is within this ambit that "man's freedom reaches its high point. There too his responsibility is greatest. There occurs the emergence of the existential subject, finding out for himself that he has to decide for himself what he is to make of himself. It is there that individuals become alienated from community, that communities split into factions, that cultures flower and decline, that historical causality exerts its sway."[55]

The fourth role of meaning is that it is necessarily *communicative*. In other words, "meaning" speaks of itself and thereby "becomes common meaning."[56] There is a historical cumulative process involved here. It has been described as follows: "Common meanings have histories. They originate in single minds. They become common only through successful and widespread communication. They are transmitted to successive generations only through training and education. Slowly, and gradually they are clarified, expressed, formulated, defined, only to be enriched and deepened and transformed, and no less often to be impoverished, emptied out, and deformed."[57]

Our task in this chapter has been to develop a philosophy of the free economic order using Lonergan's analysis in order to retrieve the human meaning of the economic process. Lonergan outlines how a combination of the "constitutive and communicative functions of meaning" gives rise to three pivotal ideas of "community, existence, and history." I hold that we could express what Lonergan calls "community" as analogous with the concept of "order." He explains how "community [order] coheres or divides, begins or ends just where the common field of experience, common understanding, common judgement, common commitments begin and end. So communities [orders] are of many kinds: linguistic, religious, cultural, social, political . . . [and economic]."[58]

We've now discussed the various roles of meaning as they apply to the economic sphere and I have already referred to the questioning of meaning by the practitioners of economics themselves. But it is often in the experience of "devaluation" of significance that one regains a more

55. See Lonergan, *Collection*, 255.
56. See Lonergan, *Method in Theology*, 78.
57. Ibid.
58. Ibid., 79.

comprehensive understanding. John F. Crosby observes that it "is a well known psychological fact that a thing often shows itself with particular clarity when we are deprived of it, or when we see the thing being violated or ignored where it should be noticed." He develops this in terms of an adequate philosophical appreciation of the personalistic value of the human person. He uses a moving piece from Dostoevsky's *Brothers Karamazov* "in which Zosima strikes his servant in the face: as he is later tormented by the humiliated, bloody face of the boy, he is overwhelmed with a sense of the dignity, the preciousness of the boy as a human being; this sense is so strong that it is the beginning of his conversion."[59] I mentioned in the previous chapter about the economic narrative which speaks of the "discontents" of the free market economy. There is the reality of the drama of economic inequality playing out on a global scale resulting in famine and hunger, telling a "tale of two cities" in the contemporary world.[60] Undeniably, it is in situations like these that different questions about meaning raise their head. Lonergan advises that "such devaluation, distortion, corruption may occur only in scattered individuals. But it may occur on a more massive scale, and then the words [economic terms] are repeated, but the meaning is gone . . . [The economic doctrines may be promulgated], but one wonders whether the home fires . . . [are] still burning. The sacred name of [economic] science may still be invoked but, as Edmund Husserl has argued, all significant scientific ideals can vanish to be replaced by the conventions of a clique."[61]

Indeed, Lonergan once wrote, "culture has become a slum."[62] The "economic slum," I suggest, is the situation in which we use language solely in an everyday sense. In these circumstances we are quite content to stay at the appearance level and just compare and contrast the supply and demand curves of a particular economic analysis and not see the "human person" behind the "zigzag" lines. We have previously commented on Alfred Schutz's remarks on economic methodology when he asks, "Is it not the 'behavior of prices' rather than the behavior of men in the market situation which is studied . . . the 'shape of the demand curves'

59. See Crosby, *Selfhood of the Human Person*, 9–10.

60. See Dickens, *A Tale of Two Cities*. Piketty's *Capital in the Twenty-First Century* and Atkinson's *Inequality: What Can Be Done?* addresses these issues.

61. See Lonergan, *Method in Theology*, 80.

62. Ibid., 99.

rather than the anticipations of economic subjects symbolized by such curves?.[63]

It is one thing to be able to distinguish between supply and demand curves but "there is a secondary, reflexive level, on which we not merely employ but also say what we mean by everyday [economic] language."[64] This is why the *communicative* dimension is so important because unless the meaning of the economic order is elaborated and spoken about its significance even on the anthropological level will be eclipsed from the overall understanding. These essential functions of meaning, that is, the *cognitive, effective, constitutive* and *communicative* can, I believe, be helpful in the retrieval of the human meaning of the free economic order. Just as in the shift from the Ptolemaic to the Copernican viewpoint when Nicolaus Copernicus proposed a heliocentric system rather than the widely accepted geocentric system of that time, I am speaking of a comparable transition in meaning toward the development of a more person-centered philosophy of economics. We've to be careful in the use of analogies because it must be remembered that it is arguable that economics was more person-centered prior to the mechanistic vision of market theory which started with the works of Augustin Cournot (1801–1877) among others. So, rather than a Copernican change we could speak of it as economic theory returning to its roots.

III. Toward a Differentiation of "Good of Order"

We can profitably ask now at this juncture: what is the specific end, goal and common meaning of a particular system like the free economy and the human economic activity associated with that process? The historical anthropologist Christopher Dawson's analysis of the elements constitutive of the transformation of primitive culture is insightful in this regard. He points out that it was in Susa and Mesopotamia that evidence of a certain differentiation occurs with "the great discovery [that] was made by which the tamed animal was put to labour, and the ox was taught to draw the plough." He emphasizes that

> this discovery was made at some definite period by a single people . . . [T]he coming of this new discovery wrought a profound change in culture . . . The old idle life of the savage . . . gave place

63. See Schutz, *Collected Papers*, 1:34–35.
64. See Lonergan, *Collection*, 256.

to a life in which all the productive forces of the community were employed . . . There was not just a great heightening of economic productivity, there was a new organised social activity, which prepared the way for a further division of labour, and for new forms of work and of leisure. Man had become an organiser and an *economist*, as well as an adventurer and an artist.[65]

Man becomes an "*order-er*" within his own experience and this is found on all levels of life. Dealing with the economic development of Mesopotamian culture, Dawson observes how this economic "ordering" goes beyond the local or domestic horizon. He writes, "It is clear that we are not dealing with mere domestic industry for the needs of the temple community, but with a production on a large scale for commercial ends . . . Thus in the course of the third millennium there grew up in Mesopotamia a regular money economy, based on the precious metals as standards of exchange, which stimulated private wealth and enterprise and led to a real capitalistic development."[66]

The discovery of the great Hammurabi and other legal and commercial tablets give sufficient proof of this economic differentiation. Dawson gives an analysis of the discovery of the power of trade. He describes how the Eastern Mediterranean "derived its power and prosperity neither from agriculture nor from war, but from trade and the control of the seaways."[67] Throughout his anthropological study Dawson makes reference to a process of "differentiation." He observes that "if a people possess a well-defined and distinctive culture, it will probably possess an equally well-marked type of language, and the *differentiation* of a common culture into several distinct regional types is usually accompanied by a similar process in the linguistic sphere . . . [E]ach of the cultural provinces of the European Bronze Age was an area of characterisation for a new social type which owed its character to the diverse elements out of which it was *compounded* . . . It was this process of *differentiation* which produced the different European peoples."[68]

A key agent in the movement from compactness to differentiation within culture is the rational human person. It is vital to keep in mind and especially in the economic arena that human beings are not just led by the nose and they are not solely intellect but that they have intellect

65. Dawson, *Age of the Gods*, 92–93, my emphasis.

66. Ibid., 130.

67. Ibid., 169.

68. Ibid., 320–21, my emphases.

that they apply to concrete reality.[69] Lonergan usefully describes liberty as a "disjunctive determination," that is, it involves a choice between two or more things and this is equally true within the economic drama of human life. The human will is understood as the faculty by which the human person not just acts but acts "reasonably" and therefore "well."[70] Mises further outlines this in his treatise on economics where he devotes Part one of his study to an analysis of *Human Action*. He writes that "human action is purposeful behavior. Or we may say: Action is will put into operation and transformed into an agency, is aiming at ends and goals . . . [it] is a person's conscious adjustment to the state of the universe that determines his life."[71]

A short economic history of the world from Paleolithic times to current times written by Rondo Cameron and Larry Neal illustrates the movement from *compactness* to *differentiation* in terms of human insights and decisions.[72] They, for example, in speaking of the early temple cities of Sumer, observe a movement from what they term "undifferentiated [compact] society to a stratified [differentiated] society,"[73] and they point to the fact that some Marxist analysis traces the transition from the "compact" to the "differentiated" as due to the creation of the institution of private property. I am primarily concerned here with an economic differentiation within human culture and history. Eric Voegelin has analyzed this movement from "compactness" to "differentiation." He remarks that "one of the fundamental problems in every philosophy of history turned out to be the constancy of reality experienced throughout the process of compactness and transition to differentiation . . . What happens between, say, the Neolithicum and the Modern Age are the events of differentiation. The thinker who first became aware of this problem and stated its structure was Aristotle in the first two books of *Metaphysics*."[74]

Voegelin explains how "when a new differentiation occurs, the area of reality newly articulated will be understood as an area of particular importance."[75] I would argue that when we speak of a specific economic

69. See Lonergan, "Analytic Concept of History," 19–20.

70. See Lonergan, "*Pantôn Anakephalaiôsis*," 142.

71. See Mises, *Human Action*, 11.

72. See Cameron and Neal, *A Concise Economic History of the World*.

73. Ibid., 30.

74. Voegelin, *Autobiographical Reflections*, 108.

75. Ibid., 109.

order, that is, in our case of the free economy, it can be understood in the Voegelinian sense as an evolution of a human insight into the reasonable economic "ordering" of humanity. It is the human will acting "reasonably" within the economic arena. Aristotle already in the *Politics* had outlined what he regarded as a "cycle of political forms." His attempt was to investigate whether there was any rule of thumb or *reason* in respect of how the various regimes follow one another. Aristotle's analysis is focused on the political constitution but it has economic implications. He writes that "we should begin by assuming the fundamental starting point. Many constitutions have come about because although everyone agrees on justice, that is, proportionate equality, they go wrong in achieving it."

He proceeds then to examine the reasons for changes within political order by stating that "which causes conditions leading to change is chiefly and generally what we have just been speaking of: inequality. For those who are bent on equality resort to faction [*stasis*] if they believe that though having less, they are yet the equals of those who have more. And so too do those who aim at inequality and excess, if they think that though unequal they do not have more, but equal or less."[76] Voegelin explains that Aristotle actually recognizes "a rule of seriation" to be found in the "process of civilizational saturation." It is the "economic order" that enables the process of differentiation, and so Voegelin explains how

> the phenomenon of saturation is called forth by transformations in the structure of the economy. To be sure, there was not an industrial revolution in Aristotle's time. But the progress from agrarian economy to the production of goods for the market, the development of trade relationships, of wealth through the business of import and export, is effective enough to elicit that degree of saturation that forces changes of the regime. Especially impressive were the shifts in the proportions of population groups in Athens due to the empire and the development of a fleet, just as in our industrial revolution there developed new groups of trade, shipping personnel, boat-construction and harbor laborers who quantitatively distorted the balance of the older polity forever and drove the political process forward in the direction of democracy.[77]

The English philosopher Michael Oakeshott in an essay titled "The Political Economy of Freedom" refers to the work of the Chicago

76. See Aristotle, *Politics*, 1301a25, 1302a22.
77. See Voegelin, "Man in Society and History," 199–200.

economist Professor Henry C. Simons. Although Simons was ostensibly concerned with the issues of banking, currency and monetary policy, he "was well aware that in every proposal of economic policy there lies an often undisclosed preference for a society integrated in one way rather than another. And in order to make his preferences in this matter secure against superstition, he went to some trouble to bring them out into the open and to put them in order. They do not amount to anything so elaborate as a political philosophy, indeed he claims for them only the title of 'a political *credo*'; there is nothing pretentious in this attempt to hold 'economics' and 'political' [order] together."[78]

It is important to remember Simons's approach, that is, that a specific societal and economic order is compatible with human freedom, has been espoused by many other economists and thinkers. We can mention here also Frank Knight, Milton Friedman, and Henry Wallich.[79] Knight, for example, in relation to "freedom and economic order," contends that what

> can be said about the form of economic . . . [order] is essentially a particular application of the more general political principle that democracy implies maximum individual liberty in all fields of action . . . .Relations of economic cooperation present in a somewhat special degree—or at least in a peculiarly obvious form—the combination of harmony or mutuality, and conflict of interest. The tremendous gain in the efficiency of action through association, and particularly through specialization and organization, forms a community of interest of great power . . . [T]he primary ethical principle is freedom, meaning mutual consent. And the obvious meaning of mutual consent is *free exchange*, with each party in the position to deal with any other and hence to select the "other" who offers the best terms.[80]

We have spoken in this chapter of a "differentiation" in terms of an economic system as being understood in terms of a "good of order" and this is what is implied in the argument that the free economy pertains to an "order" that enables the adequate unfolding of human action and the actualization of all of its anthropological dimensions within the economic arena. Michael Federici notes how, in terms of Voegelin's analysis

78. See Oakeshott, *Rationalism in Politics*, 385.

79. See Friedman, *Capitalism and Freedom*; Friedman and Friedman, *Free to Choose*; and Wallich, *The Cost of Freedom*.

80. See Knight, *Freedom and Reform*, 237–38, my emphases.

of experiences of differentiation, it can be observed that when this happens "then corresponding institutional changes are necessary to bring the institutions in harmony with these experiences [and insights]."[81] Thus, anthropologically, I would argue there is a concomitant responsibility to unfold the truth of the reality that it is the human person who is the bedrock of the free economy. In *Order and History* Voegelin illustrates how the "anthropological principle" orders "order" when he describes how "the discovery of transcendence, of intellectual and spiritual order, while occurring in the souls of the individual human beings, is not a matter of 'subjective opinion'; once the discovery is made, it is endowed with the quality of an authoritative appeal to every man to actualize it in his own soul; the differentiation of man, the discovery of his nature, is a source of social authority."[82]

Even if we go back to the times of Xenophanes we can discover the attempt at differentiation within new experiences "as an actualization of the common essence of man."[83] The search for the "good of order" is perceived as a constant struggle, and ignorance that there is such an order in terms of what Voegelin called the "quaternarian structure" of God and man, world and society is seen as a negation of what is essential in terms of human reality.[84] Thus, applied to our study, the economic order we have can be understood as being part of the actualization of the reality of the human person in which the drama of human life is enacted in the economic horizon. There is a constant struggle and responsibility to delineate and differentiate the anthropological legacy within the drama of humanity but unless we participate in its enactment we can reach what Alexander Solzhenitsyn called "a turning point at which settled concepts suddenly become hazy, lose their precise contours, at which our familiar and commonly used words lose their meaning, becoming empty shells . . . It's the sort of turning point at which the hierarchy of values to which we are dedicated all our lives, which we use to judge what is valuable and what is not, and which causes our lives and our hearts to beat, is starting to waver and may perhaps collapse."[85]

81. See Federici, *Eric Voegelin*, 99.
82. Voegelin, *World of the Polis*, 186–87.
83. Ibid.
84. See Voegelin, *Israel and Revelation*, 1.
85. See Solzhenitsyn, *Communism*, 21.

IV. Economic Narratives: Why Do Economic Lives Differ?

In the concluding part of this chapter, let me attempt a brief explanation of what we mean when we speak of an economic system as being representative of a "good of order" in the contemporary context. It is often the personal economic and historical narratives underlining the process that unfolds the meaning and consequences of any particular economic system. The philosopher Paul Ricoeur commenting on the power of "narrative" says "the story of a life includes interactions with others. One author, Wilhem Schapp, goes so far as to say in his book *In Geschichten Verstrickt* that our being caught up in the interwoven stories, far from constituting a secondary complication, must be taken as the principal experience in such matters."[86]

Take the following economic narrative case studies, for example, and then let us ask: why do economic lives differ? Are the differences merely due to accidents of geography and environment or are they caused by anthropological factors?

> Roger and Sandra live with their two children in a four-bedroom house in the [San Francisco] Bay Area. They bought the house ten years ago for $320,000; just as well, they sometimes think, because that house is now worth $750,000 and they could not afford to buy it today. Roger earns $8,000 per month as a manager in an insurance company, having graduated in engineering for the University of California at San Diego. There he met Sandra, who was studying history, and who gave up her job as a teacher when their first child was born and now earns pocket money from part-time tutoring.
>
> Roger's drive into San Francisco to his office takes about thirty-five minutes in normal traffic in their Toyota Camry; Sandra drives an old minivan. On weekends, they enjoy hiking in the hills around their home, and in the winter may drive up to ski at Lake Tahoe. Last summer, they took a week off to drive up the West Coast to Seattle . . .

On the other hand we find the case of Ravi, who

> is cycling to his job at the State Bank of India in Mumbai, where he earns $320 per month. Ravi is a recently qualified accountant, and also married. Ravi and his wife, Nandini, live with Ravi's

---

86. See Ricoeur, *The Course of Recognition*, 103–104.

parents in a two-bedroom apartment in the favored district of World. The rent of the apartment is $280 per month, paid by Ravi's father. Nandini does not work. It is relatively uncommon in India for the wives of men of Ravi's income and social status to seek employment. A housekeeper visits each morning to clean and cook; she is paid around $25 per month.[87]

It seems indeed like a "tale of two cities" for all concerned. If I take examples from Latin America or Africa, the contrast is all the more striking and still more painful. For instance, we can take the following examples:

> Raoul . . . is a skilled and experienced machinist in a factory [owned by an American corporation] in northern Mexico. He earns $700 per month, a good wage in Mexico. His brother Pedro works illegally as a kitchen porter in a Los Angeles restaurant. Pedro takes home twice as much as Raoul. Raoul has sometimes thought of joining Pedro, but he prefers to stay with his friends and family in Mexico. He thinks money is only part of life.
>
> Sicelo owns his own farm . . . in a small village in KwaZulu-Natal. He lives in a hut with his own wife, the two wives of his brother, Patrick, and five of the six children of the marriages. The hut has no electricity or sanitation. Sicelo earns $150 per month from the sale of milk and vegetables. The women help on the farm and contribute to household earnings by making baskets. Patrick works in a gold mine in Carletonville, five hundred miles away. He earns $250 per month and sends most of this back to support the family. He usually returns to the village twice a year. Sicelo's eldest son is a domestic worker in Durban and sends $75 per month to his parents.[88]

We can, as we have said, justifiably ask: why the differences in the human situations outlined and what can we do to change the circumstances? The answer is necessarily complex. The economic process of globalization seems to help in some cases but in others it merely highlights the differences and inequalities. The flow of capital is good for Raoul in that he can earn a good wage by Mexican standards and also enjoy the company of his friends and family and "happiness depends far more on personal relationships" than on quantitative measurements.[89] Yet, for

87. See Kay, *Culture and Prosperity*, 22–24.
88. Ibid., 25.
89. Ibid.

Sicelo and his family, the simple pumping in of capital, which the global capital market allows for, could be even more disastrous. The economic foundations are simply not there to facilitate such capital injections.[90] If Sicelo could benefit from straightforward education in land and animal husbandry he could then operate equipment that others might finance. If there were suitable roads he could then get his crop and animals to a market for sale. The existence of a bank, a credit union or micro-credit system would encourage investors to invest and earn a profit for their risk taking. The problem is that none of these institutions exist in this case. So, even in the contemporary context, as the economist John Kay asserts, the economic system you are in clearly makes a difference. He contends that "economic differences persist because output and living standards are the complex product of the economic environment intersecting with social, political, and cultural institutions. The economic lives of individuals are the products of the systems within which they operate."[91]

This is, of course, not the whole story. It also depends on the initiatives taken by the individual economic agents; in the cases just cited all are willing participants in improving their circumstances but this is not always the case. The narratives we have chosen demonstrate that there are indeed fundamental issues to be addressed regarding the orientation and adequacy of our current economic order. The concerns are not just limited to the economic efficiency of the current paradigm. The consequence of the situation where the market economy apparently leads to such a "tale of two cities" posits specific questions to the theoreticians as to the legitimacy and sufficiency of the essential model and whether it is after all conducive toward the "good of order."

These narratives and questions are not just a matter for armchair theoreticians. They concern people's lives and for some can be the difference between life and death. Direct experience of poverty envelopes us as Ricoeur suggests in the "interwoven" nature of our lives. A student from University College Dublin, Ireland, who on a trip to Delhi participated in an overseas project based in a slum, has described their experience as follows:

> Arriving in Delhi feels like life has been unleashed upon you. Your eyes are blasted open by sights of absolute poverty,

90. The Asian financial crisis of the 1990s was caused by such capital inflows. See ibid., 28.

91. Ibid., 29.

unqualified beauty and utter simplicity. You become entwined
into a whole new realm of experience and are blitzed by issues
that need to be considered and acknowledged. Although the city
itself seems like it has nothing to offer its inhabitants, there are
thousands of people working towards change and I was privi-
leged to be one of them.[92]

If, for example, I wake up in the *favelas* in São Paulo, Brazil, I have,
as you would expect, the desire to fill my stomach with something to
satisfy my hunger. This may be a scrap of bread I have retrieved from a
rubbish tip; nevertheless it is a good that fulfills a particular desire. Of
course, if I awake in Manhattan, in New York, it could be a cup of cof-
fee and a bagel that satisfies my need. On the level of the satisfaction of
desires the solution in addressing a particular need is relative. The slum
dweller and the New Yorker are seemingly satisfied even if the stark difference in circumstances is alarming. In other words, a customer in a
Manhattan bar might frown at a scrap of bread but to a slum dweller it is
like manna from heaven; however, both in the end seem fulfilled.

The customer in Manhattan might be watching CNN or Sky News
and see scenes of famine or indigence on the TV screen. Similarly, the
slum inhabitant might catch glimpses of wealth around the corner from
his dwelling in neighboring hotels or wealthy suburbs. This is the product
of globalization. It is evident how it in itself with the ensuing revolution
in satellite communications changes perspectives. As the German philosopher Habermas observed, the 9/11 event became "the first historic
world event in the strictest sense" in that it was witnessed by means of
TV in front of the "universal witness" of a global public. So too, world
poverty like that witnessed in Darfur cannot be ignored. By means of
a globalized communications network I can witness the differences in
terms of income and wealth and even observe that there seems to be a
"common humanity" shared by us. The political commentator Mohamed
Sid-Ahmed, writing on the phenomenon of globalization, remarked that
"as the planet shrank, it brought into sharper focus the discrepancies between societies and between people within the same society. What came
to be called the global village syndrome also invested once distant events,
toward which people were more or less neutral, with a new intensity,
forcing them to adopt stands that often brought them into conflict with

92. See McNerney, *New Horizons*, 4, and Coote, *Colour on a Grey Canvas*. See
www.ucdvo.org for information on the projects.

one another. Perceptions changed as distances from and between events seemed to vanish."[93]

To return to our slum dweller and New Yorker—both might desire then to know: *why* is this disparity the case? Lonergan points out that the human desire to know is unlike any other, that is, "it is not content [merely] with satisfaction."[94] He observes that the yearning to know

> heads beyond one's own joy in one's own insight to the further question whether one's insight is correct. It is a desire to know and its immanent criterion is the attainment of an unconditioned that, by the fact that it is unconditioned, is independent of the individual's likes and dislikes, of his wishful and his anxious thinking. Now through this desire and the knowledge it generates, there comes to light a second meaning of the good. Besides the good that is simply the object of desire, there is the good of order. Such is the polity, the economy, the family as an institution.[95]

It is interesting that Wilhelm Röpke, in discussing whether the standpoint of liberalism as a particular economic order was a right one for him as an economist, commented, "yes . . . If it is liberal to entrust economic order, not to planning, coercion, and penalties, but to the spontaneous and free co-operation of people through the market, price, and competition, and at the same time to regard property as the pillar of this free order, then I speak as a liberal when I reject socialism . . . These are the facts, and they demand the adoption of a firm position . . . *for* the liberal kind of economic order."[96] He declared that it is an "appalling sin to reduce man to a means" and that "each man's soul is something unique."[97] It is because of this that he says, "I champion an economic order ruled by free prices and markets . . . this is the only economic order compatible with human freedom."[98] As I have remarked already, Lonergan's analysis on the notion of the good is also insightful at this point. He writes that the economy (the free market process in our case), the polity or family is

93. See Milanovic, *Worlds Apart*, 155.

94. It was Aristotle who stated that fundamental to all human beings is the desire to know. See Aristotle, *Metaphysics*, Book I, 982a32.

95. See Lonergan, *Inight*, 596.

96. Röpke, *Humane Economy*, 3.

97. Ibid., 5.

98. Ibid.

not the object of any single desire, for it stands to single desires
as a system to systematized, as universal condition to particulars
that are conditioned, as scheme of recurrence that supervenes
upon the materials of desires and the efforts to meet them . . .
The good of order is dynamic, not merely in the sense that it
orders the dynamic folding of desires and aversions, but also in
the sense that it itself is system on the move. It posses its own
normative line of development, inasmuch as elements of the
idea of order are grasped by insight into concrete situations, are
formulated in proposals, are accepted by explicit tacit agreements, and are put into execution only to change the situation
and give rise to still further insights.[99]

If we accept the "order" aspect of the "good of order" perspective,
the question as to the "good" of "good" in terms of economic life is of
course open to debate. The political economist Bertrand de Jouvenel, in
a discussion with Eric Voegelin, Michael Polanyi, Raymond Aron, and
others called "The West and the Meaning of Industrial Society," describes
how the science of economics has been "swayed by concepts such as 'productivity' and methods such as 'econometry.'" This reductive approach
ends up merely considering "man as a 'factor of production.'" But he asks,
"How can he [the human person] ever know the 'good life' if his existence
is divided into joyless working hours and meaningless consumption
hours? It would seem to me that the 'good life' should presuppose that
man finds self-realization and self-fulfillment both in his work and in his
leisure."

Voegelin develops the debate when he remarks that a rational analysis as to the good or bad nature of a political or economic institution
involves the presupposition that

there is such a thing as human nature, and if we can discover
what it consists of we can offer advice as to how society ought
to be organized, since the organization of society should aim at
the full flowering of human nature. However, there is no sense
talking about good or bad institutions or making concrete sug-
gestions about this or that social problem unless we first know
what purpose or end these institutions are supposed to serve.
This we cannot know unless we are familiar with the human nature that is going to develop within this social context. Thus the
focal point of political science [and economics] should always

99. Lonergan, *Insight*, 596.

be what today we call philosophical anthropology, which in fact corresponds to the first chapter of *The Nicomachean Ethics*.[100]

This is why I suggest that the focal point of our study is on the anthropological dimensions of the free economy. A thoroughgoing critique or understanding of the free market economy must be made on the basis of its originary anthropological roots; otherwise we fail to get to the kernel of the problematic. As Dermot Quinn observes, "The proper measure of mankind is man, said Alexander Pope. Man is also the proper measure of economics."[101]

V. Conclusion

In respect of the "good of order" as applied to economic systems, politicians and economists can get it wrong, which of course can cost human lives. There is no doubt, for example, that the great famine of 1932–33 in Ukraine was the result of "the new system" or communist economic order in which six million people died due to this alone.[102] In other words, the economic order we live in is of great importance and not just a matter for academic discussion. The economist James Buchanan clearly adverts to this, and using Hayek's phrase the "fatal conceit," he asks,

> Why did economists share in the *fatal conceit* that socialism represented? How were economists, who claimed scientific competence in analysis of human choice behaviour and the interdependent interactions of choices within institutional structures, duped or lulled into the neglect of elementary principles? Why did economists, who model man as *homo economicus* in analyzing markets, fail to recognize that incentives remain relevant in all choice settings? Why did economists forget so completely the simple Aristotelian defence of private property? Why did so many economists overlook the psychology of value, which locates evaluation in persons not in goods? Why did so many professionals in choice analysis fail to recognize the informational requirements of a centrally controlled economy in both the logical and empirical dimensions? Why was there the

100. See Voegelin, *Drama of Humanity*, 95–96, 100.
101. Quinn, Introduction to Röpke, *Humane Economy*, xii.
102. Hayek, *Fatal Conceit*, 159.

near total failure to incorporate the creative potential of human choice in models of economic interaction?"[103]

Similarly, Hayek, writing on the mistakes of socialism in his study, states that "this book [*The Fatal Conceit*] argues that our civilization depends, not only for its origin but also for its preservation, on what can be precisely described only as the extended *order* of human cooperation, an *order* more commonly, if somewhat misleadingly, known as capitalism."[104] He furthermore comments that "if it were for instance true that central direction of the means of production could effect a collective product of at least the same magnitude as that which we now produce, it would indeed prove a grave moral problem how this could be done justly. This, however, is not the position in which we find ourselves. For there is no known way, other than by the distribution of products in a competitive market, to inform individuals in what way their several efforts must aim so as to contribute as much as possible to the total product."[105]

I have sketched in this chapter a possible philosophical reading of the human meaning of the free market order. The central point is that there is a profound anthropological reason for "an economy governed by free prices, free markets, and free competition implies health and plenty."[106] The reason just does not revolve around the question of "efficiency." It is because the free market order "releases and utilizes the extraordinary forces inherent in individual self-assertion," which allows for the realization of personal dignity in creative human action.[107] I am reminded here of the work of Hernando de Soto. He wrote *The Mystery of Capital: Why Capitalism Triumphs in the West and Fails Everywhere Else.* There he comments on how private property ownership is but the tip of the iceberg in understanding the mystery of capital. He notes that "the rest of the iceberg is an intricate man-made process that can transform assets and labour into capital. This process is not created from a blueprint and is not described in a glossy brochure. Its origins are obscure and its significance buried in the economic subconscious of Western capitalist nations. How could something so important have slipped our minds? It is

---

103. See Buchanan, "Economics in the Post-Socialist Century," 17–18.

104. Hayek, *Fatal Conceit*, 6–7. My emphases.

105. Ibid.

106. Röpke, *Humane Economy*, 5.

107. Ibid., 6.

not uncommon for us to know *how* to use things without understanding why they work."[108]

Equally, it is my view that the mystery of the truth of the human person is the rest of the iceberg which lies beneath the working of the free economic order. As such, the free economy seeks to adapt economic principles to the human person and not the person to the economic standard. It is based upon the "good" of that "anthropological order" which allows for a free, creative and other-centered subject.[109]

108. Soto, *Mystery of Capital*, 9.

109. See Zięba, *Papal Economics*, 118.

4

Entrepreneurial Perspectives I: The Primacy of Person-Centered Economic Creativity in the Free Market Process

Each man himself, as an individual, should render his account to God. No third person dares venture to intrude upon this accounting between God and the individual. Yet the talk, by putting its question, dares and ought to dare to remind man, in a way never to be forgotten, that the most ruinous evasion of all is to be hidden in the crowd . . . No one may pride himself at being more than an individual, and no one despondently think that he is not an individual, perhaps because here in earth's busyness he had not as much as a name, but was named after a number.[1]

—Søren Kierkegaard (1813–55)

Always be prepared to make a defense to any one who calls you to account for the hope that is in you, yet do it with gentleness and reverence.

—1 Peter 3:15

I. A Fractured Relationship: Toward Recapturing the Human Creative Aspect

The cover story of an edition of *The Economist* in October 2008 ran with the headline "Capitalism at Bay." The subheading asked, "What went

1. Kierkegaard, *Purity of Heart*, 184–86.

wrong and, rather more importantly for the future, what did not." The opinion piece writer also commented on President Nicolas Sarkozy's remark that "laissez-faire" was finished. He wrote that

> over the past century and a half capitalism has proved its worth
> for billions of people. The parts of the world where it has flour-
> ished have prospered; the parts where it has shrivelled [*sic*] have
> suffered. Capitalism has always engendered crises, and always
> will. The world should use the latest one, devastating though it
> is, to learn how to manage it better . . . History suggests that a
> prejudice against more rules is a good idea. Too often they have
> unintended consequences, helping to create the next disaster.
> And capitalism eventually corrects itself. After a crisis investors
> (and for that matter regulators) seldom make exactly make the
> same mistake twice . . . For all its flaws, it is the best economic
> system man has invented yet.[2]

The contemporary popular analysis seems to give the impression that the central agents of the free market that we live in actually are just the investors (let us read "*capitalists*" here) and financial regulators. In other words, the free economy is all about the Wall Street inhabitants who have built various cathedrals to the gods of capital; meanwhile, the Main Street dwellers, those who simply seek to survive and earn a living, have no relationship with the others who, as "Masters of the Universe," really control the entire process. But this explanation is somewhat like claiming to hit the bullseye when, in fact, all one has done is to select certain easy targets, drawn the circle around them, and declared to have hit the mark and solved the question of the originating source of the problem in the first place. The free market economy has, I have argued, a far wider anthropological horizon that constitutes its actual operation. It is therefore not just a one-man drama with the sole actor being the investor-capitalist or producer.

In fact, one of the cardinal points in the functioning of the whole free economy is the part that we call "*creativity*" as evidenced in human "enterprise." The habit of enterprise is, in fact, "the propulsive factor in economics."[3] Within the economic arena this is often referred to as "entrepreneurial creativity" or function.[4] George Reisman in his

---

2. *The Economist*, 18–24 October 2008, 13–14.

3. Gronbacher, *Economic Personalism*, viii.

4. See Soto, *The Austrian School: Market Order and Entrepreneurial Creativity*, and Kirzner, *Discovery and the Capitalist Process*.

study entitled *Capitalism* observes that a "division of labor society" actually enables individuals to focus on their strengths, which facilitates the development of human creativity at all levels even the "artistic and musical." The individual in the free market can concentrate on "the kind of work for which he is best suited by virtue of his intellectual and bodily endowment."[5] I propose in this chapter to examine the primacy of person-centered creativity which is at the basis of the whole free market process. It is this aspect that is more often than not sidelined in most explanations of the economic process.

Actually, Eric Voegelin in an interesting essay wrote about how entrepreneurs "have been apparently forced onto the defensive by an image of the entrepreneur whose characteristics come from attacks of labor and clichés of the intellectuals."[6] He speaks equally of "a gnostic psychology of demonization of partners" in understanding, be it of the workers or entrepreneurs in the market economy. This can be seen clearly in the various populist commentaries on the Great Recession and the financial crisis. The emphasis in *The Economist's* leader piece on investors and regulators is quite understandable in the context of the economic crash that started back in 2007. Indeed, there is no doubt that there is still a fractured relationship between Wall Street and Main Street.[7] The global financial crisis and recession are commonly portrayed as evidence of the excesses of "unrestrained capitalism."[8]

The *hubris* of greed is seen as the primordial causation of the rapid international financial implosion. There is evidence certainly that unreserved and even morally hazardous innovation in terms of the creation of new financial instruments contributed to this global disaster and the Great Recession. For example, in the United States and elsewhere lenders issued what were called "NINJA loans". Just to clarify the ninja reference here: In Japanese history, a ninja (忍者, ninja) is a warrior, trained in martial arts and specializing in a variety of unorthodox arts of war. The methods used by ninja included assassination, espionage, stealth, camouflage, and specialized weapons, and a vast array of martial arts were added during the twentieth century. The mutant version of the free market process unleashed during the banking crisis created within the

5. Reisman, *Capitalism*, 125.

6. Voegelin, "Democracy and Industrial Society," 207.

7. See Rajan, *Fault Lines: How Hidden Fractures Threaten the World Economy.*

8. Casey, *Murray Rothbard*, 121.

sector a shadow world in which bad loans were camouflaged as good, packaged and sold on to others. The term "NINJA" as applied to the loans meant that the real borrowers were "no income, no job, and no assets" and would not normally qualify for loans in the first place. This gave rise to the whole subprime mortgage debacle in the United States that then spread to Europe and beyond.

Subprime lending (near-prime, non-prime, or second chance lending) is a financial term that was popularized by the media during the "credit crunch" of 2007 and involved financial institutions providing credit to borrowers deemed "subprime" (sometimes referred to as "under-banked"). Subprime borrowers had a heightened perceived risk of default, such as those who had a history of loan delinquency or default, those with a recorded bankruptcy, or those with limited debt experience. The problem was that these risk instruments became so complicated (that is, human judgment ended up being eclipsed out of the equation and even if judgment was included it was reductionist and limited to the short-term story). It failed to capture the actual reality of the human person who got the loan. The failure to perceive in a lot of cases was deliberate! The big problem was that subprime lending operated on a model of spreading or distributing the risk. The risk became so spread out, like the many roots of a giant oak tree, that no one knew how far the debt extended or which loan was toxic, that is, could not be paid back, because the loan should not have been made in the first place.

There is no doubt that human innovation in the banking world certainly created the financial instruments necessary to spread the risk because of the default nature of the actual borrowers. But at the same time, I believe, it is important to remember that there was no central mind orchestrating this unfolding drama. The financial vehicles and the human creativity involved were not necessarily mistaken. As Alan Kirman observes about the crisis, "This is a story of interaction and interdependence and the *breakdown of relations of trust* which had emerged" in the market.[9] Trust is one of the essential human dimensions of the free economy; its deconstruction results in the elimination of the very anthropological roots it is centered on. It is not just modern economists who advert to the "centrality of 'trust' and the multi-dimensional human aspects of economic life." For example, the eighteenth-century economist-philosopher Antonio Genovesi and leader of the Neapolitan

9. Kirman, *Complex Economics*, 5, my emphases.

school of economics developed an anthropological and relational view-point which emerges particularly well in his analysis of "trust" or "public trust."[10]

Just as "trust" can be eroded so, too, we can perhaps begin to understand how the *entrepreneurial role* can be lost sight of in the free market process. Indeed, the "obscurification" or "contraction" in understanding the role of the entrepreneur in the economy results in fracturing the relationships of cooperation that constitute the free economy. The *"entrepreneurial function"* in Voegelin's view and in that of various economists refers to human alertness[11] and the capacity on the economic level to innovate and gain insight into "creative initiatives for the order of society,"[12] which result in economic progress. This particular role, Voegelin claims, is actually spread out within modern economic society. Thus, it does not necessarily concern just one person involved in the process. As Kel Kelly, in a discussion on how the economy progresses, states, "Our rising standards of living can be attributed not to us single workers, but to entrepreneurs, capitalists and business people who create, finance and run these companies. Innovative entrepreneurs seeking profits think up ingenious ideas for ways to make our lives more enjoyable or to produce things we currently produce more efficiently."[13]

Kelly calls these different functions "entities" but stresses that "they may or may not be the same person, or any two of them could be the same person."[14] This is similar to Voegelin's reference to a type of democratization of the function of the entrepreneur in the free economy.[15] In order to grasp an adequate understanding of the role we cannot simply hold onto an outdated image that the model of the "industrial entrepreneur" actually gives.[16] The concept of a "diffusion" of the function in modern society could, of course, result in its very demise, but we can return to this objection later on. The entrepreneurial dimension of human action and its anthropological significance are therefore important and they need retrieval and further elucidation. This is the reason why we focus

10. See McNerney, "Wealth of Persons," 73.

11. John Meadowcroft observes, "Economic coordination demands that people are entrepreneurially alert" (*Ethics of the Market*, 25).

12. Voegelin, *Published Essays, 1953–1965*, 209.

13. Kelly, *Case for Legalizing Capitalism*, 39 n. 11.

14. Ibid.

15. See Voegelin, *Published Essays, 1953–1965*, 211, 221.

16. Ibid., 208.

in this chapter on the primacy of person-centered creativity in the free market process. As already outlined there is evidence of certain "contractions" in an adequate comprehension of the anthropological dimensions in economic thought, especially as this pertains to the entrepreneurial perspective. If price, for instance, has an epistemological function in the free market process, then, I argue, "the entrepreneurial function" has an anthropological purpose too. There is a need to attend to the philosophical basis of this dimension in the free market reality, otherwise economic reflection runs the risk of cutting itself off from its "own roots in philosophy."[17] This ends up in obscuring the actual human reality the free economy actually presupposes. Voegelin in his essay "The Eclipse of Reality" refers to the dangers of this "disease of contraction." This can be applied to the entrepreneurial nature of human action. He comments that the one who suffers from this type of anthropological ellipsis "is not inclined to leave the prison of his selfhood, in order to remove the frictions. He rather will put his imagination to further work and surround the imaginary self with an imaginary reality apt to confirm the self in its pretence of reality; he will create a Second Reality . . . in order to screen out the First Reality of common experience from his view."[18]

This results in what Voegelin calls a "partial view as the whole of reality."[19] Applied to economic thought, just as in other areas, this can lead to serious anthropological derailment. A shrunken view of the hu-

---

17. See Walsh, *Growth of the Liberal Soul*, 90. Walsh recalls that Nietzsche's warning was addressed to a liberal politics that had cut itself off from its own philosophical and Christian roots. Interestingly, he notes that Pope Leo XIII gave a very similar warning at the same time in the encyclical *Libertas Praestantissimum* (On the Nature of Human Liberty). See ibid., 328 n. 12.

Pope Leo wrote,

> For, once ascribe to human reason the only authority to decide what is true and what is good, and the real distinction between good and evil is destroyed; honor and dishonor differ not in their nature, but in the opinion and judgment of each one; pleasure is the measure of what is lawful; and, given a code of morality which can have little or no power to restrain or quiet the unruly propensities of man, a way is naturally opened to universal corruption. With reference also to public affairs: authority is severed from the true and natural principle whence it derives all its efficacy for the common good; and the law determining what it is right to do and avoid doing is at the mercy of a majority. Now, this is simply a road leading straight to tyranny.

See *Libertas Praestantissimum*, no. 16, http://www.papalencyclicals.net/Leo13/l13liber.htm.

18. Voegelin, *What Is History?*, 111–12.

19. Ibid., 112.

man person and their role in the free economy can therefore distort our understanding and insight into the whole reality of the free market and its participants. Actually, it was against such "contractive" views in economics that the Austrians sought to recapture the creative human perspective that is related to the "*entrepreneurial function*" in the free economy.[20]

So, as I have said in order to achieve an adequate understanding of the free economy, an appropriate appreciation of the importance of person-centered creativity as evidenced in the entrepreneurial function is indispensable. Otherwise, we can run the risk of what Voegelin calls a kind of "anti-world" complex. Or, to paraphrase Yeats, we simply don't want to put our hands into "the greasy till" of human reality.[21] This is in the end a "lack of responsibility that should be seen, not in the rosy light of ennobling inwardness and the domain of 'beautiful souls,' but in the harsher light of laziness when it comes to thinking and fear when it comes to work."[22] I will discuss Joseph Schumpeter's reflections and some of the Austrian school's contributions that resulted in a reawakening in economic thought of the entrepreneurial perspective.[23] We will then

20. Among the modern Austrians, Israel M. Kirzner's work, for example, develops a particular understanding of the entrepreneur's task as not just limited to pure economic *calculation* but rather as a "*discovery process.*" See Kirzner, *Discovery and the Capitalist Process*; *The Meaning of Market Process*; *How Markets Work*; and *The Driving Force of the Market*. The German economist Ludwig Lachmann and others develop different emphases in the debate on the role of entrepreneurship and the dynamic of change in the free market economy. See Lachmann, "From Mises to Shackle," 54–62.

21. Yeats's poem "September 1913" is said to be a scathing attack on the Dublin merchants and employers who locked out their workers from August 1913 to January 1914. Yeats wrote,

> What need you, being come to sense,
> But fumble in a greasy till
> And add the halfpence to the pence
> And prayer to shivering prayer, until
> You have dried the marrow from the bone?
> For men were born to pray and save:
> Romantic Ireland's dead and gone,
> It's with O'Leary in the grave.

See Yeats, *Poems*, 159.

22. Voegelin, *Published Essays, 1953–1965*, 219.

23. The famous Canadian-American economist John Kenneth Galbraith is favorable in his assessment of Schumpeter and the emphasis he puts on the entrepreneur but adjudges the other Austrian economists differently. Galbraith says the Austrians "were Ludwig von Mises (1880–1973), Friedrich A. von Hayek (1899–1992), the more pliable Fritz Machlup (1920–1983) and, a lesser figure, Gottfried Haberler (1900–1995). All arrived eventually in the United States, some by way of Geneva or London, as had

hopefully arrive at a broader understanding of "human creativity" and the resulting primacy of a person-centered economics.

II. Joseph Schumpeter, Prophet of a "Creative Anthropology": A Life

It is appropriate at this stage of our study to present a brief biography of Joseph Schumpeter, because he's seen in modern economic thought as one of the principal protagonists who put the emphasis back on the entrepreneur as the primary locomotive in the free market economy. His contemporaries, like Ludwig von Mises (1881–1973), were amongst the very many admirers of his "colorful portrayal of the role of the innovative entrepreneur in driving social and economic evolution."[24] The economist Mark Blaug claims: "Schumpeter traced all economic change to innovations and identified the innovator as the entrepreneur."[25] Furthermore, Blaug adjudges his influence on modern entrepreneurial theory "as overwhelming."[26] He uses Schumpeter as the criterion for judging the adequacy of all other economic approaches to the question and agrees that the theory has "been given a new lease of life by the modern Austrian School, descending from Ludwig Mises and Friedrich Hayek."[27]

---

their fellow countryman Joseph Schumpeter by way of Bonn. All, but especially Mises, were dogmatic in the view that any departure from classical orthodoxy was an irreversible step toward socialism" (*History of Economics*, 190). Mark Blaug also attacks the Austrian school because it "was markedly conservative and given over to attacks on socialism and the espousal of laissez-faire." However, he does applaud Schumpeter's "influence on entrepreneurial theory." He comments that his insights have largely been neglected but "the theory of entrepreneurship has been given a new lease of life by the modern Austrian School, descending from Ludwig Mises and Friedrich Hayek . . . Israel Kirzner has recently sought again to persuade his fellow economists that the properties of disequilibrium states deserve as much attention as those of equilibrium states." See Blaug, *Economic Theory in Retrospect*, 287, 446–47. Harry Landreth and David Colander, while considering the Austrian school as unique, state that "they maintained a steadfast adherence to viewing individuals as purposeful actors, not as a type of utilitarian machine that reacted to pleasure or pain. This, in part, led to a strong Austrian emphasis on entrepreneurship." See Landreth and Colander, *History of Economic Thought*, 494.

24. Hülsmann, *Mises*, 165.
25. Blaug, *Economic Theory in Retrospect*, 446.
26. Ibid.
27. Ibid., 446–47.

Schumpeter was born in 1883 (the same year as John Maynard Keynes and the year of Karl Marx's death) and lived in a small village called Triesch south of Prague. His life spanned the era of the Austro-Hungarian Empire and its ultimate demise. He lived through the rise of Communism, the Great Depression of 1929, and two World Wars. Both his academic career and personal life were eventful and colorful. They would perhaps influence his very dynamic perspective on the economic process. He initially studied law in the University of Vienna under his famous teacher Eugen von Böhm-Bawerk. Eric Voegelin described the rich "intellectual horizon" within the university milieu at the time, observing that along with Hans Kelsen's Theory of Pure Law, Alfred von Verdross and Adolf Merkl, "there was the Austrian School of Marginal Utility . . . Among the younger economists there was Ludwig von Mises, famous because of his development of money theory. Joseph A. Schumpeter was in Graz at the time, but his work of course was studied."[28]

It was Schumpeter, in fact, along with some other Harvard academics, who helped secure an immigration visa for Voegelin because he had to flee the Nazis.[29] After his undergraduate studies Schumpeter traveled extensively. Among the places he visited were Berlin, Paris, and London. He became a research student at the London School of Economics and like Marx spent considerable time reading in the British Museum. While in England for a year, he also met Alfred Marshall and other academics like Philip Wicksteed and Francis Y. Edgeworth. After his marriage to a British woman called Gladys Seaver, they moved to Cairo for a year in 1907 where Schumpeter practiced law. Schumpeter actually married three times, his second wife Annie Reisinger died while in childbirth. Returning in 1908 to the university of Vienna, he taught there for a short time. Schumpeter became an associate professor of economics and government in the university of Czernowitz (known as Chernivtsi in modern-day Ukraine) in 1909. In 1911 he moved to the university of Graz, Austria, all within the same geographical area of the then Austro-Hungarian Empire. He stayed there until the end of the First World War. He became a minister of finance in the Austrian government during the difficult postwar years (1919–20). During the period 1920–24, he even acted as president of the private Biedermann Bank.[30] That bank, along

28. Voegelin, *Autobiographical Reflections*, 1.

29. Ibid., 43–44. Voegelin attended the *Privatseminar* of Mises in Vienna. See Sennholz, *Notes and Recollections*.

30. See McCraw, *Prophet of Innovation*. McCraw tells the interesting story of how

with a great part of the regional economy, collapsed in 1924, leaving
Schumpeter bankrupt. He never really recovered financially from this
until his move to the United States. He held a chair in Bonn University
from 1925 to 1932. But like many other Austrian and German intellectuals Schumpeter left Europe during the rise of Nazism. He took up a
teaching position in Harvard in 1932 where he stayed until his death.
He died on the 8th of January 1950 in Taconic, in rural Connecticut. His
third wife, Elizabeth Boody, found him comatose in bed and he died a
few hours later.[31]

III. The Context of the Eclipse of Economic Reality: A Contribution toward an Anthropological Retrieval

In the midst of his hectic life, Schumpeter was also a prolific writer. His
chief writings are to be found in *The Theory of Economic Development:
An Inquiry into Profits, Capital, Credit, Interest, and the Business Cycle*;
*Business Cycles: A Theoretical, Historical, and Statistical Analysis of the
Capitalist Process*; *The Economics and Sociology of Capitalism*; *Essays on
Entrepreneurs, Innovators, Business Cycles and the Evolution of Capitalism*; *Capitalism, Socialism and Democracy*; *Ten Great Economists: From
Marx to Keynes*; and his magnum opus, *History of Economic Analysis*. I
will refer to some of these writings in terms of the overall theme on the
role of human creativity in the free market process. But his greatest work,
History of Economic Analysis, has been seen as the *apogee* of all his economic thinking, especially on of the role of the entrepreneur and his dynamic understanding of the free economy. McCraw finds that the book's
"extensive discussion of entrepreneurship . . . represents Schumpeter's
final statement on a subject that had fascinated him since the beginning
of his career."[32] It had a wide readership and was the most reviewed of all
his works; Fred Lawrence even claims it became the philosopher Bernard
Lonergan's *vade mecum*.[33]

Schumpeter left the Austrian government and his short career as a banker thereafter
(ibid., 105–9).

31. Elizabeth would see to the posthumous publication of Schumpeter's *History
of Economic Analysis* in 1954. For a brief synopsis of Schumpeter's life, see Medearis,
Joseph A. Schumpeter, 1–33.

32. McCraw, *Prophet of Innovation*, 457.

33. See the editor's Introduction to *Macroeconomic Dynamics*, xliii.

Mises actually disavows Schumpeter's membership of the Austrian school of economics *per se* but concedes that he could be counted among "the Austrian-born economists."[34] This argument does not really relate to our thematic here. The American economist Murray Rothbard clearly holds Schumpeter in high esteem for his curative approach to the rectification of mistaken viewpoints in economic thought. For example, he refers to a flawed perspective on the understanding of Scholastic economics taken up subsequently by Frank Knight and others in the Chicago school of economics. The Scholastics, for instance, already had developed a theory of economic value that focused on the human person as constitutive of *value*. In other words, they had already outlined a *"subjective theory of value."* Rothbard stresses the importance of Schumpeter's analysis, because he sees his attempts as a significant contribution toward the retrieval of lost dimensions like the Scholastic contribution within economic thought. He says "the much-needed corrective to the older view has at last become dominant since World War II, led by the enormous prestige of Joseph Schumpeter and by the definitive research of Raymond de Roover."[35] De Roover carried out research on Scholastic economic writers like St. Bernardine of Siena.[36] De Roover wrote, "Economists may be dismayed at the uncomfortable thought that two toothless emaciated and ascetic saints should perhaps be considered as the originators of utility theory. Incredible as it may sound, such seems to be the case. San Bernardino and Sant'Antonio developed a value theory based on scarcity and utility, both objective and subjective."[37]

Rothbard's and de Roover's claims, for instance, concerning the need for a "corrective" in terms of the proper recognition and understanding of the Scholastic contribution to economic thought, suggest that there is a missing link that needs restoration in terms of an adequate knowledge of a theory of value in economics.[38] George Reisman, for example,

34. See Greaves, *Austrian Economics*, 73.

35. See Rothbard, *Economic Thought before Adam Smith*, 79. See also de Roover's *Rise and Decline of the Medici Bank, 1397–1494.*

36. See de Roover, *San Bernardino of Siena and Sant'Antonio of Florence: Two Great Economic Thinkers of the Middle Ages.*

37. Ibid., 41.

38. It is important to note here that T. S. Lowry critically reviews Rothbard's *Austrian Perspective on the History of Economic Thought* in the *Journal of Economic Literature* 34 (1996) 1336–40. See http://www.jstor.org/stable/2729509. Lowry outlines what he considers significant lacunae in the Rothbardian approach. Rothbard fails to recognize, for example, the extent "to which marginal utility was bandied about" in

dismisses the role of medieval thinkers in one sentence. In a discussion on "pseudoeconomic [*sic*] thought," he says, "The scholastics contributed nothing to sound economics."[39] His book is titled *Capitalism: A Treatise on Economics*. The dust cover title is even more interesting. It reads: *Capitalism: A Complete and Integrated Understanding of the Nature and Value of Human Economic Life*. Interestingly, during the summer of 2007, while on study break at the University of Berkeley, California, I came across a prepublication edition dated 1995, and it contained the same sentence; so Reisman obviously never changed his views.[40] John Maynard Keynes's attitude was also scathing of the contribution of Scholasticism to economics. In one of his lectures he asked, "What degree of precision is advisable in economics? There is the danger of falling into scholasticism, 'the essence of which is treating what is vague as what is precise.' A generalization to cover everything is impossible and impracticable."[41]

Regardless of the intentions involved, whether deliberative or not, this shows how the anthropological perspective can be lost or simply become overshadowed in economic thinking. There is a certain philosophical equivalence between this tendency of "occlusion" in economic theory (mentioned here in terms of the Scholastics' contribution to a subjective value theory) and Lonergan's use of the term *scotosis* or blind spot which results from *bias* that can arise in the unfolding of human understanding. I have already mentioned this before but Lonergan explains how "incomprehension, isolation, and duality rob the development of one's common sense of some part, greater or less . . . Let us name such an aberration of understanding a scotosis, and let us call the resultant blind spot a scotoma."[42] He discusses four biases that can interfere with the development of common sense. They are: *dramatic bias, individual bias, group bias,* and *general bias.*[43] *Dramatic bias* can occur at the psychiatric

---

the earlier Greek culture (ibid., 1339). He agrees that reference is made in Rothbard's biographical essay to the Norwegian economist Odd Langholm's study *Price and Value in the Aristotelian Tradition: A Study in Scholastic Economic Sources*. It should be noted that Langholm in his later work *The Legacy of Scholasticism in Economic Thought* argues against "Rothbard's absurd notion . . . that the scholastics were 'proto-Austrians' and that references to labor in connection with value on their part were mostly regrettable slips of the pen" (87 n. 36).

39. Reisman, *Capitalism*, 6.
40. See *Capitalism: A Treatise on Economics*, Prepublication, Interim Edition, 6.
41. See Bateman, *Keynes's Uncertain Revolution*, 135.
42. Lonergan, *Insight*, 214–15.
43. Ibid., 214–27, 244–50, and 250–67, respectively.

level, resulting in "a withdrawal from the outer drama of living" and an "introversion" that prevents one from accumulating insights through interaction with others.[44] *Individual bias* is a personal closure to reason resulting in an egoism that fails to ask, "can one's solution be generalized? Is it compatible with the social order that exists?" It is "an incomplete development of intelligence."[45] *Group bias* is a socio-political closure to reason and can manifest itself in terms of class conflicts. The group by its very nature "is prone to have a blind spot for the insights that reveal its well-being to be excessive or its usefulness at an end." In this way the bias of development involves a distortion in which practical ideas for social or economic development can end up "mutilated" by group interests.[46] While *general bias* is the result of the long-term historic and cultural consequences of individual and socio-political closure to reason. It is in this context that "theory is reduced to the nature of myth that lingers on to represent the frustrated aspirations of detached and disinterested intelligence."[47] Lonergan argues that these *biases* can interfere with the growth of common sense and they can, I think, be equally applied to certain distortions in the development of economic thought. In other words, progress is not inevitable and bias can limit us in terms of human progress and economic development. Discussing *general bias* Lonergan observes that "every specialist runs the risk of turning his specialty into a bias by failing to recognize and appreciate the significance of other fields. Common sense almost invariably makes that mistake; for its incapable of analyzing itself, incapable of making the discovery that it too is a special-ized development of human knowledge, incapable of coming to grasp that its peculiar danger is to extend its legitimate concern for the concrete and the immediately practical into disregard of larger issues and indiffer-ence to long-term results."[48]

Lonergan is discussing here the general bias of common sense but as I have said this can be applied to economic reflections. Simply stated, the general bias of common sense needs correction by learning, and for this it needs a higher viewpoint. Lonergan's argument is in terms of cog-nitional structure and the higher perspective needed to correct that bias

44. Ibid., 214.
45. Ibid., 245.
46. Ibid., 248–49.
47. Ibid., 257.
48. Ibid., 251.

is a theory of history. In economics there is the analogous need for a "higher viewpoint" and in *Wealth of Persons* we can see this broader perspective recaptured by unfolding and explicating an adequate anthropology. Lonergan describes this when he explains how "the needed higher viewpoint is the discovery, the logical expansion and the recognition of the principle that intelligence contains its own immanent norms and that those norms are equipped with sanctions that man does not invent or impose."[49] In my view a careful reading of Murray Rothbard, in fact, suggests that similar blind spots seem to permeate some economic areas of thought. As we've seen there is a failure to recall the significant Scholastic contribution to economic thought in regard to value theory.[50] Rothbard seizes upon Adam Smith as one example among many in the articulation of a partial view in economics on the subject of economic value. He writes,

> Adam Smith's doctrine on value was an unmitigated disaster, and it deepens the mystery in explaining Smith. For in this case, not only was Smith's theory of value a degeneration from his teacher Hutcheson and indeed from centuries of developed economic thought, but it was also a similar degeneration from Smith's own previous unpublished lectures. In Hutcheson and for centuries, from the late scholastics onward, the value and the price of a product were determined first by its subjective utility in the minds of the consumers . . . In his lectures, furthermore, Smith had solved the value paradox neatly, in much the same way as had Hutcheson and other economists for centuries . . . But in the *Wealth of Nations*, for some bizarre reason, all this drops out and falls away.[51]

The "bizarre reason" for the occlusion might have something to do with Smith's Scottish Presbyterian background and the university milieus in Edinburgh and Glasgow. This is not merely a religious argument since the Protestant Reformation obviously had cultural and intellectual consequences in the countries wherever it occurred.[52] Nicholas Phillipson,

49. See Matthews, *Lonergan's Quest*, 259.

50. See Casey, "Scholastic Economics." Casey claims that "despite what is widely believed, the Scholastic thinkers made a significant contribution to economic thought" (ibid., 70).

51. Rothbard, *Economic Thought before Adam Smith*, 448–49.

52. Bryan Fanning's study interestingly "examines a selection of debates about the human condition that place ontological beliefs at their centre so as to emphasise that even in the secular West . . . beliefs matter, that social positions are debated from

writing about the Enlightenment in Scotland, observes that after the shock of the Jacobite rebellion of 1745 (Smith's *Wealth of Nations* was published in 1776), ministers and others had to rethink their role and professions in a post-Culloden state.[53] Phillipson points out that to this end "what they wanted was a disciplined Church that would coexist amicably with civil society and develop a form of Presbyterianism which was fertilized with the sort of learning, letters and culture that would identify ministers as polite gentlemen. As ministers they thought of themselves in Hutchesonian terms. They wanted a religion that was based on philosophy, natural theology and the cultivation of practical morality rather than the truths of revealed religion and the teaching of the Church Fathers."[54]

It seems that some of these leaders actually attended Smith's lectures on rhetoric. They "found his new approach to the study of the mind a welcome alternative to that of the logicians and metaphysicians."[55] Historians are sometimes critical of presumptions about Smith's belief or absence of faith. But there is no doubt that there were influences on him. We cannot expand on the reasons for the obscuration of the subjective theory of value from economic reflection because our concern is chiefly with entrepreneurial creativity. But maybe it is easier to understand the demise of the entrepreneurial perspective, because when the subjective dimension is neglected so too is the "creative aspect" in economic life. So, Mark Blaug suggests, it was left to Schumpeter and the Austrians to retrieve the entrepreneurial dimension within economic theory. As outlined in this chapter the entrepreneurial aspect presupposes a certain viewpoint or vision of the reality of the economy but its basis is also fundamentally anthropological. It is interesting that Schumpeter also used the word "bias" when he spoke of the scientific process and its vision and rules of procedure. He wrote, "we are now ready to take the second step in our inquiry into the dangers of ideological bias, namely, to ask the

different ontological vantage points . . . [T]he theme of the first chapter is faith; specifically how Christian theology continues to influence understandings of human welfare and well-being." See Fanning, *Evil, God, the Greater Good*, 3. See also Brad S. Gregory's *The Unintended Reformation: How a Religious Revolution Secularized Society*.

53. The Battle of Culloden took place on 16 April 1746. It resulted in the total defeat of the Jacobite forces. Between 1,500 and 2,000 Jacobites were killed or wounded in the brief time, while Government losses were lighter with 50 dead and 259 wounded. The aftermath of the battle and subsequent crackdown on Jacobitism was brutal, earning the Duke of Cumberland the name "Butcher."

54. Phillipson, *Adam Smith*, 83.

55. Ibid., 84.

question how far does it threaten the validity of results in that narrower field that we have just described as Economic Analysis."⁵⁶

As previously noted Rothbard referred to a "bizarre reason" for Smith's apparent blindness in respect of an adequate economic theory of value.⁵⁷ The historian, Emil Lauder came up with an explanation for this blind spot or eclipse of reality in terms of the development in economic theory of the concept of marginal utility. I think it gives us a useful and insightful perspective into the core of an anthropological approach in economics. In a discussion on the philosophical background to marginal utility theory, Lauder explains that during his research he made a very interesting discovery. It was that prior to the nineteenth century "the writers interested in consumer value were Frenchmen and Italians, while the defenders of cost theory were of British origin."⁵⁸ He declares that this could not just happen accidentally. He writes: "it seems likely that different religious backgrounds help to explain the fact that the French and Italian economists worked at cross-purposes with the British economists."⁵⁹ The Protestant Reformation set off a seismic shock that fractured the intellectual world into two streams of distinct thought. These were "either a Catholic-Thomistic or a Protestant-Puritan pattern of thought."⁶⁰ This subsequently resulted in different "specific social outlooks."⁶¹ Thus, when it comes to the economic analysis of concepts like value, this bifurcation is evident and emerges in the predominance of the "labor theory" of value over the "subjective theory" of value. The historian R. H. Tawney in *Religion and the Rise of Capitalism* sought to illustrate, for example, how "determinist metaphysics" combined with a particular economic anthropological viewpoint and resulted in differing economic perspectives. As Bryan Fanning outlines, "the Calvinist could not aim for personal salvation. The goal instead was the glorification of

56. Schumpeter, *History of Economic Analysis*, 41.

57. James Otteson gives a very insightful reading of Smith's lacunae in "What Smith Got Wrong," in his *Adam Smith*, 135–49. Otteson argues that it is true that Smith "intends labor as an objective criterion" but he actually emphasizes "the subjective nature of the relevant 'labor.'" Therefore, Otteson calls Smith's concept a "*subjective-labor theory of value*" (ibid., 139).

58. Kauder, *History of Marginal Utility*, 3.

59. Ibid., 4.

60. Ibid. Of course, Max Weber's seminal work *The Protestant Ethic and the Spirit of Capitalism* explored how the Protestant Reformation triggered a set of motivations that he saw as giving rise to capitalism.

61. Kauder, *History of Marginal Utility*, 4.

God through active labour . . . The elect were spurred into an active life of individual agency. The evidence for spiritual salvation was to be found in material success."[62]

It is within this context, I would suggest, that economists like Carl Menger and others from the Austrian school of economics sought to recover the "subjective dimension" or "person-centered" horizon that had been excluded from economic thought.[63] In his *Principles of Economics*, Menger argued, "I have already pointed out that a goods-character is not a property inherent in the goods themselves . . . The order of a good is nothing inherent in the good itself and still less a property of it . . . The value of goods arises from their relationship to our needs, and is not inherent in the goods themselves."[64] It is for this reason the Austrian tradition in economics develops an emphasis on the subjective dimension in terms of a theory of value. In light of this Schumpeter and the Austrian perspective make a significant contribution toward developing an adequate understanding of the human entrepreneurial dimension of the free economy. As I have said earlier, just as a "blind spot or a scotoma" can arise in our human understanding, so too it can arise in various economic approaches and reflections.[65] This is why Rothbard and some other Austrian economists believe that Adam Smith's analysis in the *Wealth of Nations* of a theory of value actually diverted "the writers of the English Classical School into a *cul-de-sac* from which they did not emerge . . . for nearly a century."[66] But, of course, the Rothbardian presumption here is that nothing can be learned from a detour because it merely ends in an intellectual dead-end. But on a more positive side, I believe that an apparent *cul-de-sac* can lead to the discovery of how to enter into a more open heuristic process in terms of an adequate theory of human knowledge and economics. This can be equally applied to the

62. Fanning, *Evil, God, the Greater Good*, 31.

63. Menger lived between 1840 and 1921 and is regarded as the founder of the Austrian school of economics. Joseph Salerno considers that Menger merits this title because "he created, out of whole cloth, the system of value and price theory that constitutes the core of Austrian economic theory. But Menger did more than this: he also originated and consistently applied the correct, praxeological method for pursuing theoretical research in economics. Thus, in its core Austrian economics always and will forever remain *Mengerian* economics." Salerno, "Carl Menger: The Founding of the Austrian School," in Holcombe, *15 Great Austrian Economists*, 71–100.

64. Menger, *Principles of Economics*, 58, 120.

65. Lonergan, *Insight*, 215.

66. Ibid., 450.

development of our economic understanding and assist us in the further elaboration of the role of the human person in the free economy. Thus Schumpeter's reflections are a major contribution in the rediscovery of the primacy of person-centered economic creativity in the free economy. This is well illustrated in the example of the acting person's functioning as "the entrepreneur" in the economic drama which occurs throughout his writings. The human action of the entrepreneur was as we've seen eclipsed from economic thought and reflection on the free economy and it is the common task of philosophers and economists to regain this personalistic entrepreneurial perspective.

IV. Dynamic Economic Creativity: A Schumpeterian Vision

If you survey most financial journals with the search word "Schumpeter," you will invariably come up with two terms at least. They are "creative destruction" and "the entrepreneur."[67] These concepts are usually found in this order and there is a good reason for this. The former refers to an understanding of the economy in terms of its dynamic process and the latter relates to a function or role of human agency in the economy. If we

---

67. While conducting research for this book I kept a database on such articles. For example, in the *Financial Times* there have been numerous mentions of Schumpeter and his ideas. Between 2003 and 2010 the terms "creative destruction" and "entrepreneur" were mentioned many times directly or indirectly. Niall Ferguson, in "The Great Dying: A Memo to Market Dinosaurs; It Really Is Darwinian Out There," noted, "As Schumpeter wrote more than 70 years ago: 'This economic system cannot do without the ultimate ratio of the complete destruction of those existences which are irretrievably associated with the hopelessly unadapted.' Creative destruction, in his view, meant nothing less than the disappearance of 'those firms which are unfit to live'" (*Financial Times*, 14 December 2007). Jesse Norman, in "Human Beings Are Not Mere Selfish Agents," remarked, "At its deepest level, the crash arose because people and markets did not behave in the way described in economic textbooks. People are not always economically rational . . . We are daily conditioned to think of human beings as 'economic agents': as purely self-interested, endlessly calculating costs and benefits and highly sensitive to marginal gains and losses. But a problem arises when this economic image feeds back into society and becomes our default picture of human motivation . . . We need a different vision and a richer conception of humanity in our public policy. Such a vision starts by recognising the limits of human nature. It emphasises the importance of independent institutions, competition and entrepreneurship as factors driving prosperity. It rejects the idea that humans are merely passive vehicles for utility, in favour of a far more dynamic conception of human capability" (*Financial Times*, 5 December 2008).

consider Schumpeter's *History of Economic Analysis* we can try to summarize the main points, firstly, in relation to the model we have of the economic process. Schumpeter speaks about how any work of analysis is preceded by a "preanalytic cognitive act that supplies the raw material for the analytic effort."[68] He calls this cognitive act "Vision."[69] I have discussed this concept in previous chapters and we noted how Schumpeter saw "vision of this kind not only must precede historically the emergence of analytic effort in any field but also may re-enter the history of every established science each time somebody teaches us to *see* things in a light of which the source is not to be found in the facts, methods, and results of the pre-existing state of the science."[70]

Attempting to explain the importance of the economic "vision" we might have, Schumpeter gave the example of John Maynard Keynes and his *General Theory of Employment, Interest, and Money*.[71] He said critics and admirers alike agreed that this work "was the outstanding success of the 1930's."[72] He explained how Keynes's study was obviously designed to describe facts about "the world in which we live."[73] Keynes saw a clear dichotomy between "vision" and "praxis"; his point was that the classical theorists claimed to propound a general theory, but in fact it was not "general" at all.[74] That's why he calls his work *The General Theory*. In his

68. Schumpeter, *History of Economic Analysis*, 41.

69. Ibid.

70. Ibid.

71. There is a vast amount of literature on Keynes, who lived from 1883 to 1946. A classic biography is Robert Skidelsky's three-volume *John Maynard Keynes*; a one-volume abridged edition of the same study has been published as *John Maynard Keynes: Economist, Philosopher, Statesman, 1883–1946*. Other works on Keynes include Moggridge, *John Maynard Keynes*; Clarke, *Keynes: The Twentieth Century's Most Influential Economist*; and Skidelsky, *Keynes: The Return of the Master*. There are critical works such as Lewis, *Where Keynes Went Wrong*, and Hazlitt, *The Failure of the "New Economics"*. Schumpeter wrote a chapter on Keynes also in his book *Ten Great Economists: From Marx to Keynes*. Bradley W. Bateman has written an interesting work on Keynes titled *Keynes's Uncertain Revolution*. He comments that Keynes's attempt to introduce uncertainty into his theoretical revolution can be understood as "an honest effort at theoretical innovation." This could result in seeing Keynes as "an ally of some contemporary schools of thought: Austrian, Post-Keynesian, Rational Expectationist" (164–65).

72. Schumpeter, *History of Economic Analysis*, 41.

73. Ibid.

74. Keynes notes that the term "classical economists" was invented by Marx to include David Ricardo and James Mill and their predecessors. Keynes adds that in using

introduction he states clearly that "I shall argue that the postulates of the classical theory, are applicable to a special case only and not to the general case, the situation which it assumes being a limiting point of the possible positions of equilibrium. Moreover, the characteristics of the special case assumed by the classical theory happen not to be those of the economic society which we actually live in, with the result that its teaching is misleading and disastrous if we attempt to apply it to the facts we experience."[75]

Schumpeter argues that Keynes's approach is essentially that of an English intellectual, in that it is based on a certain vision or conception of economic reality. It was concerned, he said, with "the characteristics of England's aging capitalism."[76] Robert Skildesky agrees with this interpretation when he says that "Keynes was a product of his class and background and therefore tended to see the economic problem from a particular point of view—that of the 'educated bourgeoisie' located at the centre of a declining empire."[77] Schumpeter stresses that this vision or conception predates any analytic research on Keynes's part. The real Keynesian standpoint can be seen clearly in what Schumpeter judges to be "a few brilliant pages of Keynes's *The Economic Consequences of the Peace* (1919)."[78] In his essay on Keynes, Schumpeter explains that

> every comprehensive "theory" of an economic state of society consists of two complementary but essentially distinct elements. There is, first, the theorist's view about the basic features of that state of society, about what is and what is not important in order to understand its life at a given time. Let us call this vision. And there is, second, the theorist's technique, an apparatus by which he conceptualizes his vision and which turns the latter into concrete propositions or "theories." In those pages of the *Economic Consequences of the Peace* we find nothing of the theoretical apparatus of the *General Theory*. But we find the whole vision of things social and economic of which the apparatus is the technical complement. The *General Theory* is the final result of a long struggle *to make that vision of our age analytically operative.*[79]

the term he has in mind the followers of Ricardo, including J. S. Mill, Alfred Marshall, Francis Edgeworth, and Arthur Pigou. See *General Theory*, 9 n. 1.

75. Ibid., 9.
76. Schumpeter, *History of Economic Analysis*, 42.
77. Skildesky, *John Maynard Keynes, 1883–1946*, xvii.
78. Schumpeter, *History of Economic Analysis*, 42.
79. Schumpeter, *Ten Great Economists*, 268.

In his *History of Economic Analysis*, Schumpeter describes how it is clearly possible for what Lonergan called "bias" to enter into this process. He wrote that "there is a wide gate for ideology to enter . . . In fact, it enters on the very ground floor, into the preanalytic cognitive act."[80] He reminded his readers "the first thing a man will do for his ideals is lie."[81] I am reminded here of Alexander Solzhenitsyn's essay "'Live Not by Lies." He wrote, "The simplest, the most accessible key to our liberation: *a personal non-participation in lies!* Even if all is covered by lies, even if all is under their rule, let us resist in the smallest way: Let their rule hold *not through me!*"[82] Indeed, some of Solzhenitsyn's writings have been interpreted as a diagnosis of "the lie as a form of existence." Raymond Aron wrote how "Solzhenitsyn's message can be summarized, it seems to me, in two fundamental sentences: There is something worse than poverty and repression and that something is the Lie; the lesson this century teaches is to recognize the deadly snare of ideology, the illusion that men and social organization can be transformed at a stroke."[83]

It is hugely significant that Schumpeter as an economist speaks also of how it is almost impossible to drive out "conscious dishonesty" from economics or any of the other social sciences.[84] Aware of this ongoing challenge, I similarly believe that an adequate understanding of the anthropological roots of the free market process requires a continual striving in terms of moving toward a more satisfactory capturing and articulation of this reality. This all occurs in the context of what I would call an "anthropological agnosticism" on the part of most economic thinkers.[85] So, we always live within the existential tension of trying to narrow down and locate the blind spots within our own vision and approach; this applies equally to economic perspectives. In Schumpeter's assessment, it is important to dynamically question the "vision" being proposed in any economic analysis. This standpoint brings to mind

80. Schumpeter, *History of Economic Analysis*, 42.

81. Ibid., 43 n. 10.

82. See Solzhenitsyn, "Live Not by Lies," in *The Solzhenitsyn Reader*, 558.

83. Aron, *In Defense of Political Reason*, 123. See also Aron's *The Opium of the Intellectuals*.

84. Schumpeter, *History of Economic Analysis*, 43.

85. Maciej Zięba observes how today "a political and economic agnosticism . . . led to an anthropological agnosticism, where it is impossible to speak with certainty about the nature of man or to judge his choices, and finally to a metaphysical agnosticism, where there is no absolute truth" (*Papal Economics*, 188).

Hans-Georg Gadamer's emphasis on the dialogical nature of philosophy and human existence. In a discussion on the logic of question and answer, he wrote that "we can understand a text only when we have understood the question to which it is an answer . . . The close relation between questioning and understanding is what gives the hermeneutic experience its true dimension . . . *To understand the questionableness of something is already to be questioning.* There can be no tentative or potential attitude to questioning, for questioning is not the positing but the testing of possibilities. Here the nature of questioning indicates what is demonstrated by the actual operation of the Platonic dialogue. A person who thinks must ask himself questions . . . To understand a question means to ask it. To understand meaning is to understand it as the answer to a question."[86]

Thus, Schumpeter questions the conceptions Adam Smith and the classical economists had of the workings of the economy. It is against this background that he unfolds his understanding of the economy. He attributed a central role to human creativity in view of what he termed "*creative destruction*" and the essential role of the "*entrepreneur*" in the process.[87] Smith and the classical economists applied the term "*stationary state*" in reference to the economy. It was used both to describe the current situation and a condition that would emerge in the future. It is important to point out here that the use of the "stationary state" does not necessarily imply a failure to see the dynamic nature of the market. It was used primarily as a foil rather than as an actual description of the world. Alfred Marshall, for instance, did not subscribe to the view since he believed in the truly dynamic nature of the world.

In any case the problem, according to Schumpeter, is the actual "vision" or model the classical theorists and Smith had in the first place. Their model, in fact, fails to explain the dynamic nature of the free market process. Schumpeter explained that "from Smith on, most of the English 'classics' used the term Stationary State. But this stationary state was an actual condition of the economic process which they expected to materialize sometime in the future."[88]

86. Gadamer, *Truth and Method*, 363, 367, 368.

87. The Schumpeterian focus is on the *producer as entrepreneur*, which runs the risk of leaving out of the analysis the essential role of the *consumer as entrepreneur*. See Leen, "The Consumer in Austrian Economics." Leen observes, "The modern Austrians impute . . . the entrepreneurial role in the competitive process to the producer . . . This is in spite of the fact that the ultimate king in the market process is without doubt the consumer" (ibid., 49).

88. Schumpeter, *History of Economic Analysis*, 562.

The result of this, he says, is that we end up with "the Stagnationist Thesis of our own time."[89] This is "the notion that the capitalist system has spent its powers; that the opportunities of private enterprise are giving out."[90] Schumpeter then proceeds to categorize and outline three types of theory of economic development and their associated economists, where each has a different model or understanding of the economic process. The first group he labels the "pessimists." The pessimists are people like Thomas Malthus, David Ricardo, and James Mill. They emphasized factors like growth of population, decreasing returns in agriculture and falling net returns to industry. Schumpeter argues that the most interesting thing to note about the "pessimists" is "the complete lack of imagination which that vision reveals."[91] He claims they did not take account of present reality: for example, they lived during the Industrial Revolution and yet they wrote about want and scarcity.[92] As we have seen, Keynes referred to a similar dichotomy. The classical economists "were convinced that technological improvement and increase in capital would in the end fail to counteract the fateful law of decreasing returns."[93] For them their particular model became the reality because "they all expected, for the future, the advent of a stationary state, which here no longer means an analytic tool but a future reality."[94] The kernel of the problem in this vision goes back to the anthropological understanding of the *dramatis personae* and their functioning in the working of the economy.[95] What is missing and underestimated in the classical model is "the element of personal initiative."[96] It is for this reason that Schumpeter sees the need to develop his own theories about entrepreneurship and creative destruction.[97]

89. Ibid., 570. See also Schumpeter, *Capitalism, Socialism and Democracy*, 392–97.

90. Schumpeter. *History of Economic Analysis*, 570.

91. Ibid., 571.

92. Ibid.

93. Ibid.

94. Ibid.

95. Schumpeter outlined what he calls "The 'Classic' Schema of the Economic Process." In this he refers to the role of (*a*) The Actors, (*b*) The Agents and (*c*) The Model. He readily admits that the notion of "progress" is indeed controversial within economic circles. See *History of Economic Analysis*, 554–70.

96. Schumpeter, *History of Economic Analysis*, 572.

97. As mentioned previously there is a vast literature on entrepreneurship. See Casson et al., *The Oxford Handbook of Entrepreneurship*. In an explanation of the concept, the editors write, "The term 'entrepreneur' appears to have been introduced into economic theory by Richard Cantillon (1759), a French economist of Irish descent.

Schumpeter then proceeds in his *History of Economic Analysis* to mention the "second type of vision," that is, "*the 'optimistic' type.*"[98] The examples he gives here are the American economist Henry C. Carey and the German Friedrich List. They obviously did not hold the pessimists' economic conception since Schumpeter explained "they felt intuitively that the dominant fact about capitalism was its power to create productive capacity, and they *saw* vast potentialities in the near future."[99] Then the Marxian perspective represents the third type of vision. In an extensive treatment of Marxian doctrine, in his *Capitalism, Socialism and Democracy* Schumpeter discusses Marx under the title of "Prophet, Sociologist, Economist and Teacher."[100] He observes that "nothing in Marx's economics can be accounted for by any want of scholarship or training . . . He missed very few contributions of significance . . . The outstanding proof of this is in his work, *Theories of Surplus Value.*"[101]

In fact, Schumpeter stresses the point that Marx perhaps more than anyone else, understood the dynamic nature of the market economy. He wrote about how Marx "concentrated his analytic powers on the task of showing how the economic process, changing itself by virtue of its own inherent logic, incessantly changes the social framework—the whole of society in fact."[102] The American economist and political theorist Walt W. Rostow also suggests "it was the challenge posed by Marx's historical, theoretical, and polemical analysis of the dynamics of capitalism that most profoundly influenced Schumpeter."[103] On the other hand, many other economists tended to limit their discussion of the functioning of the free market system to the "stagnationist" viewpoint and concentrated particularly on prices. But Marx was at least prepared to lift the hood on the car and try to examine the engine, that is, the mode of production

---

According to Cantillon, the entrepreneur is a specialist in taking risk . . . this idea was refined by the US economist Frank Knight (1921), who distinguished between risk, which is insurable, and uncertainty, which is not . . . Popular notions of entrepreneurship are based on the heroic vision put forward by Joseph A. Schumpeter (1934). The entrepreneur is visualized as an innovator" (3). In this handbook on entrepreneurship the authors also discuss the contribution of Mises and the Austrian perspective on the market process.

98. Schumpeter, *History of Economic Analysis*, 571.

99. Ibid., 572.

100. Schumpeter, *Capitalism, Socialism and Democracy*, 5–45.

101. Ibid., 21.

102. Schumpeter, *History of Economic Analysis*, 573.

103. Rostow, *Theorists of Economic Growth*, 234.

that actually gave rise to the market system. For example, he wrote that "capitalist production completely tears asunder the old bond of union which held together agriculture and manufacture in their infancy. But at the same time it creates the material conditions for a higher synthesis in the future."[104]

Indeed, this is mirrored closely in Schumpeter's own theory of economic development, but there is a distinct and very important difference between the two standpoints. In Schumpeter's perspective, when an economic depression or downturn occurs in the business cycle this is not necessarily something negative. It is here, he asserts, that the most appropriate model to understand the free market process is the concept of *"creative destruction."* This in his view best describes and explains the free market process and the human agents operating in it. Marx, on the other hand, naturally interprets such economic downturns negatively and as being therefore inimical to the reality of the human person. There is no doubt that the Schumpeterian word "destruction" sounds negative, and he certainly does not deny that this aspect is necessarily involved in the workings of the free economy. In his concluding paragraph in *The Theory of Economic Development*, he recognizes clearly the painful but creative dynamic of the free market process. He writes,

> No therapy can permanently obstruct the great economic and social process by which business, individual positions, forms of life, cultural values and ideals, sink in the social scale and finally disappear. In a society with private property and competition, this process is the necessary complement of the continual emergence of new economic and social forms and of continually rising real incomes of all social strata. The process would be milder if there were no cyclical fluctuations, but it is not wholly due to the latter and it is completely independent of them. These changes are theoretically and practically, economically and culturally, much more important than the economic stability upon which all analytical attention has been concentrated for so long. And in their special way both the rise and fall of families and firms are much more characteristic of the capitalist economic system, of its culture and its results, than any of the things that can be observed in a society which is stationary in the sense that its processes reproduce themselves at a constant rate.[105]

104. Marx, *Capital*, 297.
105. Schumpeter, *Theory of Economic Development*, 255.

Schumpeter clearly suggests that "no therapy" can prevent the dynamics of "creative destruction" from unfolding within the free market process. Marx and Engels, on the other hand, would disagree and suggest that this economic order must be overturned. As they say, it is essentially a system that produces its own "grave-diggers."[106] Thus, they claim in *The Communist Manifesto* that "its fall and the victory of the proletariat are equally inevitable."[107] But Schumpeter has others besides Karl Marx in his sights when he argues for a "non-interventionist" approach to the economy. Earlier on, in his discussion of the business cycle, he mentions John Maynard Keynes, Irving Fisher, and Sir Ralph Hawtrey and the Federal Reserve Board.[108] In his view their "countercyclical ameliorative proposals"[109] run counter to a proper understanding of how the business cycle really works. According, to Schumpeter they get it wrong because they envisage the business sequence as essentially a "monetary phenomenon or one which has its root in bank credit."[110] But they underestimate the fact that profits or losses especially in a depression are not "meaningless and functionless."[111] They are actually signs of the inner workings of the system and they should be properly interpreted.

The failure to grasp the creative dynamic nature of the free market process, and the roles and functions of the different *dramatis personae* (the entrepreneur, for example), are some of the reasons why, I believe, modern economic thought became increasingly anthropologically derailed. In other words, to forget or simply to obscure the essential dynamic vision of the market process as one which is subject to constant change is a fundamentally mistaken understanding of the economic reality. Furthermore, the occlusion of the importance of entrepreneurial human creativity and its function within the free economy is, as Schumpeter suggests, rather "like *Hamlet* without the Danish Prince."[112] I made reference earlier to the threefold categorization of the vision that can be held in terms of understanding the economy, that is, the "pessimist," "optimist," and "Marxian" interpretations. We could add a fourth, that is,

106. Marx and Engels, *Communist Manifesto*, 233.

107. Ibid.

108. Irving Fisher was the American economist who famously stated just before the 1929 market crash that stocks had reached "a permanently high plateau."

109. Rostow, *Theorists of Economic Growth*, 626 n. 71.

110. Schumpeter, *Theory of Economic Development*, 252.

111. Ibid., 252–53.

112. Schumpeter, *Capitalism, Socialism and Democracy*, 86.

the Schumpeterian viewpoint we are discussing here, which is essentially *"dynamic"* in its approach to economic reality.[113]

I spoke at the beginning of the chapter about how following the international financial collapse and the Great Recession there was and still is a "fractured relationship" between Wall Street and Main Street, that is, between the world of the "Ninja-like financiers" and those who face foreclosure on their homes and eviction. This inevitably opens up the question and debate for all concerned about the model or vision we use in economics and how it plays out in the economy. Likewise, Schumpeter also spoke of a fragmentation of reality that often occurs within economics. He finds it hard to appreciate how other theoreticians miss the point and notes that even Marx understood this, that is, he sees the process of "creative destruction" is actually endogenous to the operation of the free economy. Schumpeter explains that the free market

> is by nature a form or method of economic change and not only never is but never can be stationary. And this evolutionary character of the capitalist process is not merely due to the fact that economic life goes on in a social and natural environment which changes and by its change alters the data of economic action; this fact is important and these changes (wars, revolutions and so on) often condition industrial change, but they are not its prime movers. Nor is this evolutionary character due to a quasi-automatic increase in population and capital or to the vagaries of the monetary system of which exactly the same thing holds true. The fundamental impulse that sets and keeps the capitalist engine in motion comes from the new consumers' goods, the new methods of production or transportation, the new markets, the new forms of industrial organization that capitalist enterprise creates . . . This process of *Creative Destruction* is the essential fact about capitalism.[114]

He emphasizes, in other words, that the free economy is not a static machine which can be controlled simply by adjusting different levers, but it is essentially a human process of continual discovery. What happens in one particular part of it may clarify details about the process but the

113. In this whole discussion it is important to keep in mind the use of the word "dynamic" in economics. Philip McShane observes that "even a static economics, one without any change of pattern from decade to decade, is dynamic" (*Piketty's Plight and the Global Future*, 42).

114. Schumpeter, *Capitalism, Socialism and Democracy*, 82–83, my emphasis. Schumpeter notes that an oligopolist industry is one that consists of a few firms.

true significance can be only understood in terms of the overall dynamic reality. This means, for example, that to adjudge in an economic analysis the "maximization principle" to mean "x" and then to universalize this "x" as the totality of the process is erroneous (like saying that "self-maximization" is the whole meaning of the process). Schumpeter gives the example of economists who investigate "the behaviour of an oligopolist industry."[115] They end up accepting the data of the current situation as if there were no past and no future (that is, the time factor is frozen). These analysts will then reach the inevitable conclusion that the "maximization principle" actually generates oligopoly. The challenge here is to see that what is "usually being visualized is how capitalism administers existing structures, whereas the relevant problem is how it creates and destroys them."[116] What's going on here is that the part is being misunderstood as the whole, and if you don't recognize this it ends up that "the investigator does a meaningless job."[117] I have spoken about the need to recapture the creative human perspective of the free economy. In this regard, Schumpeter's vision is of a dynamic process in which the "creative-destructive" dimensions of entrepreneurial action play out.

V. The Millennium Bridge Analogy

I want to give an example, which conveys to some degree an insight into understanding the dynamic nature of the free market process. The example comes from a study carried out by Professor Haresh Sapra of the University of Chicago Booth School of Business and other academics.[118] They draw upon an analogy with London's Millennium Bridge and what's called the "wobbly bridge" effect. The central theme of the paper does not actually concern us here.[119] The authors explain that it is because "we live

---

115. Ibid., 84.

116. Ibid.

117. Ibid.

118. See Plantin et al., "Fair Value Accounting and Financial Stability."

119. The theme of the authors' paper concerns the adequacy of actual accounting methods. The common understanding is that market prices give timely signals that assist the agents in decision-making. However, in a situation of volatility caused by distorted incentives, prices may in fact distort real decisions. How are accountants to account for these distortions in value? Accountants usually use two approaches to this problem. One is called "marking-to-market" or "fair-value" accounting. It refers to accounting for the value of an asset or liability based on the current market price of

in an *imperfect* world, where markets are not always fully liquid and incentives may be distorted" that accounting is relevant to us at all.[120] If you operated in the context of "completely frictionless markets" there would be no need for accounting.[121] Reliable market prices would be available to all and all that would be needed would be to photograph the given situation. But markets are dynamic and it can be argued "fair value accounting precludes the dubious practices of managers in hiding the consequences of their actions from the eyes of the outside observers."[122]

Sapra uses the example of the Millennium Bridge because it illustrates the free market process in operation. As the name suggests the bridge was part of the Millennium celebrations in London in the year 2000. The bridge was opened in June 2000 and thousands of people turned up at the opening. However, within moments of the bridge's opening, it began to shake violently. The shaking was so violent that many pedestrians clung on to the side-rails. It was immediately shut down and remained closed for the next 18 months. The engineers were called in to solve the problem. The solution to the problem was that this phenomenon is actually inherent to the human reality of walking. Try walking on a rope bridge and you will quickly understand. The engineers installed a shaking machine to send vibrations through the structure. They discovered that horizontal shaking at 1 hertz (that is, one cycle per second) set off the wobble that was witnessed on the opening day. This was a very important clue for the engineers. Normal walking pace is usually at two strides per second, which means that we are on our on our left foot every second and on our right foot every second. Our legs are apart, so our body sways from side to side when we walk and normally, this is not a problem for us. Another factor helped the engineers solve the Millennium Bridge question, and that is when soldiers cross a bridge together they are always instructed that they should break step. But the pedestrians were not soldiers marching in a uniform manner. You would think that the diversification principle, that is, that people walking in a random

---

the asset or liability, or for similar assets and liabilities, or based on another objectively assessed "fair" value. Whereas the term "book value" is usually understood as the value of the assets on the "books" (balance sheet) of the company. It would not take into account such things as market gain or depreciation. Sapra and his colleagues weigh up the different arguments in terms of these approaches to accounting.

120. Plantin et al., "Fair Value Accounting," 86.

121. Ibid.

122. Ibid.

fashion would cancel out one another's sway. What is the probability that a thousand people all walking at random will end up walking all in step? The answer is probably "close to zero." But the important point is that we have to take into account *how* people react to their environment. Pedestrians on the bridge react to how the bridge is moving. When the bridge moves, everyone adjusts his or her stance at the same time. This synchronised movement pushes the bridge that the people are standing on, and makes the bridge move even more. So, people end up adjusting their stance even more radically. In brief, the wobble of the bridge feeds on itself. When the bridge wobbles, everyone adjusts his or her step to compensate for the condition.[123]

Now Sapra asks, "What does all this have to do with accounting standards and financial markets?"[124] He gives the following insightful explanation:

> Financial markets are the supreme example of an environment where individuals react to what's happening around them, and where individuals' actions affect the outcomes themselves. The pedestrians on the Millennium Bridge are rather like modern banks that react to price changes, and the movements in the bridge are rather like price changes in the market. So, under the right conditions, price changes will elicit reactions from the banks, which move prices, which elicit further reactions, and so on.[125]

He clarifies that mark-to-market accounting actually assists in analyzing the process because it "ensures that any price change shows up immediately on the balance sheet. So, when the bridge moves, banks adjust their stance more than they used to, and marking-to-market ensures that they all do at the same time."[126] Sapra stresses that "the Millennium Bridge example points to the importance of the dual role of prices. Not only are they a reflection of the underlying economic fundamentals, they are also an imperative to action. Prices induce actions on the part of the economic agents, as well as mirror the actions of the economic agents."[127]

123. The foregoing description is given in ibid., 87–88.
124. Ibid., 88.
125. Ibid.
126. Ibid.
127. Ibid.

As I mentioned already the Sapra study is obviously written with special reference to the profession of accounting and the challenge of devising adequate methodologies of measurement. But financial development and innovation means that banks and other financial institutions are barometers of the dynamic and changing character of the free economy. The Millennium Bridge analogy demonstrates to some degree what is intended when we describe the dynamic character of the free market process. The Schumpeterian contribution arose in a certain historical context, and that was when conventional economists were apparently unwilling to alter their vision of the economic process and were subsequently unable to distinguish and account for the crucial roles of constant change and the entrepreneurial function.

VI. Conclusion

Schumpeter felt that there was a fundamental failure in economic reflection in terms of any real insight into understanding the dynamic nature of human action in the economy. It is for this reason that "entrepreneurial action" remained the invisible dimension in the whole process. It is as if the stage is set and ready for the action but the actors (the *acting person*) are almost sidelined. To put it rather more dramatically and in Lonerganian terms "the actors in the living drama become stagehands; the setting is magnificent; the lighting superb; the costumes gorgeous; but there is no play."[128] Schumpeter observes that "all the leaders of that time, such as Jevons, Walras, Menger, Marshall, Wicksell, Clark and so on, visualized the economic process much as had J. S. Mill or even A. Smith; that is to say, they added nothing to the ideas of the preceding period concerning what it is that happens in the economic process and how, in a general way, this process works out."[129]

At this point, it must be stressed that Schumpeter is very often sweeping in his generalizations and this is indeed an overall critique often made of his *magnum opus*. He frequently used dramatic effect in his writings.[130] Following his claim that the neoclassical economists added

128. Lonergan, *Insight*, 262.

129. Schumpeter, *History of Economic Analysis*, 892.

130. He once wrote, "Can capitalism survive? No. I do not think it can. But this opinion of mine, like that of every other economist who has pronounced on the subject, is in itself completely uninteresting" (*Capitalism, Socialism and Democracy*, 61).

nothing, he then explains however that their "analysis was far superior to that of the classics."[131] He also recognizes that the "entrepreneur was being distinguished from the capitalist, and his profit from interest, with ever increasing clearness as time went on."[132] It is important here to state, for example, the importance of Schumpeter's indebtedness to the Swiss economist Léon Walras. Schumpeter regarded himself as Walrasian and was influenced by Walras's equilibrium theory or what Schumpeter called the "circular flow" model. In one sense it is on the basis of Walras's general equilibrium approach that Schumpeter can see a way to integrating the reality of entrepreneurship, profits and loses (changes) into a theoretical explanation. The only way out of the general equilibrium is "creative destruction" through which Schumpeter reconciled what he observed in economic life with the Walrasian theoretical system.

It is true that in regard to the dynamic nature of the economic system, economists now sufficiently take on board Schumpeter's analysis and contribution. For instance, in a study on Schumpeter, Alain Raybaut and Franck Sosthé explain how he saw the importance of those theoreticians who firstly studied the stationary economy. They write that for Schumpeter

> the study of a stationary economy is a first step towards the analysis of other aspects of the economy . . . He clearly recognises that in describing both a stationary and a growing economy "we admit only small deviations at the margin, such as every individual can accomplish by adapting to economic the environment, without materially deviating from familiar lines" . . . However, once other forms of behaviour, such as entrepreneurial behaviour, are included in the analysis, new combinations

131. Ibid. When the neoclassical theorists emerged in economics there were considerable adjustments in the viewpoint of economic theory. There were substantial advances in terms of theories about money and of economic cycles. There were also as I mentioned the fundamental insights into the "new" theory of value. The neoclassical breakthrough is often dated to the 1870s. Characteristic of this school is its use of marginal concepts—such as marginal utility, marginal cost, and marginal revenue. The marginal principle is used to understand the human behavior that drives the market forces of supply and demand, and "marginalism" is the term often used to describe this approach. Neoclassical economics reached a high point with the publication of Paul Samuelson's *Foundations of Economic Analysis* (1947). Other significant works were those of Kenneth Arrow of Stanford University and Gérard Debreu of Chicago, who jointly wrote a paper titled "Existence of an Equilibrium for a Competitive Economy" (1954).

132. Schumpeter, *History of Economic Analysis*, 893.

have to be taken into account and a dynamic analysis of the system's evolution becomes necessary. Hence, Schumpeter clearly
embarks on an analytical transition from the theory of general
equilibrium with pure competition to a new, as yet unexplored,
approach which is required to describe the working of competition in a dynamic context.[133]

As I have previously said, some modern economic textbooks similarly
take up these Schumpeterian themes. In *Understanding Capitalism: Competition, Command, and Change*, for example, the authors interestingly
analyze the economy from a three-dimensional perspective. They say
that "the complex relationships of a capitalist economy" can be investigated in terms of three dimensions. That is, "a horizontal dimension
(*competition*), a vertical dimension (*command*) and a time dimension
(*change*).[134] They refer specifically to Schumpeter observing that for him
"change—our time dimension—had to be central to any economic theory. Among his many novel ideas are his theories regarding innovation,
on the one hand, and disruptive change, on the other."[135] They explain how
Schumpeter used the term "creative destruction" to describe the connection between innovation and dynamic change within the economy. But
he applied it not just to technological innovation but to social and orga-
nizational change as well. The Schumpeterian vision of the free market is
of one that constantly changes, that is, in "order for progress to occur, old
methods of doing business must be disrupted in a creative burst."[136] On the
other hand, the neoclassical vision views the economy as a smoothly running machine; it operates continuously and indefinitely into the future.
Any changes that occur are a result of external influences. These effects
could be things like population changes or differences in the quantities
of natural resources.[137] They could be due also to technological discoveries and changes in consumer demand. But change can also occur due to
the internal actions of human agents like the entrepreneur. We can see
therefore why a one-dimensional approach to understanding economics
and the economy cannot explain the economic reality sufficiently. Emphasis on the "horizontal" aspect alone runs the risk of focusing just on

133. Raybaut and Sosthé, "Schumpeter on Competition," 188–89.

134. Bowles et al., *Understanding Capitalism*, 52.

135. Ibid., 80.

136. Ibid.

137. Schumpeter made reference to some traces of the Malthusian thesis being found
among the neoclassical theorists. See *History of Economic Analysis*, 889–90.

competition and exchange, forgetting the multidimensional nature of the free market economy. Schumpeter's contribution in the economic debate can be summarized by viewing him fundamentally as a "prophet of innovation" in terms of understanding the centrality of the human creative dimension of the acting person in the free economy.

5

Entrepreneurial Perspectives II: A Philosophical Reflection on the Role of the Entrepreneur

I. The Entrepreneur: Who, Which, What?

BERNARD LONERGAN EXPLAINS THE mechanism of an exchange economy in the following terms: "An exchange economy is an attempt to give a continuously satisfactory answer to the continuously shifting question, *Who*, among millions of persons is to perform *which*, among millions of tasks, in return for *what*, among millions of possible rewards?"[1] So, in this chapter we'll examine *who* the entrepreneur is, *which* task he performs in the free economy and *what* incentive is there in carrying out these human actions. In a discussion about emergent probabilities Lonergan used the analogy of driving a car which might be useful when it comes to describing the economy. He comments when "driving a car you don't step on the accelerator and the brake at the same time with equal vigour . . . In so far as you understand how the economic machine works, you know what can be done and what can't be done."[2] He goes on to explain that an economic system "is a set of interrelations"[3] which has a natural and human basis. He develops the car example further, which I will briefly describe because it illustrates the role of the entrepreneur in that "set of

1. Lonergan, *For a New Political Economy*, 34.
2. Lonergan, *Caring about Meaning*, 186.
3. Ibid.

interrelations" that we call the free market process. Lonergan outlines how the function of the accelerator is basically to accelerate something else. He observes that "there is point-to-point correspondence with the standard of living, and if you are going to have accelerators there, they have to cause movement. In fact, what people do is to get the accelerators running beautifully; then, just as they are raking in the surplus income, they start accelerating something else so things start deflating and they are in a panic . . . [But] panic does not get you anywhere; it is just stupidity, loss of nerve."[4]

As we know, Schumpeter wrote a vast amount on the entrepreneur and entrepreneurship. But the most straightforward sentence he probably ever wrote on the entrepreneurial function was that "it consists in getting things done."[5] In terms of the car example, the "doing" is the driving of the economy and the one "getting it done" is the driver (the entrepreneur). To propel the vehicle the driver uses the "accelerator." The emphasis is therefore on *human action* but the focus is not just on any kind of action. The entrepreneur is like that "accelerator" who purposively innovates so as to create "more productive as well as capital goods and services."[6] The entrepreneur is not just a "man without qualities,"[7] that is, merely an egotistical opportunist operating in a tightly compact commoditized environment with no concern for others but for his own self. The role requires the application of human capacities like *deliberation, evaluation, decision, and commitment*. In other words, a certain anthropological perspective is presumed in terms of the "entrepreneur" acting in the free economy. The entrepreneurial actor carries out his role in terms of *experiencing, understanding, judging and deciding* in the economy.[8] Lonergan gives a philosophical analysis of intentional human actions, which could equally be applied to the action of the entrepreneur. He argues that "conscious and intentional operations exist and anyone who dares to deny their existence is merely disqualifying himself as a non-responsible, non-reasonable, non-intelligent somnambulist."[9] Thus, the entrepreneur is not a mindless sleepwalker in the economic drama. In other words, entrepreneurial action does not happen automatically as if in a machine.

4. Ibid., 187.

5. Schumpeter, *Capitalism, Socialism and Democracy*, 132.

6. Neeve, *Decoding the Economy*, 45.

7. See Musil, *The Man Without Qualities*.

8. See Lonergan, *Method in Theology*, 17.

9. Ibid.

In fact, Wilhelm Röpke's central criticism of John Maynard Keynes was exactly this. Keynes and his followers saw the economic system as part of a mathematical-mechanical universe, with economic activity being the product of quantifiable aggregates, such as consumption and investment, instead of a result of actions by individuals. He argued that Keynes took the human out of "human action" and reduced the economic system to a machine. Röpke remarked,

> In the logical machine so cleverly devised by Keynes . . . we find, to be sure, an inflation brake. But the machine is so constructed that the brake is depressed only when a breakneck rate of speed has been attained; and the brake has the further fatal tendency of being released as soon as the braking action is the least bit effective . . . in the teachings of Keynes . . . we find a man who has forgotten those mysterious powers of the human soul and of human society which cannot be expressed in mathematical equations, nor confined within an assemblage of statistics or the rubrics of economic planning.[10]

II. Overshadowing and Retrieval of the Human Dimension in the Free Economy

We referred in the previous chapter to the challenges involved in the articulation of an adequate philosophy of the human person. There is always the danger of occluding the totality of reality with a partial view of the truth. And this applies equally in the field of economics especially in relation to the role of the entrepreneur in economic action. An analysis of entrepreneurial action has often been neglected in economic thought and so the *human element* has been removed from the understanding of economic action. The economist Ulrich Fehl, for example, alludes to such occlusion when he states, "Equilibrium theory excludes *real time* and *human creativity* from its investigation."[11] He explains that "individuals, households and firms do not just have preferences and use a given technology, they are inclined to change them autonomously in the very process of time."[12] Naturally, *creativity* is not solely the responsibility of

10. Röpke, *Economics of the Free Society*, 227.

11. Fehl, "Spontaneous Order," in Boettke, *Elgar Companion to Austrian Economics*, 199.

12. Ibid.

the entrepreneur in the free market process, but it is a crucial anthropological dimension of which the entrepreneur is an *"exemplar."* Fehl even
goes so far as to say the "creativity of man may be considered even more
challenging for equilibrium theory than is the time problem."[13] There are,
of course, many other *"actors"* in the economic drama. Entrepreneurial
action is not merely limited to one actor but includes many others. Since
entrepreneurial initiative is an outgrowth of the anthropological reality of
the human person as a "creative subject," it is not surprising that "creativity" is not restricted to one actor. The *consumer* and not just the *producer*
also have an entrepreneurial function in the economic process. Indeed,
this is an aspect which the Austrian school of economics subsequently
failed to adequately develop.[14]

Philosophically, we can say beyond the human act there is always
the author of the action. When we plunge into the depths of this experience, "we reach the actor" in the drama.[15] The *dramatis personae* involved in the progress of economic activity are numerous (the labor of
the human person and the role of the capitalist are two examples) but
the one protagonist we reflect upon at this stage is the "entrepreneur." As
we've seen our overall proposal is that the free economy is actually based
upon fundamental anthropological principles. It is our endeavor to present a philosophical meditation or reflection upon these person-centered
dimensions and the protagonists involved in the free economy. We will
now examine briefly how the entrepreneur has been treated in economic
reflections by a variety of theoreticians. The viewpoint of the analysis will
be initially, in phenomenological terms, at the level of a description of the
who, what and *which* of the entrepreneur. We'll survey what economists
have said in the past and present on the role of the entrepreneur and
thereby attempt to "X-ray" this human experience as it occurs in economic life. With this approach we hope to arrive at an explanation of the
entrepreneurial role of the human person in the free market economy.
It is my view that entrepreneurial human action as such and the characteristics associated with it are in their own way revelatory of what it
means to be a human person. So, it is important to set out a description
of the "entrepreneur" found in some economic writings. Then we can
arrive at an understanding of the role and the human agency involved in

13. As Fehl notes, "equilibrium" can be understood in terms of assessing the economy as being "close to" or "far from" perfect coordination. Ibid., 198.

14. See Leen, "The Consumer in Austrian Economics," 41–75.

15. Voegelin, *What Is History?*, 112.

the actions of the entrepreneur. It is important to remember that "pure description is not enough. There is, therefore . . . the need to interpret, that is, to understand the essence of the phenomenon, by seeing it in the context of the whole person and of interpersonal relations."[16]

There is a certain complementarity and differentiation between "description" and "explanation" in our method. This is of fundamental importance with regard to an adequate understanding of human entrepreneurial action. We hope to grasp at what is essential, philosophically speaking, when it comes to an analysis of the entrepreneurial function. We should be able to deal with the question, what makes an entrepreneur an entrepreneur? An important observation about this whole issue in the contemporary context is that the protagonists in the free economy do not necessarily stop to think about their actions. They happen almost automatically in the process but it would be mistaken to take them and their actions for granted. Alfred N. Whitehead refers in a comparable way to the approach within the field of mathematics that uses mathematical notation as a shorthand in its understanding. He observed that "by relieving the brain of all unnecessary work, a good notation sets it free to concentrate on more advanced problems . . . It is a profoundly erroneous truism, repeated by all copybooks and by eminent people when they are making speeches, that we should cultivate the habit of thinking about what we are doing. The precise opposite is the case. Civilization advances by extending the number of important operations which we can perform without thinking about them."[17]

There is a fundamental challenge in the economic arena to press the pause button in regard to any analysis of human action, so that we can gain a greater insight and understanding into the human dynamics of the free economy and the roles played by the various protagonists. Alan Greenspan, the American economist and former chairman of the Federal Reserve, referred in his autobiography to the need to examine more closely the human anthropological principles on which the free market is based. Too often, we are like ice skaters who sail across the surface without considering the other depth-horizons that make up the substance of the economic reality we live in. It is only when there is a general collapse of the market infrastructure that we begin to reflect on the fundamentals holding up the process. Greenspan remarked that "we rarely look closely

---

16. McNerney, *John Paul II*, 15.

17. Whitehead, *Introduction to Mathematics*, 39, 41–42.

at that principal operating unit of economic activity: the human being. What are we? What is fixed in our nature and not subject to change—and how much discretion and free will do we have to act and learn? I have been struggling with these questions since I first knew to ask it."[18]

Greenspan relates a personal experience about this when he describes the events surrounding the fall of the Berlin Wall. He was invited in October 1989 by the American ambassador in Moscow to speak to a group of Soviet economists and bankers. His topic "was to explain capitalist finance."[19] His expectation was that he would instruct the Soviets on the fatal conceit of their erroneous ways. But he explains that his audience, in fact, would give him the most "extraordinary tutorial on the roots of capitalism"[20] that he ever had in his life. Greenspan explains that the free market economy was the system he was most familiar with but that his "understanding of its foundations was wholly abstract."[21] He says, "I was reared in a sophisticated market economy with its many supporting laws, institutions, and conventions long since in place and mature."[22] The experience of witnessing the collapse of the Berlin Wall and of communism, he explained, was like that of a neurologist "who learns by observing how a patient functions when a part of the brain has been impaired."[23] Observing markets trying to survive without fundamentals like property rights and the value of trust was a completely new experience for him. He described how he had studied free-market economics for most of his life but that "encountering the alternative and seeing it in crisis forced . . . [him] to think more deeply"[24] than he ever had before "about the fundamentals of capitalism."[25]

As Ludwig von Mises stressed, we must open up our horizons of human understanding when it comes to the consideration of human action in economic activity. Economics does not presuppose a one-dimensional understanding of the human person as aiming only "at what is called material well-being."[26] There is a fundamental bias involved when, for

18. Greenspan, *Age of Turbulence*, 16.

19. Ibid., 123.

20. Ibid.

21. Ibid.

22. Ibid.

23. Ibid., 124.

24. Ibid., 127.

25. Ibid.

26. Mises, *Human Action*, 884.

example, we focus solely on the entrepreneur as being, in the populist view, rather like an economic agent who cheats and appropriates what does not properly belong to him or her but is the rightful property and labor of others involved in the economic process.[27] The Marxian approach, for example, generally placed the chief emphasis on the corrosive activity of the capitalist in the economy. But Marx did not sufficiently differentiate the various roles of the human actors in the market economy. As Schumpeter highlighted, Marx really "had no adequate theory of enterprise and his failure to distinguish the entrepreneur from the capitalist" accounted for his shutting out this human reality from the dynamic economic process.[28] Marx held that it was the capitalist's search for profits and his reaction to changing rates of profit that explained the dynamics of the system. Marx's explanations of the market economy's destructive powers were indeed masterful and insightful but his emphasis on the theory of class struggle tended to derail his overall dynamic analysis of the market process. Schumpeter who is favorable to Marx in some respects contends that "one must wear blinkers"[29] when it comes to the class theory and its application to economics and historical understanding. Writing about Marx's application of this in terms of colonial history, Schumpeter explains that class struggle actually played a minor role and that the period in actual fact exhibited "some of the most striking instances of class cooperation."[30]

I am essentially concerned here in maintaining a non-reductive perspective on the actions of human persons in the free market economy. There is in economics the constant challenge to retain what I call an "anthropological balance" or median in the treatment of the human subject. This is important because if we build an analysis of the free economy on the basis of the construction and simple acceptance of a truncated concept of the human person as economic agent, we run the risk of mistaking the actual reduction for reality in itself. This could lead to the problem of

---

27. The American entrepreneur Warren Buffett makes an interesting reference to this populist view of the entrepreneurial function. He was asked, "Where did it come from, Warren? Caring so much about making money?" Buffet replied, "Balzac said that behind every great fortune lies a crime. That's not true at Berkshire." Berkshire Hathaway Inc. is the conglomerate holding company run by Buffett and his partner Charlie Munger. See Schroeder, *Snowball*, 4.

28. Schumpeter, *Capitalism, Socialism and Democracy*, 32, 53.

29. Ibid., 53.

30. Ibid.

"tilting at windmills." In that case we would in the words of Voegelin then move on "to the problem of deformation" within reality.[31] In this situation memories become dimmed as to the reality "of a fuller humanity" and in our investigation this could result in a failure to adequately outline the human dimensions of the free economy. Mises, for instance, argued strongly that economics is not reductive in its approach as it "deals with all human action, i.e. with man's purposive aiming at the attainment of ends chosen, whatever these ends may be."[32] So, being philosophically cognizant of this, we can turn now to the next section and endeavor to give a general description of the entrepreneur and entrepreneurial action in economic thought.

III. Various Perspectives on the Entrepreneur in Economic Thought

We must necessarily limit our description of the entrepreneur and refer to just a few economic thinkers. Economic writers are of the general opinion that Schumpeter and the Austrian school are seen as important contributors to the debate.[33] But it is important to keep in mind that the story and themes of the Austrian school actually begin in the fifteenth century, when the followers of St. Thomas Aquinas, writing and teaching in the University of Salamanca in Spain, attempted to explain the full range of human action and social organization, which included human economic activity.[34] However, this understanding of human action was lost down a "sinkhole" in economic thought, and it was the Austrian tradition which subsequently contributed to the overall rediscovery of the entrepreneur's role and importance of entrepreneurial human action in the free economy. I have already emphasized that the entrepreneur is not the sole originator of human creativity in the economic process.

31. Voegelin, *What Is History?*, 117.

32. Ibid.

33. The influence of the Austrian school is now also widespread in the American tradition. See Karen I. Vaughn's *Austrian Economics in America*.

34. See Chafuen, *Christians for Freedom: Late-Scholastic Economics*; Moss et al., *Economic Thought in Spain: Selected Essays of Marjorie Grice-Hutchinson*; Pieper, *Scholasticism: Personalities and Problems of Medieval Philosophy*; Spiegel, *The Growth of Economic Thought*; Grice-Hutchinson, *The School of Salamanca: Readings in Spanish Monetary Theory, 1544–1605*; Alves et al., *The Salamanca School: Major Conservative and Libertarian Thinkers*.

The entrepreneur is simply an *"exemplar"* of *human action* in the free economy. The anthropological characteristics of entrepreneurial action are shared in common with the other agents engaged in economic activity. Bettina Bien Greaves outlines clearly the anthropological basis of the economy when she claims that Mises's contribution to economic thinking was to highlight the fact that "the whole economy is the result of what individuals do. Individuals act, choose, cooperate, compete, and trade with one another. In this way Mises explained how complex economic phenomena develop. Mises did not simply *describe* economic phenomena—prices, wages, interest rates, money, monopoly and even trade cycles—he *explained* them as outcomes of *countless conscious, purposive actions, choices and preferences of individuals.*"[35]

In what follows we'll examine the contributions of Schumpeter in elaborating an understanding of the role of the entrepreneur in the free market process along with what I would call an "emergent anthropology" which was left undeveloped. In chapter six an overview of the perspectives on entrepreneurial human action in the free economy from some of the other Austrian school economists like Ludwig von Mises, Friedrich A. Hayek, and Israel Kirzner will be given. It is my contention that in each approach a particular philosophy of the human person emerges.

IV. Schumpeter's Entrepreneur: An Emergent Anthropology[36]

It was Schumpeter who claimed that the Franco-Hibernian economist Richard Cantillon (1680–1734) was the first to use the term *entrepreneur*.[37] Schumpeter noted that Cantillon "had a clear conception of the function of the entrepreneur."[38] Cantillon discussed entrepreneurship in

35. Greaves, foreword to Mises, *Human Action*, v, my emphases.

36. In using the term "emergent anthropology" I am making use of Lonergan's concept of "emergent probability." Lonergan used it to mean that the "world process is open. It is a succession of probable realizations of possibilities." But I use it here in the sense that the Schumpeterian analysis of entrepreneurial action is an open heuristic that provides hints or clues for us so that we as philosophers can outline the nascent anthropology. See Lonergan, *Insight*, 149.

37. Schumpeter, *History of Economic Analysis*, 222, 555, 646.

38. Ibid., 222. Schumpeter states, "Cantillon was, so far as I know, the first to use the term entrepreneur" (555).

his *Essai sur la nature du commerce en général* (1755). He argued there that all market agents could be classified in the role as entrepreneurs and wrote that "all the Undertakers are as it were on unfixed wages and the others of wages fixed so long as they receive them though their functions and ranks may be very unequal. The General who has pay, the Courtier his pension, and the Domestic servant who has wages all fall into this last class. All the rest are Undertakers, whether they set up with a capital to conduct their enterprise, or are Undertakers of their own labour without capital, and they may be regarded as living at uncertainty; the Beggars even and the Robbers are Undertakers of this class."[39]

Cantillon analyzed this entrepreneurial role and applied it, for example, to the case of the farmer. The farmer pays out certain contractual incomes, which are "certain" to landowners and laborers. But the farmer sells at prices that are uncertain, as do other economic agents like "drapers" or other "merchants." They commit themselves to certain payments in the expectation of receiving other income. Schumpeter explains that they can be described as "risk-bearing directors of production and trade, competition tending to reduce their remuneration to the normal value of their services. This, of course, is the scholastic doctrine. But nobody before Cantillon had formulated it so fully."[40] Schumpeter makes the interesting point, which Rothbard also states, that it was through Cantillon that the French economists retained this original insight into the role of the entrepreneur. But the insight was actually lost when it came to the English and Scottish economists. As I have mentioned already it was Schumpeter who argued that Adam Smith had in this way basically "shunted economics off on a wrong road, a road unfortunately different from that of his continental forbears."[41] In his examination of the classical economists on the theme of the *actors* in the economic process, Schumpeter claims that there was indeed significant but slow development of the distinction between what he calls "the businessman's *industria* from

39. Cantillon, *Essay on the Nature of Commerce*, 26. Higgs translated *entrepreneur* as "undertaker." Anthony Brewer notes in his introduction that "Cantillon's usage, in which entrepreneur is an independent risk-taking businessman, marked a major conceptual innovation which has passed via Say into modern economics. It has, however, come into modern economics untranslated—we now talk of an 'entrepreneur' and not of an 'undertaker'" (ibid., xi–xii).

40. Schumpeter, *History of Economic Analysis*, 222.

41. See Rothbard, *Economic Thought before Adam Smith*, 437.

the workman's *labor*."[42] But even going back to the times of St. Antoninus of Florence a "differentiation" in human economic understanding between the two functions had already taken place. In this regard we may find Voegelin's distinction between "compactness" and "differentiation" which I previously introduced in chapter three useful at this juncture. It was in the context of trying to reach a deeper understanding of the sociopolitical and philosophical problems that confronted Voegelin in the 1930s and 1940s that he used the symbols of "compactness" and "differentiation." His analysis was that if the structure of reality is constant or moreover if it is complex but if our understanding or articulation of it, is partial or incomplete, then we run the risk of a failure to account adequately for the "comprehensive reality." Voegelin's analysis was in terms of consciousness and a general theory of history. The less precise accounts of reality were often given in the form of myths, and these he described as "compact." But the more precise and "analytically deeper articulations he called 'differentiated.'"[43] Voegelin discovered in his historical investigations evidence for such "differentiation." He found that "there were indeed epochal, differentiating events . . . The experiences of a new insight into the truth of existence, accompanied by the consciousness of the event as constituting an epoch in history, were real enough. There was really an advance in time from compact to differentiated symbolizations of the order of being."[44]

This activity of "differentiation" can occur within various time periods and in different disciplines.[45] We can, I believe, actually trace a certain equivalence in terms of "compactness" within the economic process and the further development of understanding or "differentiation" about the role of the entrepreneur in economic thinking. Thomas Heilke, commenting on the Voegelinian methodology, described philosophy as "an activity of reflecting in a comprehensive way on the 'comprehensive reality' of which we are a part and in which we participate."[46] Economic agents also necessarily operate in a given anthropological reality, and

42. Ibid.

43. Heilke, *Eric Voegelin*, 79.

44. Voegelin, *Ecumenic Age*, 2.

45. John J. Ranieri gives an insightful account of Voegelin's theory of compactness and differentiation as applied to social order and the good society. Ranieri writes, "With a differentiation the structure and movement of reality comes to be understood more clearly" (*Eric Voegelin and the Good Society*, 96).

46. Heilke, *Eric Voegelin*, 65.

subsequent economic reflections need to take cognizance of this truth. However, what Schumpeter actually points to in his historical investigations is that although this "act of differentiation" in terms of the role of the entrepreneur did occur, it actually remained submerged in the forest of economic reflections. There was *amnesia* in respect of an adequate articulation the entrepreneur's role in economic action. Indeed, Heilke points to an important "act of differentiation" that can occur but not necessarily in the social sciences. This is the realization, he argues, that one can analytically engage in "accurate and useful (social) science without having a full grasp of the wider reality-context within which the activity takes place."[47] Thus, there is always a need for what I call an "anamnetic recovery" of the role and anthropological significance of entrepreneurial human action in economic life.[48]

Schumpeter observed that moving along from Cantillon and still in the French tradition, for example, Jean-Baptiste Say (1767–1832) "was the first to assign to the entrepreneur—per se and as distinct from the capitalist—a definite position in the scheme of the economic process."[49] Say understood the entrepreneur's function "is to *combine* the factors of production into a producing organism."[50] But Say failed to recognize and adequately understand the dynamic nature of what "the phrase 'combining factors'" when applied to the economic process could mean.[51] Schumpeter refers to the missed opportunity for a proper account of the role of the entrepreneur in the reflections of the English economists like David Ricardo, the Ricardians and Nassau Senior. They accomplished what he calls "an impossible feat, namely, the exclusion of the figure of the entrepreneur completely. For them—as well as for Marx—the business process runs substantially by itself, the one thing needful to make it run being an adequate supply of capital."[52] Schumpeter's reminder, therefore, to economists in terms of the function of entrepreneurial action in the

47. Ibid., 80.

48. Anamnesis in Voegelin is understood as recollection. It is "the recalling of past experiences that have become dormant in consciousness. Important concept to Voegelin's notion of recovery of experience." See the glossary in Federici, *Eric Voegelin*, 208.

49. Schumpeter, *History of Economic Analysis*, 555.

50. Ibid.

51. Ibid.

52. Ibid., 556.

free economy is the need for a reassertion and recovery of this original "act of differentiation" or insight that predated Adam Smith.

The Schumpeterian entrepreneur is described essentially as an individual "hero" of innovation who navigates in an economic system of continuous change.[53] He or she steps outside the pale of normal routine. Entrepreneurship "essentially consists in doing things that are not generally done in the ordinary course of business routine."[54] Schumpeter stresses that the important thing "is the recognition of the distinct agent we envisage and not the word."[55] In other words, his emphasis is upon what we would call the "anthropological principle" in terms of the entrepreneurial action. In his extensive analysis of business cycles Schumpeter discovered in the free market economy that the key that starts the engine and keeps it in operation is human innovation. He wrote that "without innovations, no entrepreneurs; without entrepreneurial achievement, no capitalist returns and no capitalist propulsion."[56] Marx was critical of the mystification, which dialectic suffered in Hegel's analysis and he claimed, "with him [Hegel] it is standing on its head. It should be turned right side up again, if you should discover the rational kernel within the mystical shell."[57] But Schumpeter could be adjudged to have "turned Karl Marx on his head. Hateful gangs of parasitic capitalists become" in his description "innovative and beneficent entrepreneurs."[58]

So, in an attempt to give an adequate description of the entrepreneur, Schumpeter "X-rays" five types of innovation, which are characteristic of human entrepreneurial action. Briefly, they are as follows: (1) the introduction of a new good—that is one with which consumers are not yet

53. See Schumpeter, *Essays on Entrepreneurship, Innovations, Business Cycles, and the Evolution of Capitalism.*

54. Ibid., 259.

55. Ibid.

56. See McCraw, *Prophet of Innovation*, 170.

57. See Marx, *Selected Writings*, 420.

58. McCraw, *Prophet of Innovation*, 69. It is important to note that, as we have previously seen, Marx had an important insight into the dynamic nature of the market process. Therefore, it is wrong to suggest that he never considered in some of his writings the role of entrepreneurs as efficient agents in economic development. But he still considered their function as fundamentally exploitative. See ibid., 529–30 n. 4. In Schumpeter's *Theory of Economic Development* there is a careful distinction made between innovative entrepreneurs and the capitalists who supply the necessary credit. Once again, what is important in the analysis is the human agency involved in the entrepreneurial action and not just the class or word in itself.

familiar; (2) the introduction of a new method of production, that is one not yet tested by experience in the branch of the manufacture concerned; (3) the opening of a new market, that is a market into which the particular branch of manufacture of the country in question has not previously entered, whether or not this market has existed before; (4) the conquest of a new source of supply of raw materials or half-manufactured goods, again irrespective of whether this source already exists or whether it has first to be created; and (5) the carrying out of the new organization of any industry, like the creation of a monopoly position (for example, through trustification) or the breaking up of a monopoly position.[59]

In all these cases the economic system advances "by the carrying out of new combinations."[60] Schumpeter points out that carrying out new amalgamations necessarily involves "'financing' as a special act . . . in practice and in theory."[61] He describes the banker as "the capitalist par excellence. He stands between those who wish to form new combinations and the possessors of productive means."[62] The banker "is essentially a phenomenon of development, though only when no central authority directs the social process . . . He is the ephor of the exchange economy."[63] It is when we come to the combination of new means of production and credit that the role of the entrepreneur emerges in the free economy. Schumpeter writes that "the carrying out of the new combinations we call 'enterprise'; the individuals whose function it is to carry them out we call 'entrepreneurs.'"[64] He remarks that this description of the entrepreneur simply clarifies and gives greater precision to this function. It agrees with "the fundamental point of distinguishing between 'entrepreneurs' and 'capitalists'—irrespective of whether the later are regarded as owners of money, claims to money, or material goods . . . It also settles the question whether the ordinary shareholder as such is an entrepreneur, and disposes of the conception of the entrepreneur as risk bearer. Furthermore, the

59. Schumpeter, *Theory of Economic Development*, 66.

60. Ibid.

61. Ibid., 70

62. Ibid., 74.

63. Ibid. Schumpeter frequently used military terms for economic terminology. An *ephor* (Classical Greek Ἔφορος, from ἐπί [*epi*], "on" or "over," and ὁράω [*horaō*], "to see," that is, "one who oversees") was a leader of ancient Sparta and had more power than the Spartan king. There were five ephors elected annually, who "swore on behalf of the city," while the kings swore for themselves.

64. Schumpeter, *Theory of Economic Development*, 74.

ordinary characterization of the entrepreneur type by such expressions as 'initiative', 'authority', or 'foresight' points entirely in our direction."[65]

Schumpeter essentially understands that the emergence of the role of the entrepreneur is associated with an increased differentiation in human insights in economics into the actual functioning of the free economy. He believes it is a prejudice to hold that the knowledge of the historical origin of an institution or a type is automatically accompanied by a sociological or an economic theory of it. In the case of a properly articulated theory of entrepreneurship there remains the difficulty of "compactness" in that it is often very difficult "to separate the entrepreneurial element from the other."[66] It is true that Schumpeter never gives a full philosophical analysis of human action as such. Nonetheless, there is always a nascent philosophical undercurrent in his economic reflections; it is intermingled, so to speak, with his adumbrations on the entrepreneur. The problem involved in an adequate articulation of the role is that "the entrepreneur's essential function must always appear mixed up with other kinds of activity, which as a rule must be more conspicuous than the essential one."[67] Schumpeter explains that the entrepreneur is an entrepreneur only "when he actually 'carries out new combinations', and loses that character as soon as he has built up his business . . . Because being an entrepreneur is not a profession . . . entrepreneurs do not form a social class in the technical sense, as, for example, landowners or capitalists or workmen do . . . [It] in itself signifies a class position no more that it presupposes one."[68]

He describes the entrepreneur as the one who swims against the current. In the normal "circular flow" of the economy every individual can act promptly and rationally and reacts to the other purposive individuals in the system. In the normal channels the economic participant can rely on their own ability and experience to navigate the market. But when the flow changes (in the context of economic disequilibrium) it is the entrepreneur who can operate and provide the insight necessary in the changed circumstances. Schumpeter describes the changed economic horizon as follows "what was formerly a help becomes a hindrance. What was a familiar datum becomes an unknown. Where the boundaries of

65. Ibid., 75.
66. Ibid., 77.
67. Ibid.
68. Ibid., 78.

routine stop, many people can go no further, and the rest can do so in a highly variable manner. The assumption that conduct is prompt and rational is in all cases a fiction. But it proves to be sufficiently near to reality, if things have time to hammer logic into men."[69]

V. A Rediscovery of the Meaning of Economic Action

As I conclude the Schumpeterian description of the entrepreneur, it is important to note how Schumpeter also gives important consideration to what he calls "the *meaning* of economic action."[70] In other words, we can trace here the movement from *pure description* to the *explanatory level* in his thinking on entrepreneurial action. As we previously outlined in this chapter, when it comes to the free market economy and the human agency involved therein, pure description is not enough. There is the necessity to interpret, that is, to understand the essence of the phenomenon of the human action. To do this we have to consider it in terms of the whole person, of interpersonal relations, and in the context of purposive human action.

Voegelin gives what I consider a useful reflection about science that can be equally applied to the study of economic thought and in understanding the meaning of the entrepreneurial dimension of human action. In his study *The New Science of Politics*, he analyzed the contraction of political science "to a description of existing institutions and the apology of their principles."[71] He discussed the destruction of science in the positivistic period during the second half of the nineteenth century. In Voegelin's perspective science is nothing less than the "study of reality . . . it is a search for truth concerning the nature of various realms of being."[72] The Voegelinian project, therefore, involved the attempt at a restoration of the theoretical dignity of political science through what he termed "retheorization."[73] The demolition of science in this era was, he argued, the result of "two fundamental assumptions." They were "the assumption that the methods used in the mathematizing sciences of the

69. Ibid., 80.

70. Ibid., 91. See also our discussion in chapter 3 of the retrieval of the human meaning of the free economy.

71. Voegelin, *New Science of Politics*, 89.

72. Ibid., 91.

73. Ibid., 90.

external world were possessed of some inherent virtue and that all other sciences would achieve comparable success if they followed the example and accepted these methods as their model . . . the second assumption [was] that the methods of natural sciences were a criterion for theoretical relevance in general."[74]

The combination of these two presuppositions resulted in the assertions that a proper study of reality could be considered as scientific (and thereby as having meaning) only if it applied the methods of the natural sciences. This meant that other matters like metaphysical or anthropological questions could be ignored and treated only as "illusionary problems."[75] Since the methods of science, did not allow for these questions to be asked in the positivistic era, they were treated as irrelevant in the first place. So, meaning ended up being evacuated out of its own meaning. The real danger Voegelin saw was in the second assumption, namely that the methods of the natural sciences were the benchmark for all theoretical significance. However, if we want to apply the principle of "theoretical relevance"[76] generally we must be open to the fact that "different objects require different methods."[77] Voegelin stated "if the adequacy of a method is not measured by its usefulness to the purpose of science, if on the contrary the use of a method is made the criterion of science, then the meaning of science as a truthful account of the structure of reality, as the theoretical orientation of man in this world, and as the great instrument of man's understanding of his own position in the universe is lost."[78]

These three elements, that is, a truthful account of the structure of reality, as the theoretical orientation of man in this world, and as the great instrument of man's understanding of his own position in the universe constitute the meaning of science and it is my view that they can equally apply to economic meaning as well. Any adequate philosophical explanation of the function of the entrepreneur must take into account the reality of the human person who acts in that role. So too Schumpeter's questioning in terms of the meaning or motivation for human entrepreneurial action is, I would suggest, recognition of the fact that description is not enough when it comes to understanding human action in the economic

74. Ibid., 90–91.
75. Ibid., 91.
76. Ibid.
77. Ibid.
78. Ibid.

setting. His approach could be philosophically considered as an attempt to recapture the full amplitude of the reality of the acting human person as "entrepreneur." We are not claiming that Schumpeter was necessarily aware of these philosophical dimensions in his investigations nor would they have essentially concerned him, since his primary interest was in the economic reflection on the issues. But I would say they are "emergent" since these anthropological questions are at least implied in his approach to the subject matter and are, therefore, open to elaboration and further philosophical expansion. There is a certain parallel, I argue, between Schumpeter's methodology and his attempted analysis of the human motivation behind the entrepreneurial act and Thomas Aquinas's study on human action theory in terms of the "human good." Aquinas wrote in the *Summa contra Gentiles*, "Every agent acts for an end." He shows the reason for this in his detailed philosophical exposition. He observes that "activities are distinguished by the different kinds of agents. Sometimes an action terminates in a product, as construction in a house, healing in health; but, sometimes not, as in the case of understanding and sensing ... there is in any activity something beyond which the agent seeks nothing further; were this not so, actions would extend into infinity, which indeed is impossible, because, since the infinite cannot be traversed, the agent would not even begin to act, for nothing is moved toward that which it cannot attain."[79]

The entrepreneurial action, according to Schumpeter, plays an essential part in the free economy. As we have seen he sets out an anatomy of the entrepreneurial act in terms of five types of innovation, which are characteristic of the human action. In this the entrepreneur acts as a human agent for a specific end. Schumpeter's exploration of the function of the entrepreneur can be understood as an application of a theory of human action that applies the insight that "every agent acts for an end" to human economic action. When it actually comes to the articulation of the motivation of the human person as entrepreneur, Schumpeter never really articulates an adequate anthropology of the person. It is for this reason I see that there is a positive area for the growth and development of a philosophy of the human person by way of an analysis of entrepreneurial action.

The idea of the need for the amplification of the whole concept of science is not, of course, limited to philosophers like Voegelin.

79. See Aquinas, *Selected Writings*, 260.

Hans-Georg Gadamer, for example, developed a similar theme in *Truth and Method*. He was also careful to warn against the presumption of the philosopher "who deduces from principles the way in which 'science' must change in order to become philosophically legitimate."[80] *Truth and Method* has as its main theme the point that truth cannot be adequately explained by scientific method alone, and that the true meaning of language transcends the limits of methodological interpretation. Gadamer argued the case that hermeneutics (the science of interpretation) is not merely a method of determining truth, but that it is an activity which aims to understand the conditions which make truth possible. Similarly, Schumpeter's understanding of the entrepreneurial role opens up to us the reality that entrepreneurial action "proves to be an event" in itself.[81] As he said about the entrepreneurial function, it just "consists in getting things done."[82] You can almost discern here in the Schumpeterian analysis of the entrepreneurial dimension the importance philosophically of a prioritization of human action over theory.[83] His exploration contains the seeds for an enhancement of our understanding of the *emerging human face* of economic action in the free economy.

I should mention that Schumpeter's concept of the entrepreneur is often critiqued as at best approximating a Nietzschean egotistical Übermensch type. There is, indeed, ample evidence suggesting the Schumpeterian entrepreneur is somewhat "dinosauric," that is, out of place and out of time in the modern economic context. His terminology is often militaristic and imprecise. It probably stems from his upbringing in the Austro-Hungarian Empire. Notwithstanding this, it is when he seeks to explain the motivation of entrepreneurial action that we can catch a glimpse of the anthropological clothing of the human agent which lies hidden underneath the process. I believe it is in Schumpeter that we can actually find what we can call a movement toward a "higher viewpoint" in terms of an adequate articulation of the anthropological principles underlying the free market process. As we've seen it is Bernard Lonergan who uses the concept of a succession of "higher viewpoints" in the progression of human knowledge. Describing the intellectual pattern of experience, he wrote, "One's understanding gradually works round and

---

80. Gadamer, *Truth and Method*, xxvi.

81. Ibid., 308.

82. Schumpeter, *Capitalism, Socialism and Democracy*, 132.

83. See Walsh, "Theory and Practice as Responsibility," 47–50.

up a spiral of viewpoints with each complementing its predecessor and only the last embracing the whole field to be mastered."[84]

He applies and expands this analysis, for instance, to the development of mathematical understanding. He shows how "mathematical activities and operations on a lower viewpoint can become the source of problems that cannot be answered internally" but must be answered on another, higher viewpoint.[85] A certain parallel can be traced in the Schumpeterian description of the entrepreneur at the level of economic action. To repeat the Schumpeterian dictum, once again, the entrepreneurial act "consists in getting things done."[86] This is the Lonerganian "lower viewpoint" which describes how entrepreneurial action in terms of innovation is integral to the working of the economy. But Schumpeter is not satisfied with a description of particular entrepreneurial acts because it fails to explain adequately the totality of the reality. In other words, in the human actor as "entrepreneur," the physical, chemical, organic, and psychic schemes, do not completely explicate the entrepreneurial action. The entrepreneur manifests within time and space human insights, judgments and decisions in the economic domain as do other human agents. We can describe these actions in terms of what is necessary for the workings of the economic process but to explain them more fully we must go beyond the specifically economic reality. And it is here, I argue, that we can apply the Lonerganian notion of the "higher viewpoint." The term "higher" is not used, of course, in any pejorative sense. It simply means that to explain a particular human action, for instance, our own theoretical horizons must expand in order to elaborate the truth of the reality of the human person. It is the task of an economic anthropology of human action as proposed in this book, to attempt such an articulation in terms of the "higher viewpoint" of the human person who acts as entrepreneur in the free economy.

Schumpeter's entrepreneur is not driven, he asserts, solely by the "profit motive" or by any other reason of a "hedonist kind." In normal circumstances "the *meaning* of economic action is the satisfaction of wants in the sense that there would be no economic action if there were no wants."[87] This is the understanding of the economy based upon the

84. See Lonergan, *Insight*, 210.

85. Mathews, *Lonergan's Quest*, 222–23.

86. Schumpeter, *Capitalism, Socialism and Democracy*, 132.

87. Schumpeter, *Theory of Economic Development*, 91.

notion of the reparation of the "good of desire," and I have already spoken about this in earlier chapters.[88] In the case of "the circular flow" model of the economy this is a perfectly normal and positive motivation for explaining economic action. By the expression "circular flow" Schumpeter proposes the ordinary concept of economic life as "running on in channels essentially the same year after year—similar to the circulation of the blood in an animal organism."[89] But economic life, as we all know, experiences alterations, which cannot be explained solely in terms of the circular framework. These changes "cannot be understood by means of any analysis of the circular flow, although they are purely economic and although their explanation is obviously among the tasks of pure theory."[90] The economist whose task it is to study economic reality must try to account for this and also ask, "how do such changes take place, and to what economic phenomena do they give rise?"[91]

The type of change in the economic process Schumpeter seeks to elucidate is not just *quantitative* in nature. It cannot be explained by exogenous causes alone; it is endogenous to the process itself. It is *qualitative* transformation occurring in the free market process which he tries to define. He gives the example of the construction of a railway. He explains, "add successively as many mail coaches as you please, you will never get a railway thereby."[92] There is a distinct human phenomenon which happens within the free economy when the entrepreneur acts and, indeed, displays a certain primacy in it. Thus, he argues that the intention of his analysis is to explicate the "kind of change arising from within the system *which so displaces its equilibrium point that the new one cannot be*

88. The distinction made here between the good that is the "object of desire" and the "good of order" was illustrated in an earlier chapter and shows what we are involved in when it comes to a philosophical differentiation with respect to the anthropological basis of a particular economic system. The economic aspect enters in, as I have already outlined, at the second level, that is, when I apply human insight to a given situation or circumstances subsequently resulting in deliberative human actions that end in the creation of an order leading to my good and the good of others; this can be on the personal, political, or economic level. It clearly matters what economic order one finds oneself in. One aspect of the "truth of markets" is that they are, in fact, on the level of a "good of order."

89. Schumpeter, *Theory of Economic Development*, 61.

90. Ibid.

91. Ibid., 62.

92. Ibid., 64 n. 1.

reached from the old one by infinitesimal steps.[93] He is talking here about the human culture of "enterprise," which is, he says, totally "foreign to what may be observed in the circular flow or in the tendency towards equilibrium."[94] Indeed, Schumpeter's theory of economic development attempts to investigate the occurrence of a *human creative enterprise culture* and the processes giving rise to this reality in the free market. So, the dynamic truth he analyzes is *business enterprise* and the human agent who is the author of the entrepreneurial act, namely, the "entrepreneur."

So, as I have outlined, a constitutive element of the entrepreneurial act is the human dimension of *"creative intelligence,"* which is deliberatively exercised by the entrepreneur. This is why we can see that the underlying basis for the free market economy is richly anthropological. There is a need for a philosophical reflection on this in order to recapture this fundamental anthropological reality, otherwise, it could be lost in a labyrinth of economic thought. Since Schumpeter is clearly singled out by different economists as an important contributor in the development and retrieval of the concept, we have devoted a good amount of discussion in consideration of his unique analysis of the entrepreneurial function.[95] But a considerable critique of Schumpeter's analysis of the entrepreneurial function can also be given. We cannot sufficiently deal with this here. His concept of the entrepreneur, for instance, could be considered as somewhat elitist, limited to the "vital few," and as not being necessarily integral to human nature.[96] However, Schumpeter does develop his idea of the entrepreneur and moves away elitist perspectives and adopts a more functional approach. Schumpeter's analysis is not based on

93. Ibid.

94. Ibid.

95. Some readers might think there is an overemphasis on Joseph Schumpeter in this book. This might be true, but it is merited in my view because it helps general readers and "non-economists" understand the importance of "entrepreneurial creativity" in the economic process that Schumpeter explored and unearthed. See Casson et al., *The Oxford Handbook of Entrepreneurship*. Casson writes, "Schumpeter (1939) provided one of the earliest economic applications of entrepreneurial theory" (8). Mark Blaug notes, "Schumpeter's influence on entrepreneurial theory has been overwhelming and subsequent writers on entrepreneurship have usually defined their own position by contrasting it with his" (*Economic Theory in Retrospect*, 446).

96. Casson et al. point out that Schumpeter's classification of entrepreneurship "fits well with the major forms of innovation that occurred during the 'Age of High Imperialism,' 1870–1914. The large-scale entrepreneurial exploits of the 'robber barons' of the late nineteenth century—Vanderbilt, Harriman, Rockefeller, and so on—conform well to Schumpeter's model" (*Oxford Handbook of Entrepreneurship*, 8).

any clearly outlined anthropology and it is the task of the philosopher to unearth the emerging person-centered perspective.

When he discusses the human motivation behind the entrepreneurial act, he explains, that it is not merely for hedonist reasons. Nonetheless, when it comes to any anthropological explanation this remains completely undeveloped. But if our understanding of economic action is limited merely to the "circular flow" analysis of the economy, then the entrepreneurial function does not necessarily arise.[97] The meaning of economic action in this context is the satisfaction of wants ("good of desire') and this is a normal motivation for economic action. However, we must remember this does not account for the totality of human economic action. This is because, as we've previously examined, the economy is fundamentally "dynamic" in its nature.[98] It is purposive human beings and not merely automatons who are the prime motivators acting in the free market process.[99] The driving analogy previously used is illustrative for understanding the purposive human actions involved in the free economy. An interesting economic textbook in this regard is *The Economic Way of Thinking*.[100] Its authors intentions are to assist students in achieving "more thinking, more application, more insight" when it comes to economic understanding.[101] The textbook's approach is in emphasizing "the dynamic entrepreneurial nature of the market process, themes developed by Ludwig von Mises, F. A. Hayek, Israel Kirzner, and Murray Rothbard."[102] The writers use the example of driving but place it in the context of rush-hour traffic. This might seem to be a strange example of

97. As already mentioned, with the concept of "circular flow" Schumpeter intends the ordinary concept of economic life as "running on in channels essentially the same year after year—similar to the circulation of the blood in an animal organism" (*Theory of Economic Development*, 61).

98. We've observed how Schumpeter stressed that perhaps more than anyone else Marx understood the dynamic nature of the market economy. He said Marx "concentrated his analytic powers on the task of showing how the economic process, changing itself by virtue of its own inherent logic, incessantly changes the social framework— the whole of society in fact" (*History of Economic Analysis*, 573).

99. Mises in his expansive study on human action (praxeology) declares human action "is not simply giving preference . . . But acting man chooses, determines, and tries to reach an end. Of two things both of which he cannot have together he selects one and gives up the other. Action therefore always involves both taking and renunciation" (*Human Action*, 12).

100. Heyne, *The Economic Way of Thinking*.

101. Ibid., xiv.

102. Ibid.

"purposive human action," as it could be seen instead as an example of utter chaos. But the main characteristic of the driving in rush-hour analogy "is not jam but movement, which is why people venture into it day after day and almost always reach their destinations."[103] The example is also illustrative of the *human capacities* that entrepreneurial action really involves. The point is that thousands of people leave their homes each day and head for work in rush-hour traffic. They all choose their own routes without prior consultation with anyone else. They all "have diverse skills, differing attitudes toward risk . . . The drivers all pursue their separate objectives, with an almost single-minded devotion to their own interests, not necessarily because they are selfish but simply because none of them know anything of the objectives of the others . . . There are general rules, of course, that everyone is expected to obey, such as stopping for red lights, and staying close to the speed limit . . . The entire arrangement as just described could be a prescription for chaos . . . Instead, we witness a smoothly coordinated flow."[104]

The Schumpeterian entrepreneur breaks the crust of convention and somewhat like a purposive driver in the rush hour of economic reality drives with single-minded devotion the means of production into new channels. In doing this he acts purposively in order to discover "better ways of doing things." In other words, there is no such thing as automatic economic progress or, indeed, its inverse, namely, decline. Economic development or change is the result of *human creative intelligence*. In the Schumpeterian economic world nothing is inevitable. The human person acting as "entrepreneur" is not merely "froth" and "bubble" in the stream of history but their action "consists precisely in breaking up old, and creating new, tradition."[105] This applies primarily to entrepreneurial action, but according to Schumpeter, it has also moral, cultural, and social consequences.

VI. Motivational Considerations of the Economic Act

Schumpeter sets out various reasons why the entrepreneur acts like this but the hedonist justification as we have seen is insufficient. He explains that even if we did attribute hedonistic motivations to entrepreneurs,

103. Ibid., 3
104. Ibid., 4.
105. Schumpeter, *Theory of Economic Development*, 92.

Gossen's law would ultimately come into effect.[106] Experience shows "that typical entrepreneurs retire from the arena only when and because their strength is spent and they feel no longer equal to their task."[107] Any purely selfish or pleasure seeking motivation could not adequately explain the human motivation for entrepreneurial action. A solely selfish self-seeking principle in terms of human action presupposes "consumption," which requires the leisure to do so. The entrepreneur, on the other hand, actually does the opposite and interrupts the normal "circular flow" model, which to the hedonist "would be irrational," as satiation is the prime motivation.[108] In an Aristotelian fashion Schumpeter lists other justifications in terms of an overall explanation of the human motivations for the entrepreneurial act, but none is, he concludes, altogether satisfactory. Aristotle, for instance, deals with the concept and reasons for friendship to some extent in a similar way. In his study in book VIII of the *Nicomachean Ethics* we find an analysis of the different kinds of friendship. His analysis aims to determine what constitutes "perfect" friendship. He analyzes three types, that is, those based on "utility," "pleasure," and "goodness." Friendships based upon "utility" or "pleasure" are friendships but "they love the other person not for what he is, but *qua* useful or pleasant." Aristotle regards these types of friendships as "accidental" because "the person loved is not loved on the ground of his actual nature, but merely as providing some benefit or pleasure." Friendship based upon "utility" or "pleasure" is less enduring, while perfect friendship is more enduring since it is based on "goodness." He observes, "It is those who desire the good of their friends for the friends' sake that are most truly friends, because each loves the other for what he is, and not for any incidental quality."[109] So, in an Aristotelian type mode, Schumpeter lists various

---

106. Hermann Heinrich Gossen (1810–58) formulated two laws that form the basis of the neoclassical theory of consumer behavior. Schumpeter refers to the first law and applies it to a hedonist interpretation of the entrepreneur. "The *first law* establishes the principle of decreasing marginal utility: the pleasure obtained from a good decreases as the amount consumed increases until, eventually, satiety is reached." See Screpanti and Zamagni, *Outline of the History of Economic Thought*, 90. It is true that certain economic theories are compatible with a purely self-interested motivation for entrepreneurial discovery. But the lack of sufficiency I refer to cannot be explained solely in terms of the insights of the Austrian school. So, as I have said, we need a "higher viewpoint" in order to explain the human action involved.

107. Schumpeter, *Theory of Economic Development*, 92.

108. Ibid.

109. See Aristotle, *Nicomachean Ethics* 1156b2–23.

possible reasons for human entrepreneurial action. There is, he argues, always the human desire to establish a private kingdom and perhaps a dynasty. Industrial or commercial success can seek to mirror a type of "medieval lordship."[110] There are, he observes, an endless variety of such motives "from spiritual ambition down to mere snobbery."[111] There is also "the will to conquer."[112] In this context the economic result takes second place or else it is simply used "as an index of success and as a symptom of victory."[113] These are, it is true, very different from any hedonistic motivations but they still do not adequately explain the reason for the *human action* of the entrepreneur.

Finally, Schumpeter remarks that there is an altogether different justification and that is "the joy of creating, of getting things done, or simply of exercising one's energy and ingenuity."[114] This is where, I argue, we encounter the hidden anthropological roots and reach the kernel meaning of human action in the economic drama of humanity that underlies economic thought but is too often insufficiently expostulated. In the next chapter, we'll explore how the development of the philosophical theme of the purpose of "human creativity" in the free market economy moves us toward a "higher viewpoint" anthropologically. Any analysis of entrepreneurial action which occludes the *human creative dimension* runs the risk of staying at the level of the "husk" of the action without entering into the real marrow of an adequate anthropological explanation of entrepreneurship.

Following his motivational considerations of the entrepreneurial act, Schumpeter points out that the entrepreneurial agent is, in fact, the "most distinctly anti-hedonist" type.[115] The entrepreneur, in fact, "seeks out difficulties, changes in order to change, delights in ventures."[116] There is, of course, the *profit motive* behind all entrepreneurial action. Schumpeter comments that "pecuniary gain is indeed a very accurate expression of success, especially of *relative* success, and from the standpoint of the man who strives for it has the additional advantage of being an objective

110. Schumpeter, *Theory of Economic Development*, 93.
111. Ibid.
112. Ibid.
113. Ibid.
114. Ibid.
115. Ibid., 94.
116. Ibid.

fact and largely independent of the opinion of others."[117] Entrepreneurial profit is naturally within the Schumpeterian framework a fundamental motivator and a tangible sign of a successful human enterprise.[118] But he explained that high profits were usually temporary because participants in a similar business would soon become "imitators" of the innovation.[119] Schumpeter expressed the matter regarding role of the profit motive and profits as follows, stating that "it is the expression of the value of what the entrepreneur contributes to production in exactly the same sense that wages are the value expression of what the worker 'produces.' It is not a profit of exploitation any more than are wages . . . [Profit] is at the same time the child and the victim of development . . . Without development there is no profit, without profit no development . . . Without profit there would be no accumulation of wealth."[120]

VII. Plato's *Republic* and the Need for "Anthropological Balance"

We are essentially concerned here in maintaining a non-reductive perspective on the actions of human persons in the free market process. So, in economics there is the constant challenge to retain what we can term an "anthropological balance" or the median in its treatment of the human subject. Indeed, even within philosophical reflections this task is not new because in Plato's *Republic* there is a similar emphasis on the need for equilibrium within the individual if they want, for example, to be "just." Socrates, for instance, outlines his tripartite theory of the human soul and distinguishes between: the logical (λόγος), the spirited (θυμός) and the appetitive (ἐπιθυμητής). He describes how the just man must "quite literally . . . put his own house in order, being himself his own ruler . . . and tuning the three elements just like three fixed points in a musical scale . . . he must combine them all, and emerge as a perfect unity of diverse elements, self-disciplined and in harmony with himself. Only then

117. Ibid.

118. Schumpeter outlines his theory of profit in *The Theory of Economic Development* where he devotes a whole chapter to the topic. He explains that "entrepreneurial profit is a surplus over costs. From the standpoint of the entrepreneur, it is the difference between receipts and outlay in a business" (128).

119. Schumpeter, "Capitalism," in *Encyclopedia Britannica*; reprinted in *Essays on Entrepreneurs*, 189–210.

120. Schumpeter, *Theory of Economic Development*, 153–54.

does he act, whether it is a question of making money, or taking care of his body, or some political action, or contractual agreements with private individuals."[121]

A sense of "anthropological balance" is important because if we build an analysis of the free economy on the basis of the construction and simple acceptance of a limited concept of the human person as economic agent, we run the risk of mistaking the actual truncation for reality in itself. In the *Republic* the truculent sophist Thrasymachus in his dialogue with Socrates holds the view that the social order we inhabit is solely materialistically determined and we can see an equivalence here in terms of some popular views on the economic order we live in.[122] But there is the clear danger that in the words of philosopher Eric Voegelin we get ourselves involved in an "eclipse of reality." In this situation memories become dimmed as to the reality "of a fuller humanity" and in our investigation this could result in a failure to adequately outline the person-centered dimensions of the free economy. Philosophers have reflected for centuries on the motivation for human actions in all areas of life. In fact, the discoveries made by the Austrian school of economics come from insights derived from the philosophical approach which puts the emphasis on the human person as the motivating force in valuation and these were subsequently applied to economic action.[123] But these considerations arise even earlier in philosophical writings. The Sophist Thrasymachus in Plato's *Republic* argued that the social order we are in is determined solely materialistically and this same understanding could be applied to the entrepreneur and his actions. But in the *Republic* Socrates counters the materialistic thesis with an analysis of different *arts* or *skills* when he says that they aim "at what is good for . . . [their] object, not its practitioners."[124] In the dialogue, which we cannot sufficiently enlarge upon here, Socrates gives some insights, which I feel can be usefully applied to our current discussion on the motivation of the entrepreneur. Socrates introduces into the whole discussion a reflection on the roles of the doctor or ship's captain. He explains, "because the body is defective,

121. Plato, *Republic* 443 d-e.

122. Thrasymachus holds that "justice is simply what is good for the stronger" (ibid., 338c).

123. Barry Smith outlines the singular contribution of the German philosopher Franz Brentano in his reintroduction of the concept of intentionality derived from the Scholastic philosophers. See Smith, *Austrian Philosophy: The Legacy of Franz Brentano*.

124. Plato, *Republic* 341c.

and not self-sufficient, the art of medicine has come to be invented."[125] He further clarifies that "the art of medicine does not think about what is good for the art of medicine, but what is good for the body."[126] He argues, "Isn't it a fact that no doctor, to the extent that he is a doctor, thinks about or prescribes what is good for the doctor? No, he thinks about what is good for the patient."[127] Thus, pecuniary enrichment is not the primary motivating factor in different skills because, first medicine produces health, and then earning a living produces payment. First the art of building produces a house, and then earning a living comes along afterwards and provides payment. And it is the same with the other arts or skills. Each performs its own function, and benefits the object, of which it is the art or skill.[128] Socrates slowly brings his interlocutors including Thrasymachus to the central insight that can be correspondingly applied to the entrepreneurial function, which is that, "no art or skill and no power or authority, provides what is beneficial for itself. They provide and prescribe, as we said originally, for what is under their authority. They think about what is good for *it*, the weaker and not what is good for the stronger."[129]

This naturally ends up turning totally on its head what Thrasymachus said about the whole material motivation for social order. Socrates concludes Book I of the *Republic* with an anthropological insight, which we can apply to our understanding of *entrepreneurial action*. He gives examples of the functions of seeing and hearing and asks, "do the eyes . . . also have an excellence?" Eyes are for seeing, and therefore, even Thrasymachus agrees, "they have an excellence as well." Then Socrates applies this to the human person, when he asks, if the soul has a function "which nothing else in the world could perform? Think about management or ruling, or decision-making . . . Would we be justified in attributing those functions to anything other than the soul? Could we say they belonged to anything else?"[130] In the end, Thrasymachus agrees with Socrates' anthropological insight "that there is an excellence of the soul" which pertains to it *qua person*. Applying these Socratic insights in order to recapture an

125. Ibid., 341e.
126. Ibid., 342c.
127. Ibid., 324d.
128. Ibid., 346d.
129. Ibid., 346e.
130. Ibid., 353b, 353d-e.

adequate understanding of the motivation of the entrepreneur, we can paraphrase Socrates by saying, "the art of the entrepreneur does not think about what is good for the art of *entrepreneuring*, but what is good for the *body-economic*," that is, the common good of persons who are all participants in the economic drama.[131] Indeed, the American entrepreneur Bill Gates once said something similar when he explained in an interview that "the origins of Microsoft [have] *little to do with money*."[132] The money was, he says, just an accidental by-product; the purposive force was the human creativity involved in the project.

The Austrian-born American management consultant Peter Drucker gives what I consider a useful synopsis of Schumpeter's overall contribution about the meaning and *human creativity* involved in entrepreneurial action. I think it is worth quoting in full. He wrote that

> classical economics considered innovation to be outside the system, as Keynes did, too. Innovation belonged in the category of "outside catastrophes" like earthquakes, climate, or war, which, everybody knew, have profound influence on the economy but are not part of economics. Schumpeter insisted that, on the contrary, *innovation*—that is, entrepreneurship that moves resources from old and obsolescent to new and more productive employments—is the very essence of economics and most certainly of a modern economy.
>
> He derived this notion, as he was the first to admit, from Marx. But he used it to disprove Marx. Schumpeter's *Economic Development* does what neither the classical economists nor Marx nor Keynes was able to do: It makes profit fulfil an economic function. In the economy of change and innovation, profit, in contrast to Marx and his theory, is not a *Mehrwert*, a "surplus value" stolen from the workers. On the contrary, it is the only source of jobs for workers and of labour income. The theory of economic development shows that no one except the innovator makes a genuine "profit"; and the innovator's profit is always quite short-lived. But innovation in Schumpeter's famous phrase is also "creative destruction." It makes obsolete yesterday's capital equipment and capital investment. The

---

131. This approach is obviously controversial, and many would see it as totally contrary to the insights of the Austrian school, but *Wealth of Persons* also seeks to go beyond the limits of any particular school in terms of the reality of the human person.

132. See Gideon Rachman, "Lunch with the *FT*: Bill Gates," *Financial Times*, 30–31 October 2010, http://www.ft.com/intl/cms/s/2/67672314-e2e0-11df-9735 -00144feabdco.html.

more an economy progresses, the more capital formation will it therefore need. Thus what the classical economists—or the accountant or the stock exchange—considers "profit" is a genuine cost, the cost of staying in business, the cost of a future in which nothing is predictable except that today's profitable business will become tomorrow's white elephant. Thus, capital formation and productivity are needed to maintain the wealth-producing capacity of the economy and, above all, to maintain today's jobs and to create tomorrow's jobs.[133]

VIII. Conclusion

In the preface to his book devoted to the topic of innovation and entrepreneurship, Drucker actually noted the anthropological nature of the entrepreneurial act when he observed that "innovation is a discipline, with its own, fairly simple, rules. And so is entrepreneurship. Neither of them requires geniuses. Neither of them will be done if we wait for inspiration and for the 'kiss of the muse.' *Both are work.* And only those businesses . . . who accept this are likely to survive, let alone do well, in the turbulent decade ahead."[134] A fundamental and constitutive element in economic development or change is the contribution of *human creative intelligence.* Economies basically develop or not because human beings discover "better ways of doing things."[135] In the Schumpeterian economic world and indeed in our own contemporary human drama nothing is inevitable. The human person acting as "entrepreneur" is not as I have said merely "froth" and "bubble" in the stream of history but is a freely acting person motivated toward specific ends.

Apart from functioning according to clear economic principles of how the free market actually works, the economy also operates upon the basis of fundamental anthropological principles. These principles are equally applicable "to a society of perfect altruists or completely selfish egoists."[136] The free economy can be understood essentially as being a

133. Peter F. Drucker, "Modern Prophets: Schumpeter or Keynes?," http://druckersociety.at/index.php/peterdruckerhome/texts/modern-prophets-schumpeter-or-keynes.

134. Drucker, *Innovation and Entrepreneurship,* xvi.

135. There is an extensive literature on Schumpeter and entrepreneurial innovation. The significance of the wide expanse of studies is the recognition of the central importance of *entrepreneurial action* in economic thinking. I refer the reader to a general bibliography contained in McCraw's *Prophet of Innovation,* 689 n. 10.

136. Meadowcroft, *Ethics of the Market,* 13.

catalyst or a process that allows the coordination of disparate economic actors to achieve their ends. The free market is therefore basically compatible with the principle of human creativity that lies at the heart of a free society. The entrepreneur in his or her actions can be seen as an exemplar of the human person acting toward a specific end, which is not merely economic, but fundamentally personalistic. The entrepreneurial action in the free economy moreover allows for and produces the opportunity for the realization of the *creative human subject* in the economic dimension of life. So, entrepreneurial action is not an end in itself; rather, it creates a space in which the human person can realize their personal dignity in creative action.

An important point in terms of our focus on the person-centered principles which often lie hidden beneath the free economy is to stress the fact that the "entrepreneur" and the human action involved is not limited to the business world but could as Schumpeter outlined be present "even in a primitive tribe."[137] So, it would be entirely misleading to reduce Schumpeter's analysis to a simple history of entrepreneurship. His study suggests that entrepreneurial creativity, in point of fact, predates the historical emergence of the free market economy. Actually, the Voegelinian distinction between "compact" and "differentiated" in human experience can be further applied to this Schumpeterian insight that "human creativity" predates the existence of the free economy. The activity of "differentiation" occurs within various time periods and in different disciplines. What I mean is that just because a truth, that is, the *self-determining* and *creative dimension* of the human person, remains "undifferentiated" during a specific period does not necessarily mean it is not present in a particular culture. Thus, when Schumpeter traces the existence of human initiative and creativity to a period prior to the historical emergence of capitalism this is because the anthropological dimension of human creativity pertains to the reality and constitution of what it means to be a human person. So, his point is essentially anthropological and not purely historical or economic. This is why the economist professor Yuichi Shionoya observes that human creativity is a unique phenomenon which by its very nature causes "discontinuity from preceding situations."[138] It is he says, "an enigma of human beings."[139] In the next chapter, we'll give

137. Schumpeter, *Business Cycles*, 1:223. See also Dahms, "The Entrepreneur in Western Capitalism."

138. Shionoya, *Schumpeter and the Idea of Social Science*, 175.

139. Ibid.

an overview of how some economists expanded Schumpeter's theme on the role of entrepreneurial action in the free market process. In this way we can hopefully unfold the anthropological enigma of the wealth of the human person who lies at the heart of the free economy.

6

Entrepreneurial Perspectives III: A Movement toward a Higher Anthropological Viewpoint

I. The Great Recession in Light of Praxeological and Anthropological Considerations

IN THIS CHAPTER WE'LL examine the broader development of the entrepreneurial concept in economic writers specifically in regard to an elaborated anthropology. In the study of social science there are at least three types of investigation. They are *praxeology* (the study of human action), *axiology* (the study of value), and *anthropology* (the study of human nature).[1] Our focus in this book is on the praxeological and anthropological.[2] The considerations in the previous chapter on the human motivations for entrepreneurial action by Schumpeter give rise to understanding the human person as an "axiological origin" and motivator in the free economy. It is part of what Yuichi Shionoya observed, that human creativity is a unique phenomenon even at the level of axiology

---

1. Mises spelled the name of the study as "praxeology"; many others spell it as "praxiology."

2. See Beaubout et al., *Beyond Self-Interest*, 2. In terms of the link between praxeology and economics I refer the reader to works such as Auspitz et al., *Praxiologies and the Philosophy of Economics*; Gasparski and Ryan, *Human Action in Business*; Zsolnai and Gasparski, *Ethics and the Future of Capitalism*; and Gasparski and Airaksinen, *Praxiology and the Philosophy of Technology*.

and as such it constitutes the "enigma of human beings."[3]

As we've seen, an important task in analyzing the free economy is to draw from it the philosophy of the human person upon which it is actually based. Each school of economic thought presupposes its own model or what Schumpeter calls "vision" of the human person. It then applies this theory to its various investigations. Our focus is on the human person as the "actor" in the economic drama. Nonetheless, there is no doubt that during times of economic and apparent financial Armageddon the human subject and agency ends up alienated, tossed around like flotsam and dashed up on the shores of apparent economic annihilation.[4] Indeed,

3. See Shionoya, *Schumpeter and the Idea of Social Science*, 175. In regard to the concept of praexology, Gasparski gives a very useful summary of its origins. He writes that it was initially "the *science of functions* situated in Louis Bourdeau's system of sciences, next it was the most general *science of techniques* characteristic of human action approached by Alfred Victor Espinas, then it was considered by Tadeusz Kotarbinski as a *general methodology*, and by Ludwig von Mises as a theoretical *foundation of economics*, finally Mario Bunge situated it within the family of philosophical disciplines dealing with ethics *sensu largo* or practical philosophy as *human action theory*, while Jan Zieleniewski situated it among *ergological sciences*, i.e. studies on human labor . . . One may conclude that praxiology, located between logic and ethics, offers epistemological foundations for the concept of *reflective practitioner*, pointing out the *axiological context* of human action." See Gasparski and Airaksinen, *Praxiology and the Philosophy of Technology*, 7.

4. A whole series of articles, for example, were written in the *Financial Times* on the credit crunch during August 2007. Gillian Tett and Anuj Gangahar wrote that Goldman Sachs was "forced into an embarrassing admission . . . In a rare unplanned investor call, the bank revealed that a flagship global equity fund had lost over 30% of its value in a week because of problems with its trading strategies, created by computer models. In particular, the computers had failed to foresee recent market movements to such a degree that they labelled them a '25-standard deviation event'—something that only happens once every 100,000 years or more . . . The question now being asked by some bankers—and regulators—is whether this week's events show that the modern financial industry is foolish to be placing so much faith in these complex computer driven models . . . The roots of this revolution go back to the 1970s, when computers became small and flexible enough to be easily used by bankers—and bright minds from the world of economics started to move into finance . . . Soon they started using computers not just to spot anomalies but to execute trades too. Computers are thus now using models to make trades—and often trading with other computers—with barely any human intervention . . . But while computers are often able to operate better than humans in 'normal' markets, this month's events demonstrate that during times of stress they have some crucial flaws . . . The essential danger . . . is a tendency to view models as 'cameras,' snapping pictures of market movements . . . The lesson that some bankers and policymakers may yet draw from this month's events is arguably the simplest: namely, that it could be time to reinsert humans into the trading process. One way to do this would be to improve risk management functions; another key

because we are dealing with human experience the devastation is often experienced not just on the economic horizon but also on the different levels of our being in the political, social and personal arenas.

I have presented how Voegelin characterized human existence in terms of *"participation"* within a "quaternarian structure" of being involving a multidimensional understanding of reality.[5] He explains how "God, and man, world and society form a primordial community of being."[6] He emphasizes how "participation in being . . . is not a partial involvement of man; he is engaged with the whole of his existence, for participation is existence itself."[7] Voegelin's concept of "participation" can, I argue, be applied in the attempt to comprehend the essential anthropological dimensions of the free economy. I have suggested how it is somewhat analogous to Lonergan's call for a "democratic economics."[8] Philip McShane reiterated this in respect of the need to understand and clearly explicate the economic and anthropological principles at the foundation of human economic action, since democracy by its very definition suggests participation by everyone in the political process.[9] Applied to economics this implies what Ludwig von Mises called an "activistic basis" for an adequate understanding of economics.[10] He wrote "the characteristic of man is action . . . action—is purposive conduct. It is not simply behavior, but behavior begot by judgments of value, aiming at a definite end and guided by ideas concerning the suitability or unsuitability of definite means. It is impossible to deal with it without the categories of causality and finality. It is conscious behavior. It is choosing. It is volition; it is a display of the will."[11]

---

step is to ensure that banks have the ability to switch off the models during times of stress. Anyone with a human brain, rather than algorithms, could have made money in recent days in the equity markets . . . One unexpected winner from this month's market turmoil . . . may be a newfound appreciation of human intuition—and old-fashioned common sense." See Tett and Gangahar, "System Error: Why Computer Models Proved Unequal to Market Turmoil," *Financial Times*, 15 August 2007.

5. Voegelin, *Israel and Revelation*, 1.

6. Ibid.

7. Ibid.

8. Lonergan, *For a New Political Economy*, 5.

9. See McShane, *Economics for Everyone*, 9.

10. Mises, *Ultimate Foundation of Economic Science*, 30.

11. Ibid.

Mises's reference here—to the fact that the ultimate foundation of economic science is based on conscious deliberative "human action"—is of considerable relevance to the modern challenges the free economy finds itself in. In the popular literature on the past financial crisis, for example, human greed and the economic system are often diagnosed as the principal reasons for the economic crash that is likened to the Wall Street crash of 1929. The suggested treatment for the sick economic patient is said to be increased financial regulation.[12] But the economist David Pitt-Watson, in a perceptive article titled "Lessons of the Credit Crisis Are Not Just for Regulators," remarked how

> the failures that caused the great credit crisis are the same ones which brought down Enron, Worldcom and Parmalat: lack of accountability, lack of responsibility and lack of transparency.
>
> Capital markets can serve us well. But if they lack accountability and responsibility, that is a toxic mixture. The security of our investments depends on these basic tenets. . . .
>
> In the past, when a bank made a loan, it was held on its balance sheet. It owned the loan and was therefore concerned that its customers were credit worthy. However, the bank could make more loans if they were held in a special purpose vehicle off its balance sheet. To take advantage of this, many loans were made to individuals, banks and others, then packaged up and sold on the "the market."
>
> This process of disintermediation meant that banks had less need to check credit worthiness. Instead, they had incentives simply to write more loans, take a fee and sell on the loan. To be assured that these loans were credit worthy, the market passed on this accountability and responsibility to credit rating agencies. . . .
>
> . . . Traders bet against each other and seek out performance, with little concern for the performance of the market overall. Outperformance is a zero sum game. . . .
>
> *Regulation alone is not the answer.* America has lots of regulation, yet it is there that so many financial scandals have arisen.

12. Richard Taffler and David Tuckett, in "How a State of Mind Abets Market Instability," wrote, "The solution to financial crises will not easily be found in increased regulation, more transparent information or cuts in interest rates. Rather, it lies in understanding how a market in which a paranoid-schizoid state of mind is encouraged is inherently unstable . . . Understanding the part emotions play in all investment activity should concern central banks, market regulators—and us all." *Financial Times,* 21 September 2007.

Further, regulation has the danger of adding costs and of simply shutting the stable door after the horses are long gone.

We need to constantly return to the principles on which successful capital markets are based. It is on those principles that all our investments depend. *It is only the participants, not the regulators, who can ensure the accountability, responsibility and transparency investors need.* When the post-mortem is conducted on the credit crisis, it will find the cause to be one which was identified thousands of years ago. As Aristotle said: "That which is common to the greatest number has least care bestowed upon it."[13]

So, the claim that "Gekkoism" can somehow just be legally expelled from the economic and financial system by regulation is a failure to perceive the full anthropological reality the market economy is ultimately based on.[14] Voegelin borrowed the symbol of *Apperzeptionsverweigerung* from Heimito von Doderer to describe the refusal to apperceive reality. He wrote, "The refusal to apperceive has become for me the central concept for the understanding of ideological aberrations and deformations. It appears in a variety of phenomena, of which the historically most interesting is the formal interdict on questioning demanded by Comte and Marx."[15] There is a similar failure amongst some economic writers and commentators to properly understand and articulate the multidimensional reality of the *acting human person* in the economy. Indeed, *accountability, responsibility* and *transparency* as outlined by Pitt-Watson are all characteristics of purposive human action. Their antonyms are equally the result of deliberative human actions. A philosophical reflection like ours can assist in lifting "the hood of the financial system" and help gain insight into the essential nature of the human person who acts as part of the economic *dramatis personae.*[16]

13. *Financial Times,* 5 December 2007. The reference to Aristotle is taken from *Politics* 121b32. My emphases.

14. This neologism is based on the film character Gordon Gekko, the main antagonist in the 1987 film *Wall Street* and antihero in the 2010 film *Wall Street: Money Never Sleeps* (both directed by Oliver Stone, with Michael Douglas portraying Gekko). It is claimed that the original movie is based on Ivan Boesky, an arbitrageur, who once gave a speech on greed at the University of California, Berkeley, and on Carl Icahn, an investor/corporate raider. Boesky was eventually charged for racketeering and fraud in 1989.

15. Voegelin, *Autobiographical Reflections,* 98.

16. See Tim Harford, "Post-crisis Confessions of an Armchair Economist," *Financial Times,* 4 August 2010.

There is always, of course, the possibility of derailment, exclusion and non-participation of the human person in the free market process and this can result in disorder on the individual, social, political and economic levels in which the human person acts. The solution to this problematic is not to retreat from the deeper philosophical questions and just consider the economic system as some type of robotic Cartesian machine but to attempt to recapture its anthropological roots. Indeed, the post-Enron context has seen increased critical development in research into the reasons for economic derailment. Paul Dembinski and Jean-Michel Bonvin, in an insightful essay titled "Enron: Visiting the Immersed Part of the Iceberg," comment that after thousands of pages of official reports and studies on Enron "its collapse can be attributed to a coincidence of a number of dysfunctions and malfunctions within the firm. Each of these 'local problems' has been scrutinized, analyzed, and in some most visible cases, addressed at a regulatory level. Despite all these efforts, however, a more fundamental question remains on the internal composition of the multi-causal knot that led to Enron's collapse."[17]

The authors in this study point to deeper human-based explanations for the Enron disaster. The how and the why of the debacle cannot be explained solely in terms of "technical causality," since it goes much deeper than that.[18] Dembinski and Bonvin argue that use of Aristotle's "'multi-causal' methodology"[19] is appropriate in order to dig down and account for the anthropological "strata of reality" that are the basis for human action in the matter.[20] They explain that the Aristotelian method identifies "four causes or fashions: the efficient cause, the material cause, the formal cause and the final cause. [The Aristotelian methodology] . . . aims at showing how and why (the objectives pursued or the final cause) an acting subject (an efficient cause that can be individual or collective) gives a specific shape or form (the formal cause) to an amorphous and raw material (the material cause)."[21]

Clearly, economic commentators will focus on different causes for the collapse. Those who apportion blame to the raw material of finance

17. See Dembinski et al., *Enron and World Finance*, 237. It might seem that Enron happened in the distant fog of the past but its lessons are still relevant today. We could equally apply this analysis to contemporary examples.

18. Ibid., 238.

19. Ibid.

20. Ibid.

21. Ibid.

(material cause), for example, will look on Enron as a symptom of the economic process and not simply an accident. They will see it as evidence of the malaise that lies at the heart of the free market process. Those who focus on the *telos*, the final cause, will attribute culpability to the directors of Enron and the auditors. The Aristotelian analysis can help "in grasping the complexity of a situation where differing rationalities interact and intertwine."[22] We are not directly concerned with the Enron affair in this investigation and it is long past, but the whole scandal is a counterbalance to holding a completely illusionary view about the virtues of the unencumbered operation of the free economy.[23]

When Pitt-Watson in terms of the international economic collapse suggested both that regulation is not enough and the need to return to first principles, he is pointing to the dangers of a purely procedural approach to the situation. In other words, he indicated the view that the emphasis on procedures can result in the formal cause (or process) obfuscating the final cause (substantial values). Central to an adequate understanding of economic reality is the role of human agency, the acting subject as the efficient cause in the free economy. The focus on entrepreneurial action in this *Wealth of Persons* is clearly directing our attention toward one dimension of human agency in the free market economy. Nonetheless, it is a dimension that often lies hidden in analyses of human economic action. Some of the obvious consequences of just blaming the "system" (we often hear the phrase "systemic failure") for the Great Recession are that the praxeological (*human action*) and anthropological (*human nature*) dimensions of economic action become totally occluded in such an analysis.

II. Narratives of Anthropological Economic Disintegration

It is important to elaborate a "person-centered" perspective if we want to understand the dynamics of the free economy. We've used Voegelin's concept of "participation" in order to elucidate a philosophical understanding of human action in the economic arena. But the inevitable fallout effect of the economic collapse in the Great Recession means

22. Ibid., 239.

23. I refer the reader to an excellent study on Enron by Malcolm S. Salter, *Innovation Corrupted: The Origins and Legacy of Enron's Collapse.*

that many protagonists in the free economy end up as "outsiders" in the process. Albert Camus in his novel *The Outsider* described the existential non-participation of the chief character, Meursault, as events unfolded for him in the following way: "Things were happening without me even intervening. My fate was being decided without anyone asking my opinion."[24] Equally, the employees, shareholders, and pension fund victims of Lehman Brothers could likewise justifiably claim to be human subjects who ended up atrophied by the market process.[25]

The *Financial Times* writers and other commentators devoted considerable space and time to the whole issue of why that particular collapse happened. Repeatedly the human dimension is emphasized in their causal analyses. Frank Partnoy, for instance, in "Hubris—Is Thy Name Richard Fuld?," wrote,

> Is it just coincidence that both Lehman Brothers and Bear Stearns were led by entrenched men who lost touch with their employees, businesses and mission? Did hubris cause the collapse of these two venerable banks? As 158-year old Lehman disintegrates and potential buyers sniff the carcass, it is worth asking whether blame for the fall of both Lehman and Bear might be attributable not only to a failure of risk management, but to a failure of character . . . Hubris was considered a crime in classical Athens, because it could bring down an institution. Even Mr Fuld viewed narcissism as dangerous, or so he said. In July 2005, he told *Euromoney* magazine his biggest concern was arrogance: "I worry that we could get arrogant. If you get arrogant, you lose your way, and start making mistakes."[26]

Andrew Ross Sorkin, for example, commented on Lehman saying that "in the end, this drama is a human one, a tale about the fallibility of people who thought they themselves were too big to fail."[27] Malcolm Salter in his investigation into the Enron collapse singles out "fatal thoughtlessness," "pride and hubris" as the major contributory factors rather than just fraud. He explains, "At its core, this story is about thoughtless and

24. Camus, *Outsider*, 95.

25. Before declaring bankruptcy in 2008 Lehman was the fourth biggest investment bank in the United Sates. Its bankruptcy filing was the largest in US history and its collapse is said to have played a major part in the unfolding of the late-2000s global financial crisis.

26. *Financial Times*, 15 September 2008.

27. Sorkin, *Too Big to Fail*, 7.

incompetent leadership, the ethical drift that inevitably followed, and a breakdown in oversight and control by the company's board of directors and external watchdogs."[28] The jury's judgment in the case actually sent out two important messages. The central points were that "the jury's verdict reflected the legal principle that in matters of alleged fraud, intent to deceive trumps compliance with arcane legal rules. The verdict was consistent with the long-established ethical principle that the moral status of an act should be judged not only by its consequences, but also by the intentions of the actor."[29]

What all these financial stories of derailment illustrate is the fact that they are also in essence narratives about how *we act* as human persons. The reality is that we often inhabit grey areas in terms of human action and this is true equally in economic action. Salter refers to Owen D. Young, the former chairman of General Electric, as speaking of "the '*shadowed space*' or '*penumbra*' between the clear light of right doing [*sic*] and the clear light of wrongdoing, where the law is unclear and spirit of the law is open to interpretation."[30] It was actually within this penumbra that Jeffrey Skilling, Kenneth Lay, and many others in Enron and in other cases lost their way. A purely procedural approach therefore fails ultimately to adequately deal with the fact that We are dealing in a praxeological sense with what Mises called "volitional beings" when we come to consider human persons acting in the economic sphere. As Mises observed "Man is not, like the animals, an obsequious puppet of instincts and sensual impulses. Man has the power to suppress instinctive desires, he has a will of his own, he chooses between incompatible ends. In this sense he is a moral person; in this sense he is free."[31]

III. Self-Determination: The Reality of "Bias" in Human Action

A study of human action in the different horizons of existence reveals "self-determination" as a vital aspect of the human person. Mises explains, for example, how the historian approaches this aspect of praxelology. He notes that

28. Salter, *Innovation Corrupted*, 2, 15.
29. Ibid., 4.
30. Ibid., 5–6, my emphases.
31. Mises, *Ultimate Foundation of Economic Science*, 51.

the historian refers to the spiritual milieu and the past experience of the actor, to his knowledge or ignorance of all the data that could influence his decision, to his state of health, and to many other factors that could have played a role. But then, even after full attention has been paid to all these matters, something remains that defies any attempts at further interpretation, viz., the personality or individuality of the actor. When all is said about the case, there is finally no answer to the question why Caesar crossed the Rubicon than: because he was Caesar. We cannot eliminate in dealing with human action reference to the actor's personality.[32]

An investigation into entrepreneurial action reveals the "*self-determining*" characteristic of the human person in economic action. The Scottish philosopher John Macmurray saw that "action, then, is a full concrete activity of the self in which all our capacities are employed."[33] Even when human action results in disintegration in the economic sense as in the case of a global financial crisis, this still can be analyzed in terms of human causality. Previously we have given consideration to the Schumpeterian creative and destructive nature of the free market process. Disintegration is essentially a part of the anthropological dimension of the human person acting in the economic horizon. To ignore or to jettison this from our understanding of the process occludes the multidimensional reality we are dealing with.

Indeed, Lonergan took up this concept of the rhythm "of both growth and disintegration" in his studies on economics.[34] Economic disintegration at the micro-level of companies like Lehman Brothers or other corporate collapses and at the macro-level of the whole economic system can occur when the process is distorted by "*bias*." Lonergan's fourfold pathology of bias in terms of the "dramatic," "individual," "group," and "general" levels of its occurrence, as outlined in previous chapters of this book, can be applied to the economic disintegration. Dick Fuld, former CEO of Lehman Brothers, is an example of the general "bias" of all "good" men of common sense. Reuters reported in an article that

> "Fuld went wrong in not taking seriously enough the impairment of his balance sheet," said Charles Peabody, analyst at independent research firm Portales Partners. He had the typical

32. Ibid., 53.
33. Macmurray, *Self as Agent*, 86.
34. See Mathews, *Lonergan's Quest*, 111.

hubris that any long-term CEO has: "I built this thing, and it's got more value than the marketplace understands." As the credit crisis worsened, Fuld was Wall Street's one seemingly teflon chief executive, keeping his job unchallenged even as CEOs fell at rivals like Bear, Merrill Lynch Cos Inc and Citigroup and as Fuld's own underlings including Chief Financial Officer Erin Callan were pushed out.[35]

The *Financial Times* columnist John Gapper wrote,

> Lehman's collapse is worrying for financial markets and for Wall Street as a whole. It is also a tragedy for its 24,000 employees, who were drilled into unwavering loyalty and cohesion by Mr Fuld. Many held a lot of their wealth in Lehman shares, which have lost most of their value. It is also a tragedy for Mr. Fuld, in the classical Greek sense. He had devoted so much of his personality into moulding the bank that he could not accept its decline. If he had sold out earlier, Lehman might have survived but he was too proud. It was hubris, followed by nemesis.[36]

Individuals in this situation are illustrative of general bias because they value "the illusion that their single talent, common sense, is omnicompetent, insisting on procedures that no longer work, convinced that the only way to do things is to muddle through, and spurning as idle theorizing and empty verbiage any rational account of what has to be done."[37] The human reality is that there is a Dick Fuld in each one of us because through the biased mind there can be a cumulative evasion of fresh insights.[38] This is constitutive of the reality of the human person too who acts in the economic domain. There is a distorting effect of all such bias in the whole process of growth on the individual, social, political and economic levels. As Lonergan observed, the "longer cycle" of decline

---

35. Christian Plumb and Dan Wilchins, "Lehman CEO Fuld's Hubris Contributed to Meltdown," 14 September 2008, http://www.reuters.com/article/idUSN134105912 0080914?pageNumber=1.

36. Gapper, "A Tragedy of Pride and Fall for Fuld," *Financial Times*, 15 September 2008.

37. Lonergan, *Third Collection*, 105.

38. Lucy Kellaway wrote an article in the *Financial Times* titled "There Is a Fred Goodwin or Dick Fuld in All of us." She commented that "such is the human propensity to err in the office that there is a Fred Goodwin or Dick Fuld or even Andrew Fastow lurking inside most of us ready to be brought out in the right circumstances. This theory isn't terribly appealing, but I fear it may be partly right." See *Financial Times* 16 March 2009.

caused by general bias wreaks havoc and can only be reversed by the attainment of a higher viewpoint in man's self-understanding as a human person.[39] And this essentially involves *"a conversion in the subject"* which necessarily entails the person's "solution to the problem of living."[40] But in a testimony before a congressional committee Dick Fuld denied any responsibility for the collapse of Lehman Brothers and declared, "the short sellers did it . . . with the benefit of hindsight, I can now say I and many others were wrong."[41] In my view he is an example of what Lonergan described in the development of bias over the long run, when he observed what often happens in this cycle is that "incomplete ideas, mutilated ideas, enthusiasms, passions, bitter memories and terrifying bogies" are transmitted.[42] He explained how "the objective social surd will be matched by a disunity of minds all warped but each in its private way. The most difficult of enterprises will have to be undertaken under the most adverse of circumstances, and under the present hypothesis that the general bias of common sense remains effective, one cannot but expect great crises that end in complete disintegration and decay.[43]

There is a parallel here, I would suggest, between Alexander Solzhenitsyn's literary exploration of the role of personal efficacy in human action and the responsibility of the *"I act"* in the economic drama of life. The whole tragedy that unfolds in Solzhenitsyn's writings is its diagnosis of a type of *Apperzeptionsverweigerung* (failure to apperceive) in terms of the *"I act"* of the human person on the personal, social, historical, and cultural levels. So too in the free economy, we can comprehend economic progress as a consequence of the *"I act"* of the person, whether they are acting in that horizon as a worker, investor or an entrepreneur. But "decline" is also a concomitant of the *"I act"* on all levels of reality. The blame game subsequent to various economic crashes and other financial debacles is in one sense a failure to realize and accept the *"self-determining"* characteristic of the human being. And this is a flight from human understanding in itself. Solzhenitsyn was also careful to outline the fallible and limited nature of the human subject. He once remarked, "So let the reader who expects this book to be a political exposé slam its covers shut

39. Lonergan, *Insight*, 258.

40. See Lonergan, *Phenomenology and Logic*, 291.

41. Kirchgaessner and Farrell, "Fuld Insists the Short Sellers Were to Blame," *Financial Times*, 7 October 2008.

42. Lonergan, *Insight*, 258. Similar scenarios played out in the Libor scandal.

43. Ibid.

right now. If only it were so simple! If only there were evil people somewhere insidiously committing evil deeds, and it were necessary only to
separate them from the rest of us and destroy them. *But the line dividing
good and evil cuts through the heart of every human being. And who is
willing to destroy a piece of his own heart? During the life of any heart this
line keeps changing places. Socrates taught us: Know thyself!*"[44]

The politician and writer Jesse Norman, speaking about the economic crisis and subsequent downturn, adverted to the need for an adequate anthropological analysis. He wrote that

> at its deepest level, the crash arose because people and markets
> did not behave in the way described in economic textbooks.
> People are not always economically rational . . . We are daily
> conditioned to think of human beings as "economic agents": as
> purely self-interested, endlessly calculating costs and benefits
> and highly sensitive to marginal gains and losses. But a prob-
> lem arises when this economic image feeds back into society
> and becomes our default picture of human motivation . . . *we
> need a different vision and a richer conception of humanity in
> our public policy.* Such a vision starts by recognising *the limits
> of human nature.* It emphasises the importance of independent
> institutions, competition and entrepreneurship as factors driv-
> ing prosperity. It rejects the idea that humans are merely passive
> vehicles for utility, in favour of a far more *dynamic conception of
> human capability.*[45]

Entrepreneurial action is, I believe, one example of human creative
capability unfolding in the economic realm. Norman stresses that we
need a "richer conception of humanity" because the "default picture" of
the human person is inadequate. As we've examined, Schumpeter, in his
study of the entrepreneur, obviously gained an essential insight into the
creative dimension of human action in the free economy. An investigation into entrepreneurial action reawakens within us a greater appreciation of personal efficacy, of the reality of the "*I act*" and "*I will*" of the
human person as it unfolds in economic life. We turn to the contribution
of Ludwig von Mises who enhances our understanding of entrepreneurial

---

44. Solzhenitsyn, *Gulag Archipelago*, 168, my emphases. He denies any attempt by
individuals to escape responsibility with his forceful remark, "History is us." See *From
Under the Rubble*, x.

45. See "Human Beings Are Not Mere Selfish Agents," *Financial Times*, 5 December 2008, my emphases.

creative action and shows how its roots are to be found in the constitution of the human person.

IV. Misesian Entrepreneurial Action and Expansions

Indeed, a whole study could be devoted to Ludwig von Mises's (1881–1971) contribution to understanding human action and the role of the entrepreneur in the economic framework. It is interesting to note that although Mises was older, he was also a contemporary of the philosopher Eric Voegelin (1901–85). In making this connection I am not claiming that they were in any way economic bedfellows.[46] Nonetheless, the cultural, political, and economic milieus they addressed were in very different ways similar. Voegelin notes that when he was at the university of Vienna he came into contact with the "Austrian School of Marginal Utility."[47] He notes that "among the younger economists there was Ludwig von Mises, famous because of his development of money theory. Joseph A. Schumpeter was in Graz at the time."[48] It was through the private seminar of Mises that Voegelin formed connections with Friedrich von Hayek, Oskar Morgenstern, Fritz Machlup, and Gottfried von Haberler. The sociologist Alfred Schutz was also a member of the group. The contacts Voegelin made in the private seminar were important later when he needed a visa to travel to the United States. It was said that when Mises eventually emigrated to America he "could have resumed his old private seminar: all its members were there in New York."[49]

The cultural context in which Mises lived and worked undoubtedly influenced his contributions to a theory of human action in economics. Mises saw the controversies that occurred between the dominant German intellectuals in social science and the Austrian economists led by Carl Menger, and consequently by Eugen von Böhm-Bawerk, as having a meaning extending far beyond a mere question about the methodology of economics.[50] It was in such a charged ideological context that Mises

46. See Gordon, "The Fallacies of Voegelinian Antiliberalism."

47. Voegelin, *Autobiographical Reflections*, 1.

48. Ibid.

49. Hülsmann, *Mises*, 795.

50. I have already referred to the dispute on methods in economic research that occurred in the 1880s in German-speaking countries and is called the *Methodenstreit*. See Sandelin et al., *Short History of Economic Thought*, 50, 62, 71. Landreth and Colander note, "This *Methodenstreit* (controversy over method) was one of the most intense

formed ideas which helped him gain insights for a study into human action. Mises saw the Mengerian School, for instance, as the champion of the freedom of the human person and of his or her economic agency. Just as we referred to the significance of the cultural collapse of the Austro-Hungarian Empire in reference to Schumpeter, so too for Mises, the disintegration of the empire would see the emergence of various crisis points which he would seek to address. There were the hyperinflations of the 1920s and the dangers posed by statism and Marxism. If a civilized society was to be created and preserved, he saw the importance of articulating an adequate theoretical foundation for economics.

V. Mises on Human Action

Mises's seminal work titled *Human Action* was a contribution toward the appreciation of the vital importance of economic understanding for the safeguarding of freedom and civilization in human society. As we've seen Lonergan also made similar references to the crucial need for human insight into *how* the economy works. There is, he contended, an intelligibility pertaining to economic events that needs continual unfolding. This requires a correct understanding of the human intelligence that functions in the "drama of human living," be it on the artistic or practical levels, as in the case of economics.[51] The intervention of the human factor of intelligence is correspondingly evident in economic progress. This is evidenced, Lonergan explains, in the concept of "capital formation," when things are "produced and arranged not because they themselves are desired but because they expedite and accelerate the process of supplying the goods and services that are wanted by consumers . . . Each step in the process of technological and economic development is an occasion on which minds differ, new insights have to be communicated, enthusiasm has to be roused, and a common decision reached. Beyond the common sense of *the laborer, the technician, the entrepreneur* there is the political specialization of common sense."[52]

The Misesian understanding of entrepreneurial action develops the Schumpeterian insight of its essential role in the free market process. But

methodological controversies ever to occur in the development of economic theory" (*History of Economic Thought*, 325).

51. Lonergan, *Insight*, 232.

52. Ibid., 234, my emphases.

in Mises's viewpoint, *all human action* has an entrepreneurial dimension to it. The function is therefore not just limited to entrepreneurial or economic action *per se*. So, Mises "develops a theory of entrepreneurship, understood as the capacity of human beings to create and recognize the subjective opportunities for profit."[53] Mises extends the entrepreneurial concept to include all human action in the economic arena because "creativity" is constitutive of the human person in himself or herself. It is part of the human drama, of the unfurling of the "*I act*," that is, the self-determination of the human person upon the stage of economic reality.

Eric Voegelin referred to Plato's phrase "that a polis is man written large"[54] and called it the "anthropological principle."[55] This insight, that society is an expression of the kind of people who constitute it can, he claims, be used as "a general principle for the interpretation of society"[56] but it can also be used as "an instrument of social critique."[57] It can be applied, I believe, equally to our understanding of the economy. Indeed, Mises's broadening of the entrepreneurial aspect in his economic writings has in my opinion deep anthropological roots. Voegelin suggested that the anthropological principle could actually be "a heuristic principle."[58] In other words, if you want to understand political society, then one of the first ways to do so, is to "ascertain the human type that expresses itself in the order of this concrete society."[59] This can be applied likewise to understanding economics and the economic system we are in. The economic order of the free market can be interpreted as an expression of the fundamental anthropological characteristics of the human person that are at its basis. The free economy is, in other words, the human person "written large" and *acting* in the economic horizon. The *anthropological principle* can, of course, be applied equally as means of critique of the type of person who is "written large" in the economy. The economic and financial scandals and subsequent economic disaster are clear evidence of the need for a proper critique of the model of the human person used in economic theory. As I have suggested with particular reference to the

---

53. Soto, *Austrian School*, 70.
54. Voegelin, *New Science of Politics*, 136.
55. Ibid.
56. Ibid., 137.
57. Ibid.
58. Ibid.
59. Ibid.

global economic crash and cases of corruption, the human person "written large" in the economy often turns out to be a neglected, truncated, devalued, or even alienated subject. Just as, in the words of Lonergan, the human world "does not come into being or survive without deliberation, evaluation, decision, action, without the exercise of freedom and responsibility," so, too, the economic order of the market economy is based upon specific personcentric principles.[60] When these essential factors are omitted in praxis then the economic actors risk becoming meager puppets or just stagehands in the economic drama where, as we've seen, "the setting is magnificent, the lighting superb, the costumes gorgeous but there is no play."[61] When the house lights go up in this setting, the participants in the economic drama may be like Hans Christian Andersen's small child seated in the audience, who to the embarrassment of all, simply and correctly cries out about the emperor that "he isn't wearing anything at all!"

VI. The "Human Creativity" of the Entrepreneur

Mises outlines clearly the essential constituent of entrepreneurship is the human capacity for creativity. He declares that "only the human mind that directs action and production is creative . . . Production is not something physical, material, and external, it is a spiritual and intellectual phenomenon. Its essential qualities are not human labor and external natural forces and things, but the decision of the mind to use these factors as a means for the attainment of ends. What produces the product are not toil and trouble themselves, but the fact that the toiling is guided by reason. The human mind alone has the power to remove uneasiness."[62] It is in light of these Misesian reflections on entrepreneurial action that "the entrepreneur" and his action can be interpreted as a "heuristic principle" which actually facilitates us in understanding the creative dimensions of the human person as a whole. In a discussion on the characteristics of the market Mises emphasizes the point that "the market is not a place, a thing, or a collective entity. The market is a process, actuated by the interplay of the actions of various individuals cooperating under the division of labor. The forces determining the—continually changing—state of the

60. Lonergan, *The Subject*, 30.

61. Lonergan, *Insight*, 262.

62. Mises, *Human Action*, 141–42.

market are the value judgments of these individuals and their actions directed by these value judgments."[63]

The entrepreneur from Mises's perspective cannot be trained to act in a specific way. Rather, a person acts as an entrepreneur when he seizes "an opportunity" and fills a gap that results in an adjustment to the production process.[64] To do this they actuate "keen judgment, foresight and energy."[65] In an insightful section in *Human Action* Mises gives consideration to human action in the world and discusses what he calls "the law of marginal utility, the law of returns, human labour as a means, immediately gratifying labour and mediately gratifying labour, the creative genius and production."[66] An important point he makes in terms of our theme is that *creativity is singular to human beings.* Human beings are irreducibly different. Thus, to study human nature we "cannot abandon reference to meaning and purpose."[67] All that we do is done with a view to the whole reality of who we are as persons and this is established through the maxims of our human action. Historically, he explains, a customary distinction was made between "the production of tangible goods"[68] and the supplying of "personal services."[69] He gives the example of the carpenter and the doctor. He observes, "the carpenter who made tables and chairs was called productive; but this epithet was denied to the doctor whose advice helped the ailing carpenter to recover his capacity to make tables and chairs. A differentiation was made between the doctor-carpenter nexus and the carpenter-tailor nexus. The doctor, it was asserted, does not himself produce; he makes a living from what other people produce, he is maintained by carpenters and tailors."[70]

Mises says that contemporary economists may laugh at these untenable differentiations. They may ridicule the French physiocrats'[71] view that,

63. Ibid., 257.
64. Ibid., 314.
65. Ibid.
66. Ibid., 119–40.
67. Ibid., 28.
68. Ibid., 140–41.
69. Ibid.,141.
70. Ibid.

71. The physiocrats had essential insights into the interrelatedness of the different parts of the economy. Their intellectual leader was François Quesnay (1694–1774). They "believed that a natural order existed that was superior to any possible human design, and they conceived of the economy as largely self-regulating and thus rejected

for example, held "all labor was sterile unless it extracted something from the soil."[72] But such economists, he says, "should rather cast the beam out of their own eyes."[73] In terms of conceptual reversal in economic theory, he gives the example of the labor theory of value that holds "in toiling and overcoming the disutility of labor man adds something to the universe that did not exist before."[74] But this is erroneous from Mises's viewpoint because the "productive forces" that underlie the market economy are, in fact, not material at all. They are, he asserts, "a spiritual, intellectual, and ideological phenomenon."[75] He affirms that what actually differentiates our situation from that of our ancestors "is not something material, but something spiritual. The material changes are the outcome of the spiritual changes."[76] So, an essential Misesian insight is the reality that economics is not solely concerned with the material circumstances of human life. Production is essentially a transformation of a given reality according to the use of human reason. Mises claims "human action is a manifestation of the mind. It is in this sense praxeology can be called a moral science (*Geisteswissenschaft*)."[77]

When it comes to an adequate articulation of what "mind" actually is, Mises takes on a Wittgensteinian tone and is silent.[78] He notes "of course, we do not know what mind *is*, just as we do not know what motion, life, electricity *are*. Mind is simply the word to signify the unknown factor that has enabled men to achieve all that they have accomplished: the

---

the controls imposed by the mercantilist system. The proper role of government was to follow a policy of *laissez faire*." See Landreth and Collander, *History of Economic Thought*, 62. But in terms of a theory of value the physiocrats "broke with centuries of sound economic reasoning . . . rejected subjective value and insisted that the values of goods are 'objective' and mystically embedded in various goods irrespective of consumers' subjective valuations." See Rothbard, *Economic Thought before Adam Smith*, 375. Adam Smith wrote, "This system [the physiocrats'], however, with all its imperfections is, perhaps, the nearest approximation to the truth that has yet been published upon the subject of political œconomy . . . Though in representing the labour which is employed upon land as the only productive labour, the notions which it inculcates are perhaps too narrow and confined" (*Wealth of Nations*, 388).

72. Mises, *Human Action*, 141.

73. Ibid.

74. Ibid.

75. Ibid., 142.

76. Ibid.

77. Ibid.

78. The seventh, most famous, proposition in Wittgenstein's *Tractatus Logico-Philosophicus* was, "Whereof one cannot speak, thereof one must be silent."

theories and the poems, the cathedral and the symphonies, the motorcars and the airplanes."[79] Clearly, Mises lacks an explicit anthropology and so he cannot fully account for human action or entrepreneurial action in particular. Nonetheless, the characteristics he outlines in his investigations into human action are essential qualities of the human person. The human agents in the free market framework are, according to him, *rational, deliberative and purposive human beings*. Mises does not develop a distinct philosophy of the person but we can, I contend, capture in his reflections on human action and in particular on entrepreneurial action a philosophical profile of the person. Philosophy can in a collaborative way help contribute to the development of a more "personcentric profile" in order to elaborate an adequate economic anthropology.

VII. The Threat of Anthropological Anorexia: A Never-Ending Story

There is no doubt there is a type of "anthropological lag" in economic theory in its failure to account for human action in all of its wide-ranging dimensions. Mises is well aware of the various horizons where human action is manifest but he is still unable to account for what he calls the "unknown factor."[80] It is obvious, for instance, that if the participants in the free market process are treated merely as "aggregates" (as in John Maynard Keynes's approach) instead of as individual actors (as in Mises's analysis) "then experts are needed to do their thinking for them . . . [and] planners are needed to tell them what to do."[81] But if people are understood not as aggregates but as "persons, intelligent and reasonable, free and responsible," then economic theoreticians will be better able to account for the human actor's intelligence and freedom as applied in human action.[82] Lonergan observes that what you actually witness in "planned society" is the total opposite, that is, "a regimentation of human living, a mechanization of human activity, a levelling down of human aspirations. The worker is to have his every movement planned for him by some more intelligent expert on methods . . . Education ceases to transmit a culture

79. Mises, *Human Action*, 142.
80. Ibid.
81. Lonergan, *Shorter Papers*, 123.
82. Ibid.

that passes judgment on society and becomes an ever more efficiently organized department of bureaucratic government."[83]

Economic writers point to the fact that a fundamental difference in the *Weltanschauung* among economists actually emerges when you analyze how they view economic reality. Henry Hazlitt confirms the view that John Maynard Keynes approached economics methodologically from the perspective of the "aggregate." Hazlitt adjudged that "his [Keynes's] 'aggregate' or 'macro-economics' is not a step in advance; it is a retrograde step which conceals real relationships and real causation . . . 'Aggregate' or 'aggregative' economics, they [Keynesians] tell us, has displaced 'special' or 'partial' economics, or 'the economics of the firm.' The 'macroscopic' has displaced the 'microscopic' view . . . [Keynes] thinks in aggregates, in averages, in abstractions which are mental constructs that have lost touch with reality."[84] It is not our task in this study to resolve specific economic arguments but the issue has clear philosophical implications. The economist George Reisman in a robust critique of Keynesianism asserts that "aggregative" economics is basically incompatible with "common sense and the love of liberty . . . it is incompatible with the traditional Anglo-Saxon acceptance of the political philosophy of limited government . . . Keynesianism is consumptionism *par excellence*. For no doctrine is more adept in claiming that parasitism is a source of actual enrichment for its victims."[85] As we've remarked, apart from the economic disagreements involved in the real economic debate there are also anthropological reasons for differing methodological approaches taken by various economists to the free economy. We've examined how the entrepreneurial function in some of the economic literature can be easily marginalized in the account of human economic action. It is this very "occlusion" that Schumpeter, Mises, Israel Kirzner, and others have sought to remedy in economic thought.

I referred to the "anthropological principle" in this chapter and how it can be applied both interpretatively and as a critique. I believe that we can philosophically critique the anthropological principle that is at the core of economic theory. If and whenever economic theory does not sufficiently explain or measure up to the reality of the human person,

83. Ibid., 124–25.

84. Hazlitt, *Failure of the "New Economics"*, 28, 274, 278.

85. Reisman, *Capitalism*, 864, 865, 888.

it makes the human person less than they really are.[86] The eclipsing of the entrepreneurial role from economic writings can be interpreted as a dumbing down of the human-centered reality of economic life and a "depersonalization" of the market process. Economists like Schumpeter, Mises and Kirzner want to incorporate a restorative anthropological balance into the overall understanding of the free market process. They do this by giving an adequate account of the entrepreneurial role in economic action.

Israel Kirzner, in a tribute paid to Mises, wrote that during the twentieth century, the dominant schools of economics developed a "mechanistic framework" in their analysis of the market.[87] But Mises really sought to refute this "with every ounce of energy."[88] This depersonalized account, in fact, "did violence to the subtle insights a more powerful awareness of the market is able to confer."[89] Kirzner explains it as follows:

> the market came to be seen as a kind of computer, grinding out the equilibrium solution compatible with the basic data of the system—a task which presumes that the economic actors already possess perfect knowledge. The theory of the market came to mean the solving by the theorist of the computation problem. Moreover this theory came to be seen as equally suited to the needs of societies choosing to allocate their resources by central direction; the socialist planner could, it came to be thought, simulate the success with which the market allocates resources by merely addressing himself to the very same computation problem which it was thought to be the function of market theory to solve.[90]

I speak of the idea of an "anthropological anorexia" occurring in economic writings. Just as "entrepreneurial action" was jettisoned from economic analyses and it was Schumpeter and the Austrians who reawakened us to this reality, so, too, there has been a "devaluation" of the "human person" in economic thought and praxis. But the challenge to recapture the anthropological reality is always a part of the human drama and it is an essential dimension of the philosopher's task to do this. Lonergan uses the phrase "the existential gap" to express something similar. He

86. See Lonergan, *Phenomenology and Logic*, 296.

87. Kirzner, *Driving Force of the Market*, 276.

88. Ibid.

89. Ibid.

90. Ibid.

says "the existential gap consists in the fact that the reality of the subject lies beyond his own horizon."[91] The "lag" or "gap" is constitutive of who we are as persons and so it will always be inherent to the human sciences. The "existential opening" is "the difference between what is one's reality and the measure of one's reality that is within one's own horizon."[92] It is for this reason we must learn to continually broaden our horizons to fill in the anthropological fissure, what Walker Percy diagnosed in his essay "The Fateful Rift: The San Andreas Fault in the Modern Mind."[93]

There is no doubt that the cataclysmic meltdown in global financial markets and the consequent economic recession also point to evidence of "anthropological anorexia," which can occur in the economic system. But there is always the temptation to blame pure human greed or to hold that the free market system itself leads inherently to global inequality.[94] But the elephant in the room is the fact that *human action* in the free economy is often blocked by too much interventionism by governments and other parties. In other words, there is not too much *freedom* but too little. Thomas Woods, for instance, in a discussion on how governments can actually cause the "boom-bust" cycle, refers to the interference of central bankers in the process.[95] He describes how

> the central bank's lowering of the interest rate therefore creates a mismatch of market forces. The coordination of production across time is disrupted. *Long-term* investments that will bear fruit *only in the distant future* are encouraged at a time when the

91. Lonergan, *Phenomenology and Logic*, 281.

92. Ibid., 284.

93. See Percy, *Signposts in a Strange Land*, 271–92.

94. Indeed, Thomas Piketty's analysis in *Capital in the Twenty-First Century* is somewhat similar in his attribution of the fundamental source of "inequality" as being found in the historical unfolding of the capitalist system itself. But the question to be addressed is the equality of persons, which cannot be measured in purely economic terms.

95. In regard to the role of central banks in the financial system, Colin Teese wrote, "The world's central banks, which control little more than a tenth of total liquidity, are now small players. They no longer have any real influence over the creation of most credit—indeed of monetary policy. Central banks, especially in the English-speaking world, have been pretending otherwise—while the world money market was being transformed before their eyes." He argues that the real focus should be redirected away from the financial sector, "towards what *really* matters—the real economy, and especially the domestic manufacturing sector." See "Unlocking the Riddle of the Global Financial Crisis," *News Weekly*, 20 December 2008, 5–6, http://www.newsweekly.com.au/articles/2008dec20_e.html.

public has shown no let-up in its desire to consume *in the present*. Consumers have not chosen to save and release resources for use in the higher stages of production. To the contrary, the lower rates encourage them to save less and thus *consume more*, at a time when investors are also looking to *invest more* resources. The economy is being stretched in two directions at once, and resources are therefore being misallocated into lines that cannot be sustained over the long term.[96]

This is essentially Mises's argument, that the market is not something artificial like a computer "grinding out solutions to sets of simultaneous equations."[97] Economist and *Financial Times* columnist John Kay wrote precisely about this mistaken approach to the financial markets. He discussed the funding model in the United States, where universities were funded by results of investment performance. But with the collapse of shares on the Wall Street market, he noted that

> Yale reported in December that its endowment had lost a quarter of its value . . . the model seems to be in question . . . Quantitative portfolio management relies on measures of correlations between asset classes. These historical correlations are not universal constants but the products of particular economic conditions. Unless you *understand* the behaviour that produced them, you cannot assess durability . . . Anyone in the financial world knew these things: but computers, churning through reams of data, did not . . . *Diversification is a matter of judgment not statistics. A model will tell you only what you have already told the model and can never replace, though it can enhance, an understanding of market psychology and the factors that make for successful business.*[98]

VIII. The Fragility of the Human Person in the Free Economy Process: Gnostic Themes

Mises outlines how the market is a fragile process where in the context of ever changing circumstances (Schumpeter's dynamic nature) and with limited information "the *decisions* of market participants are, through

96. Woods, *Meltdown*, 68.

97. Kirzner, *Driving Force of the Market*, 276.

98. John Kay, "Financial Models Are No Excuse for Resting Your Brain," *Financial Times*, 28 January 2010, http://www.ft.com/cms/s/0/eced7976-ecdc-11dd-a534-0000779fd2ac.html. My emphases.

their interplay in the market, brought into steadily more dovetailing adjustment. In this process the key roles are played by *restless, active, ever alert entrepreneurship*, and by its counterpart, the merciless, ceaseless, impartial court of active competition."[99] The fragility of the free economy often results in what I identify as Gnostic solutions or tendencies, such as "interventionism" in the market, because someone or some group claims to "know" better than the participants. In his study titled *Socialism*, Mises, while discussing the methods of destructionism, wrote, "State interference in economic life, which calls itself 'economic policy,' has done nothing but destroy economic life. Prohibitions and regulations have by their general obstructive tendency fostered the growth of the spirit of wastefulness. Already during the war period this policy has gained so much ground that practically all economic action of the *entrepreneur* was branded as violation of the law."[100]

"Interventionism," according to Mises, can result in decommissioning the role of profits in the market process. But there seems to be a convenient "forgetfulness" that "loss" is a corollary of "profit," and that it is the entrepreneur who incurs the loss. Mises observes, in fact, that "profit and loss are the instruments by means of which the consumers keep a tight rein on all entrepreneurial activities. It is profit and loss that makes the consumers supreme in the direction of business . . . On the unhampered market a man can earn profits only by supplying the consumers in the best and cheapest way with the goods they want to use . . . The consumers suffer when the laws of the country prevent the most efficient entrepreneurs from expanding the sphere of their activities."[101]

The core of Mises's and the Austrian economists' critique of communist "collectivism," which they invariably identified with "totalitarianism," was that it was fundamentally based upon specific "epistemological" considerations which were "Gnostic" in origin. "Interventionism" presupposes the possession of a "wider" kind of knowledge than what is just specific to market participants. Mises, for instance, clearly outlines what he considers as the chiliastic dimensions of socialism. He mentions that scholars have actually traced "the main notions of the materialist or economic conception of history" back to pre-Marxian writers.[102] These theories are usually based upon the presumption of a pre-existing

99. See Kirzner, *Driving Force of the Market*, 276, my emphases.

100. Mises, *Socialism*, 424, my emphasis.

101. Ibid., 487.

102. Ibid., 249–50.

"Golden Age, from which man is moving farther and farther away, only to return finally to an equally good, or, if possible, even better, age of perfection."[103] What is required, therefore, to return to this "ideal age" is a certain type of "salvific knowledge" that permits the construction of an economic paradisiac structure. Mises observed that there was an obvious link between "Christian Chiliasm" and "philosophic Chiliasm" which

> in the eighteenth century was a rationalist reinterpretation of Christianity; and thence, through Saint Simon, Hegel, and Weitling to Marx and Lenin. Curiously enough, it is this particular Socialism, derived in this way from mystical ideas whose origin is lost in the darkness of history, which has called itself scientific Socialism, while it has tried to disqualify as "Utopian" the Socialism that is derived from the rational considerations of the philosophers . . . In its prophecy is found the same strange mixture of ecstatically extravagant phantasy with uninspired commonplace and coarse materialism as is found in the most ancient messianic prophecies.[104]

My central point here is that economic "interventionism" often presupposes that "enlightened" knowledge is held by the "interventionist(s)," and it ineluctably involves the occlusion of some of the market participants, for example, the entrepreneur. I see a parallel here between this gnostic-type interpretation of interventionism and Voegelin's analysis of the metamorphosis of Gnosticism within culture. Voegelin initially became aware of the problem of Gnosticism and its possible application as a critique of modernity through the work of Hans Urs von Balthasar.[105] He subsequently developed his reflections in *The New Science of Politics* and expanded them in *Science, Politics and Gnosticism*. Gnosticism is basically engendered in the context of dissatisfaction with the world as it is. This results in the aspiration to transform the world through human action, be it on the political, social or economic levels.

---

103. Ibid., 251.

104. Ibid., 253. Mises referred to Auguste Comte, secretary to Saint-Simon, whose central belief was that in understanding world history, it was essential to look for truth in the past. He cites Comte: "But now I, Auguste Comte, have discovered the truth. Therefore, there is no longer any need for freedom of thought or freedom of the press. I want to rule and to organize the whole country" (*Marxism Unmasked*, 45).

105. Voegelin, *Autobiographical Reflections*, 66.

Voegelin outlined six main characteristics of the Gnostic attitude that can, I believe, be applied to the development of economic theory too. A summary of the main points is as follows:

1. The Gnostic is dissatisfied with his situation.

2. The belief that the drawbacks of the situation can be attributed to the fact that the world is intrinsically poorly organized.

3. The third characteristic is the belief that salvation from the evil world is possible.

4. The belief that the order of being will have to be changed in a historical process.

5. The belief that a change in the order of being lies in the realm of human action, that this salvational act is possible through man's effort.

6. Knowledge—Gnosis—of the method of altering being is the central concern of the Gnostic.[106]

Voegelin claimed that one variant or another of these attitudes were to be found in various gnostic movements. He commented that it was observable in science in the development of "scientism." He claimed, in fact, that "scientism has remained to this day one of the strongest gnostic movements in Western society; and the immanentist pride in science is so strong that even special sciences have each left distinguishable sediments in the variants of salvation through physics, economics, sociology, biology, and psychology."[107] He later on expanded his viewpoint and agreed that many other factors, besides Gnosticism, have to be taken into consideration in order to give an adequate account of modernity.[108] But these "gnostic themes," I argue, can be equally found in the economic analyses offered by Mises and some of the other Austrian economic writers. It is frequently employed as a diagnostic tool and often emerges in economics in the context of what's called the "knowledge problem."[109] Indeed, Mises wrote about the limited nature of human knowledge and about the fallibility of the human agents involved in the economic process, noting how

106. See Voegelin, *New Science of Politics*, 297–98.

107. Ibid., 192.

108. See Heilke, *Eric Voegelin*, 120 n. 73.

109. It was Friedrich Hayek who had the insight into the "knowledge problem" within economics. See Kirzner, *Meaning of Market Process*, 152–59.

men are affected with all the frailties and weaknesses of human existence. What determines the real course of events, the
formation of prices and all other phenomena commonly called
economic as well as all other events of human history, is the
attitudes of fallible men and the effects produced by their actions liable to error. The eminence of the approach of modern
marginal utility economics consists is the fact that it pays full
attention to this state of affairs. It does not deal with the actions
of an ideal man, essentially different from real man, but with the
choices of all those who participate in social cooperation under
the division of labor.[110]

Thus, in this context the entrepreneur is the "antihero" of the "gnostic prophet" who claims to be in the singular possession of secret knowledge. The gnostic type is very different to Schumpeter's description of
the entrepreneur in terms of a "prophet of innovation" and indeed the
Misesian development of the concept so as to include all human action
within its scope. The "gnostic prophet" is unprepared to "lose," whereas
the real entrepreneur understands profit and loss as coessential aspects
of entrepreneurial action. In fact, Mises argued that entrepreneurs are
known not primarily by their profits but by their losses. He remarked,
"There is a simple rule of thumb to tell entrepreneurs from non-entre-
preneurs. The entrepreneurs are those on whom the incidence of losses
on capital employed falls. Amateur-economists may confuse profits with
other kinds of intakes. But it is impossible to fail to recognize losses on
the capital employed."[111]

In Friedrich Hayek's (1899–1992) critique of scientism the theme
of Gnosticism can be similarly detected.[112] In an essay titled "The Use of
Knowledge in Society" he asked, "What is the problem we wish to solve
when we try to construct a rational economic order?" He explains that if

110. Mises, *Ultimate Foundation of Economic Science*, 68–69.

111. Mises, *Planning for Freedom*, 145.

112. See Cubeddu, *Philosophy of the Austrian School*, 109. Hayek wrote an essay titled "Scientism and the Study of Society," in *The Counter-Revolution of Science: Studies
on the Abuse of Reason*. There he said, "During the first half of the nineteenth century
a new attitude made its appearance. The term *science* came more and more to be confined to the physical and biological disciplines which at the same time began to claim
for themselves a special rigorousness and certainty which distinguished them from
all others. Their success was such that they soon came to exercise an extraordinary
fascination on those working in other fields . . . Thus the tyranny commenced which
the methods and techniques of the Sciences in the narrow sense of the term have ever
since exercised over the other subjects" (*Counter-Revolution of Science*, 20–21).

every one possesses all the relevant information, have a given set of preferences and complete knowledge of available means, then the problem
that remains "is purely one of logic."[113] But economic reality is not like
this. He describes that

> the peculiar character of the problem of a rational economic
> order is determined precisely by the fact that the knowledge of
> the circumstances which we must make use of never exists in
> concentrated or integrated form but solely as the dispersed bits
> of incomplete and frequently contradictory knowledge which
> all the separate individuals possess. The economic problem of
> society is thus not merely a problem of how to allocate "given"
> resources—if "given" is taken to mean given to a single mind
> which deliberatively solves the problem set by these "data." It
> is rather a problem of how to secure the best use of resources
> known to any of the members of society, for ends whose relative
> importance only these individuals know. Or, to put it briefly, it
> is a problem of the utilization of knowledge which is not given
> to anyone in its totality.[114]

It is interesting to note that Michael Polanyi (1891–1976) likewise
developed a polycentric approach to knowledge and human decision-
making in the free economy. Polanyi believed that "the social orders most
important to human well-being are *spontaneous orders,* that is, orders that
result from the interplay of individuals mutually adjusting their actions to
the actions of others. Spontaneous orders are the result of human action
but not of human design."[115] The fundamental difficulty with a centrally
planned economy is not necessarily a question of economic inefficiency;
the problem is primarily anthropological. The philosopher Karol Wojtyła
intuited similarly that the "main problem with Marxism is not merely a
question of the inefficiency of a social system: it is something far more
deep-seated. He [Wojtyła] sees the core difficulty as anthropological."[116]

Hayek acknowledged the contribution of Polanyi to the idea of
"spontaneous order." In *The Constitution of Liberty,* there is a discussion
on the concept of "order without commands." He comments that most
opposition to freedom under a general set of laws arises because some
people are unable to think of effective coordination of human action

113. Hayek, *Individualism and Economic Order,* 77.
114. Ibid.
115. See Polanyi, *Logic of Liberty,* xi.
116. See McNerney, *John Paul II,* 153.

without a commanding deliberative intelligence. Hayek argues, in fact, that one of the major contributions of economic theory has been to elucidate "how such a mutual agreement of the spontaneous activities of individuals is brought about by the market."[117] He acknowledges that Polanyi had already called this approach "the spontaneous formation of a 'polycentric order': 'When order is achieved among human beings by allowing them to interact with each other on their own initiative—subject only to the laws which uniformly apply to all of them—we have a system of spontaneous order in society . . . The actions of such individuals are said to be free, for they are not determined by any *specific* command, whether of a superior or a public authority; the compulsion to which they are subject is impersonal and general.'"[118]

Lonergan also speaks about the fragility or "dilemma" of the human subject. He describes how "human act, subject, act, object differ, for not only is the act finite, but also the subject does not know himself by his own essence."[119] He sees human knowledge as in process and at any stage in its development you can differentiate a threefold division. That is, firstly, the "*known*: the range of questions I can raise and answer." Secondly, the "*known unknown*: the range of questions I can raise, find significant, worthwhile, know how they might be solved, but *de facto* cannot answer and I know I cannot answer. *Docta ignorantia*." Thirdly, the "*unknown unknown*: *Indocta ignorantia*, the range of questions that I do not raise; if raised I would not understand nor find significant nor judge worthwhile nor know how to go about solving." The "*horizon* is the limit" and it is important to recognize the boundary between the *known unknown* and *unknown unknown* even in the human sciences.[120] The *unknown unknown* is not just because of human frailty, it is part of who we are as persons. It pertains to human knowledge as such; it is "not any matter of biochemistry or synapses."[121] The human being brings this "unknown factor" into the human sciences, like philosophy, theology, psychology and economics.

It is interesting that contemporary economists like Roman Frydman and Michael Goldberg also take up this theme of the "knowledge problem" in their research. If the model of the economy is one in which

117. Hayek, *Constitution of Liberty*, 159.

118. Ibid., 160.

119. Lonergan, *Phenomenology and Logic*, 197.

120. Ibid., 198–99. The triad, commonly attributed to US Secretary of Defense Donald Rumsfeld, was coined by Bernard Lonergan in 1958.

121. Ibid., 282.

endogenous change occurs then there must be room for the *"unknown"* factor and the free exercise of entrepreneurial action. If things are pre-determined because everything is *known* then there is "no possibility for the actors in the economy to create something unforeseeable, surprising, [and] genuinely innovative."[122] Frydman and Goldberg in their study wrote that

> on the occasion of his 1974 Nobel lecture Friedrich Hayek, appealed to fellow economists to resist the "pretence of exact knowledge" in economic analysis. Drawing on his prescient analysis of the inevitable failure of central planning, Hayek warned against the lure of predetermination . . . Decades later, experience as a Federal Reserve chief led Alan Greenspan to concur with Hayek. He told the economists assembled at a 2004 meeting of the American Economic Association that central banking requires creativity. Central bankers, just as all individuals, *act in a world of imperfect knowledge.*[123]

122. Edmund S. Phelps, Foreword to Frydman and Goldberg, *Imperfect Knowledge*, xvi.

123. Ibid., 3, my emphases.

7

Entrepreneurial Perspectives IV: Eastern Awakenings and Western Alertness

I. Outside the Window: János Kornai's Discovery of the "Human-centered-ness" of Economic Life

THE HUNGARIAN ECONOMIST JÁNOS Kornai's (b. 1928) discovery of the centrality of the anthropological perspective in economic thinking is strongly reminiscent of the Misesian-Hayekian perspective.[1] Kornai, unlike the other remarkable group of émigré Austrians and Hungarians, actually remained in Hungary during the Second World War and the subsequent communist takeover. The former group included scholars like Friedrich Hayek, Joseph Schumpeter, Paul Rosenstein-Rodan, Ludwig von Mises, and Gottfried von Haberler. Whereas all of these made significant contributions in the West, Kornai "stands apart by having made his [contribution] in the east."[2] He wrote "from the concrete experience of a centrally planned economy."[3] Kornai in his memoir *By Force of Thought* describes his intellectual awakening and the influence of Hayek on him. He says:

> I found Hayek's critique thought provoking. He drew his main arguments from practical considerations rather than theory.

1. Four of Kornai's main works are as follows: *Overcentralization in Economic Administration*; *Anti-equilibrium*; *The Economics of Shortage*; and *The Socialist System*.

2. Padma Desai, "How the East Was Won," *Financial Times Magazine*, 24–25 November 2007, 44.

3. Skidelsky, "Winning a Gamble with Communism."

193

How will central planners be able to trace the supply and demand of a million types of product at once? His arguments pushed my nose into something that I knew well enough: the *limitations of centralized knowledge*. Hayek rightly pointed out that the market was not simply a balancing mechanism. Knowledge in society is decentralized. Only a decentralized market and a private owner-ship can make it possible for anyone receiving a direct incentive to make the best use of the knowledge in his or her possession. Reading Hayek directed my attention to the close tie between knowledge, incentives, and property.[4]

Kornai explains that the change in his ideas began "on a meta-ratio-nal, not a rational plane."[5] He describes how "my *faith* in communism was shaken as I recognized the lies and brutality around me. The collapse was in the moral foundations of my worldview."[6] He mentions Hayek and Schumpeter as exerting a great influence on his thinking but does not directly mention Mises.[7] Nonetheless, I contend that a Misesian un-derstanding can be detected in his economic perspective. This especially regards Kornai's insight into the importance of human choice. Kornai explains that the clichéd phrase often repeated in the 1950s was "that was not by chance, Comrades."[8] It was not that Marxian philosophy in itself reflected a strict "predeterminism" but that the teachers and those involved in the planning offices "liked to imply that there was *no alternative*."[9] Kornai describes how "the economic plan was drawn up in a singe 'version' that every organization, though formally entitled to accept it or reject it, had to endorse."[10] It was in the latter half of the 1950s that other sources like dramatic plays by Hungarian writers opened up the opposite idea to him, that is, "there *was* choice."[11] He describes how the plays he read illuminated "the alternative solutions to great tragic di-lemmas and the pain of having to choose."[12]

4. Kornai, *By Force of Thought*, 126, my emphases.

5. Ibid., 79.

6. Ibid.

7. Ibid., 334.

8. Ibid., 132.

9. Ibid.

10. Ibid.

11. Ibid.

12. Ibid.

During this time he read some of the writings of the existential-
ist philosophers and in this way he discovered that "it was vital to understand that *I* was responsible for my decisions and *I* could not blame
circumstances."[13] By now Kornai had also come across the "rational
choice" model in economics. He would later criticize this theory, but the
essential insight was that the model at least was open to the fact "that
there *is* a choice."[14] From what we have discussed about Mises in the
previous chapter, especially in relation to the entrepreneurial function,
we can see that *human choice* in itself is a rich Misesian theme. Indeed,
Mises is careful to elucidate, for example, that the movement from the
classical theory of value in economics to the subjective theory is not just
a simple substitution of one explanation of market exchange for another
one. What Mises says is worth quoting here. He states that

> the general theory of choice and preference goes far beyond the
> horizon which encompassed the scope of economic problems
> as circumscribed by the economists from Cantillon, Hume, and
> Adam Smith down to John Stuart Mill. It is much more than
> merely a theory of the "economic side" of human endeavors and
> of man's striving for commodities and an improvement in his
> material well-being. It is the science of every kind of human ac-
> tion. *Choosing* determines all human decisions . . . No treatment
> of economic problems proper can avoid starting from *acts of
> choice*; economics becomes a part, although the hitherto best
> elaborated part, of a more universal science, *praxeology*.[15]

Since self-determination, choice, and decision are inherent to human nature, the Misesian perspective is illuminating of the fundamental
"personcentric dimension" at the core of economic life. We can discover
it likewise in the writings of Schumpeter, Hayek, and Kornai. Kornai
significantly entitles one chapter in his intellectual memoir "Against the
Current." This was because he was a voice in the wilderness prepared
to speak against what Osip Mandelstam called in a similar context "the
atomization . . . of personal existence." Indeed, his "choice" was to stay in
Hungary and try to dialogue with communism on his home ground. At
a book launch for his autobiography, Harvard economist Francis Bator
commented, "Some might think a blemish Kornai's choice, as he puts it
in the book, 'not [to] indulge in heroic, illegal forms of struggle against

13. Ibid., 133, my emphases.
14. Ibid.
15. Mises, *Human Action*, 3, my emphases.

the communist system . . . [instead] to contribute to renewal through . . . scholarly activity.' Not so. If you want your bold ideas to affect the real world, you have sometimes to restrain your impulse to be bold. It is the courageous tradeoff of a quintessentially autonomous man."[16]

In Kornai's intellectual memoir, he speaks about his book *Anti-Equilibrium* and points out that it "underscores, as one virtue of capitalism, something acknowledged in Marx and Engel's *Communist Manifesto* and central to Schumpeter's theory: *technical advance* and *continual innovation* are the central driving forces constantly generated by the intrinsic attributes of the capitalist system."[17] He describes his developing intellectual unease with Marxism. The deepest level of discontent for him was at the moral level. But then he also objects at the rational level, that is, to "the *epistemological* basis of Marxism."[18] He explains how Marxism regarded itself as a scientific theory of socialism and considered unscientific accounts as "naïve and utopian."[19] But he holds that it was exactly on these grounds, that is, the "scientific," that he broke away from Marxism. He is well aware that in itself this is controversial because there is, he asserts, no consensus "on what makes a statement 'scientific' or even on when the truth of a statement can be deemed to be confirmed."[20]

II. Kornai's Barometer of Anthropological Reality: A Person-Centered Perspective

Kornai outlines that he ultimately broke with Marxism when he used the "barometer" of reality to assess the theory. The result for him was that it was measured and found wanting. He analyzed economic questions, such as "how did the 'theory of value' relate to prices?"[21] He refers to the influence upon him of Eugen von Böhm-Bawerk's critique of Marx in *Karl Marx and the Close of His System*. But Kornai mentions one essential factor in his intellectual conversion and then rapidly skips over it, and that is what he calls the "*bitter experience of being deceived.*"[22] He

16. Warsh, "Kornai's Choice," 20 May 2007, http://www.economicprincipals.com/issues/2007.05.20/249.html.

17. Kornai, *By Force of Thought*, 191, my emphases.

18. Ibid., 79.

19. Ibid.

20. Ibid.

21. Ibid.

22. Ibid., my emphases.

describes how the Marxian theories "performed badly" in comparisons made with other models.[23] But the failure was not just at an economic level because much more importantly the assumptions simply "failed to match reality."[24] Now, it seems to me Kornai never actually articulates an understanding of what "reality" is, but I hold that beneath the surface of his reflections the "devaluation" of the reality of the human person emerges as the kernel of his critique.

The notion of "*deception*" he speaks about is reminiscent, I think, of Voegelin's diagnosis of the Western crisis. Voegelin described how the human person could end up being deceived when "the power of society is thrown on the side of appearance."[25] This can become an "impossible" burden for the many, "and hard to bear for the few."[26] Interestingly, Kornai summarizes his main objection as that the theory of "economics failed to answer the *big* questions, to assist in a deeper understanding of capitalism and socialism, or to indicate how the world might be 'improved.'"[27] In this instance, he's actually referring to the motivation for writing his book called *Anti-Equilibrium*. He explains how "sticking to theoretical convictions is rather like being in love. I had blindly and passionately attached to Marxism, and abandoning it was traumatic. Then I developed a slight affection for neoclassical theory . . . My eyes were soon opened and I began to be annoyed, and later furious, that neoclassical theory was not giving me satisfactory answers to the questions that were torturing me—or, worse still, that I sensed the answers were wrong."[28]

He reiterates that he had turned away from Marxism because it did not "compare its theories with reality."[29] And he had similar suspicions about neoclassical theory. He has in mind the Walrasian equilibrium model devised by the French Swiss economist Léon Walras in the later part of the nineteenth century. Kornai writes that "equilibrium, harmony, the best state possible under the given conditions—that is the image of the society projected by this theory."[30] He says the theory is strictly

23. Ibid.

24. Ibid.

25. Voegelin, *Plato and Aristotle*, 79.

26. Ibid.

27. Kornai, *By Force of Thought*, 180–81.

28. Ibid., 179.

29. Ibid.

30. Ibid., 180.

speaking logical. It captivated him until he *"woke up"* to some other questions.[31] Peter Leeson sums the matter up by saying, "For Kornai, like for Mises, the world of equilibrium, or what Mises called the 'evenly rotating economy,' is an indispensable mental tool for understanding economic theory. But it is demonstrably not about the world we live in and cannot tell us about the actual economic problems—'the big questions,' to use Kornai's language—we actually face."[32] The experience of deception suggests that one is actually deceived by the duplicity and Kornai readily admits to this. He describes how he was *awakened from his slumbers* by some disturbing experiences. Like, for example, the meeting with the former prisoner Sándor Haraszti who had been imprisoned for many years. Haraszti retold his own story of betrayal and deception. Kornai comments, "it was dreadful to hear all this from the one who had suffered in the drama. The tragedy was enhanced for me because I knew the other player, the one who had tormented the hero—and not a man inherently evil, but as someone who had started life with noble intentions. I found this revelation shocking because it demonstrated that the tragedy was not caused by the personal characteristics of the participants. There was something fatally wrong with the system itself."[33]

Kornai voluntarily admits, "I had believed the lie."[34] Here, I believe, we are dealing with fundamentally the "undying struggle," *mache anthanatos*, to make sure that theory, be it on the social, political or economic level, really measures up to the truth of the human person.[35] As Voegelin points out "this is the crucial point on which the meaning of theory depends. Theory is not just any opining about human existence in society; it rather is an attempt at formulating the meaning of existence by explicating the content of a definite class of experiences. Its argument is not arbitrary."[36]

Aristotle was one of the first philosophers to advert to this requirement when it comes to any theorizing about the human person and his actions. Indeed, he developed Plato's anthropological principle as the

31. Ibid.

32. Leeson, "We're All Austrians Now: János Kornai and the Austrian School of Economics," www.peterleeson.com/We_re_All_Austrians_Now.pdf.

33. Kornai, *By Force of Thought*, 60.

34. Ibid.

35. Voegelin adapts this term from Plato's *Laws*. See Voegelin, *Published Essays, 1966–1985*, xxii, 365.

36. Voegelin, *New Science of Politics*, 138.

source of order in terms of political reality. His basic point is we must posses a systematic understanding of the nature of the human person if we want to develop a coherent political science. Similarly, this can be applied to economic reality and assist us in understanding the role of different human agents in the free economy. Kornai's investigations are another example of someone awakening from dogmatic slumbers in economics and recapturing the "person-centered" principles that underlie the free market economy.

The American philosopher David Gordon, for example, explains the philosophical origins of the Austrian approach to economics we've referred to in this book. The Austrian emphasis upon human action, for instance, can be traced back to Aristotle's *Nicomachean Ethics*. And on another level too Gordon says, "One can point to the role of individual substances in the *Metaphysics*."[37] There are also many other philosophical influences, like those of Franz Brentano and his theory of "intentionality," which influenced the subjective theory of value developed by the Austrians.[38] In any case, Gordon concludes, "at every stage in the development of Austrian economics, philosophy has been an accompanying though not dominating presence. Action, that leitmotif of praxeology, has in the Austrian tradition received a distinctly Aristotelian analysis. Austrian economics and a realistic philosophy are made for each other."[39]

In his investigations, Aristotle sets out in search of the true nature of what it is to be human, in order to understand what is the highest good in human action. Aristotle used the term "*spoudaios*, the mature man"[40] to describe the one who has "maximally actualized the potentialities of human nature."[41] Applied to our economic-philosophical thematic we can say: unless an economic theory attempts to explicate the reality of the human person and his or her potentialities, it results in a reductive understanding of human action. Then the theory risks becoming a lie that creates "the impression of empty talk."[42] In this scenario you can "talk the talk" and "repeat the words" but the meaning is missing "because the ho-

---

37. Gordon, *Philosophical Origins of Austrian Economics*, 26.

38. Barry Smith notes "intentionality is a form of relational contact with reality. It is this thesis which lies at the heart of Austrian philosophy as this was developed by Brentano's disciples" (*Austrian Philosophy*, 332).

39. Gordon, *Philosophical Origins of Austrian Economics*, 41.

40. Voegelin, *New Science of Politics*, 139. See Aristotle, *Nicomachean Ethics* 1113a, 29–35.

41. Ibid.

42. Ibid.

rizon is not broad enough" to comprise the many different aspects of the truth of the human being.[43] This explains why Kornai felt so deceived in terms of the "theory" he encountered and how it was experienced in the real lives of those around him in Hungary and the Eastern bloc countries.

Science essentially concerns the study of reality and in this respect it must have "*theoretical relevance*" not just in terms of a method but also in terms of its subject matter. This holds true too in terms of our economic understanding. But I also want to use the term "*anthropological relevance*" or "*dignity*" here in relation to the economic arena. In any discussion of the entrepreneurial function in the market economy, the maximization of the monetary dimension is important but so also is the maximization of the human creative capabilities which the entrepreneurial process involves and unfolds for us. It is not necessarily the task of the economist alone to articulate this reality. Thus, there is a *responsibility* to create an opportunity for multidisciplinary collaboration in our approach. I spoke at the beginning of *Wealth of Persons* about the need for a "creative collaboration" between scholars and practitioners. Such an economic anthropology can contribute toward a fuller articulation of human action and the human agents involved in the free economy. Nonetheless, there is always the "tension" between theory and praxis, and once that "tension" escapes us, we can in a sense lose an apperception of the permanent "metaxical" or "in-between" nature of human existence.[44] Kornai's intellectual and existential "deception" became exposed for him because he discovered that although there was a rational or logical part to Marxism, it was after all a "logical speculation about a fragment of reality that purported to be the whole of reality."[45] Kornai attests in this regard: "I had complete trust in Marxist-Leninist ideology. I was convinced that every word was true . . . As I think back on that period, in the appalling knowledge of what really took place, I have often felt that a comparison with a sleepwalker was just."[46]

43. See Lonergan, *Phenomenology and Logic*, 283.

44. See Voegelin, *Autobiographical Reflections*, 72–73.

45. See Federici, *Eric Voegelin*, 25.

46. Kornai, *By Force of Thought*, 44–45.

III. Kornai's Entrepreneur as "System-Specific"

In a study titled "Some System-Specific Features of Capitalism," which is symptomatic of his intellectual awakening, Kornai lists *"dynamism, innovation* and *enterprise"* as "system-specific" to capitalism.[47] He asks, "Why is it right to call the central role of the entrepreneur in capitalism (and only capitalism) a characteristic, *system-specific* feature? How is it possible to claim in this case that this is a relation of cause and effect, i.e. the capitalist system makes a protagonist of the entrepreneur?"[48] He outlines four essential characteristics of capitalism that describe the *specificity* of entrepreneurial action in the market economy. They are (1) *Freedom of enterprise.* I will trade if I wish. I will not trade if I do not so wish. I am not ordered or forbidden by a higher authority to be an entrepreneur. (2) *An exceptionally strong incentive.* Entrepreneurs can gain huge rewards if they manage to do what they wish. But they suffer grave losses if they do not. Success can be a matter of economic life and death, since the outcome of failure is *exit*, destruction of the business. (3) *Competition among sellers.* Sellers (and ultimately producers) compete for buyers primarily by offering new products or services. The socialist system is marked by a shortage economy where a sellers' market applies. Buyers are pleased to obtain the product or service at all and there is no need to entice them with innovation. Competition among sellers for the buyers' attention and ultimately their propensity to buy is one of the strongest driving forces behind dynamism, innovation, and technical progress. The opposite of that is that a chronic shortage economy curbs or distorts the dynamism of the economy, cools the spirit of enterprise inside many people, stands in the way of innovation, condemning the economy to stagnation and trailing idly behind the rapid technical advances of developed capitalism. And finally, (4) *the presence of free, untied capital.* Its owners seek chances to place it usefully. The capital market making capital available to entrepreneurs is flexible. Kornai explains that some readers may have read his *Economics of Shortage* (1980) and even remember it. There is no slack (usually unused) capital in a shortage economy. Everything is allocated, indeed over-allocated beforehand. There is no money available for unplanned investment projects, let alone experimentation or uncertain undertakings. The rigid machinery of bureaucratic centralism leaves no room for the form of investment of *venture capital*, where great profit is

47. Kornai, "Some System-Specific Features of Capitalism."
48. Ibid., 7.

sought at a venture and obtained from the venture if successful, but at a risk.[49]

It is a fundamental methodological error, he contends, when social scientists fail to compare different systems.[50] His study of comparison between socialism and capitalism titled *The Socialist System: The Political Economy of Communism* was written when the Berlin Wall was still standing. But by the time he wrote the introduction in the spring of 1991, it had collapsed and the greatest social, political, and economic "laboratory experiment" in Europe had come to an end. He's careful to emphasize that the analysis in his writings are not made on the basis of a critique of the personalities of the top leaders or mistakes made by planners. He believes the "system is incapable of stepping away from its own shadow"[51] because it is "unable to renew itself internally."[52] He discovers, for instance, that the causes of shortage and inflation in the "classical socialist economy" are indeed multifaceted. Leaving the "phenomena and causes of shortage"[53] aside, he shows that "classical socialism, in spite of its promises, is not capable of a high level of efficiency."[54] He admits that there is no one reason for economic inefficiency and lack of technical progress. But one characteristic feature of the classical socialist economy is that *human innovation "does not produce a particular advantage, and a poor performance does not lead to a failure."*[55] In fact, any inefficiency or waste is actually forgotten about because of "soft budget" constraints.[56] On the other hand, participants in the free market economy are open to the possibility of both "loss" and "gain." He describes how it "allows entrepreneurs to undertake the introduction of a new technology, a new form or organization, or a new product . . . The socioeconomic mechanism described by Schumpeter [in *The Theory of Economic Development*] is an explanation of decisive importance for the dynamism of a capitalist

---

49. Ibid., 7–9.

50. David L. Prychitko writes, "The collapse of the Soviet Union and the Eastern Bloc after 1989 seems to suggest that there is empirical power to the Austrian analysis, and has already rekindled some outside interest in the school's approach to comparative analysis (see Kornai, 1990, for example)" ("Comparative Economic Systems," 227, 229). The Kornai reference is to his book *The Road to a Free Economy*.

51. Kornai, *Socialist System*, xxv.

52. Ibid.

53. Ibid., 292.

54. Ibid., 293.

55. Ibid., 297, my emphases.

56. Ibid.

economy."⁵⁷ Finally, Kornai argues that many books are published "on the present [free] economy without comparisons being made with the social- ist system even at the most obvious points. The latter is seen as over and done with, yet authors should be comparing the present with the earlier system precisely because it failed. It failed, for one thing, *because it would not let Schumpeterian enterprise develop.*"⁵⁸

IV. Israel Kirzner: On Human Alertness in the Free Economy

I begin this section with a discussion of the English-born American economist Israel Kirzner's understanding of the development of entre- preneurial action in the free economy. His contribution recaptures and brings into sharper focus the "person-centered" roots of the whole pro- cess. How you evaluate the free economy depends on whether you believe that it actually works. Kirzner understands it as an *ongoing process of cre- ative discovery.* His theory builds on the insights of Mises and Hayek and their understanding of "human action" and the "problem of knowledge" question, respectively. However, into the theory of entrepreneurship he introduces a new dimension into the concept of human action. Entrepre- neurial action expresses itself, according to Kirzner, through the underly- ing category of *human alertness.* Schumpeter and Kirzner are somewhat similar in their views in that they hold "the essence of entrepreneurship lies not necessarily in bearing risk (or even uncertainty) but in stepping outside existing cognitive frameworks."⁵⁹ As we've noted before, the Schumpeterian entrepreneur goes against the current of convention and is guided basically by human "intuition." But the Kirznerian entrepre- neur, on the other hand, is "alert to previously unnoticed possibilities."⁶⁰

Entrepreneurial action, according to Kirzner, is manifest in circum- stances when the entrepreneur is *observant* enough to see the economic

57. Ibid. In support of his assertions Kornai cites the analysis of Peter Murrell in *The Nature of Socialist Economies: Lessons from Eastern European Foreign Trade* and in "An Evolutionary Perspective on Reform of the Eastern European Economies." These studies show "the lack of Schumpeterian entrepreneurs as the gravest shortcoming of both the prereform and the reformed socialist economy." See Kornai, *Socialist System,* 297 n. 42.

58. Kornai, "Some System-Specific Features of Capitalism," 9, my emphases.

59. Langlois, "Risk and Uncertainty," 121–22.

60. Ibid., 122.

opportunities (*profits*) that have not yet been exploited by others. The entrepreneur acts *creatively*, he argues, by discovering novel opportunities mapped out by free market conditions. He clearly sees great similarities between his own theory of entrepreneurship and the Misesian perspective. Profit opportunities, for Kirzner, emerge in imperfect situations when you have price differentiation between sellers and buyers. In a situation of perfect equilibrium, that is, in a perfectly coordinated economic world, any profit advantages have already been taken up. Thus, there is no need for human entrepreneurial action. But that is not economic reality, as we know it. Instead, in the *real world* there are problems with proper economic harmonization. This is a result of the *"knowledge problem"* which was explained in the previous chapter, that is, the fact that human knowledge and information even in the free market are limited. It is important to observe here that you essentially have a *"knowledge problem"* in the market economy because human freedom is at work. As we have seen János Kornai outline, in the classical socialist economy there is really no knowledge predicament because the *"unknown"* is *"known"* by the planner, or, at least the solution is the dilemma for the central controller. Here Kirzner builds upon Hayek's epistemological focus of placing the knowledge dilemma at the center of the free market dynamic.[61] This is why I suggested in the preceding chapter that the *"socialist calculation debate"*[62] is ultimately an *"anthropological"* one since it concerns what Lonergan called the *"dilemma of the human subject"* who's the one who is knowing. The central planner can never fully know the *unknown unknown*, and so he can never solve the *human predicament*. This nature of human knowing "is essential to man," as it is "this which constitutes the ontological basis of his dignity."[63]

Indeed, it is interesting that the Nobel Prize–winning economist Joseph Stiglitz, in outlining how standard economic theory eschewed the topic of human "innovation," refers directly to Schumpeter's and Hayek's contributions. He observes that as "mainstream economists grasped the importance of innovation, they began to try to develop theories that explained its level and direction. As they did so, they re-examined some

61. Mises wrote on epistemological issues too in his *Epistemological Problems of Economics*.

62. This refers to the ongoing discussion about how a socialist economy could perform economic calculation given that various elements like the law of value, money and financial prices for capital goods and the means of production would be missing. See Mises's *Socialism*.

63. See Zięba, *Papal Economics*, 159.

ideas that had been put forth by two great economists of the first half of the twentieth century, Joseph Schumpeter and Friedrich Hayek, that somehow had been left out by the mainstream."[64] So, in line with a growing understanding of the role of knowledge and entrepreneurial action in economics, Israel Kirzner, rather like Hayek, claimed that "the kind of 'knowledge' required for entrepreneurship is 'knowing where to look for knowledge' rather than knowledge of substantive market information. The word which captures most closely this kind of 'knowledge' seems to be *alertness*. It is true that '*alertness*,' too, may be hired; but one who hires an employee alert to possibilities of discovering knowledge has himself displayed alertness of a still higher order."[65]

The free economy rather than being "*monocentric*" is "*polycentric*" in nature and is composed of purposive individuals. No one mind can possess all the necessary knowledge and information for the free market process to function adequately. Kirzner explains this process in his study *Competition and Entrepreneurship*. He describes how "my understanding of the Misesian view of the entrepreneur and of its similarity to my own can be expressed by characterizing the Misesian view of profit as well as my own as an '*arbitrage*' theory of profit. Profit opportunities arise when the prices of products on the product markets are not adjusted to the prices of resource services on the factor markets. In other words, 'something' is being sold at different prices in two markets, as a result of imperfect communication between the markets . . . The entrepreneur notices this price discrepancy before others do."[66]

The objection could be made here, that the Kirznerian entrepreneur is, therefore, a pure opportunist, and unlike other market participants really "does no work."[67] He is basically a "free rider" in the market process.[68] After all, "the opportunities which he sees . . . are already there . . . even though no other economic agent has as of yet perceived them."[69] But this critique rather than being fatal actually opens up an essential human dimension that is vital in understanding entrepreneurial action. What can be properly questioned in this instance is the very concept of "work,"

64. Stiglitz, *Freefall*, 271.

65. Kirzner, *Competition and Entrepreneurship*, 68, my emphases.

66. Ibid., 85.

67. Grassl et al., *Austrian Economics*, 19.

68. With the term "free rider," I essentially mean that the entrepreneur is seen as taking "profit" without doing anything in return for it.

69. Grassl et al., *Austrian Economics*, 19.

which, it is claimed, the entrepreneur does not do. Let me explain what I mean. Kirzner in his discussion of the entrepreneur makes an important distinction between what he terms "*economizing*" behavior and the "broader Misesian notion of *human action*."[70] Why does he make this differentiation? It was Lionel Robbins (1898–1984) who was responsible for the famous definition of economics as "the science which studies human behaviour as a relationship between ends and scarce means which have alternative uses."[71] Kirzner believes, and I would agree, that this characterization of human action in the free market is misleading and incomplete. He's essentially saying that the concept of human action conceived of in this Robbinsian perspective is not anthropologically adequate and it is a reductive understanding of human action in the economic sphere.

Kirzner argues along with Mises for broader horizons in any study of human action and in terms of the very concept of entrepreneurial action itself. He observes, "as developed by Mises, the concept of *homo agens* is capable of all that can be achieved by using the notions of economizing and of the drive for efficiency. But the human-action concept, unlike that of allocation and economizing, does not confine the decision-maker (or the economic analysis of his decisions) to a framework of *given* ends and means."[72] In Robbins's economic perspective *human choice* was, of course, central to the economic element of life. There are obviously strong Austrian influences on Robbins in this respect. Indeed, the economist Jörg Guido Hülsmann remarks how the Austrian influence on the London School of Economics "developed slowly during the 1920s, especially through Mises's impact on the young Lionel Robbins."[73] But still the Robbinsian concept of choice is restricted to the "given ends and means" context. One is left with the questions: what is the "choice" of the "choice"—or indeed, how and why is it arrived at? In other words, if the ends are already given, as are the means, then the choice is not a real choice because the human action is thereby necessary. A necessary choice in this sense is not a free choice at all. Kirzner elaborates this point when he writes, "Human action, in the sense developed by Mises, involves courses of action taken by the human being 'to remove uneasiness' . . . *Being broader than the notion of economizing, the concept*

70. Kirzner, *Competition and Entrepreneurship*, 32–33.

71. *Essay on the Nature and Significance of Economic Science*, 16.

72. Kirzner, *Competition and Entrepreneurship*, 33.

73. Hülsmann, *Mises*, 481.

of human action does not restrict analysis of the decision to the allocation problem posed by the juxtaposition of scarce means and multiple ends.[74]

Human decisions and actions by their very nature cannot be arrived at merely "by mechanical computation."[75] The implicit suggestion of a "given means and ends" framework, as presupposed within some standard economic theories, implies perhaps such a solution. However, the real choice involved in dynamic human action is also inclusive of "*the very perception of the ends-mean framework* within which allocation and economizing is to take place."[76] Human action obviously encompasses economizing action but not all human action is necessarily economizing. The human person has the aptitude to act efficiently and acts therefore in a way typical of the Robbinsian economizers. But the human person cannot be reduced to this function alone but also has the capacity for what Kirzner calls the *alertness* necessary to act so as to "identify which ends to strive for and which means are available."[77]

If any analysis of human action in the economic dimension is limited solely to economizing type behavior it runs the risk of jettisoning an important element of human action. We return here to the central point that Kornai, for example, struggled with in terms of the possible fracture between economic theory and human reality in economics. He witnessed this personally and it led to a conversion in his own intellectual journey. As previously described, Voegelin and other philosophers also reflected on this challenge and the "undying struggle" there is in terms of the acquisition of "theoretical relevance" or what I have called "theoretical dignity" as a satisfactory account for understanding the "acting person" in the free economy. In contrast to any positivist understanding of science Voegelin argued that science is about the "study of reality,"[78] or, at least the search for the truth of that reality. An essential element in the meaning of science is as I have already said that it can be considered "as a truthful account of the structure of reality."[79] Thus, any investigation into the reality of human action and the role of the human person as he or she functions in the economy must measure up to the truth and wealth of the human person.

74. Kirzner, *Competition and Entrepreneurship*, 33.

75. Ibid.

76. Ibid.

77. Ibid., 34.

78. Voegelin, *New Science of Politics*, 91.

79. Ibid.

My overall viewpoint is positive since I think economic writers in general take into account the importance of an adequate economic anthropology. Certainly, there is evidence of an increasing prioritization of the "human person" in their reflections and the locating of the driving force of the free economy in the "inner dynamic of human existence."[80] There is a parallel, I believe, between the philosopher David Walsh's suggestion "that philosophy, beginning with Kant, has explicitly shifted from an account of entities and concepts to an existential meditation on the horizon within which it finds itself" and a similar "anthropological shift" in economic writers like Kirzner and others.[81] The legitimacy of their particular anthropological model is obviously always open to discussion and philosophy can make a worthwhile contribution in this area. It is important to avoid what Voegelin terms any *Frageverbot* or restriction where the anthropological question cannot be simply addressed in the intellectual inquiry.[82] Economics is not philosophy nor is philosophy economics but each can enrich the other in the search for the truth of human reality. I actually have no doubt that most economists are cognizant of the fact that economics is actually based upon a philosophical perspective about the human person. Stiglitz, a case in point, adverts to the importance of the anthropological question when he reminds us that the two critical questions which preoccupied him as a graduate student were the assumptions "concerning information and those concerning the nature of man himself."[83] The continuous challenge for the philosopher is to draw out the philosophical image of the human person whose actions are the subject of analysis in economic thinking. That "person" is, admittedly, often—like Adam's Smith's "invisible hand"—active but perhaps "ghostly" and hidden beneath the economic drama.

Stiglitz actually challenges the model of the human person often employed in economics. And I view this in a positive light because to have the question in the first place is often the beginning of knowledge. Stiglitz suggests it is the classic *Homo economicus* who repulses most people, that is, the model of "a calculating, rational, self-serving, and

80. See Walsh, *Modern Philosophical Revolution*, 95.

81. Ibid., xiii.

82. David Walsh writes, "Voegelin identifies the points at which in one way or another that awareness is countered by the *Frageverbot*. Certain questions are not permitted." See Walsh, introduction to Voegelin, *Crisis and the Apocalypse of Man*, 23.

83. Stiglitz, *Freefall*, 248.

self-interested individual."[84] There seems to be no space in this for "human empathy, public spiritedness, or altruism."[85] Stiglitz is rather caustic here and suggests that the economist or indeed the student of economics usually ends up becoming the image and likeness of their own model. But he does mention in passing that in *The Theory of Moral Sentiments* Adam Smith had already outlined a positive set of human characteristics associated with the acting person in economics.[86] Smith's development of a theory of morality in this work which he revised contemporaneously right up to the writing of the *Wealth of Nations*, actually reveals an understanding of morality based on the principle of reciprocity. Smith wrote, "every faculty in one man is the measure by which he judges of the like faculty in another. I judge of your sight by my sight, of your ear by my ear, of your reason by my reason, of your resentment by my resentment, of your love by my love. I neither have, nor can have, any other way of judging about them."[87]

It is true that even going back to Smith there is always been a consideration of the importance of the "other" in economic and moral thought. If you look at Smith's earlier but little studied book *The Theory of Moral Sentiments* (1759), you'll find him making reference to the importance of concepts like sympathy, or as we might say, putting oneself in the other's shoes in order to make moral decisions. He gives the example of torture and explains that in order to understand the "other" we've to "enter as it were into his body, and become in some measure the same person with him."[88] Smith also speaks of the use of the "impartial spectator" who acts like a "mirror" (the "Other as Me"), which helps me reflect upon the decisions I should make in human action. He states that the human person "naturally desires, not only to be loved, but to be lovely; or to be that thing which is the natural and proper object of love. He naturally dreads, not only to be hated, but to be hateful; or to be that thing which is the natural and proper object of hatred."[89]

Later on, of course, in Smith's more famous *Wealth of Nations* (written in 1776, the same year as the Declaration of Independence) he applies

84. Ibid., 249.
85. Ibid.
86. Stiglitz, *Freefall*, 249 n. 21.
87. Smith, *Theory of Moral Sentiments*, 19.
88. Ibid., 9.
89. Ibid., 113–14.

the insight of the significance of the "other" to economic life, when he speaks about the importance of a "division of labor" and "specialization" in human action, if an economic society is to develop. So, we can see clearly, that Smith and others know that society works better if we facilitate the "interdependent" dimension of human reality. But it is true to say that this dimension is eclipsed from our normal understanding of economics. We've ended up not necessarily knowing *why* we need the "other" or *who* they are. So, they can really remain strangers to us in the whole process.[90]

V. Toward a More Comprehensive Vision of the Acting Human Person

So, Kirzner's contribution to the debate on the anthropological model used in economics stresses that an adequate understanding of the human person who is the progenitor of action in the economic dimension cannot be arrived at by an analysis limited to "*economizing behavior.*" If we constrain ourselves to one aspect of economic action in terms of economic efficiency and try then to comprehend economics in this sense alone, we will never adequately account for the reality of the human person or economic action as such. This is to analyze a fragment of the reality of the human person and their behavior and interpret it as the whole. Entrepreneurial action, for example, cannot be understood in terms of the category of "economizing action" alone. Indeed, the entrepreneurial act interpreted as being in the Schumpeterian sense "destructive" of the status quo could be said, in fact, to be wasteful and inefficient economic action.

As previously suggested, Kirzner favors the much broader Misesian perspective on human action in order to explain the economic drama. This is significant, I suggest, in terms of arriving at an adequate philosophical interpretation of human entrepreneurial action. You can develop a wider understanding of the concept of human action in economics only if you have a more comprehensive concept of the human person. We've seen that most economists do not necessarily outline a specific anthropology. But it is possible to philosophically "X-ray" their writings

90. This is a corrective to Murray Rothbard's reading of Adam Smith, which I have covered in chapter 4. See also the reference to Otteson's approach in the same chapter.

and try to discern the nature of the human person who "*acts*" in the economic framework. For Mises, for example, all knowledge of human action depends on the important methodological distinction between the study of human beings and the study of "things" like "stones, molecules, or atoms."[91] There is a profound difference between the two, according to him, because "individual human beings are conscious . . . they adopt values, and make choices—*act*—on the basis of trying to attain those values and goals."[92] A philosophy that treats "people as if they were stones and atoms, whose behavior could be predicted and determined according to quantitative laws"[93] cannot, for instance, satisfactorily account for entrepreneurial action nor indeed explain the working of the free market economy.

Thus, Mises and Kirzner seek to guard against any such philosophically reductive approach in their treatment of economic action and of entrepreneurial action in particular. And current economic writings reflect this increasing awareness of the need for a comprehensive philosophy of the human person. An essential point in the study of the reality of entrepreneurial action is that no one can actually predict this action in the free economy and this is a unique anthropological characteristic. Kirzner clearly shows that the entrepreneur in his or her actions within the free market process can be understood as efficient, or to use the economic term, as "economizing." But grafted into entrepreneurial action, because of its inherent human nature, is the further possibility of *alertness or insight* regarding "fresh goals and the discovery of hitherto unknown resources with which *homo agens* is endowed."[94] If economic inquiry focuses solely on an analysis of the act of choice within a purely given "ends-means" perspective, it obfuscates the human *insight* and capacity that enables choice to be made in the first place. Choice, in order to be true human decision, must initially be a choice between alternatives. Choice is after all a consequence of the unique human capacity of *alertness* and this presupposes understanding the human person in a broader perspective.[95] To have the choice to choose and be *alert* to this capacity is a singularly human act and a distinguishing attribute.

91. Rothbard, *Ludwig von Mises*, 44.

92. Ibid.

93. Ibid., 45.

94. Kirzner, *Competition and Entrepreneurship*, 34.

95. There is a certain parallel here, I suggest, with Voegelin's "understanding of consciousness in the fullness of its dimensions" and as not just limited to "the

This dimension of human awareness or alertness that "is absent from the notion of economizing but very much present in that of human action"[96] is what Kirzner calls, "the *entrepreneurial* element in human decision-making."[97] This opens up broader horizons in terms of moving toward a more comprehensive understanding of the anthropology that underpins economic actions. Once the entrepreneurial dimension and action is reflected upon, I argue that a more dynamic picture of the human person is revealed—a person who is "active, creative, and human rather than [understood] as passive, automatic, and mechanical."[98] Therefore, human decision-making can no longer be explained just "in terms of maximization, of 'passive' reaction that takes the form of adopting the 'best' course of action" as dictated by the circumstances.[99]

Kirzner observes that there are clear connections with the Misesian understanding of the entrepreneur. For Mises, too, the unit of analysis "is *not* the act of choice" in the limited "ends-means" context.[100] The verb "to act" in Mises's understanding includes the original *discovery* of different opportunities for human action. This implies openness to learning by the economic participants in the economy. The entrepreneur is open to "profit" but also to the possibility of failure and "loss." This reality actually "facilitates heuristic learning among market participants."[101] Kirzner argues that any analysis of entrepreneurial action that limits itself to purely "allocative explanations,"[102] will fail in its attempt to understand "the pattern of change in an individual's decisions"[103] which is the heuristic outcome resulting from "the unfolding experience of the decisions themselves."[104]

If knowledge were perfect there would be no need for the entrepreneurial element. The human person could perfectly well operate and act toward specific "ends" using known "means." As Kirzner describes it, "In

consciousness of objects of the external world." See Voegelin, *Autobiographical Reflections*, 99, 71.

96. Kirzner, *Competition and Entrepreneurship*, 35.

97. Ibid.

98. Ibid.

99. Ibid.

100. Kirzner, *Ludwig von Mises*, 86.

101. Meadowcroft, *Ethics of the Market*, 23.

102. Kirzner, *Competition and Entrepreneurship*, 36.

103. Ibid.

104. Ibid.

such a world there would be no scope for the entrepreneurial element. If each individual knows with certainty what to expect, his plans can be completely explained in terms of economizing, of optimal allocation, and of maximizing—in other words, his plans can be shown to be in principle implicit in the data which constitutes his knowledge of all the present and future circumstances relevant to his situation."[105]

But human life and the economic drama we act in are not like this. In the situation where perfect knowledge and economic equilibrium are presumed, change certainly can only be explained by external circumstances. An earthquake, for example, can quickly change the "means" that are at our disposal and this can account for alteration in the economy. This model nonetheless cannot explain the normal transformation that occurs in the free market process. In the economic realm alteration mostly occurs within, that is, internally. Economic research shows that most innovation comes from the inside. Some innovators do come from outside, like the American Internet entrepreneur Jeff Bezos, who had no prior knowledge of selling books and so on. He originally worked at a hedge fund but he went on to create Amazon.com. Dramatic transformations from outside are actually rather rare. For example, Bill Gates and Paul Allen were "attuned to the opportunity presented by the launch of personal computers in 1975 because they had been computer hackers at high school."[106] Google too had internal origins since it "grew out of search algorithms that Larry Page and Sergey Brin developed as PhD students at Stanford."[107]

This type of change and innovation cannot be accounted for if we treat the participants in the market economy as things, as "molecules or atoms," or, as Kirzner describes them, as mere "economizing" agents. It is only if we enlarge our horizons in our interpretation of human action that we can seek to explain the dynamics of transformation constitutive of the market economy. When we widen our perspectives on human action this necessarily implies and leads to what I call an "*enhanced anthropology.*" This philosophy of the human person is, I believe, central to understanding the workings of the economy. Unfortunately, a clear articulation of a proper understanding of the reality of the human person in terms of the social, political, or economic dimensions of human life often goes

105. Ibid., 37.
106. Bhidé, *Call for Judgment*, 33.
107. Ibid.

"unsaid." It is rather like Gandhi's allegedly saying about Western society that "it would be a good idea" but it has never fully put into practice.[108]

It might seem somewhat paradoxical to claim that it is in the context of an "imperfect articulation" that distinctly anthropological features of the free market process emerge into clearer relief. But this is not unknown in other fields like that of anthropological research. As previously mentioned John F. Crosby, for instance, observes, "It is a well known psychological fact that a thing often shows itself with particular clarity when we are deprived of it, or when we see the thing being violated or ignored where it should be noticed."[109] This suggests it is through a type of *via negativa* investigation that we can gain greater insights into an understanding of human action and more specifically into entrepreneurial action. This moreover requires a Kirznerian type of *alertness* or *awareness* of the different methods we employ in our investigation. In terms of the methodological question Voegelin observed that, obviously, "different objects require different methods."[110] This is why even in terms of "theoretical relevance" I believe that investigation into the anthropology at the basis of the free economy is useful, because it helps us capture a satisfactory account of the structure of economic reality. Voegelin remarked, "If the method has brought to essential clarity the dimly seen, then it was adequate; if it has failed to do so, or even if it has brought to essential clarity something in which we are concretely not interested, then it has proved inadequate."[111]

It is my view that Mises and Kirzner bring to light important anthropological dimensions like the focus on human action and alertness respectively, which are important factors in the operation of the free market process. These are also developed and highlighted by some modern-day economists.[112] Many criticisms have also been made of Kirzner's theory of entrepreneurship. I will just mention two important ones. Firstly, critics mention how "the central concept of alertness" is analytically weak.[113] Kirzner's analysis of the market process has the notion of error at

108. See Casey, *Murray Rothbard*, 122.

109. Crosby, *Selfhood of the Human Person*, 9.

110. Voegelin, *New Science of Politics*, 91.

111. Ibid., 92.

112. I refer the reader to economic studies discussed in this chapter, such as Frydman and Goldberg, *Imperfect Knowledge*. See an interview with Frydman, "Kicking Over Former Models," *Business and Finance*, 1 February 2008, http://www.econ.nyu.edu/user/frydmanr/pdf/20080201_ireland.pdf; and Amar Bhidé's *A Call for Judgment*.

113. Gloria-Palermo, *Evolution of Austrian Economics*, 105.

its center but "the idea of individual erroneous behaviour in this context does present some problems."[114] It is the case that the concept of alertness allows Kirzner "to play at will with various levels of perception."[115] But at the same time it is important to keep in mind that "error stems from a lack of alertness on the part of an agent"[116] who has made a decision "on the basis of less information than he could have used with a little more concentration."[117] Rothbard develops the critique when he observes that

> Kirzner sees the only function of the entrepreneur, and his only necessary quality, to exercise "alertness": to catch the market signals earlier than the next guy. In Kirzner's favorite metaphor, a $10 bill lies on the ground. Many people do not see that bill; but the entrepreneur is more alert than his fellows, and so he is the first to see, and to snatch that bill. Superior alertness, alertness to the truth out there, accounts for entrepreneurial profits . . . If superior alertness accounts for entrepreneurial profits, what in the Kirznerian world can account for entrepreneurial losses? The answer is nothing.[118]

Secondly, Kirzner's theory undervalues the speculative and creative aspects of entrepreneurial action. This is clearly seen when you contrast the Schumpeterian profile of the entrepreneur with the Kirznerian perspective. Kirzner writes that in Schumpeter

> the essence of entrepreneurship is the ability to break away from routine, to destroy existing structures, to move the system away from the even, circular flow of equilibrium. For us, on the other hand, the crucial element in entrepreneurship is the ability to see unexploited opportunities . . . For Schumpeter the entrepreneur is the disruptive, disequilibrating force that dislodges the market from the somnolence of equilibrium; for us the entrepreneur is the equilibrating force whose activity responds to the existing tensions and provides those corrections for which the unexploited opportunities have been crying out.[119]

114. Ibid., 106.

115. Ibid., 106–7.

116. Ibid., 107.

117. Ibid.

118. Rothbard, "The Present State of Austrian Economics," https://mises.org/library/present-state-austrian-economics.

119. Kirzner, *Competition and Entrepreneurship*, 127.

Clearly, the Schumpeterian theory of entrepreneurial action is seen in terms of the activity of *creation* whereas the Kirznerian philosophy looks upon it as the activity of human *discovery*. The visions of the role of entrepreneurial action are very diverse among economists and even between members of the Austrian school. But notwithstanding these differences, this points to the fact that the varying accounts of the crucial role of the entrepreneur in the free market process are all based upon particular perspectives about human knowledge, human nature and capacity. In other words, the various views themselves are based upon anthropological perspectives on the human person who is *Homo agens* in the free economy.

There is ample evidence of a Copernican-type shift in economic writers where *Homo agens* as opposed to *Homo economicus* becomes increasingly more central in the interpretation of the free market process.[120] This is seen in the resurgence of interest in the Austrian insights into economics that I have outlined. The contemporary economist William J. Baumol, for example, places human entrepreneurial *action* at the center of the free economy. He comments, "in accounting for the extraordinary growth performance of the capitalist economies . . . we cannot overlook the role of the entrepreneur."[121] Baumol explains how the entrepreneur is indeed "one of the most intriguing and elusive in the cast of characters that constitutes the subject of economic analysis."[122] Schumpeter and Frank Knight, he says, succeeded somewhat in "infusing this character with life"[123] but then like a disappearing stream, the entrepreneur seems to disappear underground until "entrepreneurs have . . . virtually disappeared from mainstream theoretical literature."[124] He refers to recent empirical studies that have shown "that the entrepreneurial function is a vital component in the process of growth of output and productivity."[125] He concludes his discussion on the significance of the entrepreneur by declaring that "the absence of entrepreneurs is sometimes stated as a significant obstacle to growth. Whether or not they are assigned the starring

120. Even though I mentioned in chapter 3 that this idea of a "Copernican shift" has to be qualified since we are dealing with a rediscovery of the original anthropological roots of the free economy.

121. Baumol, *Free-Market Innovation Machine*, 58.

122. Ibid.

123. Ibid.

124. Ibid.

125. Ibid.

role, they are clearly not considered minor characters."[126] Baumol refers to the elusive nature of the concept of entrepreneurial action insofar as the economic theorist is concerned. This is because human "innovation" is by its very nature a *"heterogeneous act."* A creative act like economic innovation is something new "that has never been carried out before," and if it is repeated it is no longer new and therefore no longer innovative.[127]

As we've remarked, economic theorists rarely refer to what their anthropological model is, so questions about the nature of the human person arise more often than not indirectly. Although Baumol does not directly discuss the question of a human anthropology, the issues he deals with suggest the importance of such a philosophical perspective. The adequate articulation of an economic theory of innovation remains "elusive" primarily because "creativity" is after all an imprint of the reality of the acting human person. This is by its very nature difficult to characterize and it cannot be explained in purely economic categories. The very irreducibility of the human person accounts for the difficulty in arriving at a clear articulation of entrepreneurial action. As Baumol observes, "There is a good reason why entrepreneurship should elude the theorist, because by its very nature we cannot describe exactly what entrepreneurs do."[128]

VI. Economics' Need for a Higher Anthropological Viewpoint

Kirzner's distinction between "economizing" and "entrepreneurial" action, for instance, suggests to me the necessity for the articulation of a satisfactory philosophy of the human person in order to explain human action more comprehensively in the economic domain. Mises in his analysis of human action also stresses the need for a thoroughgoing explanation in the praxeological attempt to "describe what it is" in terms of human action at the level of economics.[129] He observes that "the science of human behavior—as far as it is not physiology—cannot abandon reference to meaning and purpose. It cannot learn anything from animal psychology . . . .The subject matter of praxeology is human action. It deals with acting man, not with man transformed into a plant and reduced to a

126. Ibid.
127. Ibid.
128. Ibid.
129. Mises, *Human Action*, 29.

merely vegetative existence."[130] So, if we are not to fall into a "general bias" resulting in decline rather than progress in a particular area of research, we must perforce take cognizance of the broader issues or, as Lonergan terms them, the "higher viewpoints." Previously we noted how Lonergan commented that "every specialist runs the risk of turning his speciality into a bias by failing to recognise and appreciate the significance of other fields. Common sense almost invariably makes that mistake; for it is incapable of analyzing itself, incapable of making the discovery that it too is a specialized development of human knowledge, incapable of coming to grasp that its peculiar danger is to extend its legitimate concern for the concrete and the immediately practical into disregard of larger issues and indifference to long-term results."[131]

Likewise, economists need to "appreciate the significance of other fields" and in this regard economic anthropology can perform an *integrating function* in economic reflection.[132] Mises alludes to this when he challenges economics as a science to forego any postulation based on a reductive concept of the human person. He wrote "economics does not assume or postulate that men aim only or first of all at what is called material well-being. Economics as a branch of the more general theory of human action, deals with all human action, i.e., with man's purposive aiming at the attainment of ends chosen, whatever these ends may be."[133] The concept of a "higher viewpoint" is not meant in a pejorative sense. In the Halifax lectures Lonergan offers some reflections on the role of philosophy and the necessity of higher viewpoints that are useful in understanding the Misesian focus upon human action if any worthwhile investigation into economics is to happen. Lonergan says that

> many human scientists are trying to ride the bandwagon of the physicists and chemists, and a science of man is pursued as though man were just another electron or another atom. As long as human science is of that type, as long as it is carried out in that manner, we shall have creeping socialism. For if the scientific knowledge of man is in terms of the types of knowledge that are possible of electrons and atoms, then there is no question of developing a science of man that can speak to man. Rather, we simply develop scientists who are consultants to government,

130. Ibid.
131. Lonergan, *Insight*, 251.
132. Ibid.
133. Mises, *Human Action*, 884.

thereby giving government more power to control man. If philosophy is not attempting an *integration* of the sciences in the
proper sense, then it cannot exert an influence upon the human
sciences.[134]

Human actions speak of the human person who is the author of
those actions. The "broader Misesian notion of *human action*" and the
subsequent Kirznerian perspectives are, I suggest, cognizant of the need
for a "higher anthropological viewpoint" when it comes to an adequate
articulation of entrepreneurial action in the free economy.[135] When the
entrepreneur, for example, comes up against opportunities (profits) or
difficulties (losses), he or she has to be alert and to use his or her intelligence to reformulate original conceptions. Lonergan's philosophical
description of the role of "higher viewpoints" can be applied in trying
to explicate the anthropological principle underlying the entrepreneurial
act. He describes how "when it [human intelligence] comes up against
difficulties, intelligence starts all over again, reformulating all of its fundamental conceptions. This is the result of further insights that constitute
a *higher viewpoint* with respect to the previous set of insights."[136]

The necessity of a higher viewpoint is evident even in areas of study
like mathematics, chemistry and physics. Lonergan describes how "for
the forms on any given level, there is a set of laws."[137] Then "schemes of
recurrence" can be developed from the set of laws.[138] The mathematician,
physicist or chemist possesses the ability to be able to bring to light these
recurrent patterns. Normally, the events that occur within chemistry,
for example, can be explained on the level of the laws of chemistry but
sometimes this is not the case and there is need for a "higher viewpoint"
in order to understand the occurrence. Lonergan writes,

> In the biological unit of the cell, there is taking place a continu-
> ous release of chemical actions, and every one of those actions
> occurs in accordance with the laws of chemistry. But if it is not
> possible through chemical laws and the schemes of recurrence
> that can be devised in chemistry to account for the regularity
> with which those chemical processes take place in the cell, you
> have to appeal to a *higher viewpoint* [my emphasis] to account

134. Lonergan, *Understanding and Being*, 95–96, my emphasis.
135. Kirzner, *Competition and Entrepreneurship*, 32–33.
136. Lonergan, *Understanding and Being*, 204, my emphasis.
137. Ibid.
138. Ibid.

for the regularity, and you introduce conjugate forms on the biological level with their laws and schemes. If in the animal you find regularities that cannot be accounted for by the totality of laws and schemes of recurrence on the biological level, you postulate another higher level.[139]

If you "X-ray" human entrepreneurial action what essentially emerges is the need for a specific anthropological level, that is, Lonergan's "higher viewpoint," in order to comprehensively explain the human action involved in the entrepreneurial "act." This has been outlined in the brief expositions on the Misesian and Kirznerian theories of entrepreneurship but will be developed philosophically in the final chapters. As we've seen Kirzner clearly states how "entrepreneurial action" cannot be explained solely by "economizing action." He explains that "economizing consists in the allocation of scarce resources among competing ends. *Acting*, in the praxeological sense, consists in selecting a pattern of behavior designed to further the actor's purposes. Of course, the particular allocation that, in any given situation, will be made of scarce means in respect of different ends will constitute a course of action, a pattern of conduct designed to further the achievement of as many of those goals . . . as possible. But the *concept of action is wider* and at the same time more fundamental than that of economizing."[140]

In the next chapter I give an outline of how the real wellspring of human wealth, namely the human person, is revealed in the example of the Foxford Woolen Mills entrepreneurial project in Ireland. We'll see how the entrepreneur Agnes Morrogh-Bernard, just as she harnessed the powers of the river Moy, also unfolded and recaptured the truth of the "creative" reality of the human person. Hers is an example of the "prioritization of the human subject" over theoretical abstraction because she understood that alienation couldn't be reduced to a purely material level as in Marx, and that human dignity can be realized in creative action by all the participants in the economic drama of life.

139. Ibid., 205.
140. Kirzner, *Economic Point of View*, 161, my emphases.

8

The Real Wellspring of Human Wealth Revealed: An Example from the Foxford Mills Entrepreneurial Project

I. Introduction: An Illuminating Visit to Foxford

DURING RESEARCH FOR THIS book, I made a trip to visit the Providence Woolen Mills, Foxford, County Mayo, in Ireland. Agnes Morrogh-Bernard, of the Irish Sisters of Charity founded the Woolen Mills there in 1892.[1] At the time of my visit I was reflecting on the primacy of person-centered economic creativity in the free market process. I was preparing a philosophical reflection on the role of the entrepreneur, using the writings of Austrian economists like Joseph Schumpeter and others. The occlusion of the importance of entrepreneurial human creativity and its function from the free market process is evident as we've seen. As I said in chapter five Schumpeter had traced the existence of human initiative and creativity to a period prior to the historical emergence of capitalism. This is because the anthropological reality of human creativity actually pertains to the reality and constitution of what it means to be a human person and is therefore not solely an economic phenomenon. So the visit to Foxford was significant because it gave me an insight into and an example of the unfolding of the "*charismatic entrepreneurial spirit*" in the drama of human life on my own island of Ireland. It is thought provoking that if we go back, in fact, to Schumpeter's original notion of the entrepreneur, the German

---

1. The Congregation are now called the Religious Sisters of Charity.

word *Unternehmergeist* actually suggests "the external and technical aspects of entrepreneurship"[2] but also includes the idea of "the 'spirituality' of the entrepreneurial person."[3] The Franco-Hibernian economist Richard Cantillon (1680–1734) was the first to use the term *entrepreneur*.[4] As we've already seen Schumpeter noted how Cantillon "had a clear conception of the function of the entrepreneur."[5] In earlier chapters we've covered how Schumpeter actually recovered the originating sense of the role of the entrepreneur in human economic action.

In our discussion on Schumpeter, I stated how he makes the interesting point, which Murray Rothbard also makes, that it was through Cantillon that the French economists retained this original insight into the role of the entrepreneur. But the insight was actually lost or eclipsed when it came to the English and Scottish economists. And as we know Schumpeter argued that Adam Smith had in this way basically "shunted economics off on a wrong road, a road unfortunately different from that of his continental forbears."[6] In his examination of the classical economists on the theme of the *actors* in the economic process, Schumpeter claimed that there was indeed significant but slow development in the distinction between what he calls "the businessman's *industria* from the workman's *labor*."[7] Even going back to the times of St. Antoninus of Florence a "differentiation" in human economic understanding between the two functions had already taken place.

In the contemporary context, I want to refer to the emergence of interesting new horizons in philosophical thinking applicable to economic reality. I have in mind the writings of Professor David Walsh, an American political philosopher.[8] His philosophical *oeuvre* is singularly enlightening in the context of the emergence of new revolutionary philosophical perspectives in terms of our understanding of a person-centered

2. See Habisch and Loza Adaui, "Entrepreneurial Spirit," 219.

3. Ibid.

4. Schumpeter, *History of Economic Analysis*, 222, 555, 646.

5. Ibid., 222.

6. Rothbard, *Economic Thought before Adam Smith*, 437.

7. Ibid.

8. Walsh is a professor of politics at the Catholic University of America. He has written a trilogy concerning the modern world: *After Ideology: Recovering the Spiritual Foundations of Freedom*; *The Growth of the Liberal Soul*; and *The Modern Philosophical Revolution: The Luminosity of Existence*. He also edited three volumes of the Collected Works of Eric Voegelin. His *Politics of the Person as the Politics of Being* (2015) is his most recent book.

economics. It can be applied in particular to giving philosophical dignity
to the role of the human person as "entrepreneur" or to use the Schumpeterian terminology the *Unternehmergeist* in the free market process. The
German word *Geist* ("spirit") is rich in meaning. Some commentators
remark how in German idealism "*Geist* refers to a form of rationality able
to unlock the moral and political spirit of a given sociocultural context."[9]
So, *Unternehmergeist* "would indicate the ability of the entrepreneur
to respond adequately to the societal" and human demands of his own
time and place.[10] The entrepreneur is therefore literally the person who
"undertakes" to unfold the spirit of human economic creativity within a
given space and time.[11]

Walsh's writings are a contemporary meditation on the philosophical truth of the reality of the human person. He writes, "A human being
is not just part of the whole; he is also a part that contains the whole."[12]
I consider that his philosophical insights, when applied to human economic action, assist us greatly in understanding that the human person is
not just at the service of the free market process but that a free economy
actually has a "human face." The person is at the heart of the process and
is not merely incidental to its development. He explains that the "human
being is a process or a project, and it is up to each one to take charge of
its development. We are responsible. We are free . . . We create ourselves,
not in the sense that we are the source of our own existence and that our
powers are unlimited, but in the sense that we participate in the work
of self-creation. This is the source of the dignity by which we surpass all
other realities we know.[13]

Otherwise, he argues, we are shrunken "to the level of things,"[14]
reduced to persons "without the need to think,"[15] "to the level of
instruments."[16] If there is no need for the human to reason, no requirement to innovate, the result is an anthropological reduction in itself. A
close reading of economic theorists shows there is plenty of evidence of

9. See Habisch and Loza Adaui, "Entrepreneurial Spirit," 219.

10. Ibid.

11. See Cantillon, *Essay on the Nature of Commerce*, 26.

12. Walsh, *Modern Philosophical Revolution*, 419.

13. Walsh, *Guarded by Mystery*, 26.

14. Ibid., 33.

15. Ibid.

16. Ibid.

the overshadowing of what lies at the heart of the working of the free market system, namely, the essential reality of the human person. This is why modern economic crises cannot be explained in economic terms alone, because all reflections must be guarded by the mystery of the human person and any adequate articulation must seek to illuminate these horizons.

Throughout *Wealth of Persons* we've given consideration to a missing link in economic reflection, that is, the forgotten "anthropological dimension." I turn now to a very specific example of "entrepreneurial creativity" because it is in the creativity of entrepreneurship that we see the real enlargement of the human person occurring. I present a case study of Sr. Arsenius (the name she took on her profession), who founded the Foxford Woolen Mills in Mayo in post-famine Ireland more than a hundred years ago.[17] In this historical case study the "higher viewpoint" in terms of the reality of the human person acting in the economic drama is disclosed where the excitement of creation far outweighs anything purely material. Economics is thus revealed at its core as a spiritual activity. There is no doubt in my mind that the Providence Woolen Mills project innovated by the charismatic Agnes Morrogh-Bernard is a paradigmatic case of the central role of the entrepreneur in the economic process. But it is far more than this because it cannot be analyzed solely on this basis. It is principally an example of the unfolding in the economic dimension of human life of the "creativity" which is constitutive of the human person. It is a paramount illustration of what Walsh describes as "the endless fecundity of human creativity."[18] It is for this reason that we will reflect now in this chapter upon the project itself and the role of its central innovator.

II. The Story of an Irish Industry: A Case in History

Agnes Morrogh-Bernard was born in 1842 at Cheltenham, Gloucestershire, England, at her mother's home. But her early years were spent in County Cork before the family moved to an estate at Sheheree, Killarney, County Kerry. She was born into privilege and wealth, her father being a landed Cork gentleman and her mother being a member of an old English Catholic family. Agnes witnessed at first hand the ravages of famine and rural poverty as Ireland was hit by years of potato blight

17. See Molloy, *Agnes Morrogh-Bernard.*
18. Walsh, *Guarded by Mystery,* 39.

and famine in the 1840s. When she was a small child she had an experience that left "an indelible impression on her mind."[19] The story is told
of a starving woman who came into her father's kitchen while "nettles
were being prepared for the poultry. The poor woman begged to be allowed to satisfy her hunger by eating what was prepared for the farmyard
fowl. The impressionable child was horrified. But more harrowing scenes
could be witnessed in the neighbourhood."[20] The Famine years in Ireland
were cataclysmic with dystopian consequences for both people and society. Cecil Woodham-Smith, the famous narrative historian described
how in 1846 the "autumn was now passing into winter. The nettles and
blackberries, the edible roots and cabbage leaves on which hundreds of
people had been eking out an existence disappeared; flocks of wretched
beings, resembling scarecrows, had combed the blighted potato fields
over and over again until not a fragment of potato that was conceivably
edible remained. Children began to die. In Skibbereen workhouse more
than fifty per cent of the children admitted after October 1, 1846, died;
the deaths, said the workhouse physician, were due to 'diarrhœa acting
on an exhausted constitution.'"[21]

In County Cork where Agnes lived with her parents for some time
the central relief committee of the Society of Friends had reported ter-
rible conditions even in 1846. They observed "a labourer with his wife
and two children sitting round a bit of fire, a younger child lying dead in
its cradle; the poor woman herself suffering want, and the family unable
to provide a coffin for the deceased."[22] The letter of a Cork magistrate sent
to the Irish-born Duke of Wellington is truly shocking. He wrote,

> My Lord Duke, I presume . . . to present . . . the following state-
> ment of what I have myself seen within the last three days . . .
> I entered some of the hovels . . . In the first, six famished and
> ghastly skeletons, to all appearances dead, were huddled in a

19. Gildea, *Mother Mary Arsenius of Foxford*, 12.

20. Ibid.

21. Woodham-Smith, *Great Hunger*, 141–42. There is a rich literature on famine
and on the Irish Famine in particular: Mokyr, *Why Ireland Starved*; Kinealy, *This Great
Calamity*; Ó Gráda, *Black '47 and Beyond*; Ó Gráda, *Eating People Is Wrong*; Ó Gráda,
Famine: A Short History; Ó Gráda, *The Great Irish Famine*; Ó Gráda et al., *Ireland's
Great Famine*; Ó Murchadha, *The Great Famine*; Coogan, *The Famine Plot*; Crowley
et al., *Atlas of the Great Irish Famine*; Delaney, *The Curse of Reason*. Yang Jisheng has
written a book on the Great Famine in China titled *Tombstone: The Untold Story of
Mao's Great Famine*.

22. Gildea, *Mother Mary Arsenius of Foxford*, 13.

> corner on some filthy straw . . . I approached with horror, and
> found by a low moaning they were alive—they were in fever,
> four children, a woman and what had once been a man. It is im-
> possible to go through the detail. Suffice it is to say, that in a few
> minutes I was surrounded by at least 200 such phantoms, such
> frightful spectres as no words can describe, either from famine
> or from fever. Their demoniac yells are still ringing in my ears,
> and their horrible images are fixed upon my brain.[23]

In Foxford, County Mayo, the situation was representative of "the spread
of starvation mortality in the country as a whole."[24] Historical documen-
tation shows that in villages "between Pontoon and Foxford . . . 'entire
families' were 'lying and many dying.'"[25] Parents in Castlebar "were reported to be putting children to bed during the day, in order 'to sleep off
the hunger which was gnawing at their hearts.'"[26]

Agnes Morrogh-Bernard entered the Irish Sisters of Charity in
1863. From 1866 to 1877 she was assigned to teaching and other roles.
But it was in 1890 that she went to the village of Foxford. Thomas Finlay,
professor of classics, philosophy, and political economy in University
College Dublin described the abject poverty of the region at the time. He
wrote that

> the bleak and dreary aspect of nature in this ill-favoured region
> reflected with fidelity the conditions of human life within its
> borders . . . There is a poverty which is pathetic without being
> repellent . . . And there is a poverty which is at once repulsive and
> pitiable, like a disease which disfigures while it kills, a poverty
> in which privation dulls the higher sensibilities and self-respect
> seems extinguished, in which rags and squalor are acquiesced
> in . . . It was a poverty of this latter type which prevailed in the
> district round Foxford. Within a radius of five miles from the
> village some 1,500 human habitations might be counted on
> which it had its seal.[27]

It was into the aftermath of the real dystopian reality of the Irish
famine that Agnes entered. The community reflection on the effects of
the famine even a hundred years after it was, "*Mharbh an gorta achan*

23. Woodham-Smith, *Great Hunger*, 162.

24. Ó Murchadha, *Great Famine*, 62.

25. Ibid.

26. Ibid.

27. Finlay, *Foxford and the Providence Woollen Mills*, 7.

rud," that is, "The Famine killed everything."[28] This included human self-determination, self-esteem and dignity. Ó Murchadha notes how "communal interdependence was replaced by a new familial nuclearity, and a distancing in societal relationships that brought with it a deep personal loneliness and alienation . . . Emigration perpetuated a spiritual and cultural weakening that, when added to continuing hunger and material depreciation, left those remaining on the land confused and demoralized."[29]

But each crisis is also an opportunity for the human spirit to triumph. It can be perhaps an opportune time to try to recapture the truth of the reality of the person-centered dynamic at the heart of a truly free society and economy. The journalist and political activist A. M. Sullivan, writing in post-famine Ireland, observed that in spite of the cataclysmic situation, "other values" were actually characteristic of the post-famine period.[30] These included qualities like a "'great seriousness of character,' as well as 'providence, forethought, economy,' and a greater 'method, strictness and punctuality in business transactions' than had existed before."[31] It is within this context that Agnes Morrogh-Bernard emerges in poverty-stricken Ireland.

The village of Foxford is located on the river Moy, which gathers its waters from a wide area. Its source is close to the Ox Mountains. The river then flows southwards and eventually flows through the village of Foxford. In the village, "it encounters a ledge of granite stretching across its path, and supporting a bridge of six arches . . . A moment later it plunges down to a steep declivity, churned into foaming chaos by a litter of boulders that strew its path."[32] Finlay points out that a visitor who in 1890 stood on the bridge, "if of a practical turn of mind,"[33] would have remarked upon the large force exerted by the swirling river. And "would have asked himself why this force was not turned to useful purpose."[34] In fact, there was evidence that others had similar thoughts because there was a ruin on the right bank of the river. The "structure, a long-disused

28. Ó Murchadha, *Great Famine*, 182.

29. Ibid., 185.

30. Ibid., 189.

31. Ibid.

32. Finlay, *Foxford and the Providence Woollen Mills*, 3.

33. Ibid.

34. Ibid., 5.

corn-store, had once been attached to a mill that in other times utilised the forces of the Moy for the benefit of the surrounding district."[35]

Finlay describes how "the squalid poverty which brooded over this locality"[36] had been unaffected even by the works of the Congested Districts Board[37] or through private philanthropy. There was one person's action, however, which could not be deterred. Finlay dramatically sets the scene:

> One day—a happy day for Foxford and its neighbourhood—a Sister of Charity stood upon the Bridge of Foxford surveying the bleak and dreary landscape which it commanded. She had a quick eye for the evidences of human misery, and they abounded before her . . . Her ambition was stirred. To carry hope into the cheerless gloom of these dismal cabins, to strengthen and uplift the souls which their squalor degraded; in some degree to dispel ignorance, and to diminish the suffering which they housed—this was an enterprise worthy of the service to which she was vowed . . . Given the liberty to act, she would consecrate her energies to the task.[38]

Agnes Morrogh-Bernard eventually established a Woolen Mills at Foxford, harnessing "the unceasing din of the tumultuous waters" of the river Moy for a new industry.[39] But before she did this she sought to make improvements in the social conditions of the local population. She and her community firstly acquired property on which they erected a school and a convent. They then ran community literacy projects for adults, imparting knowledge about new standards of sanitation and housekeeping. Horticulture and animal husbandry were also taught to the inhabitants. Four years after the arrival of the sisters, Mr. Standish O'Grady McDermott stated, "It is no exaggeration to say that all the Acts of Parliament ever passed have not effected in these remote rural districts as much in the cause of sanitation and health, as has been done in a few months by the example and gentle influence of the Sisters of Charity."[40]

35. Ibid.

36. Ibid., 11.

37. Chief Secretary Arthur Balfour established these in 1891 to alleviate poverty and congested living conditions in the west of Ireland.

38. Finlay, *Foxford and the Providence Woollen Mills*, 11–13.

39. Ibid., 19.

40. Gildea, *Mother Mary Arsenius of Foxford*, 94.

Critics of the Irish often spoke of their indolence, of the "listlessness and apathy in regard to economic improvements."[41] But maybe this was not so surprising since, as the bishop of Meath, Dr. Nulty, exclaimed, "Is it in human nature that any one could have the heart or the enterprise to expend his labour and capital on the permanent improvement of the soil exclusively for the benefit of others, and with a certainty that he will be charged an increased rent for the use of his own property?"[42] Nulty's point is, I would argue, neither merely economic nor sociological; it is richly anthropological in that it opens up the great question and reality of what it means to be a human person. As David Walsh clearly outlines, it is in the human being we encounter "the dignity of self-determination"; and its very annihilation leads to our depersonalization.[43] This is true also in terms of the economic horizon in which we live out part of the drama of our own lives. As Saint John Paul II observed, the fundamental failure of Communism could not just be understood in terms of economics, in that it was totally inefficient in the distribution of goods. But its economic system itself was based upon an "anthropological lie." As I have said elsewhere, philosopher Karol Wojtyła (later known as Saint John Paul II) intuited that the main problem with Marxism is not merely a question of the inefficiency of a social system; it is far more deep-seated. He sees the core difficulty as anthropological.[44] It deconstructed the very roots of what it means to be a fulfilled human person, that is, the fecund irreducibility of the creative dimension within us all and the need for its realization. Any suppression of this reality is a denial of the human person's "very nature as a free subject, that is, the *anthropological truth* that humans are creatures capable of choosing how they act."[45]

So, Morrogh-Bernard was well aware that simply tackling questions about literacy, sanitation, health and agriculture would not result in "the root of the distress of Foxford"[46] being addressed.[47] The people she looked upon in that forlorn village and the countryside around had the creativity of their human spirits annihilated and this creativity needed

41. Ibid., 81.
42. Ibid., 83.
43. Walsh, *Guarded by Mystery*, 39.
44. McNerney, *John Paul II*, 153.
45. See Gregg and Preece, *Christianity and Entrepreneurship*, 87.
46. Finlay, *Foxford and the Providence Woollen Mills*, 19.
47. See Lonergan, *Insight*, 596.

to be restored. Mere philanthropic hand-outs could not recover it. She was not just going to tap into the power of the river Moy but also the far deeper strength of human creativity for the common good found in every person. I have made numerous references in this study to Lonergan's useful distinction in terms of his analysis of the good that is the "object of desire" and the "good of order." This can be equally applied to our philosophical investigation into Morrogh-Bernard's entrepreneurial action. For her "human economic action" can be understood in terms of this second level, that is, as concerning a "good of order."

Her charismatic entrepreneurial project was an example of what Walsh in his *Politics of the Person* has called the "flash of self-transcendence." The true path to human progress lies in the human person because economic action or work has human significance. In his final encyclical Pope Benedict XVI unfolds the meaning of what I am suggesting in his articulation of "the full development of the person."[48] He describes how "business activity has a human significance, prior to its professional one. It is present in all work, understood as a personal action, an '*actus personae*,' which is why every worker should have the chance to make his contribution knowing that in some way 'he is working "for himself"' . . . With good reason, Paul VI taught that 'everyone who works is a creator.'"[49]

It is in post-famine Ireland that we find someone like Agnes Morrogh-Bernard emerging with the charismatic entrepreneurial intuition to tap into the power and truth of a "person-centered" understanding of economic development. But she was not alone of her kind. The economic historian Luigino Bruni remarks that within the whole European context, for example,

> the story of humanity is studded with civic and economic experiences that derive from spiritual currents . . . Europe, for example, would not be, as we know it today, also under a social and economic profile, without the Benedictine movement, or the Franciscan one, from which fundamental innovations sprang forth that then laid the groundwork for a market economy . . . The social charisms of many founders of religious orders between the XVIII and XIX centuries, which gave life to hospitals, schools and charitable works, marked the birth and development of the modern welfare state. These are all experiences with ideal and spiritual motivations, certainly, but which

48. Walsh, "Person as the Heart of Benedict's New Evangelization," 6.

49. Benedict XVI, *Charity in Truth: Caritas in Veritate*, no. 41.

have enriched and in some cases also determined the economic and social advancement of our civilization.[50]

III. Agnes Morrogh-Bernard: A Charismatic Entrepreneur of the Human Person

Agnes Morrogh-Bernard searched for assistance from like-minded entrepreneurs in furthering her planned new industry at Foxford. She found great help from a Mr. John Charles Smith of the Caledon Mills, County Tyrone. She wrote to him and explained the situation. They were "without any capital in the most congested poverty-stricken district of the West . . . [they were] anxious to start a Woollen Mills for the relief of destitution."[51] She invited Smith and his business partner Mr. Sherrard to visit her in Foxford. Smith's letter of reply has not been preserved but memories of the first few words of his reply have been recollected. He is said to have replied, "Madam, are you aware that you have written to a Protestant, and a Freemason?"[52]

On 6 June 1891 Smith arrived at Foxford railway station. He went immediately to meet Agnes at the convent. She explained her views and showed him the river, the corn-store and their own household. Gildea relates how "naturally the man of experience scoffed at the idea of un-trained, penniless women secluded from the world, without a knowledge of machinery or business, succeeding when an experienced capitalist like Guinness had failed to make his woollen factory on the [river] Liffey a success."[53] After viewing the area and listening to the plans Smith said, "Well, Madam, the best advice I can offer you is to abandon the idea."[54] Agnes replied, "I am deeply grateful for your kind advice and for your transparent honesty: but I may tell you that we will go on without you. Providence will provide."[55] Smith took off his hat with a courteous bow and said, "Madam, I place myself and my experience of twenty years at

50. See Bruni, "First Challenge: Economy," talk given at Volunteerfest, Buda-pest, 16 September 2006, my translation. See http://www.edc-online.org for Bruni's publications.

51. Gildea, *Mother Mary Arsenius of Foxford*, 98.

52. Ibid.

53. Ibid. Arthur Guinness was an Irish entrepreneur who later went on to found the world-famous Guinness Brewery in Dublin, Ireland.

54. Ibid., 99.

55. Ibid.

your disposal."[56] The encounter had unforgettable repercussions that are felt even today.[57]

A British Member of Parliament, Mr. Burdett-Coutts, was invited to open the first bale of wool. On visiting the factory he declared that after the long journey he had made through the congested districts, "one of the most useful, one of the most productive, one of the most elevating efforts that could be made for the people of Ireland was represented by just such an enterprise as that, which would take the raw material produced by the people, and convert it by their labour, for which they would be duly paid, into a valuable article, and eventually dispose of it in the ordinary commercial market."[58] A Protestant official records an amazing tribute to Agnes's entrepreneurial venture. His name was William J. D. Walker and he was the owner of Glenbanna Mills, Laurencetwon, Co. Down. He was an adviser to the Congested Districts Board and he wrote a confidential report on the Foxford project. He observed,

> In a place like Foxford the difficulties are extraordinary. Where everyone requires to be taught everything, and all at the same time, the management would require to be omnipresent . . . It is only after the lapse of a very considerable time that a place with every factor which contributes to economical production against it, can be expected to hold its own, and I should anticipate that it is only recently that it has become at all possible at Foxford to reach a position where Profit and Loss might be nearly balanced. At Foxford great difficulties have been surmounted, *only ceaseless watchfulness and the most anxious care* have retained the same result in the same time. I had everywhere the clearest indication of this . . . My opinion is that the outlook for Foxford is most hopeful . . . The workers of Providence appear to me to be *active, attentive* and *intelligent* . . . The thorough nature of the work and the enthusiasm of . . . [the workers] astonished me. And there *is a unity and interdependence* pervading the entire business which indicates the *rarest quality of organising ability* . . . Your Board need have no anxiety about the investment. The

56. Ibid.

57. The Foxford Woollen Mills and Visitor Centre is still open today. For information about the actual products sold, profit returns, and the company's progress over the years, see www.foxfordwoollenmills.ie. The company has spent over three million US dollars in major investment in the business and diversified its product range. It originally produced wool blankets and rugs but this diversified into throws, duvet covers, and contemporary furnishings.

58. Gildea, *Mother Mary Arsenius of Foxford*, 108.

return is there already, *in the social and moral elevation of the people*, now for the first time placed within reach of earning competency at home. The interest on capital, which I consider the smallest part of the return, is certain to follow . . . I shall conclude by saying that I have my Northern prejudices, just as markedly accentuated as most men, and if the above report is favourable, it is not because I went there to praise what I saw, but because I have stated nothing but what I believe to be true.[59]

Just as in Plato's parable of the cave[60] where one prisoner is depicted as being set free to painfully ascend toward the light of the Good, Agnes Morrogh-Bernard has been described in her entrepreneurial action as unbolting "the prison in which the workers and their ancestors had been incarcerated for centuries, and given them time to accustom their dim eyes to the light into which she was leading them . . . [Then] the *listless* worker became *industrious*, *clumsiness* was supplanted by *dexterity*, *timidity* gave way to *courage*. The bright gleam was beginning to break through the clouds of darkness."[61] A writer in the *Irish Peasant* observed that "nowhere . . . referring to Foxford . . . have we been struck with the personality of the individual worker as here. He is altogether a different type from the ordinary operator . . . Here he seems an individual who has got an ideal to attain, whose life's sole effort is not confined to the earning of a weekly wage . . . And in this—the actual influence of the mills on the social life of the worker—is the point on which Foxford scores high."[62]

The Irish political economist Thomas Finlay who taught in University College Dublin from 1883 to 1909 had an early intuition into the charismatic entrepreneurial insights of Agnes. He also worked with Horace Plunkett, a member of an ancient Anglo-Irish family, to found the Irish Agricultural Co-operative Movement. Plunkett reports that it was

59. Ibid., 113–15, my emphases.

60. See Plato, *Republic*, Book VII, 514a–520a. "Then think what would naturally happen to them [prisoners] if they were released from their bonds and cured of their delusions. Suppose one of them were set loose, and suddenly compelled to stand up" (515 c-d). Eric Voegelin comments, "The philosophers must go down, as the saviors like Socrates, in order to help the prisoners in the Cave. Since they have seen 'the truth of the beautiful, the just, and the good,' they can discern much better than the dwellers 'There' the obscure things, the shadows of the real things. Since they have seen the Agathon, the polis under their rulership will be governed with a wake mind and not ruled, as most poleis are today, darkly as in a dream (520c-d)" (*Plato and Aristotle*, 171).

61. Gildea, *Mother Mary Arsenius of Foxford*, 117, my emphases.

62. Ibid., 153. William P. Ryan was editor of the *Irish Peasant*.

Finlay[63] who informed him about "the appalling conditions of Dublin slums, where some 20,000 families—perhaps 100,000 souls—were living in one-room tenements. It was clear from what he [Finlay] had said that much of his spare time was devoted to that baffling problem."[64] In the Jesuit journal *Lyceum*, a forerunner to the later *Studies*, Finlay explained the philosophy behind his motivation and involvement in the economic cooperative movement. His approach was totally unlike that of Karl Marx or Ferdinand Lassalle, both of whom proposed a system which, he maintained, "could never be more than a 'utopian ideal' that testified 'to the philanthropic ambitions of its authors' . . . [Their paradigm] was out of touch with human nature and the selfishness and idleness inherent in it. The system, which he advocated, took account of self-interest, enabling workers, by means of co-operation, to become capitalists—'to be owners of wealth which assists labour, as well as furnishing the labour itself.'"[65]

Finlay explained how in the "co-operative system, its members, who were producers and consumers, aimed to become their 'own agents for the sale and purchase of commodities' which they held."[66] The use of the cooperative scheme did not just result in increased economic advantages but also promoted an increase in what Finlay called "mental and moral improvement."[67] The whole process involved the human person in the application of "business capacity, an understanding of the ways and means of commerce, a rigid observance of business rules, a knowledge of the right method of expending money as well as saving it, a capacity to test things by their practical results."[68]

Finlay therefore clearly saw how Morrogh-Bernard had the ingenuity and courage to found a woolen mills in Foxford village. As we have seen, the entrepreneur John Charles Smith from northern Ireland recognized her entrepreneurial gifts early on. A commentator observes that Smith "must have recognised the same [entrepreneurial] qualities in her . . . what the Sisters lacked in business training and capital, they made up

63. In the Irish political landscape of the time their cooperation was unusual, Plunkett being a Unionist member of parliament for South Dublin and Finlay being a Roman Catholic priest and a nationalist.

64. Morrissey, *Thomas A. Finlay, SJ*, 77.

65. Ibid., 82.

66. Ibid.

67. Ibid., 86.

68. Ibid.

THE REAL WELLSPRING OF HUMAN WEALTH REVEALED   235

for in sheer resourcefulness, courage and the will to succeed."[69] Finlay
gave an outline of her philosophy in his *Foxford and the Providence Wool-
en Mills*. He describes how in medieval times religious communities took
a major part in "promoting the material interests of people."[70] But in the
new industrial era of the eighteenth century this role had been somewhat
obscured. So, Agnes was in a situation where "the life of the cloister gives
no facilities for the training of the entrepreneur."[71] However, "in industry,
as in literature, genius can supply the place of education, and in the case
of the organiser of the Foxford enterprise" this was self-evident.[72] Finlay
declares that Foxford and its woolen mills are worthy of careful study
because "we have here the solution of a social problem which elsewhere
perplexes statesmen and philanthropists."[73]

Finlay points out that the common view in regard to wealth creation, that all that is needed is capital, is mistaken. He argues,

> This assumption is at variance with the accepted economic
> theory that real business ability rarely fails of success for want
> of capital . . . It certainly finds no support in the history of
> Foxford Mills. The capital with which they began would have
> been lost . . . had not the *business ability* necessary to make it
> fructify guided its application. The story of the Foxford industry
> is the story of a prolonged struggle against singularly adverse
> conditions, a struggle in which success was achieved by *ability*
> which, in its own order, might be characterised as *genius, and by*
> *a resolute, systematic, and persevering fortitude, which fell little*
> *short of heroism* . . . There are other districts in Ireland where
> population is as dense and poverty as piteous as in Foxford . . .
> Why is there not a similar scheme of manufacturing industry
> there? The answer is obvious. Such a scheme may be devised
> without difficulty. But it is not easy to assure its success. And this
> is for the reason that the *essential factor* in its successful working
> is not to be had for the asking, will not at once be forthcoming
> in response to a newspaper advertisement. Nor will it be evoked
> by the mere offer of a tempting salary.[74]

69. See Joyce, *Agnes Morrogh-Bernard*, 9, 16–17, 31; see also *The Life and Work of
Mary Aikenhead*, 447–52.

70. Finlay, *Foxford and the Providence Woollen Mills*, 19.

71. Ibid., 21.

72. Ibid.

73. Ibid., 25.

74. Ibid., 29, my emphasis.

The nearby natural resources and the stark human need were, of course, factors in the woolen mills' founding. But Morrogh-Bernard's concept of economic rationality was lucid and based upon a rich philosophy of the human person; it was at the same time rooted in the knowledge that, as Adam Smith (quoting Hobbes) wrote, "wealth is power."[75] The causes of human poverty could not according to her perspective be put simply at the door of systemic and ideological obstacles. If it were left at that, the people would still be the victims. But the free market as a process, in fact, has the power and capacity to facilitate the economic well-being and development of the human person.

The *"essential factor"* of production Finlay alludes to is the genius of Agnes's entrepreneurial *"creativity"*—a capacity for innovation which is actually constitutive of our nature as human persons. Morrogh-Bernard intuitively knew this and acted upon it. Her manager, Frank Sherry, said of her that time and time again she put forward projects to him which he considered wrong and "unbusiness-like."[76] After some time of deliberation "she would finally say 'something is telling me to do so-and-so.'"[77] The economic and social poverty she witnessed was evidence of extreme alienation. But the economic manifestation of this in Foxford and its environs could not explain the totality of the dehumanization she saw, nor could it be solved solely in those terms. The words of Hobbes' *Leviathan* came alive in that Mayo village. For its populace experienced indeed the reality that "the life of man . . . [is] poor, nasty, brutish, and short."[78]

To plot any exit strategy out of the human catastrophe they were in, Morrogh-Bernard understood the need to take cognizance of the "flash of transcendence" discovered in each human person she encountered in the village of Foxford. She decided to focus her attention upon "human action," and in so doing she mapped out otherwise unforeseen anthropological horizons for the people of Foxford and those who would come to study the project. The foundational key lay in recapturing the truth and harnessing the power of the reality of "human action" in the economic horizon of life. Her entrepreneurial acumen was the spark that ignited the bright star of a small industry in post-famine Ireland.[79] Her entire

75. See Smith, *Wealth of Nations*, 37.

76. Gildea, *Mother Mary Arsenius of Foxford*, 196.

77. Ibid.

78. Hobbes, *Leviathan*, XIII, [62].

79. Morrogh-Bernard can be classified more as a "social entrepreneur" than a purely "market entrepreneur." See Licht and Siegel, "The Social Dimensions of Entrepreneurship," 511–39.

approach can be understood in light of the perspective of the Austrian school of economics we've been examining. As we've seen, for them, *"human acts"* are the basis of economic activity, and if we want to understand or change "economic life in commercial society"[80] we must focus our attention upon "human persons."[81] As I outlined in earlier chapters, Carl Menger had been very influential in initiating this whole approach in economics. In 1871 he had published his *Principles of Economics* where he suggested that the best way to understand macro-phenomena, "was to break them down into their component parts."[82] So, Menger helped recapture the truth of the reality about economics, that is, "the individual is at the center of economic inquiry—not the hedonistic social atom of Benthamite utilitarianism."[83] Then Mises took up this analysis and observed that human action "is not simply giving preference. Man also shows preference in situations in which things and events are unavoidable or are believed to be so. Thus a man may prefer sunshine to rain and may wish that the sun dispel the clouds. He who only wishes and hopes does not interfere actively with the course of events and with the shaping of his own destiny. But *acting man chooses, determines, and tries to reach an end.* Acting therefore involves both taking and renunciation."[84]

As previously discussed, Mises described how his "subject matter of praxeology is human action."[85] The Austrians considered "praxeology" as a general theory of human action. As such it concerns flesh-and-blood human beings who are seen as "creative actors and the protagonists of all social processes."[86] Thus, Mises explained how "praxeology does not deal with the external world, but with man's conduct with regard to it. Praxeological reality is not the physical universe, but man's conscious reaction to the given state of this universe. Economics is not about things and tangible material objects; it is about men, their meanings and actions. Goods, commodities, and wealth and all the other notions of conduct are not elements of nature: they are elements of human meaning and

---

80. Gregg, *Commercial Society*, 54.
81. Ibid.
82. Ibid., 55.
83. Ibid.
84. Mises, *Human Action*, 12, my emphasis.
85. Ibid., 29.
86. Soto, *Austrian School*, 5.

conduct. He who wants to deal with them must not look at the external world; he must search for them in the meaning of acting men."[87]

Any worthwhile economic investigation, if it is to measure up adequately to the reality of the human person, should deal with "acting man, not with man transformed into a plant and reduced to a merely vegetative existence."[88] Morrogh-Bernard's "falcon's eye"[89] was fixed upon "human action" because its authors can, "unlike animals," actually "shape the reality around them through their choices and action."[90] She had unspoken "person-centered" philosophical presuppositions in her approach to post-famine Foxford, its people and challenges; and these are worthy of careful consideration. It is interesting to examine again the comments of various visitors to the woolen mill because we can trace the characteristics of a "person-centered" dynamic in them. Most of them focus not on the products produced but on the "human action" encountered therein. Finlay described how "the factory becomes a school where much more is learned than spinning and weaving. Character has a value—even an economic value—no less than tweeds."[91]

Visitors note the transformation in the workers involved in the entrepreneurial project. There was an interior alteration. It is not just the raw materials that were transformed by the mechanical processes. As we've seen in Foxford: "the *listless* worker became *industrious, clumsiness* was supplanted by *dexterity, timidity* gave way to *courage.*" And as the businessman William Walker's remarked "the workers of Providence appear . . . to be *active, attentive* and *intelligent* . . . The thorough nature of the work and the enthusiasm of . . . [the workers] astonished me. And there *is a unity and interdependence* pervading the entire business which indicates the *rarest quality of organising ability.*"[92]

This illustrates well how "economic initiative does more than create things and benefit others. As a work-*act* of the creative subject, entrepreneurship involves man's *self-realisation* of moral good."[93] Morrogh-Bernard's entrepreneurial insight and initiative went beyond mere theorizing.

87. Mises, *Human Action*, 92.

88. Ibid.

89. Gildea, *Mother Mary Arsenius of Foxford*, 189.

90. Gregg, *Commercial Society*, 54.

91. Finlay, *Foxford and the Providence Woollen Mills*, 27.

92. Gildea, *Mother Mary Arsenius of Foxford*, 114.

93. Gregg and Preece, *Christianity and Entrepreneurship*, 87.

She put her innovative understanding into practice. I am reminded here of David Walsh's reference to the "genius [which] derives from the Tocquevillian prioritization of practice over theory."[94] Agnes could be said to have illustrated a uniquely *"feminine genius"* in this regard.[95] This resulted in the recapturing and cultivating in her co-workers the power of their own "creative subjectivity."[96] The Misesian entrepreneurial theory likewise envisages everyone as being capable of participating in entrepreneurial human action. Mises states, "in order to succeed in business a man does not need a degree from a school of business administration . . . An entrepreneur cannot be trained. A man becomes an entrepreneur in seizing an opportunity and filling the gap . . . No special education is requires for such a display of keen *judgment, foresight, and energy.*"[97]

"Creativity" is constitutive of *how* we are as human persons. It is integral to *who* we are as human beings. Mises alludes to this when he claims that entrepreneurial action is "not the particular feature of a special group or class."[98] It is, in fact, "inherent in every action."[99] He observes that in using the term "entrepreneur" we should keep in mind the view that "every action is embedded in the flux of time and therefore involves speculation."[100] Such action is therefore a constitutive element of who we are. The founder of the Foxford Woolen Mills unfolded this essential aspect of the human person within the space and time of her own contemporaries. Indeed, she saw everyone as a "candidate" for the flourishing and enactment of this anthropological truth. The fundamental "self-esteem" (dignity) of the workers in the woolen mills was based upon the actualization of this unique human capacity. Paul Ricoeur asks in his book *The Just*, "in terms of what then . . . can we esteem or respect

94. Walsh, "Theory and Practice as Responsibility," 47–50.

95. The founder of the Focolare Movement, Chiara Lubich, often spoke of the "feminine genius." See Lubich, "The Feminine Genius," Trent, Italy, 1995, http://www.centrochiaralubich.org/en/documents/texts/145-text-en/1025-the-feminine-genius.html. She subsequently initiated the Economy of Communion project in 1991 in São Paulo, Brazil. It involves a network of more than seven hundred businesses worldwide that seek to make a positive contribution toward recapturing the truth of the reality of a person-centered dynamic in business and economics. For further information on the Economy of Communion, see www.edc-online.org.

96. John Paul II, *Sollicitudo Rei Socialis*, no. 15.

97. Mises, *Human Action*, 314, my emphasis.

98. Ibid., 252–53.

99. Ibid., 253.

100. Ibid.

ourselves?" He explains how "self-esteem" and "self-respect" essentially pertain "to a capable subject."[101] But at the same time he stresses how there is the concomitant need for the actual conditions for the actualization of the subject's capacities to be realized. Morrogh-Bernard was the prime instigator of the realization of these very "human capacities" within her co-workers but her journey was not easy. We are told that "difficulties did not disappear . . . there was much development of brain and muscle before they [the workers] grew into such sturdy young folk."[102] In his later work *The Course of Recognition*, Ricoeur recognized too how "the road to recognition is long, for the 'acting and suffering' human being, that leads to the recognition that he or she is in truth a person 'capable' of different accomplishments. What is more, this self-recognition requires, at each step, the help of others."[103] In the case of the charismatic entrepreneur, Agnes Morrogh-Bernard, existential problems were not just to be solved but had, in fact, to be loved. She did this because she perceived the integral development of the human person an enterprise worthy of her attention and as such it was something "that is truly 'too big to fail.'"[104]

We have noted how the Austrian school of economics in particular sought to develop a systematic reflection on a theory of entrepreneurship. It was scholars like Mises, Hayek, and Kirzner who contributed significantly to the whole debate. But many philosophers and theologians alike have elaborated on the same themes. As I have already said Mises lacks any explicit anthropology so he cannot fully account for human action or entrepreneurial action in particular. Nonetheless, the characteristics he outlines in his investigations into economic action are essential qualities the human dimensions involved. The human agents in the free market framework are, according to him, rational, deliberative and purposive human beings. Morrogh-Bernard's entrepreneurial project can be analyzed in a similar way and in itself gives rise to the retrieval of where the real wellspring of wealth lies, that is, in the human person. And as I have said it is the task of philosophy to contribute to the development

101. See Ricoeur, *The Just*, 4.

102. Finlay, *Foxford and the Providence Woollen Mills*, 23.

103. Ricoeur, *Course of Recognition*, 69.

104. See Benedict XVI, "Meeting with Representatives of British Society, Members of the Diplomatic Corps, Academics and Business Leaders," Westminster Hall-City of Westminster, 17 September 2010, http://www.vatican.va/holy_father/benedict_xvi/speeches/2010/september/documents/hf_ben-xvi_spe_20100917_societa-civile_en.html#.

of a "higher viewpoint" in the elaboration of a more adequate economic anthropology.

In terms of an enlargement of our minds and hearts in this regard, I have in mind Saint John Paul II's encyclicals *Laborem Exercens* and *Centesimus Annus*. In these, his themes on "human work" and "entrepreneurial initiative," respectively, are reflected upon as constitutive dimensions in the enactment of the drama of the human person. Actually, David Walsh, in his essay "The Person as the Heart of Benedict's New Evangelization," also sees in Pope Benedict's "theological personalism" a radical departure in Christian thought. He remarks that "John Paul II had made the person central to his whole intellectual framework, often quoting the Council's remark that the Church is an expert in humanity, on the side of the person in his or her innermost reality. Benedict began to work out what this more personalist emphasis would mean for the way Christianity understands itself in the heart of the secular world. The Church would change the world neither by separating itself from it nor submitting to it, but by revealing the eschatological secret that lies buried within it."[105] Indeed, Pope Francis stresses the importance of "integral development" in our world. "Integral development" is inclusive of the multidimensional reality of the human person and is "non-Cyclopean" in not reducing the reality of the person to a mere component of the totality. Pope Francis outlines how "we urgently need a humanism capable of bringing together the different fields of knowledge, including economics, in the service of a more integral and integrating vision" because this demonstrates "yet again that 'the whole is greater than the part.'"[106] There is no doubt that Pope Francis has initiated a fresh debate about global poverty. Indeed, Piketty's *Capital in the Twenty-First Century* also enters into the discussion with his analysis of the global inequality of wealth.[107] But I would suggest that any appeal to the well-intentioned and vital question of poverty and its alleviation is no substitute for an adequate grasp of the role and importance of "wealth creation" in society.

Actually, in this book we've taken up a challenge to move away from any "undifferentiated and one-dimensional paradigm" used in an economics subverted by its anthropological oblivion.[108] And it is

---

105. Walsh, "The Person as the Heart of Benedict's New Evangelization."

106. Pope Francis, *Laudato Si: On Care for Our Common Home*, no. 141.

107. Piketty, *Capital*, 59–69.

108. Pope Francis, *Laudato Si: On Care for Our Common Home*, no. 106.

true that whatever model is used in economic theory it presupposes an understanding of the human person. Pope Francis adverts to this problematic when he critically comments on the characteristic in today's world "to make the method and aims of science and technology an epistemological paradigm which shapes the lives of individuals and the workings of society."[109] But I hold that by means of a radical "X-raying" of the "human action" involved in the Foxford Woolen Mills entrepreneurial project we can unearth how Morrogh-Bernard takes a distinctive approach in the face of the assuagement of the frightful poverty she witnessed around her. In her perspective we can rediscover the "eschatological secret that lies buried within" human action in the economic realm.[110] We are able to uncover the reality of the human person *acting* as a "self-transcender." There is a fundamental "uneasiness" in our being, and in the words of Walsh "no state of satiety can assuage" our human searching.[111] This is because "every fiber of . . . [our] being reaches toward a horizon that is beyond" all that we are and have humanly accomplished.[112] This is the "flash of transcendence" that is alive in our hearts. Indeed, I am reminded again of those visitors' impressions of the woolen mills project given to us in the various reports, articles, and letters and cited in this chapter. Walsh's reflections seem quite appropriate in trying to articulate the new philosophical horizons, which seem to emerge from Morrogh-Bernard's entrepreneurial action. He describes how "by transcending the self, by rubbing off the rust of selfishness in the mutually sustaining struggle, the heart is enlarged to the point that it glimpses the unseen measure that had previously eluded it. The 'growth of the soul' puts the individual in touch with the really real that surpasses the self."[113]

We can also see perhaps in Gildea's remarks a corresponding reality when he observed that Agnes's burning zeal was for the salvation of the human soul; this "was like a golden thread running through the warp and woof of her existence. All her activities were subordinated to that end."[114] It is striking to recall here Mises's similar remark on the ultimate "*spiritual nature*" of the commercial process. As we've observed he said

109. Ibid., nos. 106–7.

110. Walsh, "The Person as the Heart of Benedict's New Evangelization."

111. Walsh, *Guarded by Mystery*, 39.

112. Ibid., 38

113. Walsh, "Theory and Practice as Responsibility," 47–50.

114. Gildea, *Mother Mary Arsenius of Foxford*, 136.

that "production is not something physical, material, and external; it is a *spiritual and intellectual phenomenon*. Its essential requisites are not human labor and external natural forces and things, but the decision of the mind to use those factors as means for the attainment of ends. What produces the product are not toil and trouble in themselves, but the fact that the toiling is guided by reason. The human mind alone has the power to remove uneasiness."[115]

In other words, what's revealed in the philosophical analysis of human economic action I have sought to employ in this chapter in regard to the Foxford project, is the fundamental truth of the human person. That is, the person, described by Walsh as "that capacity to become more than we are."[116] It was, I believe, the mystery of that truth which Morrogh-Bernard tapped into. As we've noted, just as she harnessed the powers of the river Moy, she also unfolded and recaptured the truth of the "creative" reality of the human person. Her famous catchphrase was "Providence, providence will provide."[117] The originating choice in her life was that of the "transcendent," the choice of God as active in history. One of her English Protestant friends wrote, "It is quite true that some Higher Power looks after your firm."[118] She lived this in practice with others, knowing that an understanding of the economy which excluded the "transcendent" is in the end an inhuman one because it overshadows the actual truth and beauty of the human person.[119]

115. Mises, *Human Action*, 141–42, my emphases.

116. Walsh, "Person as the Heart of Benedict's New Evangelization," 6.

117. Gildea, *Mother Mary Arsenius of Foxford*, 99.

118. Ibid., 157.

119. "Without God man neither knows which way to go nor even understands who he is . . . Man cannot bring about his own progress unaided . . . *A humanism which excludes God is an inhuman humanism*." See Benedict XVI, *Caritas in Veritate*, no. 78.

9

Toward a Philosophical Anthropology of the Free Market Economy: Recapturing the Human Wealth of its Person-Centered Roots

I. A Reorientation of Economics: The Turn toward the "Human Subject"

A S WE OBSERVED IN chapter 8, Morrogh-Bernard's entrepreneurial project unfolded the truth of the "creative" reality of the human person. But it is important to keep in mind that this discovery of the "creativity" of the human person as the essential wellspring in the creation of human wealth should not remain just a "dinosauric" remnant of the distant past. Many contemporary economists and scholars are increasingly discovering the need to sufficiently account for and recapture the human dimension of economic and social reality in their theoretical reflections and which have evaporated from the landscape around us. The economist Tony Lawson in his study *Reorienting Economics*, for instance, outlines the thesis that the discipline of modern economics is in need of a significant change of orientation. In fact, he speaks about an "ontological turn" in economics. He explains, "By ontology I mean enquiry into (or a theory of) the nature of being or existence. It is an endeavour concerned with determining the broad nature, including the structure, of reality."[1] Lawson,

---

1. Lawson, *Reorienting Economics*, xv.

while being critical of the Austrian school's perspective, mentions their unique contribution.[2] Indeed, Lawson is of the opinion that although the "mathematizing tendency" in modern economics is mainstream, it cannot necessarily claim to be any more successful than the other, older traditions in terms of the "explanation" of economic reality. In fact, he holds that the "heterodox traditions" (and the Austrian tradition is considered as "heterodox" by leading economists) are actually more successful in their attempts to articulate economic reality.[3]

The overall argument in this study is that in the fundamental characteristics of the free economy there already exists what I call an "emergent" anthropological paradigm and that a *person-centered* focus is not necessarily detrimental to the economic process. On the contrary, these personalistic principles are presupposed by the workings of the free market process. However, just as in the case of the entrepreneurial function these can, of course, end up being jettisoned from the framework of our overall economic understanding. We've seen that as in the other human sciences there are various schools or traditions with different emphases and so economics and economists can take different approaches each one developing specific themes. After the Industrial Revolution, for example, in the history of economic reflection you had a divergence in the development of different schools of thought in regard to the theory of value. In chapter 4 we spoke about the development of the "labor theory of value" by Karl Marx and Ferdinand Lassalle, on the one hand, and on the other the "subjective theory of value" proposed by Leon Walras, William Stanley Jevons and Carl Menger. These schools of thought would later develop in the twentieth century into socialism, communism, welfare economics, economic planning and Keynesianism on the labor theory side and the neoclassical, Chicago, and Austrian school approaches of the "subjective value" perspective. The hidden or very often forgotten *dramatis personae* in most of these approaches are "human persons." Consequently, the so-called subjective turn in economic thought can, I believe, be seen as an attempt to recapture and understand the "person-centered" roots of the free market process. In this "turn" there is, of course, the evident danger of a "reductionism" in which society is "understood as an aggregate of individuals" and the resulting "methodological individualism" can then become the predominant paradigm in economic research.[4]

2. Ibid., 247.
3. Ibid.
4. See Grassl, *"Pluris Valere,"* 317.

Therefore, to avoid the "sinkhole" of any "rugged individualistic" solipsism which might be suggested by the reorientation toward the "subjective" in the Austrian tradition, it is important to keep in mind the insight that "the economic unit is the human person."[5] The French philosopher Jacques Maritain makes useful clarifications in regard to any possible dichotomy between the "individual" and the "person." He explains how there is clearly a difference between the individual and the person but that the most important thing is "to understand the distinction correctly."[6] He outlines how it is that "individual realities exist" designating that "concrete state of unity and indivision required by existence, in virtue of which every actually or possibly existing nature can posit itself in existence as distinct from other beings."[7] Bernard Lonergan makes a similar point in his discussion on the general notion of the Thing. He observes how "the notion of a thing is grounded in an insight that grasps ... a unity, [an] identity" which takes data in its "concrete individuality."[8] It is quite clear that human beings are individuals since the common characteristic of all existents is that in order to exist they must be individual, that is, "undivided" and "distinct" from every other existent.[9] So, it is the case that as individuals we are a "fragment of a species, a part of nature," but that is not all we are since each of us is also a "person."[10] We exist not just by reason of our individual physical nature but also by virtue of who we are as human persons. Fundamental to this nature as human persons is *"being more."*[11] Thus, we discover that the "person" is distinguished by being "a source of dynamic unity, of unification from within."[12] The "subjectivity" we are concerned with in terms of the reality

5. Jacques Maritain applied the same principle to society when he wrote "the social unit is the person" (*Person and the Common Good*, 47).

6. Ibid., 34.

7. Ibid.

8. See Lonergan, *Insight*, 271.

9. Maritain, *Person and the Common Good*, 34.

10. Ibid.

11. Pope Benedict XVI has written that "man is constitutionally oriented towards 'being more.'" See *Caritas in Veritate*, no. 14.

12. Maritain, *Person and the Common Good*, 41. I would also refer the reader to other background studies of the person such as that in John F. Crosby's *Selfhood of the Human Person* and *Personalist Papers*.

of the human person has nothing to do with "the isolated unity, without doors or windows, of the Leibnizian monad" or of any Austrian hybrid.[13]

Maritain outlines how, in fact, it is a fatal "anthropological error" to mistake the distinction between the "individual" and the "person" as a separation which sets up the belief that there are "two separate beings."[14] He summarizes the argument as follows: "In order to avoid misunderstandings and nonsense, we must emphasize that they [the individual and the person] are not two separate things. There is not in me one reality, called my individual, and another reality, called my person. One and the same reality is, in a certain sense an individual, and, in another sense, a person. Our whole being is an individual by reason of that in us which derives from matter, and a person by reason of that in us which derives from spirit. Similarly, the whole of a painting is a physico-chemical mixture by reason of the coloring stuff of which it is made, and the whole of it is a work of beauty by reason of the painter's art."[15]

The human person is not just an individual but also a "whole" who transcends in their very own "ontological capacity . . . the whole of the relational social order" because they are "directed to the knowledge and boundless love of other 'wholes.'"[16] Indeed, in our own study we've investigated an example of this in the case of Agnes Morrogh-Bernard and the Foxford entrepreneurial project (see chapter 8). I contend that this sketches out for us the "broader anthropological horizon" which any adequate study of the human person in the economic drama necessarily calls for. So, the reorientation of economics toward the "human subject" need not end up in "methodological individualism" but actually pushes us toward regaining an "anthropological and relational view" of economic life.[17] Economics thus can have a realism about it that is helpful to any philosophy based on *what* is. In our study we described the retrieval of these forgotten anthropological principles as they re-emerged in the pioneering work of Joseph Schumpeter. These personcentric insights were further developed in the works of Raymond de Roover, Marjorie Grice-Hutchinson, and John T. Noonan.[18] We noted too in chapter 4 how the

13. Ibid.

14. Ibid., 45.

15. Ibid., 43.

16. See Schall, *Jacques Martian*, 154. See also Pope Francis, *Laudato Si*, no. 141.

17. See Bruni, *Wound and the Blessing*, 67.

18. Rothbard, *Economic Thought before Adam Smith*, x.

cultural roots of the amnesia concerning the "personcentric" dimension in economics could be traced back to the Protestant Reformation but this theme does not directly concern us here.[19]

II. The "Subjective-Objective" Dimension in Economics

It is important to clarify what the "subjective-objective" dimension means in the economic context. The popular meaning of "subjective" suggests that something is personal, individual, possibly one-sided or maybe even biased. But this is not the meaning intended in economics. Hayek gives what I consider an insightful explanation of the "subjective" meaning in economics and it clearly has philosophical implications. In an essay titled "The Subjective Character of the Data of the Social Sciences" he outlines the meaning of the term "subjective" as it occurs in economic thinking. Hayek's discussion takes place in the context of his argument against "scientism." He refers to the "slavish imitation of the method or language of Science"[20] as "scientism" and differentiates the subject matter of the social sciences as concerning "the relations between men and things or the relations between man and man."[21] In other words, its scope is also on the interpersonal horizon. You can, he asserts, study certain areas of human life by means of the natural sciences. He gives examples of investigations into "the spread of contagious diseases . . . the study of heredity, or the study of nutrition."[22] But these areas do not concern "human action" *per se*. He contends, "Wherever we are concerned with unconscious reflexes or processes in the human body there is no obstacle to treating and investigating them 'mechanically' as caused by objectively observable events. They take place without the knowledge of the man concerned and without his having power to modify them."[23]

19. An interesting study in this regard by Brad S. Gregory is *The Unintended Reformation: How a Religious Revolution Secularized Society*. Gregory writes, "What transpired five centuries ago continues today to profoundly influence the lives of everyone not only in Europe and North America but all around the world, whether or not they are Christians or indeed religious believers of any kind" (1).

20. See Caldwell, *Hayek's Challenge*, 242.

21. Hayek, *Counter-Revolution of Science*, 41,

22. Ibid.

23. Ibid., 42.

The social sciences, on the other hand, are concerned with "man's conscious or reflected actions, actions where a person can be said to choose between various courses open to" them.[24] Of course, the intentionality of human actions can be explained as the consequence of the influence of external stimuli, but this explanation is not sufficient and if we limit ourselves to this approach, according to Hayek, "we would confine ourselves to less than we know about the situation."[25] Thomas Aquinas, of course, made a similar distinction in his action theory analysis, between "human acts" (*actus humani*) and "acts of man" (*actus hominis*). Aquinas observed that "those acts alone are properly called 'human' of which man is master. Now, a man is master of his acts through his reason and will. Therefore, free will is said to be a faculty of the will and the reason. Thus those acts are properly called 'human' which proceed from deliberate choice."[26] So, Hayek's "unconscious reflexes," as for example in reflex actions, would come under Aquinas's categorization of "acts of man," and Hayek's "man's conscious" actions could be considered as Aquinian "human acts." Human acts as such are therefore free acts and are purposive.[27]

The Austrian philosophers and economists of that tradition were not just "*subjectivist*" in their approach but also "*objectivist*" in their theories. But as Barry Smith points out this was often forgotten because "the practitioners of Austrian economics, not only as this was classically conceived, but also in its Misesian, Rothbardian, and Kirznerian varieties" rarely felt the need to emphasize this fact.[28] The point is that there is an objective dimension too since these are constituted by "*facts* of economic reality" and these are also established by human purposive acts.[29] The means to apprehend these facts happens to be through a study of *human action*. If you analyze the human person merely in terms of "wishes and hopes" you will never gain an insight into "human acts" in the economic arena. Ludwig von Mises explains this when he says, "A man may prefer

24. Ibid., 43.

25. Ibid.

26. *Summa Theologiae*, Ia, IIae, 1, 1.

27. The prologue to the second part of Aquinas's *Summa Theologiae* concerns "people precisely as *principium*, source, of their own deeds, having free choice [*liberum arbitrium; libera electio*] and power [*potestas*] over those deeds. Indeed, as he [Aquinas] promptly adds, one's deeds (acts, actions) are really human only if one is fully in charge—ruler, master, owner [*dominus*] of them." See Finnis, *Aquinas*, 20.

28. Smith, *Austrian Philosophy*, 319.

29. Ibid.

sunshine to rain and may wish that the sun would dispel the clouds. He who only wishes and hopes does not interfere actively in the course of events and with the shaping of his own destiny. But acting man chooses, determines, and tries to reach an end. Of two things both of which he cannot have together he selects one and gives up the other. Action therefore always involves both taking and renunciation . . . Action is a real thing. What counts is man's total behavior, and not his talk about planned but not realized acts."[30]

Attention to these economic realities is important when it comes to understanding *how* the free economy functions. Lonergan gives, in my view, a useful explanation of "objectivity" which can be equally applied to economic understanding. He describes objectivity as the consequence of "authentic subjectivity, of genuine attention, genuine intelligence, genuine reasonableness, genuine responsibility."[31] He explains that while mathematics, science, philosophy, and ethics all have different subject matter, a common characteristic is that their objectivity is "the fruit of attentiveness, intelligence, reasonableness, and responsibility."[32] Likewise, the Austrian economists we've referred to in this study, and as seen in the diffusion of their insights in the United States through various authors, all judge that there are "*objective*" facts of economic reality. They all hold, for instance, that there are "acts of entrepreneurial perception, that value is a function of individual valuing acts that is subject to the law of marginal utility, that there are unintended consequences of human action, that time preference is positive."[33]

Thus, "objectivity" means that "economic reality" is constituted by "human acts and actions, interacting together over time in complex ways."[34] In light of this approach, it is the task of the economist to try to unearth the contents of these human actions. Within this perspective it emerges that the theorist and his or her theory do not "create" the economic reality he or she is focused on. Rather, the human person and his actions are the *site* we must quarry to arrive at an adequate understanding of economic reality. I believe that the "subjective *Kehre*" in economics can be understood in this way, that is, as the realization that there is a need for

30. Mises, *Human Action*, 12–13.

31. Lonergan, *Method in Theology*, 265.

32. Ibid.

33. Smith, *Austrian Philosophy*, 319.

34. Ibid.

a "person-excavation" to reach a higher anthropological viewpoint where economic action is explained more comprehensively. As Karen Vaughn says, "Ideas within the Austrian tradition—ideas about processes, subjectivism, learning, time . . . suggest new ways of theorizing about human beings as they go about pursuing their projects and plans using concrete resources."[35]

III. An Enhanced Understanding of "Human Intentionality"

It is clear that the universal Austrian school foundational principle in economic thinking is the primacy of "*human purposefulness.*" But this extends philosophically far more broadly than they intended and is not just limited to saying that a particular action (economic action in this case) is the expression of egoistic, or selfish greed. As Lionel Robbins recognized, it is reflections on the dependency of economic phenomena upon human "purposive action" that enable us adequately to dismiss the "oft-reiterated accusation that Economics assumes a world of economic men concerned only with money-making and self-interest."[36] Simply stated, there seems to be no such individual like the *Homo economicus* envisaged by some economic theorists, or if he really exists in this way, then he does so only as a *shadowlike* reality of the real acting human person. If we reduce our understanding of economic actions and "*intentionality*" in such a way and thereby interpret this as being equivalent to the totality of human action, we run the concomitant risk of disgorging from the framework the reality of what it means to say that all human action is purposeful. If we accept the premise of the "purposiveness" of human action we cannot subsequently necessarily limit what that might entail. Hayek and the other Austrian economists would refer to the "uncertainty" principle in this situation, since different individuals have varying purposes which we can never know. But from the perspective of philosophical anthropology, we can also use the term "*mystery*" when applied to the acting person. Thus, we can say the human person in the economic drama is always guarded by the mystery of their reality.

This, of course, opens up the need for the development of the anthropological perspective which lies at the heart of the free economy. As

35. Vaughn, *Austrian Economics in America*, 177.

36. Robbins, *Essay on the Nature and Significance of Economic Science*, 87.

we said, Mises does not focus on or develop an explicit anthropology. Yet what he is seeking to account for in his analysis of economics requires an anthropology in order to explain the human actions involved. The Austrian economists and their followers naturally do not develop this theme because for them it is strictly speaking "noneconomic." Nonetheless, we've seen from a philosophical perspective in our investigation into the role of the entrepreneur, how when we phenomenologically "X-ray" "entrepreneurial action" aspects such as *judgment, choice, innovation, initiative, alertness* and *creativity* clearly emerge and are revealed as crucial human characteristics. This suggests that the entrepreneurial function cannot be fully understood or completely explained if it is left merely at the level of being a function of monetary motivations, because these elements refer to qualities and capacities that are constitutive of the *acting human person*. They necessarily pertain to the individual characteristics *qua* human person and cannot be explained solely in material or monetary terms. This can be further explained by reflecting on the motivation of entrepreneurs and *how* they "act" in the free economy. I have mentioned in chapter 5 how in an interview with the *Financial Times*, Bill Gates explained the motivation behind his own entrepreneurial action. The interviewer, Gideon Rachman, commented that

> Gates's account of the origins of Microsoft . . . *has little to do with money*. He founded the firm in 1975, after dropping out from Harvard to indulge his passion for computing. "When I decided to go and start Microsoft, it wasn't because it was some lucrative career. Paul Allen [his childhood friend and co-founder of Microsoft] and I were just excited about the personal computer and it was something we were surprised nobody else was working on . . . We were in on the ground floor." As Gates tells it, *the money was almost an accidental by-product*: "Really, if you develop good software, the business isn't that complicated . . . The business side is pretty simple; you try to take in more than you spend."[37]

We are led again to what I have referred to as a "broader anthropological viewpoint." The economic arena just happens to be one such dimension where these human capacities are unfolded.[38] The same human

---

37. See Gideon Rachman, "Lunch with the *FT*: Bill Gates," *Financial Times*, 30–31 October 2010, http://www.ft.com/cms/s/2/67672314-e2e0-11df-9735-00144feabdc0.html#axzz140KOKluo. My emphases.

38. I have in mind here, for example, the aesthetic dimension of human existence,

faculties are enacted at the various levels in which the human person *acts* in the drama of human living. So, when we turn our attention to the economic life-world we discover that it is inhabited by "real, flesh-and-blood agents" and not by solitary machine-like automatons that perform in a one-act play where the principal actor is only *Homo economicus*.[39] An adequate investigation of this reality suggests you can only have a broader theory of human action that accounts for the truth of economic reality if you have a wider concept of the human person.

I have mentioned various Austrian economists in the story of the "subjective" turn in economic understanding. This "existential shift" can be seen as movement toward capturing that wider concept of the person I have drawn attention to. The idea I have here is not that these economists have necessarily reached and successfully captured the whole reality and are in possession of a "paradisiacal" theory of the human person. In fact, due to the "irreducible" nature of the person this search remains an ongoing pursuit for philosophers and economists alike. Nonetheless, this does not mean that the search in itself is fruitless because it can at least approximate toward what we call a truthful account of the reality of the human person. We mentioned in chapter two Eric Voegelin's three elements constitutive of the meaning of science; they are that it is seen as "a truthful account of the structure of reality, as the theoretical orientation of man in this world, and as the great instrument for man's understanding of his own position in the universe."[40] So, my argument essentially is that when the Austrian economists and their followers came upon an anthropological "*outcrop*" on the economic topography, that is, the insight that *humans act for reasons*, they initiated a movement back toward the source of all value and economic action, namely, the human person. It is true that they did not necessarily fully understand the full implications of what they were dealing with but at least they could then try to account for the structure of economic reality and explain the anthropological principles on which it is based. But in doing this it is important to keep in mind that they also discovered the fragility of their and our own subject matter because as Walsh said, "Human beings are notoriously difficult to study."[41]

---

which involves human initiative and creativity, to mention but a few anthropological qualities.

39. See Madison, "Phenomenology and Economics," 40.

40. See Voegelin, *New Science of Politics*, 91.

41. Walsh, *Guarded by Mystery*, 26.

Indeed, it is important to highlight that Mises understands the transition from "the classical theory of value to the subjective theory of value" as something that cannot just be understood at the level of the substitution of one theory of market exchange for another.[42] This change cannot be understood at this level alone. Lonergan, for instance, formulates a world-view constituted by an ordered series of viewpoints and each more wide-ranging perspective adds a higher system of intelligible terms.[43] So, too, the "subjective turn" in economic theory can be understood, I argue, as a "growth point" in the exploration of the intelligibility of *human action* in economics. This whole transformation Mises sees as having far deeper import, and I suggest it is an indication of a movement toward a broader *anthropological viewpoint*. Mises believed that up until the late nineteenth century economics as a science was "atomized" in that it "remained a science of the 'economic' aspect of human action."[44] This meant that it continued primarily as a "theory of wealth and selfishness."[45] It focused on human action only in so far as "it is actuated by what was . . . described as the profit motive."[46] Other aspects of human action were not considered as falling under the remit of economic investigation. But the rise of "modern subjectivist economics"[47] actually shifted economics away from being "merely a theory of the 'economic side' of human endeavors and of man's striving for commodities"[48] toward economics as the "science of every kind of human action."[49]

Although Mises and Hayek do not refer directly to Aquinas in the sources I have cited, there are parallels between Aquinas's theory of human action and the Austrian "subjective" approach to human action in economics. In *Human Action*, for instance, and in other writings, Mises, in my opinion, outlines an analysis of human action in which specific attention is given to "*intentionality*." In fact, Barry Smith, in *Austrian Philosophy: The Legacy of Franz Brentano*, gives an insightful reading of Austrian economics in light of Brentano's philosophy of mind and ontology.

42. Mises, *Human Action*, 3.
43. See Rixon, "Derrida and Lonergan on Human Development," 231.
44. Mises, *Human Action*, 3.
45. Ibid.
46. Ibid.
47. Ibid.
48. Ibid.
49. Ibid.

He explains how "Austrians have wanted to emphasize the central role in their theory of the *acting, valuing, human subject* (as opposed to abstract equilibrium models and the like). In Menger's eyes the very possibility of economics as a theoretical science tests the thesis of subjectivism in this sense, for it is this which implies that one can *understand* the workings of an economy by coming to an understanding of how the value of goods at earlier stages in the process of production is derived from the value to actual consumers of the products of the later stages."[50]

This is therefore a uniquely human theory since only human persons can *act* and *choose*.[51] Mises observes how "choosing determines all human actions . . . no treatment of economics proper can avoid starting from acts of choice."[52] Mises's *opus magnum* can be interpreted as an anthropological manifesto in which he attempts to initiate a recovery in an understanding of the *acting person* as participant in the reality of the free market process. If Marx's overall opus is understood in light of an investigation into *Das Kapital*, then the Austrian perspective in economics can be summed up as turning the spotlight upon *der menschliche Person in Wirtschaftswissenschaften*.

Indeed, Hayek specifically mentions Mises's "consistent development"[53] of the subjective perspective in economics. Hayek succinctly explains the "subjective" approach in economics as follows:

> What is true about the relations of men to things is, of course, even more true of the relations between men, which for the purposes of social study cannot be defined in the objective terms of the physical sciences but only in terms of human beliefs. Even such a seemingly purely biological relationship as that between parent and child is in social study not defined in physical terms and cannot be defined for their purposes: it makes no difference with regard to people's actions whether their belief that a particular child is their natural offspring is mistaken or not . . . All this stands out most clearly in that among the social sciences whose theory has been most highly developed, *economics*. And *it is probably no exaggeration to say that every important advance in economic theory during the last hundred years was a further step in the consistent application of subjectivism*. That the objects of economic activity cannot be defined in objective terms but

50. Smith, *Austrian Philosophy*, 319.

51. See Grassl and Smith, *Austrian Economics*, 175.

52. Mises, *Human Action*, 3.

53. Hayek, *Counter-Revolution of Science*, 52 n. 7.

only with reference to a human purpose goes without saying. Neither a "commodity" or an "economic good," nor "food" or "money," can be defined in physical terms but only in terms of views people hold about things.[54]

IV. The British Economist Philip Wicksteed's Emphasis: The "Economic Relationship"

The Austrians were not alone in contributing to the "existential shift" in economic reflection, nor were they the first to have this insight; in fact, the "hidden roots" of a more "personcentric" understanding in philosophical and economic thought reach back to the Scholastics.[55] The British economist Philip Wicksteed (1844–1927), for example, also got involved in the attempt to redirect the focal point of economic reflection away from the material objects of the classical inquiry to the implications of individual human choices and decisions. Indeed, Wicksteed was often called the English Austrian. In his work titled *The Common Sense of Political Economy* he wrote that his point of departure "for . . . [his] study will be personal."[56] His emphasis is upon the "economic relationship" and that is his "first chosen field of observation."[57] Wicksteed describes his methodology as follows:

> We may naturally draw our first illustrations mainly from the doings of housewives; and this will have the great advantage of keeping us upon ground with which we are all broadly familiar and with which all of us, man, woman, and child are closely concerned . . . Starting then with the investigation of the management of household affairs, we will begin by taking for granted without examination the purchasing power of money and the existence of the market or current prices as facts which the housewife has to deal with . . . I shall then try to show that these principles are identical . . . with the principles that regulate the conduct of life in general, and the administration of all resources whatsoever.[58]

54. Ibid., 52, my emphases.
55. See chapter 5.
56. Wicksteed, *Common Sense of Political Economy*, 17.
57. Ibid.
58. Ibid., 18.

Wicksteed's analysis of the *"mother's problem"* opens up what the "personcentric" horizons might signify and in so doing reaches and recaptures a more comprehensive understanding of human action in economics. He emphasizes that "we must regard industrial and *commercial life, not as a separate and detached region of activity*, but as an *organic part of our whole personal and social life*; and we shall find the clue to the conduct of men in their commercial relations, not in the first instance amongst those characteristics wherein our pursuit of industry differs from our pursuit of pleasure or of learning . . . but rather amongst those underlying principles of conduct and selection wherein they all resemble each other."[59]

We cannot discuss Wicksteed's contribution in any great detail but his analysis is insightful in terms of the unearthing of the anthropological principles that are at the core of action in the economic horizon. He is somewhat revolutionary in his approach because the economic agent he settles upon for an initial analysis is the "mother" of a family household.[60] Wicksteed, in fact, in the analysis he gives of how a mother is to allocate scarce resources in terms of alternative uses, opens up the horizons of what the "existential turn" possibly signifies. In terms of methodology, Wicksteed argues that there is a certain equivalence between the economic action of the mother and human action in general. He uses the example of the mother who goes to the market and unexpectedly finds that prices of goods vary considerably. So, prices could be lower and therefore "she can fill her basket for less"[61] or if they are higher she will need to find some saving elsewhere that will allow her "to spend a little more in the market place."[62] Thus, when she knows the prices she can discover if "she can get that scarf for Bob after all" or maybe she might have to "put off binding *Grimm's Fairy Tales* a little longer."[63] Wicksteed emphasizes that "we must regard industrial and *commercial life, not as a separate and detached region of activity*, but as an *organic part of our whole personal and social life*; and we shall find the clue to the conduct of men in their com-

59. Ibid., 3, my emphases.

60. The British economist William Smart (1853–1915) in his analysis of a theory of value gives the example of the housewife and her value of butter. See *Introduction to the Theory of Value*, 39. Smart wrote, "The history of economic science is strewn with the wrecks of theories of value" (ibid., 1).

61. Wicksteed, *Common Sense of Political Economy*, 38.

62. Ibid.

63. Ibid.

mercial relations, not in the first instance amongst those characteristics wherein our pursuit of industrial differs from our pursuit of pleasure or of learning . . . but rather amongst those underlying principles of conduct and selection wherein they all resemble each other."[64]

Wicksteed's investigation is insightful for us in terms of disclosing once again in a reasoned economic reflection some of the anthropological principles and issues that are at the heart of human action in the economic horizon. Rather like the "entrepreneurial action" we've already analyzed, the mother's actions reveal essential capacities of human nature, such as "deliberate judgment," "watchfulness," "attention," "control."[65] An important point here is that there is not necessarily a dichotomy between the principles the mother's actions display in the marketplace and nonmarket human actions in general. The common denominator in the analysis of economics for Wicksteed is not just *prices* and *quantities* but "*human choice*." In the example of the "mother's problem" Wicksteed would contend that "the job of the economist is not to *tell* the mother what to do but to *understand* and *explain* what she is doing."[66] So, too, as philosophers our primary interest is not the economic problem *per se*, but if we phenomenologically analyze the mother's actions, we find that as in the case of entrepreneurial action, the human factors of *judgment, alertness* and *human choice* emerge are *constitutive of her economic action*.[67] I use the word "phenomenological" here in the sense that a pure description of the mother's actions are necessary but insufficient to *understand* and *explain* the action in itself. There is a further need to *interpret*, that is, "to understand the essence of the phenomenon by seeing it in the context of the whole person and of interpersonal relations."[68] Wicksteed begins his introduction in *The Common Sense of Political Economy* with the apt quote from Goethe: "Ein jeder lebt's, nicht vielen ist's bekannt," that is, "Everyone lives it, but not many are aware of it," and this is true in terms of a philosophical understanding of human economic action.[69] My

---

64. Ibid., 3, my emphases.

65. Ibid., 20–21.

66. Mueller, *Redeeming Economics*, 133.

67. Dermot Moran describes the phenomenological approach as attempting to get at the truth of matters, and as describing human experience "to the experiencer" (*Introduction to Phenomenology*, 4).

68. McNerney, *John Paul II*, 13.

69. The translation is taken from Mueller, *Redeeming Economics*, 408. Mises wrote, "The economist—like the biologist and the psychologist—deals with matters that are

overall approach in this book is not really to adjudicate on the different economic schools of thought from the viewpoint of economics. It is rather to place a searchlight on selected economic reflections in order to highlight the anthropological background that often lies hidden in the analysis given of the substratum of economic action. Wicksteed's choice of "*materfamilias*" is insightful because it shows the mother is someone who is in the context of a "nexus of relationships," that is, she is involved in the market in order to provide for herself and her own family.[70]

The mother's action in the free economy is to administer "her pecuniary resources and trying to make the money go as far as possible."[71] But this is not the end of the mother's problem or actions because "when her purchases have been brought home she still has the kindred task, sometimes a delicate and difficult one, of so *distributing them* amongst the various claimants."[72] In her economic actions in the market place she has to be economizing because her resources are insufficient and "the thoughtless indulgence [to the need] of one would involve disproportionate neglect of others."[73] So, the mother at home is guided by the same fundamental principle as in the market place and she must equally employ in her actions all the human faculties already adumbrated.

It is a fact of existence that as human persons our life is constituted by many choices, and this is true too in terms of the market; indeed, the "mother's problem" is illustrative of this predicament. We can say that

> the art of life includes the art of effectively and economically distributing our vital resources of every kind, and domestic administration is a branch of this art in which it is possible to pay too dear in money for the saving of time, or too dear in time for the saving of money, or too dear in thought and energy for saving in bread, potatoes, or cream . . . Whatever the nature of the alternatives before us, the questions of the terms on which they are offered is always relevant. If we secure this, how much

---

present and operative in man . . . What distinguishes him [the economist] from other people is not the esoteric opportunity to deal with some special material not accessible to others, but the way he looks upon things and discovers in them aspects which other people fail to notice. It was this that Philip Wicksteed had in mind when he chose for his great treatise a motto from Goethe's *Faust*: Human life—everybody lives it, but only to a few is it known" (*Ultimate Foundation of Economic Science*, 70).

70. Wicksteed, *Common Sense of Political Economy*, 20.

71. Ibid., 19.

72. Ibid., my emphases.

73. Ibid.

of that must we pay for it, or what shall we sacrifice to it? And is
it worth is? What alternatives shall we forgo? And what would
be their value to us?[74]

I have mentioned how Wicksteed's *materfamilias* model can be in-
structive in regard to excavating the anthropological depths of human
action involved in the economic horizon. In a chapter entitled: "Business and the Economic Nexus," Wicksteed makes a comment that is relevant to this whole discussion. He explains that the broadest definition
of economics would "confine their scope to things that can be regarded
as in some sense exchangeable, and capable of being transferred."[75] But
then he makes an anthropologically significant distinction when he says
that "the housewife's administration of her stores amongst the different
claimants at home *is not a series of acts of exchange*, but is a series of *acts
relating to exchangeable things* . . . Economics includes all dealings with
exchangeable things, but does not extend beyond them."[76]

In other words, the mother's purposive actions can be explained in
terms of "economizing actions," but *all* of her purposive actions cannot
be explained by this analysis, that is, not all of them can be interpreted
as "economizing." Thus, we can say that economizing action can be interpreted in terms of purposeful action, but not all purposeful behavior
is necessarily economizing.[77] I remind the reader of the correlation here
with the Misesian-Kirznerian development of the same point in terms
of their understanding of entrepreneurial action.[78] Kirzner, for instance,
states, "being broader than the notion of economizing, the concept of
human action does not restrict analysis of the decision to the allocation
problem posed by the juxtaposition of scarce means and multiple ends."[79]
The human person and his actions cannot be reduced to the economizing
function alone because they also have the capacity for what Kirzner calls
the *alertness* necessary to act so as to "identify which ends to strive for
and which means are available."[80] We can perceive this too in terms of the

74. Ibid., 21.

75. Ibid., 160.

76. Ibid., 160, 162. John Mueller brings out this point in *Redeeming Economics*,
135, my emphases.

77. See Beaubout et al., *Beyond Self-Interest*, 29.

78. See chapters 6 and 7.

79. See Kirzner, *Competition and Entrepreneurship*, 33.

80. Ibid., 34.

actions of the mother in that she is involved in dealing with acts involving exchangeable things and acts concerning "nonexchangeable things like the persons she loves" at home.[81]

Wicksteed describes economic action essentially as an *"economic relation"* and, following his *materfamilias* analysis, attests that this relationship is entered into for multidimensional "human purposes and impulses, and rests in no exclusive or specific way on an egoistic or self-regarding bias."[82] He maintains that it is, of course, feasible and of use "to make an isolated study of the economic relation and the economic forces."[83] But this hypothesis should never be taken in point of fact as existing because in reality the *"economic relation,"* as well as being connected to other relations, is by its very nature generative of "other relations."[84]

In my opinion, we have here the beginnings in economic thought of a movement toward an enhanced economic anthropology. Wicksteed at least recognizes in his analysis of the *"mother's problem"* that some of her actions cannot be reduced to transactions or just as maximizing utility. Indeed, the mother is not the only one who acts in this way, so do other market participants, such as the entrepreneur we have often referred to in our study. So, the mother's actions actually mirror the actions of others, since in them there are reflected elemental anthropological principles that any adequate theory of human action must seek to account for. It is the case, then, that the *materfamilias* reality opens up our horizons to the fact that, as Mises says, economics actually "deals with the real actions of real men. Its theorems refer neither to ideal nor to perfect men, neither to the phantom of a fabulous economic man (*homo oeconomicus*) nor to the statistical notion of the average man (*homme moyen*)."[85]

Wicksteed does not actually go on to describe the acts, which cannot be strictly portrayed as "acts of exchange." John Mueller argues that Wicksteed has difficulty describing economic action with regard to the

81. Mueller, *Redeeming Economics*, 135.

82. Ibid.

83. Ibid., 170.

84. Wicksteed, *Common Sense of Political Economy*, 170.

85. Mises, *Human Action*, 651. Mises took the term "catallactics" from the economist and Anglican Archbishop of Dublin Richard Whately (1787–1863). Mises wrote that "the subject matter of catallactics is all market phenomena with all their roots, ramifications, and consequences . . . Acting man is always concerned both with 'material' and 'ideal' things. He chooses between alternatives . . . catallactics is the analysis of those actions" (ibid., 3, 233).

mother because the type of action Wicksteed is dealing with "is essentially gift."[86] The neoclassicals had no terminology for dealing with the action of "gift" "except by assuming that they are disguised exchanges."[87] But Wicksteed cannot be necessarily faulted for this since, I believe, the "higher anthropological viewpoint" was at the time still something that possibly lay beyond the immediate concerns of economic science. In any case, it is interesting that Wicksteed develops his own type of anthropology, which he describes as "*non-tuism.*" He famously wrote that the "economic relation" essentially ignores both egotistic and altruistic motives. He says, "The specific characteristic of the economic relation is not its 'egoism,' but its 'non-tuism.'"[88] Wicksteed understands by this the fact that the economic relation "does not exclude from my mind every one but me, it potentially includes everyone but you."[89] In light of this the very essence of an economic transaction is that I am not considering "*you*" at all other than "as a link in the chain."[90] This means, according to Wicksteed, that I may, of course, be "other-centered" in my actions but they are "certainly not for your sake."[91] Another important insight Wicksteed had was that "the mother is a person, not an individual . . . even a shipwrecked Robinson Crusoe—is not an *individual* but a *person*—which means, in part, an intelligent being with relationships to other persons."[92] What emerges in Wicksteed's *mother model* is the analysis of an acting "human person" where there is uncovered a whole intricate web of personal, social, cultural and economic relationships but this was left largely undeveloped or simply ignored in the froth and bubble of economic history.

V. A Polish-American Nobel Prize–Winning Economist Turns the Spotlight on the Human Person

Another example of an economic theorist who turned the spotlight upon the human person is the Polish economist Leonid Hurwicz, a Nobel Prize

---

86. Mueller, *Redeeming Economics*, 136.
87. Ibid.
88. Wicksteed, *Common Sense of Political Economy*, 180.
89. Ibid., 174.
90. Ibid.
91. Ibid.
92. Ibid.

winner who worked on "mechanism design" theory.[93] This whole area might seem somewhat contrary to "free market" dynamics since the market economy seems fundamentally opposed to the notion of deliberate design or command. Nonetheless, mechanism design theory was actually established in order to address the main challenge posed by Mises and Hayek. Peter Boettke explains that "it all starts with Mr. Hurwicz's response to Hayek's famous paper, 'The Use of Knowledge in Society.' In the 1930s and '40s, Hayek was embroiled in the 'socialist calculation debate.' Mises . . . had raised the challenge in his book 'Socialism,' and before that in an article, that without having the means of production in private hands, the economic system will not create the incentives or the information to properly decide between alternate uses of scarce resources. Without the production process of the market economy, socially desirable outcomes will be impossible to achieve."[94]

It was Hayek who published Mises's essay in English in his own work titled *Collectivist Economic Planning*. As we've previously explained Hayek basically summarized and clarified Mises's argument and showed how the economic problem society faced was not just a question of the allocation of resources but the challenge was inherently "*epistemological*," that is, "how to mobilize and utilize the knowledge dispersed throughout the economy."[95] Hurwicz embraced the challenge set up by the original Hayekian-Misesian contention, that is, the assertion that socialism could not possibly mobilize the dispersed knowledge in society so as to allow for rational economic calculation permitting the alternative uses of limited resources. Mises and Hayek held that you could not simply replace "the invisible hand of the market" with one guided by the government.[96] This is not after all *how* the economy actually works and furthermore to do this would destroy the dynamics involved in the market process. Here we can see that we are concerned not just with a question of economic efficiency but an anthropological issue as well. As I have explained the free economy presupposes the actions of many individual human purposive agents. The socialist market solution actually fails "because the accounting prices set by the planners and bureaucrats charged with managing

93. Hurwicz shared the Nobel Prize in economic science with Eric Maskin and Roger Myserson. Hurwicz was the oldest recipient of the prize.

94. Boettke, "A Market Nobel," *Wall Street Journal*, October 16, 2007, http://online.wsj.com/article/SB119249811353060179.html.

95. Ibid.

96. Ibid.

the economy cannot perform the *epistemological function* demanded of them in the absence of fully functioning markets in consumer and capital goods; prices can only reflect the relative value of goods and services . . . if they are generated by *genuine markets* driven by the *polycentric choices* of consumers and producers."[97]

Hurwicz's project which eventually led to his being awarded the Nobel prize, was to see whether Mises and Hayek were right or wrong in their assumptions; suppositions which in the first place have deep anthropological roots. Hurwicz and his colleagues understood clearly that economic activity does not take place in a vacuum. Economic action occurs in the context "of institutions and frameworks"[98] that have their own "laws, customs, formal organizations."[99] Hurwicz and Reiter called these structures "*mechanisms*."[100] In a modern economy like that of the United States, to describe economic activity only in terms of production, consumption or exchange would be inadequate because they claim that a large amount of what is considered as economic activity actually involves "*creating* or *operating* a mechanism."[101] Hurwicz's conclusion was basically that Mises and Hayek were correct in their understanding of what the essential elements of the free market were and that "to function properly, any economic system must . . . structure incentives so that dispersed and sometimes conflicting knowledge in society is mobilized to realize the gains from exchange and innovation."[102]

In *Designing Economic Mechanisms* the authors explain that the book's aim is

> to present systematic methods for designing *decentralised* economic mechanisms whose performance *attains specified goals* . . . Economic activity has been classified as production, consumption, and exchange. These activities are constrained by restrictions on resource availabilities, and *on knowledge* of technological possibilities . . . Knowledge of resource constraints and of technological possibilities is generally *distributed among economic agents*. Consequently no economic agent . . . can know the totality of what is *feasible* and what is not. The preferences

97. Meadowcroft, *Ethics of the Market*, 23, my emphases.
98. Hurwicz and Reiter, *Designing Economic Mechanisms*, 15.
99. Ibid.
100. Ibid.
101. Ibid.
102. Boettke, "A Market Nobel."

of economic agents are also distributed among agents; they are typically interpreted as private information . . . They play a dual role: they understand the *motivations of agents* . . . and they also play a role in determining the criteria of economic efficiency and hence in defining the goals of economic activity.[103]

It was the "existential shift" in Austrian economic thinking and the challenges it inevitably unfolded which provided Hurwicz's original inspiration. It is the fundamental discovery that the design of all designs in the free market process and that upon which an adequate model can be built is the freely *"acting"* human person. Mises and Hayek stressed that the "private-property rights that come with the rule of law, freedom of contract, and freedom of association" are essential and a *conditio sine qua non* for an effectively functioning economy.[104] This is because human beings act for intended purposes, which are not just accidental, but are constitutive of their very nature. If the social, political or economic environment severely limits these personalistic principles then economic action runs the risk of serious derailment. It appears therefore that such economic action is not contrary but integral to human nature because, as Mises wrote, "Thinking and acting are not contrary to nature; they are, rather, the foremost features of man's nature. The most appropriate description of man as differentiated from nonhuman beings is: a being *purposively* struggling against the forces adverse to his life."[105]

I believe that Hurwicz and other economists developed their theories on the basis of what I call the irreducible "anthropological projection" of the acting human person in the economic arena. Hurwicz and Reiter in explicating mechanisms and design state that "if there is only one way of organizing, then there is nothing to choose."[106] In other words, they understand economic activity as a "multidimensional" reality and, as they describe, varying "across, space, time and types" of economic action.[107] This dynamic nature of economic life can be explained because of the nature of the human agents who are the source and origin of the drama. A relevant philosophical question, which we can continually keep before us concerns, the adequacy of any theory of the human person

103. Hurwicz and Reiter, *Designing Economic Mechanisms*, 14, my emphases.

104. Boettke, "A Market Nobel."

105. Mises, *Human Action*, 882.

106. Hurwicz and Reiter, *Designing Economic Mechanisms*, 19.

107. Ibid.

we have. And this applies equally to Mises and other economic thinkers. Mises's praxeology, for example, accounts for a great deal of human action but not its totality. It is true to say that his overall emphasis on the "subjective nature of human action led him to neglect the possibility of objective realities" which might also account for human action.[108] Any philosophical anthropology must be measured by its openness to the multidimensional reality of human action otherwise it remains reductive in itself. Scholars raise these legitimate concerns regarding "economic models of human nature" employed by various economic schools. Even the economist Murray Rothbard is critical of the Austrian school and its development of the subjective value theory. Some theorists have taken the theory too far, he argues, and the problem that emerges is that "everything is subjective and economics as a science dissolves."[109] Rothbard holds that Austrian economics "must not be equated with the endless repetition of the words 'subjectivism' and 'uncertainty.'"[110] On the other hand, if you take the Chicago and Virginia schools of thought, for instance, they rely on differential calculus and assume that "human action takes place in finitely small, but discrete steps."[111] This involves the whole area of calculus but the philosophical challenge or question is always to see if human purposeful action can be totally measured in this way. The challenge is to retain what we've called the "anthropological balance" in the perspectives we adopt and not jettison a proper concept of the human person from the economic process. This is because in the long-term this results in the "debunking" of economics and turning it into something it is not.

VI. Human Action: Toward an Anthropological Enhancement

So, having surveyed various economic and philosophical writers in this book with a view to disclosing some of the personcentric principles that are at the heart of the drama of the free economy, we conclude this chapter with a discussion of the possibilities for the elaboration, growth and possible development of what I have referred to as the need for a

108. See Beaubout et al., *Beyond Self-Interest*, 100.

109. See Gordon and Hoppe, "Introduction," in Rothbard, *Logic of Action*, 1:xiii.

110. Ibid.

111. Donohue-White et al., *Human Nature*, 65.

"higher anthropological viewpoint" in economic reflection. Just as in the Austrian school of economic thought, so too various philosophers have attempted to focus on human action in their anthropological thematizations. They open up interesting areas for a possible elaboration of what some commentators refer to as the need for an enhanced praxeology.[112] Indeed, various Austrian economists recognize the limitations of a strictly praxeological approach perceiving that there are positive areas for development in terms of the overall investigation into capturing the truth of the reality of the acting human person. This is not only in the area of economics but also in the different dimensions of human existence, making applications to themes like the ethics of human liberty. Rothbard clearly articulated the need for a broader perspective[113] when he wrote, "Praxeology or economics, as well as the utilitarian philosophy in which this science has been closely allied, treat 'happiness' in the purely formal sense as the fulfilment of those ends which people happen—for whatever reason—to place high on their scales of value. Satisfaction of those ends yields to man his 'utility' or 'satisfaction' or 'happiness.'"[114]

The subjective theory of value presupposed by the formal science of praxeology or of economic theory is, according to Rothbard, "perfectly proper."[115] But this does not mean that value or utility is purely subjective and depending on individual choice alone. This is because in another sense value is also "objective" as it is "determined by the natural law of man's being, and here 'happiness' is for man considered in the common-sensical, *contentual* sense."[116] In other words, the well-being or the "good" of the human person is constitutive of what it means and necessitates to be a fulfilled being, that is, to be "who" I am as a person and not just as a "solipsistic" individual. Rothbard explains that "the natural law ethic decrees that for all living things, 'goodness' is the fulfilment of what is best for that type of creature."[117] So, in the case of the human being, goodness or badness is determined "by what fulfils or thwarts what is best" for the person's nature.[118] This is not therefore merely dependent on individual

112. See Beabout et al., *Beyond Self-Interest*, 101.

113. See Casey, *Murray Rothbard*, 42.

114. Rothbard, *Ethics of Liberty*, 12.

115. Ibid.

116. Ibid.

117. Ibid.

118. Ibid.

human choice (that is, the "subjective"), since I cannot necessarily just decide on *being* a "*content-less*" creature. This implies that human value has "*content*," that it is "objective" and cannot be arrived at in a purely formal sense only.

We are concerned here with the anthropological enlargement of a theory of human action and its possible implications and applications in the field of economics. It is interesting to note that Rothbard elaborates on this wider discussion by drawing on the writings of various thinkers including the American philosopher Henry Veatch. Veatch was a neo-Aristotelian and a proponent of rationalism, authoring *Rational Man: A Modern Interpretation of Aristotelian Ethics*. Rothbard quotes from Veatch's *For an Ontology of Morals* recalling that "it is in virtue of a thing's nature—i.e., of its being the kind of thing that it is—that it acts and behaves the way it does. Is it not also in virtue of a thing's nature that we often consider ourselves able to judge what that thing might or could be, but perhaps isn't?"[119] Indeed, Veatch in his work *Swimming Against the Current in Contemporary Philosophy*, while mentioning other studies also singles out Rothbard's *The Ethics of Liberty* as having been particularly helpful to him in his philosophical investigations.[120] This multidisciplinary approach to an adequate elaboration of an economic anthropology isn't surprising since the truth about the reality of the human person requires it. Rothbard sees positive areas for the development and application of Veatch's philosophical perspective in order to open up an enhanced understanding of praxeology, that is, of human action. Actually, there are examples, for instance, of the attempt to apply the Aristotelian perspective to economics and business. These developments also widen the horizons of our understanding of the amplitude and significance of human action. Tom Morris's *If Aristotle Ran General Motors*, for example, is a very popular book that takes the four transcendentals—Truth, Beauty, Goodness, and Unity—and applies them in order to obtain a broader understanding of the concept of human action in work. Themes covered include "the intellectual dimension at work . . . the aesthetic . . . creativity and the meaning of life . . . the challenge of ethical action . . . [and] the spiritual dimension at work."[121] Likewise, Wolfgang

---

119. Ibid., 11 n. 7.

120. Veatch, *Swimming Against the Current*, 175 n. 2.

121. Morris, *If Aristotle Ran General Motors*, vii–viii.

Grassl's work is interesting in this regard since it seeks to apply Aquinas's human action theory to business management.[122]

Elaine Sternberg gives a robust academic study of human action in business and economics in *Just Business: Business Ethics in Action*. Sternberg explains that the focus of her study is to understand that business is a distinctive activity; it is therefore paramount to understand the business of business. Similarly, I claim, that it is equally important to understand the anthropological framework of the free economy. Sternberg's overall contribution in her study is in the field of business ethics. She points out that most approaches in business ethics actually lack any adequate philosophical basis and argues that "theories that cannot accommodate *human action* have little hope of making sense of ethics or of business."[123] That's why an enhancement in our understanding and the development of a higher anthropological framework or viewpoint and applying it to economics "makes the *world of action* more, not less, intelligible."[124]

122. See Grassl, "Aquinas on Management and Its Development," https://www.academia.edu/203178/Aquinas_on_Management_and_its_Development.

123. Sternberg, *Just Business*, 3.

124. Ibid., my emphases.

10

Being More: A Trinitarian Model Applied to Economic and Social Life

I. The Trinitarian Model as a Paradigm for the Intrinsic Integration of Economic Life

SOME PHILOSOPHERS AND THEOLOGIANS have made significant contributions in their investigations into "human action" by broadening our viewpoint on it and recognizing the implications of human existence being defined by the free choice of individuals who may, in fact, act on the basis of the reality of a "Trinitarian anthropology."[1] The Trinitarian model can be used in economic analysis because it measures up to the transcendent nature of human beings. From this perspective civil society is seen as composed of "real communities of persons" and any adequate account of human action must include this dimension.[2] One example of these new studies is by Enrique Cambón, who wrote *Trinità modello sociale* (*Trinity: Model of Society*) where he applies Trinitarian anthropological categories to the acting person in the social and economic world.[3] Our own study has focussed on economic human action and on broadening our interpretative horizons so are not directly concerned with Trinitarian

---

1. See Gold, *New Financial Horizons*, 57.

2. See Pope John Paul II, *Centesimus Annus: On the Hundredth Anniversary of Rerum Novarum*, no. 49.

3. See Cambón, *Trinità modello sociale*; Cambón, "Communione trinitaria e sviluppo sociale" [Trinitarian Communion and Social Development], 7–13. See also Giacinto Magro's essay "Trinità e vita sociale" [Trinity and Social Life].

models from a particularly confessional perspective. But in terms of any adequate theory of human action the significance of a Trinitarian model is that apart from accounting for individual action, as human agents we also participate in the reality of "intersubjectivity." Thus, any theory must be at least cognizant and explicatory of the "relational" nature of human persons.

Indeed, there have been calls from scholars for an *"enlargement of economic reason"* to embrace the multidimensional nature of us as human persons.[4] Vilfredo Pareto of the Lausanne school of economic thought, for example, once described how "the same man, which I consider as *homo oeconomicus* for an economic study, I can consider as *homo ethicus* for a moral study, as *homo religiosus* for a religious study etc. . . . [As] the physical body comprehends the chemical body, the mechanical body, the geometrical body, etc.; [so] the real man comprehends the *homo oeconomicus*, the *homo ethicus*, the *homo religiosus*, and so on."[5] In this regard various contemporary philosophers, theologians and economists maintain that Trinitarian categories can assist us in giving an enhanced explanation of the human person and indeed account for one other unique characteristic of human action, that is, that it can go beyond itself and its own self-interest. If we cannot account for this dimension of "human action" then, as Saul Bellow describes, there is the danger of not seeing "the lack of the human in the too-human" and failing to understand how life's drama involves us in the perpetual struggle "to free ourselves" from the "imprisoning self."[6] Actually, it can be argued that a philosophical-theological elaboration of human action allows us go beyond the clear boundaries and limitations of praxeology which we've discovered in our study.[7] If for instance, as Mises states, the central approach of praxeology is to deal "with the real actions of real men," then perforce it must attempt to account for the *"transcendent"* dimension in human action too.[8] The word "transcendent" here refers to the fact that some human actions cannot be explained only in terms of the maximizing "self-interest" hypothesis. We mentioned in chapter 7 how Israel Kirzner's contribution to the anthropological model debate in economics stresses that an adequate understanding of the human person, as the progenitor of action

4. See Grassl, *"Pluris Valere."*

5. Pareto, *Manual of Political Economy*, 18.

6. See Bellow, *Dangling Man*, 153.

7. See Casey, *Murray Rothbard*, 42.

8. Mises, *Human Action*, 651.

in the economic dimension, cannot be arrived at by an analysis limited to "economizing behavior." Likewise, we cannot, for instance, satisfactorily account for entrepreneurial action or indeed for the overall working of the free economy if our concept of human action is too reductive and limited. Consequently, an adequate account of human action cannot be given if some actions are excluded from an investigation leading to the general anthropological theory.

Mises set out the prerequisites of human action when he stated that

> acting man is eager to substitute a more satisfactory state of affairs for a less satisfactory . . . The incentive that impels a man to act is always some uneasiness. A man perfectly content with the state of his affairs would have no incentive to change things . . . But to make a man act, uneasiness and the image of a more satisfactory state alone are not sufficient. A third condition is required: the expectation that purposeful behavior has the power to remove or at least alleviate the felt uneasiness. These are the general conditions of human action. Man is the being that lives under these conditions. He is not only *homo sapiens*, but no less *homo agens*.[9]

Mises actually took this concept of "uneasiness" from John Locke's account of human action. Locke explained that what determines the will in human action is the "*uneasiness* a man is at present under."[10] This restlessness can certainly be the motivation of some human action but it clearly is not the driving force for all human action. Human actions can also be motivated by objective and transcendent values where the self-interest paradigm is insufficient to explain the action satisfactorily. This is where we must go beyond the praxeological confines in order to account for human action appropriately, as when the human person reveals himself or herself in their actions as *Homo donator*. In a discussion on the limitations of Misesian praxeology, Gregory Beabout poses insightful questions we can ask about an adequate theory of human action. He asks: "is love for the poor nothing more than the alleviation of uneasiness? Is charity nothing more than the most enlightened form of self-interest? Such categories of human motivation [that is, self-interest] break down as they are pressed against types of human action motivated by values that

---

9. Ibid., 13–14. In chapter 6 we already mentioned Mises's concept of the power of the mind to remove human "uneasiness."

10. Locke, *Essay Concerning Human Understanding*, 233.

call for a response from individuals beyond that of self-actualization."[11] It is also the case that modern business practices invariably go beyond traditional categories. Grassl points out how the "entrenched social dichotomies," as in market participants being "either consumers or producers," are actually "breaking down as value co-creation allows consumers to participate in the production of their goods." According to Grassl, open source software and shared online resources such as Wikipedia and music file sharing networks are all examples of the *"logic of gift"* being added to the "commercial logic."[12]

So, if at least like Ludwig von Mises we want to focus on "grasping the meaning of action" then we have to allow ourselves follow through wherever human action may lead us, and investigate it accordingly, so that the theory can be adequately interpretative of action. I have spoken about detecting a movement toward a higher anthropological viewpoint in some of the economic reflections we've considered in this study. Actually, it is in the reflections of philosophers and theologians and their application of the Trinitarian model to social reality that we can trace a development toward a "universal viewpoint" in regard to the articulation of an adequate theory of human action. In his inquiry into the nature of human understanding Lonergan explains what I have in mind. He explains how an investigation "must begin from a minimal viewpoint and a minimal context; it will exploit that minimum to raise a further question that enlarges the viewpoint and the context; it will proceed with the enlarged viewpoint and context only as long as is necessary to raise deeper issues that again transform the basis and terms of reference of the inquiry; and clearly, this device can be repeated . . . as often as required to reach the universal viewpoint and the completely concrete context that embraces every aspect of reality."[13]

A "viewpoint" can be interpreted as "an intellectual perspective based on sets of questions and insights into a related set of truths."[14] Lo-

11. Beabout et al., *Beyond Self-Interest*, 100.

12. See Grassl, "*Pluris Valere*," 323, 328. It is interesting to note clear references to these concepts in *Caritas in Veritate*. Pope Benedict XVI observes that if "economic, social and political development" is to be authentically human, then it must make room for the "the logic of gift" (nos. 34, 36). There is also reference to "hybrid forms of commercial behavior" which "aim at a higher goal than the mere logic of the exchange of equivalents, of profit as an end in itself" (no. 38).

13. Lonergan, *Insight*, 18. In chapter 4 I also outlined Lonergan's perspective on the importance of a "universal viewpoint."

14. Mathews, *Lonergan's Quest*, 413.

nergan's philosophical quest, for example, was primarily to try to give an adequate account of human knowledge.[15] The issues we've been more immediately concerned with in this investigation are to uncover the anthropological principles underlying the free economy and to obtain insights into the truth of the reality of the human person participating in the economic drama. Lonergan defines a universal viewpoint as "a potential totality of genetically and dialectically ordered viewpoints."[16] His conception of the movement toward a "universal viewpoint" can be applied to the development of a more comprehensive theory of human action. He stressed the fact that "the universal viewpoint is concerned with the interpreter's *capacity to grasp meanings*."[17] I hold that Mises's reflections on economics actually imply this too and he asserted that we have the capability to do this: "because we are human beings, we are in a position to grasp the meaning of human action, that is, the meaning that the actor has attached to his action. It is this comprehension of meaning that enables us to formulate the general principles by means of which we explain the phenomenon of action."[18] The overall Misesian-Austrian approach to and explanation of human action is understandable insofar as it goes but it is not a *terminus ad quem*—on the contrary, it is a *terminus a quo*. In terms of a general movement toward a "universal viewpoint" in understanding human action it is a foundational point. Taken therefore from what we can call a "minimum" viewpoint and context, this methodology starts with human action, with the acting subject at its core. We've seen how this perspective is central to many of the Austrian economists. As we've already noted throughout this book, Mises stated that the subject matter of "praxeology is human action. It deals with acting man, not with man transformed into a plant and reduced to a mere vegetative existence."[19] This is certainly a beginning in constructing an adequate economic anthropology but in no way would I regard it as sufficient. That's why various philosophers' and theologians' contributions and their application of the Trinitarian model to economic and social reality can, I believe, contribute to a more thoroughgoing understanding of human action.

15. Lonergan, *Insight*, 13.
16. Ibid., 587.
17. Ibid., 588, my emphasis.
18. Mises, *Epistemological Problems of Economics*, 137–38.
19. Mises, *Human Action*, 29.

Indeed, we shouldn't be especially surprised by references to the writings of theologians in trying to outline a more comprehensive understanding of human action in the economic drama. As economic life expanded throughout Europe in the Middle Ages, for example, clerics found an increasing number of people consulting them on issues and asking questions: "What was the just price? When was a person no longer obliged to adhere to a contract? When was charging interest legitimate?"[20] And so it was that theologians then reflected on these social and economic questions. It is in this context that the unique contribution of the Scholastics to economic theory emerges, and as I mentioned in chapter 4 Joseph Schumpeter's *History of Economical Analysis* recaptured this dimension in the history of economic thought. The historical scholar Jürg Niehans observed how "the scholastics thus found it necessary to descend from theology into the everyday world of economic reality, of early capitalism, foreign trade, monopoly, banking, foreign exchange and public finance. What one knew about these things in the School of Salamanca was hardly less than Adam Smith knew two hundred years later, and more than most students know today."[21] Thus, if the medievals looked to the Scholastics for help in reflecting on social and economic dimensions, it is not incongruous for us to apply the insights of contemporary philosophers and theologians who find in the interpersonal life of the Trinity not just a spiritual or theological abstraction but a "social model." These reflections are not therefore "dinosauric," that is, out of place and out of time, but can actually assist us in recapturing the reality and full amplitude of the acting person in the economic drama of life.

I have mentioned the writings of Enrique Cambón, mostly published in Italian, but in the English-speaking world the contribution of the American philosopher and theologian Michael Novak can also be cited.[22] His 1982 book *The Spirit of Democratic Capitalism* was novel at the time in its theological and philosophical articulation of the free market as the process that creates innovative opportunities for human flourishing and as not being necessarily inimical to the Christian tradition. Novak does not develop any economic reflections based on the interpersonal life

20. See Gregg, *Tea Party Catholic*, 69.

21. See Niehans, *History of Economic Theory*, 16; cited in Gregg, *Tea Party Catholic*, 70.

22. The work of the English academic Edward Hadas can also be referred to. See *Human Goods, Economic Evils: A Moral Approach to the Dismal Science*, along with many other books published in the area.

of the Trinity in his 1982 work but in his subsequent writings he moves beyond any notion of the human person as understood solely as a "self-maximizing" agent in economic life. Novak explains how openness to the truth of human action propels us toward understanding the human person also as a "self-transcender." He explains how we essentially move beyond pure egoism when he says "we imagine that self-interest sets man against man, and drives individuals apart in centrifugal directions. We forget that human action is full of intelligence. Action is not random, wholly undirect. Free persons are intelligent and self-correcting. They have an interest in order . . . What actually moves them is their own practical intelligence."[23]

In the Anglo-Saxon world reflections on an elaborated economic anthropology based on a Trinitarian dynamic are slowly emerging.[24] I refer here to two books in particular, both of them authored by Lorna Gold: *The Sharing Economy: Solidarity Networks Transforming Globalisation* and *New Financial Horizons: The Emergence of an Economy of Communion*. In a discussion on the model of business used by a worldwide network of companies involved in a project called the Economy of Communion, Gold explains their "Trinitarian perspective." She points out how even in the history of Christianity the doctrine of the Trinity has been invariably treated as "an unfathomable mystery" and how it has ended up being understood as having "nothing to do with human life" or indeed with economic life. She explains how "Kant once wrote that the doctrine of the Trinity does not mean anything in practice." Furthermore, indicating the abject failure among theologians and others to reflect on the role of the Trinitarian dynamic in human existence, Karl Rahner once remarked, "that if the doctrine of the Trinity was to be eliminated from theology nothing would change in theory—nor in practice in the life of Christians."[25]

In fact, the Italian theologian Piero Coda, who has influenced many writers in the Bologna school of economics, can be seen as a corrective in this regard.[26] He highlights the centrality in Hegel's thinking of both the death of Christ and of the Trinity for a thoroughgoing understanding of

23. See *Free Persons and the Common Good*, 78.

24. See Grassl, "Integral Human Development," 135–55.

25. See Gold, *New Financial Horizons*, 56.

26. I will explain the viewpoint of the Bologna school of thought later. They fundamentally try to develop a personcentric understanding of economic, social, and political realities.

human history. He prefaces his book on Hegel, *Negation and the Trinity: A Hypothesis Concerning Hegel*, with two quotations from Hegel: "the death of Christ is the central point around which everything hinges" (*Lectures on the Philosophy of Religion*) and that "whoever does not know that God is Trinity, knows nothing of Christianity. This new principle is the axis around which the history of the world turns" (*Lectures on the Philosophy of History*).[27] Coda speaks of the necessity of a "Trinitarian humanism" applied to the "ethical-political" field and I would complement this with a similar need in the "economic" dimension. The challenge he sees is "for contemporary thought to project an integral humanism . . . which . . . could be called a *trinitarian humanism*."[28] The philosopher Gennaro Cicchese in an essay titled "Pensare l'intersoggettività. Contesto antropologico e provocazione teologico" (Intersubjective Thought: The Anthropological Context and Theological Ramifications) suggests in light of the Trinitarian paradigm the need for a rethinking of "intersubjectivity." He speaks about "il 'di più' antropologico," literally, "the anthropological extra" or the "higher viewpoint" I have mentioned which the Trinitarian perspective contributes to. He says that a "Christian-inspired anthropology contains not only an original interpretation, but also a new solution of the relationship with the 'other.'"[29] Coda also comments on the centrality of the theme of "intersubjectivity based ultimately on the trinitarian model" in modern ethical and political thought.[30]

Joseph Ratzinger (later Pope Benedict XVI) likewise observed the importance of the connection between the Trinity and human existence. He wrote that "just as we have reached the extreme limit of theory, the extreme of practicality comes into view: talking about God discloses what man is; the most paradoxical approach is at the same time the most illuminating and helpful one."[31] Pope Francis emphasizes how St.

27. See Coda, *Il negativo e la Trinità: Ipotesi su Hegel*, my translation. Other interesting scholarly contributions on the theme of the application of Trinitarian categories to contemporary thought can be found in Coda and Tapken, *La Trinità e il pensare: Figure percorsi prospettive* [The Trinity and Thought: Figures, Paths and Perspectives]. Piero Coda and the philosopher Massimo Donà have written *Pensare la Trinità: Filosofia e orizzonte trintario* [Thinking the Trinity: European Philosophy and Trinitarian Horizons].

28. Coda, *Il negativo e la Trinità*, 418, my translation. See also Purcell, "Towards a Trinitarian Humanism," 247–71.

29. Coda and Tapken, *La Trinità e il pensare*, 321–30, my translation.

30. See Coda, *Il negativo e la Trinità*, 418, my translation.

31. Ratzinger, *Introduction to Christianity*, 190.

Francis of Assisi "points out to us the challenge of trying to read reality in a Trinitarian key." He describes how in the Trinitarian model we can "discover a key to our own fulfilment. The human person grows more, matures more and is sanctified more to the extent that he or she enters into relationships, going out from themselves to live in communion with God, with others and with all creatures. In this way, they make their own that Trinitarian dynamism which God imprinted on them when they were created."[32]

Lorna Gold shows in her studies how Chiara Lubich, a charismatic proponent of the concept of the Trinity as a social model, equally understands the far-reaching social and economic implications of the doctrine. Lubich was the founder of the international Focolare Movement and launched the Economy of Communion project in 1991 in São Paulo, Brazil. Her originating insight was the application of the interpersonal life of the Trinity to social, political and economic reality. Today the Economy of Communion project comprises a network of more than eight hundred businesses worldwide.[33] She sees that the reality of the Trinity is not just a matter of faith but "that all social relationships, including the economic, can be re-interpreted in such a way as to cast light onto the interpersonal dimension of human existence."[34] So when we come to investigate economics with this "higher viewpoint" in mind, what's involved in this challenge is basically an extensive remapping of economic theory so that it measures up to the reality of the human person who lives and works in a multidimensional and "intersubjective" context. Lubich's critical insight is her suggestion that the Trinitarian model can illuminate our understanding of the *acting person* even in the economic drama of human life. Throughout this book we've seen how in economic literature the economic agent is frequently viewed as a *purely self-maximizing agent*. But this one-dimensional perspective conceals the reality of who we are as human persons and it is not truly an authentic account of how the human person acts in the free economy. Indeed, the economist Wilhelm Röpke explains how such a view of the human person as "*homo sapiens consumens* loses sight of everything that goes to make up human happiness apart from money income and its transformation into goods." This perspective is he says, "a false anthropology, one that lacks wisdom, [and]

32. *Laudato Sì*, nos. 239–40.

33. See http://www.edc-online.org/en/ for an explanation of the economic project.

34. See Gold, *New Financial Horizons*, 56.

misunderstands man." He asks, are we then just to give in to the interpretation of the market economy as being based upon the "icy water of egotistical calculation," which lets people gain the world but lose their souls? In fact, Röpke also calls for a "new humanism" and that we should "adopt a philosophy which, while rendering unto the market the things that belong to the market, also renders unto the spirit what belongs to it."[35]

A living economic reality can only be understood "through *continuous recourse to real life experience*."[36] For example, many of the Economy of Communion entrepreneurs throughout the world are discovering through their own experiences that "the true meaning of all their economic activities lies not in economic transaction *per se*, but in making it a 'meeting place' in the deepest sense of the word: a place of communion."[37] We can recall that even Bill Gates when asked about what motivated him to enter into business did not explain it solely in monetary terms. All commercial life is therefore influenced by a particular culture or vision and that is something, of course, which Max Weber also investigated.[38] Wicksteed's "mother model" (outlined in the previous chapter) was an example of the fact that the model of the human person who participates in the free economy should also be inclusive of the one "who could [also] be called *homo donator*."[39] Similarly, participants in the Economy of Communion project are motivated by a vision or culture which gives rise to "the category of gift or sharing" in their businesses and this can be called "a culture of giving."[40] It is based on the nature of the human person as someone who is open to going beyond their own self-interest. This characteristic is actually constitutive of who we are as human persons, and economic models and reflections must moreover measure up to the truth of this reality. Professor David Schindler also speaks about an economy of gift in a very interesting essay titled "'Homelessness' and Market Liberalism: Toward an Economic Culture of Gift and Gratitude."

---

35. Röpke, *Humane Economy*, 102, 113, 116.

36. See Bruni, *Economy of Communion*, 12.

37. Ibid., 17. The Economy of Communion networks of businesses are not the only ones that use "hybrid business models." The Compagnia delle Opere is another project composed of "for-profit" and "non-profit" businesses associated with Comunione e Liberazione. See Nanini, "A Catholic Alternative to Globalization?," 47–76.

38. See *The Protestant Work Ethic and the Spirit of Capitalism*.

39. Ibid., 22.

40. Ibid.

In it he gives an outline of what he would consider "to be an adequate anthropology" or model in the free market system.[41] He goes on to suggest "what this anthropology implies for an economy of gift and gratitude" and once again like Wicksteed he refers to the paradigm of the mother's action in the economic drama.[42] He refers to how restaurateurs often advertise their food as "home-cooked" or the way Grandma used to prepare it. They never just claim that the food "they serve is storepackaged and mechanically prepared."[43] No, they sell it based upon the difference of what a "home-cooked" meal means. And this has both an anthropological and an economic significance. Schindler sums up his approach by explaining "the mother's love, in brief, is not merely a matter of an intention remaining external to the food. On the contrary, her love *takes form* in the food, such that the food itself now takes on the form of love."[44] Schindler also analyzes Adam Smith's famous example where he says, "It is not from the benevolence of the butcher, the brewer, or the baker, that we expect our dinner, but from their regard to their own interest. We address ourselves, not to their humanity but to their self-love, and never talk to them of our own necessities but of their advantages."[45] But Schindler, just as I suggest, sees how "an anthropology of gift and gratitude transforms the original meaning of an economy and indeed of *homo economicus* as such."[46] This vision of the economy actually "deepens the reality . . . enhances the worth of *everything and everyone involved in the production and exchange of goods: self, thing and other.*" According to this perspective, baking out of the paradigm of love "by no means excludes baking also for profit." But the focus is now "person-centered" because "profit now is put into the service of and thereby integrated into the good of the person and of the thing in their proper created and artifactual reality as gift."[47]

Actually, a further development of this new "anthropological perspective" on the implications of a Trinitarian model in economics can be seen in the work of several economists and philosophers who have

---

41. See Bandow and Schindler, *Wealth, Poverty, and Human Destiny*, 349.

42. Ibid.

43. Ibid., 359.

44. Ibid., 360.

45. See Smith, *Wealth of Nations*, 22.

46. Bandow and Schindler, *Wealth, Poverty, and Human Destiny*, 362.

47. Ibid., 363, 364.

introduced the concept of "relational goods" into the theoretical debate. Luigino Bruni mentions the contributions of the philosopher Martha Nussbaum and the economists Benedetto Gui and Carole Uhlaner to this whole debate.[48] He outlines how Gui "defines relational goods as 'immaterial goods, and yet not services that can be consumed individually, but connected to interpersonal relationships.'"[49] This is the interpersonal dimension which is inherent to economic action but which is often excluded from consideration in rational-choice models. Gui analyzes the productive process as an "encounter" between vendor and purchaser, doctor and patient, where what is produced is not merely a tangible output like a transaction or the supply of a service but also "relational goods."[50] Bruni explains that "for both Gui and Uhlaner, relational goods do not coincide with the relationship itself: Friendship is not definable as a relational good but as a repeated interaction, a series of encounters characterized by affective states of which the relational good *is only one component*."[51] We cannot develop this theme here but I mention the theme of "relational goods" to illustrate how philosophers and economists are seeking new ways of opening up new horizons on the reality of the human person.

In this light the sociologist Vera Araùjo describes how in the Economy of Communion the "culture of giving encapsulates both the essence of the human person (by putting this relationship at the center and goal of everything) and a whole series of attitudes and behaviors that characterize human relationships."[52] In my view, the Economy of Communion venture and its Trinitarian viewpoint is an example of how an economic theory and the models employed by it could be "stress-tested" or "litmus-tested" by the reality and mystery of the human person and by the lived experiences of human existence. So, economics and theoreticians bear an essential responsibility to account for the "*person*" who is the *whole* and not just the *part* of the reality in which they find themselves. An economic theory can be subsequently measured as adequate only according to its openness to the claims and reality of what it means to be a human person; otherwise it is anthropologically and even economically

48. See Bruni, *Reciprocity, Altruism and the Civil Society*, 8. See also Uhlaner, "Relational Goods and Participation," 253–85.

49. Ibid.

50. See Bruni and Zamagni, *Civil Economy*, 240.

51. Ibid.

52. See *Wealth, Poverty, and Human Destiny*, 23.

unfit for purpose. The Trinitarian perspective applied to economic and social life is therefore an attempt to account for the "category of relation" which constitutes our very nature as human persons.[53] The theoretical developments I have outlined can, I believe, help us recapture and to appreciate the wealth of the person-centered roots which lie at the heart of economic actions in the free economy.

II. The Radical Solution: The Priority of the *Other* as *Me*

It is in light of some of these considerations that I view Cambón's treatment in *Trinità modello sociale* as a potential contribution toward the enhancement of a theory on human action. For example, he applies the perspective of "intersubjectivity" to economics when he writes, "How you treat *economic action* depends on how you conceive of relationships, be they primarily interpersonal, or social on all levels."[54] Alfred Schutz also emphasized that the world of ordinary life was "by no means my private world but is from the outset an intersubjective one."[55] Indeed, he remarked that

> if we retain the natural attitude as men among other men, the existence of others is no more questionable to us than the existence of an outer world. We are simply born into a world of others, and as long as we stick to the natural attitude we have no doubt that intelligent fellow-men do exist. Only if radical solipsists or behaviorists demand proof of this fact does it turn out that existence of intelligent fellowmen is a "soft datum" and incapable of verification (Russell). But in their natural attitude even those thinkers do not doubt the "soft datum" . . . As long as human beings are not concocted like homunculi in retorts but are born and brought up by mothers, the sphere of the "We" will be naïvely presupposed.[56]

In other words, *human action* presupposes the existence of others; therefore any theory must be inclusive of this anthropological reality. As I have said earlier on in the chapter it is interesting to see that Cambón

---

53. See Pope Benedict XVI, *Caritas in Veritate*, no. 53.

54. Cambón, *Trinità modello sociale*, 113, my emphasis.

55. Schutz, *On Phenomenology and Social Relations*, 163.

56. Ibid. I have already referred to Schutz in chapter 2.

and those associated with the Bologna school of thought do not consider Trinitarian conceptions as purely of confessional relevance. They see them as having implications in a theory of human action as well and as offering the possibility for an enhanced viewpoint and the context from which to analyze human action. In fact, Cambón explains the concept in terms of "alterity," as something that typically pertains to a Trinitarian conception of reality. This development goes well beyond the confines of Christian writers. Cambón has in mind here the work of philosophers like Emmanuel Levinas and the rich literature on the philosophy of the "Other" that has emerged in philosophy.[57] According to Levinas, when we come to the study of human action we encounter what he calls the ontological absurdity of the acting person and this expresses itself in multidimensional ways. Levinas, for instance, observes that "plants, animals, all living things hang onto their lives. For each one, it is the struggle for survival . . . And then comes the human, with the possible advent of an ontological absurdity: concern for others is greater than concern for oneself. This is what I call 'saintliness.' Our humanity consists in being able to recognize the priority of the other."[58]

Philosophers such as Martin Buber, Gabriel Marcel, Emmanuel Mounier, and Karl Wojtyła can be classified as philosophers of the "Other." The Swiss theologian Hans Urs von Balthasar also developed this area of thought in his writings. He wrote that "man exists only in dialogue with his neighbour . . . The 'I' is always indebted to a 'We.'"[59] Klaus Hemmerle, a German theologian, also attempted to apply a Trinitarian analysis to a theory of human action based on an ontology that perceives "being" as love. This opens up a dynamic and triadic conception of reality and human action occurs in this *Lebenswelt.*[60] Hemmerle's analysis of human

57. See Levinas, *Alterity and Transcendence.*

58. Levinas, *Unforeseen History,* 128.

59. See Schindler, *Hans Urs von Balthasar,* 3, 239. We can see a similar development of this theme in modern literature in the writings of the American author Walker Percy. Professor John Desmond observes how "all of Percy's fictions show a movement towards some genuine community as the novel ends, even if only between two people, a *solitude à deux,* which is for Percy the bedrock of all human community." He points out how Percy developed the idea of a "'new anthropology' based on the semiotic concepts of Charles Sanders Peirce" and how this "offered the hope for reuniting forms of knowledge and experience that have followed divergent paths at least since the Middle Ages." See Desmond, *Walker Percy's Search for Community,* 4.

60. See Norris, *Living a Spirituality of Communion,* 134. See also Hemmerle, *Dreifaltigkeit: Schlüssel zum Menschen, Schlüssel zur Zeit.*

action is based on a metaphysics of love. He wrote that: "Being is love, is relationship. The gift of one's self, therefore, is to be and if well understood, is to be lost in every other person, but so as to be reborn, in order to 'be' . . . In this way I can no longer represent the point of departure, the center and the point of arrival of my being in isolation. The Trinitarian existence can only be lived in reciprocity, as a 'we,' which at the same time does not dissolve *I* and *you* but constitutes them."[61]

These insights by sociologists, philosophers and theologians alike can, I contend, move us toward a redefinition of the person that emerges from the Judeo-Christian tradition. This understanding is very specific; it is that the *other* is another *I*. The fallout effect of this therefore in my political, social, and economic life is the challenge to understand and act according to the full anthropological measure of the reality of seeing "*oneself as another.*" This means that the "*other*" is another "*I*" and human action, therefore, must fit into this anthropological truth. It all might seem a far remove from the world of business, but it is not that remote from it and some economists and commentators are increasingly discovering this. At her conferral with an honorary doctorate in philosophy Chiara Lubich gave an interesting insight into an economy that is based on a culture of giving. She explained "there may be those who think that to affirm self implies a struggle against all that is not self, because what is not self is perceived as a limit and what is more, as a threat to the integrity of the self." But she points out that the reality is actually asymmetrical because "I am myself, not when I close myself off from the other, but rather when I give myself." She gives the example of giving away a flower: "If . . . I have a flower and I give it to someone, certainly I deprive myself of it, and in depriving myself, I am losing something of myself (i.e., non-being); in reality, precisely because I give that flower, love grows in me (i.e., being). Therefore, my subjectivity is when it is not, out of love; that is, when out of love it is completely transferred into the other."[62]

Indeed, if Descartes summed up his particular philosophy by stating, "I think, therefore I am," we can say that the Trinitarian anthropology and its dynamic inspiring the Economy of Communion vision can be summed up in the saying, "I love therefore, I am." In chapter 8 of this study, devoted to the nineteenth-century social entrepreneur Agnes

---

61. Hemmerle's original study is titled *Thesen zu einer trinitarischen Ontologie.* It was published in Italian under the title *Partire dall'unitá: La Trinità come stile di vita e forma di pensiero*, 45–46, my translation and emphases.

62. Lubich, *Essential Writings*, 211.

Morrogh-Bernard, I outlined how in her entrepreneurial innovation at Foxford, she was an exemplar of what David Walsh called the "flash of self-transcendence" of "love in action" for "others." I hold that the true path to human progress and the source of that wealth lies in the human person who goes beyond the self. Indeed, this dynamic of "self-transcendence" is intrinsic to who we are as "persons" and of necessity it spills out into all parts of our lives. Pope Benedict XVI hints at this *"intrinsicality"* when he discusses human development and progress in society and the economy. He observes how efforts are needed to ensure that the whole economy is more ethical but he suggests that this cannot happen "merely by virtue of an external label, *but by its respect for requirements intrinsic to its very nature.*"[63] Pope Francis also remarks on the unique ability of human persons to "go beyond." He observes that "human beings, while capable of the worst, are also capable of rising above themselves, choosing again what is good, making a new start" and how "no system can completely suppress our openness to what is good, true and beautiful."[64] When this understanding is applied to the human person we can understand how the radical solution of the priority of the "Other" as "Me" stems from the Trinitarian model and see how it is intrinsic even to the integration of economic life.

In this chapter, we've described how some entrepreneurs are influenced by the exemplar of a Trinitarian anthropology, which in turn casts light on their economic actions. Their discovery is that by transcending the self and moving beyond selfishness in the drama of economic life, their hearts and minds are "enlarged to the point that"[65] they can put into economic action the vision and reality of seeing the relationship between the individual entrepreneur and community as "a relation between one totality and another."[66] This is in line with Thomas Aquinas's reflection when he outlines how "the rationality of a part is contrary to the rationality of a person."[67] Thus, a central question facing all of us is, how do we build social and economic structures that respect and sustain "the freedom, integrity and creativity" of the "other"?[68] Recapturing the

63. Benedict XVI, *Caritas in Veritate*, no. 45.

64. Pope Francis, *Laudato Sì*, no. 205.

65. Ibid.

66. See Pope Benedict XVI, *Caritas in Veritate*, no. 53.

67. Ibid. Footnote 130 refers to St. Thomas Aquinas, *Sentences* III d.5, q.3, a.2. See also Walsh, "Theory and Practice as Responsibility," for reference to this point.

68. See Sacks, *Dignity of Difference*, 92.

person-centered roots of the free economy as we've sought to do in this study reveals to us that the economy can in itself be "an instance of the self-transcendence that marks a community of persons."[69] An adequate metaphysical interpretation of human economic action cannot be left at the level of description as being merely about the "exchange of things." The philosophers of the "Other" and the Christian tradition open up the horizon of "*a metaphysical interpretation of the 'humanum' in which relationality is an essential factor.*"[70] So, when it comes to an adequate articulation of an economic anthropology something more is needed than the usual models currently in use by theoreticians and social commentators. A fully systematic explanation of human economic action must take into account the fact that "in *commercial relationships* the *principle of gratuitousness* and the logic of gift as an expression of fraternity can and must *find their place within normal economic activity.*"[71] Economists, philosophers and theoreticians all bear a responsibility for the articulation of the multidimensional reality of the human person in the economic drama of life. So, we can appreciate that from this perspective the contributions by writers like Cambón, Hemmerle and others to a theory of human action are not merely idiosyncratic. They can be interpreted as the interpreter's capacity and ability to envisage the protean possibilities of the notion of human action, which varies in content with the experience, the insights, and the judgments of each individual person.[72]

Actually, Murray Rothbard clearly pointed out the need for a broader perspective in terms of achieving an adequate understanding of human action. Indeed, he adverts to this openly when he explains in his *magnum opus, Man, Economy, and State*, that "the analysis in chapter 1 was based on the logical implications of the assumption of action, and its results hold true for all action. The *application* of these principles was confined, however, to "Crusoe economics," where the actions of isolated individuals are considered by themselves. In these situations, there are no interactions between persons. Thus, the analysis could easily and directly be applied to *n* number of isolated Crusoes on *n* islands or other isolated

69. See Walsh, "The Person as the Heart of Benedict's New Evangelization."
70. See *Caritas in Veritate*, no. 55.
71. Ibid., no. 36.
72. Ibid.

areas. The next task is to apply and extend the analysis to consider inter-actions between individual human beings."[73]

Some readers may not, of course, agree with the various interpreta-tions of human action given in this study, but the analyses are all illustra-tions of the development of what I have referred to as movement toward a "universal viewpoint" in economic reflection. Indeed, the objection could be made that it is really not up to economics to account for the entirety of reality since it is simply the task of economists to devise models or to cre-ate maps to help us understand the economic process. Models are models and maps are maps and they should not be expected to show reality in its fullness. *Homo oeconomicus* some might say has its deficiencies but these can actually be useful and this may very well explain why in economics there is no outline of an anthropology beyond that of "economic man."

In one sense, there will be as many theories of human action as there are economists. But, I would argue, that since the free market economy can be understood as a process of continual creative discovery, so the human person, as the efficient cause of economic activity, is equally in-volved in a process of "self-enactment" within the economic arena.[74] It is the unfolding of this unique "human dimension" which should further-more be taken account of in economic reflections. The "existential shift" I outlined in chapter 9 as occurring in the Austrian school of economic thought can therefore be understood as an essential therapeutic moment in recapturing the anthropological reality lying at the heart of the free economy which can be easily eclipsed from our economic thinking. This has, I believe, subsequently led to a rich cross-fertilization of investiga-tions into the multidimensional nature of the human person, who in the role of the entrepreneur can be understood as an *exemplar* of the *acting person*. To paraphrase Sternberg's book title *Just Business*, if we want to make sense of the free market process we've to keep in mind one essential framework: "*Just the Person*"—and it is from this that an adequate eco-nomic understanding can unfold for us.

73. Rothbard, *Man, Economy, and State*, 79.
74. See Walsh, *Guarded by Mystery*, 46.

III. The "Person-Centered" Shift in Economic Reflections: The Bologna School of Thought

In this book I have given substantial consideration to the Austrian school's analysis of "human action" in the drama of economic life, with special reference to the role of entrepreneurial action in economic activity. We've referred to the "existential shift" found in some economic writings. This reorientation can be understood as paralleling to some degree what is termed the "existential turn" in modern philosophy. The "existential turn" in philosophy characterizes a stage in contemporary thought that prioritizes human existence and the human subject over and above a previous traditional focus on essence. David Walsh argues that two great manifestations of the modern spirit are the growth of science and technology and of the universal moral and political language of human rights. But a third great achievement of the modern movement is, he believes, the "philosophical revolution that prioritizes existence"[75] and that this philosophical shift is "the one that enables us to understand the viability of both science and rights."[76] A similar argument could be made, I contend, in relation to the shift toward the "person-centered" dimension in economic theory, and it is this movement in economics which opens up the horizon of meaning of the acting person in the free economy. We saw the beginnings of this in the Austrian school's development of the subjective theory of value as opposed to the labor theory of value promoted by Adam Smith and subsequently developed by others, most notably Karl Marx. We also observed in passing how the Scholastics and especially the Spanish theorists of the school of Salamanca with their own subjective value theory actually predated the Austrian theorists.[77]

There is no doubt that the human person and his or her actions are the indispensable presuppositions of the Austrian approach to the study of economics because only human persons "act." Their hermeneutic on economics starts and ends with the acting human person and any analysis of economic action is obviously an investigation into human action. But this does not automatically mean that "economic action" is the totality of all human action. Indeed, I have argued that the Austrian theory on human action in the economic arena is crucial to understanding the

75. Walsh, *Modern Philosophical Revolution*, xii.

76. Ibid.

77. See Moss and Ryan, *Economic Thought in Spain*; Chafuen, *Faith and Liberty*; Grice-Hutchinson, *The School of Salamanca*.

free market reality but at the same time it is not necessarily sufficient to capture the truth concerning the multidimensional nature of action and the human person.[78] The whole understanding of the basis of the free economy in contemporary economic writings has suffered greatly because of the overshadowing of what I call the "human face" in its models. The Great Recession and subsequent economic fragmentation in the world is, as we've explained, often interpreted as the end result of the free market process since it is assumed to be intrinsically flawed and inimical to the well-being of the human person. In this sense there is what I would call a resulting "bewitchment"[79] of economics; in this scenario the human mind and imagination can "cut loose from reality" and set up economic concepts that we can "call Second Reality because they pretend to refer to reality though in fact they do not."[80]

In my concluding remarks, I will briefly refer more directly to the writings of the group of economists, philosophers and thinkers sometimes called the Bologna school of thought. As I explained this school of reflection attempts to develop an adequate concept of the acting person in the free economy but also on the political and social levels. Coda speaks of how a renewed revival of "intersubjectivity" on the basis of a Trinitarian model could throw light on the ever increasing and precarious relationship between the human person and "nature and the cosmos: work and technology."[81] Most of the writings from the Bologna scholars

78. Throughout this chapter I have outlined how the concept of "self-interest" does not adequately explain "entrepreneurial action." Entrepreneurial action involves an inherent "risk" for the entrepreneur himself or herself. Nobody would necessarily set out to "undo" oneself since it is not in the "interests" of the "self" to do so. It is for this reason that we have to broaden our horizons of explanation in terms of such human action. Bruce Baker notes how "entrepreneurial risk is motivated by a desire to deliver benefits to others, not merely to oneself. There is an element of grace in entrepreneurial behavior because it rests on the willful decision of an individual to commit personal time, energy, and resources, in an effort to benefit others without any assurance that the self-sacrifice will reap benefits for others or for oneself" ("Entrepreneurship as a Sign of Common Grace," 92).

79. I have taken the concept of "bewitchment" from Emmanuel Levinas, who explains that "the first part of [Cervantes'] Don Quixote has, as its principal theme, bewitchment; the bewitchment of the appearance that sleeps in all appearing . . . The 'Knight with the Sad Face' lets himself be bewitched, loses his understanding, and assures everyone that the world and he himself are the victims of bewitchment" ("Don Quixote: Bewitchment and Hunger," in God, Death, and Time, 168).

80. Voegelin, What Is History?, 114.

81. Coda, Il negativo e la trinità, 420, my translation.

are naturally in Italian. I have discovered in them certain anthropological principles like human alertness, insight, choice, initiative, and innovation (all associated as we have seen with our earlier analysis of entrepreneurial action), which emerge as of central importance for an adequate philosophical understanding of the acting human person in the economic horizon. In a Fordham University journal Luigino Bruni and Amelia Uelmen, for example, both influenced by this school of thought, wrote that "the emergence of the modern market economy has been presented most of all as an affirmation of a *new humanism* based on a conviction which is more moral than economic—that wherever markets arrive, sooner or later, also interpersonal relationships will become more free and more equal, thus imploding feudal and caste systems."[82] This is because the "category of relation" in human economic action is not just "accidental" but is "substantive" in its very nature.[83] I will now outline some of the other salient references in this rich literature that are of interest to our general theme.[84] Luigino Bruni points us toward important insights in regaining the essential human elements of the market economy. He reminds us that

> the market when it functions properly is a place where innovations and human creativity are favored and rewarded. It is all too clear that we will never emerge from this crisis without a revival of entrepreneurship . . . The market, the competition of the market . . . can be seen, that is, if we want to understand it in its totality, as a race to innovate: whoever innovates grows and lives, whoever does not innovate remains behind and exits from the economic and civil game . . . The author who has most developed this *virtuous* dynamic of the market (the capacity to innovate is certainly a virtue, because it is an expression of *areté*, of excellence) is the Austrian economist Joseph A. Schumpeter.[85]

82. See Bruni and Uelmen, "Religious Values and Corporate Decision-Making," 667, my emphases.

83. Aristotle actually understood "relations" as merely "accidental."

84. The following is a small example of studies by these Italian scholars. Professor Stefano Zamagni is based at Bologna University—hence the name of the school of thought, although the writers come from various European countries. Some of the studies are Moramarco and Bruni, *L'economia di comunione*; Bruni and Pelligra, *Economia come impegno civile*; Bruni, *La ferita dell'altro*; Zamagni, *L'economia del bene commune*; Becchetti, *Oltre l'homo oeconomicus*; Campiglio and Zamagni, *Crisi economica, crisi antropologica*.

85. Bruni, "Su imprenditori e concorrenza," 1–14, my translation.

Professor Stefano Zamagni of the University of Bologna speaks of the urgent need to update the concept of the market economy with a more "personalistic perspective."[86] He writes about the need to turn away from any type of "hyper-minimalist" conception of the human being toward what I have described as a "higher anthropological viewpoint" on human action.[87] With this in mind he points out that "the Economy of Communion says to us that the market . . . can become an instrument which can reinforce social ties, favouring both the promotion of practices of wealth distribution through its mechanisms and the creation of an economic space in which it is possible to regenerate those values (such as *trust, sympathy, benevolence*) on which the existence of the market itself depends."[88] Indeed, John Mundell, CEO of Mundell & Associates, an Economy of Communion business, gives an example of what this means in practice in a company when he says, "The communion we build and rebuild over time is not some nebulous, idyllic, textbook concept, but a true, lived, concrete and essential reality that grows deeper and deeper as we take the steps towards each other in the daily happenings of our businesses."[89]

The philosopher Antonio Baggio in "Capitalismo e Impresa" (Capitalism and Enterprise) gives particular consideration to the role of the entrepreneur in the market economy.[90] He observes how the entrepreneur was often viewed as an exploiter but then in the era of "Reaganomics" and "Thatcherism" the situation turned around completely from a state of extreme "anti-entrepreneurism" to its exact opposite. But in either case the figure of the entrepreneur was deformed.[91] Baggio makes reference to Max Weber explaining that the kernel of his intuition concerning the entrepreneur was the fact that the market process cannot be reduced "merely to its material elements, to the unleashing of a productive capacity never experienced before by man."[92] In fact, the Weberian entrepreneurial theory, Baggio says, "carries with it a set of attitudes,

---

86. See Pavan, *Dire Persona*, 254–55.

87. Campiglio and Zamagni, *Crisi Economica*, 255.

88. See Zamagni, "On the Foundation and Meaning of the 'Economy of Communion' Experience," in Bruni, *Economy of Communion*, 134, my emphases.

89. See Gallagher and Buckeye, *Structures of Grace*, xvii.

90. Baggio, "Capitalismo e Impresa," in *Etica ed economia*, 93–140. Antonio Maria Baggio is Professor of Social Ethics at the Pontifical Gregorian University in Rome.

91. Ibid., 106–7.

92. Ibid., 108.

ideals, often religiously inspired, which are endowed, so to speak, with its very own spirit."[93] This anthropological understanding of the role of the entrepreneur as an essential participant in the economic drama was, according to Baggio, and as we have discussed, jettisoned from the economic accounts of human action in the free market theories of both Smith and Ricardo. Nonetheless, he notes that it was the continentals like Jean-Baptiste Say and the German Friedrich von Hermann who opposed the obfuscation of this appreciation of entrepreneurial action that occurred in economic writings.[94] In this regard, Murray Rothbard also refers to von Hermann, explaining that the English economist Thomas C. Banfield (c. 1800–1860) spent time in Germany and while there came under the influence of the marginal theorist Heinrich von Thünen and "the advanced Smithian Friedrich von Hermann."[95] On Banfield's return to Cambridge, he referred to von Hermann in his lectures. Rothbard observes that in the preface to Banfield's lectures published as *The Organisation of Industry* (1845), Banfield referred to the enormous changes brought about in economic theory

> during the past two decades *by the subjective theory of value*, "which demands of producers at least as much attention to the physical and mental improvement of their consuming fellow-citizens as to the mechanical operations" or production . . . It certainly seems that economics in England, by the later 1840's, was poised for a mighty "Austrian" breakthrough, for an integrated system elaborating the effect of human purposes and values and their interaction with the scarcity of resources. Yet something happened; and economics, poised for a great breakthrough, sank back into the slough of fallacies constituting the Ricardian system.[96]

Baggio explains entrepreneurship in a way already familiar to us in our study, that is, as "not being static, it is not cold calculation, it is dynamism, fantasy, creativity."[97] Whatever the history and categorization of the entrepreneur, he considers entrepreneurial action as rooted in the

---

93. Ibid.

94. Ibid., 113. Rothbard comments, "If Adam Smith purged economic thought of the very existence of the entrepreneur, J.-B. Say, to his everlasting credit, brought him back" (*Classical Economics*, 25).

95. See Rothbard, *Classical Economics*, 130.

96. Ibid. My emphases.

97. Baggio, *Etica ed economia*, 115.

freedom of the human person. Human action in the free market process involves the flourishing of some of the following virtues among the economic participants: "diligence, industriousness, prudence in undertaking reasonable risks, reliability and fidelity in interpersonal relationships, as well as courage in carrying out decisions which are difficult and painful but necessary, both for the overall working of a business and in meeting possible setbacks."[98]

These theorists clearly recognize that every economic theory presupposes a concept of the human person, that is, a particular anthropology.[99] They understand as, I do, that the figure of the entrepreneur has evolved in economic history and been developed by contemporary theorists, but that, to use Pope Benedict's terminology, this must be inclusive of the *"intrinsicality"* of the human person. Furthermore, a thoroughgoing investigation into the nature of entrepreneurial action actually reveals the "wealth of persons" which may at first might lie hidden and insufficiently explored in the history of economic thought but when unearthed can actually enrich our comprehension of economic anthropology.[100] Just as I have critiqued the Austrian tradition so the Bologna scholars do likewise. They detect in the Austrian approach the danger of a movement away from a full comprehension of the intrinsically "other-directedness" of the human person which can result in a total collapse into rugged economic individualism. This is quite possible since the Austrians never really developed an adequate philosophy of the human person because it did not necessarily concern them. While this is correct, there is a certain adequacy in their reflections to the reality of the human person because they're fundamentally open to an analysis of human action in itself. The charge of "rugged individualism" against their approach is perfectly reasonable, but we must remember in the last analysis it's the free decision of a self-appropriating and self-determining individual to be individualistic or not.[101] As such selfish individualism does not stem from the initial starting point of their analysis, that is, in "human action." But "human action" in itself is not neutral, and this was

98. See John Paul II, *Centesimus Annus*, no. 32.3; cited in Baggio, *Etica ed economia*, 115.

99. Baggio, *Etica ed economia*, 137.

100. Ibid., 126.

101. Pope Francis outlines how the reality of sin ruptures "three fundamental and closely intertwined relationships: with God, with our neighbour and with the earth itself" (*Laudato Sí*, no. 66).

insufficiently acknowledged or developed by these thinkers. Still, we are indebted to Joseph Schumpeter for recapturing and revealing the true "wealth of persons" at the heart of the working of the free economy in an analysis of entrepreneurial action, even if he too lacked an adequate understanding of the human person. Nonetheless, the Austrian perspective need not result in a "hyper-minimalist" conception of the human person as Zamagni suggests but can be the initial "gurglings" of a stream which initiates an "existential shift" in economic thought towards accommodating the transcendent nature of human existence. The Bologna school theorists are noteworthy because they clearly see the power of this "anthropological stream" and the growth areas for the development and progression towards a more personcentric economic anthropology taking into account the true wealth of the human person in creating economic reality, thereby revealing an economics with a human face.

IV. The Human Person Guarded by Transcendence and Mystery

The ultimate measure against which the economics of a free economy can be valued is whether it amply measures up to the truth of the transcendent and mysterious reality of the acting human person. Economic thought and reflection is challenged to reach up to the reality of who we are as persons, persons who have the capacity to become more than we are.[102] Nonetheless, it's always important to keep in mind, since the "actor" in human action, that is, the human person, is especially difficult to study; the context where he or she is explored can always be enlarged but the investigation can never be completed.[103] This might, indeed, explain why economists simply don't seek to go beyond the limitations of their own models. Human action can certainly be explained but the challenge lies in explaining "its innermost beginning."[104] How, for example, is an explanation of where the initiative came from attainable, if it has no other source beyond itself?[105] But the fact that our investigation into human action or the human person will always remain incomplete should not surprise us. As Saul Bellow asks, "Who can be the earnest huntsman of

102. See Pope Benedict XVI, *Caritas in Veritate*, no. 14.

103. See Lonergan, *Insight*, 18.

104. Walsh, "Persons as Beyond Good and Evil."

105. See ibid.

himself when he knows he is in turn a quarry?"[106] The truth of reality is that the secret of our preservation is contained in our participation in the "inexorable limit of mystery" because this invites us to move beyond the limits we encounter.[107] Jacques Derrida in a chapter titled "Beyond: Giving for the Taking, Teaching and Learning to Give, Death," speaks of a similar mystery when he writes about "the authentic mystery of the person" and that that "authentic mystery must *remain* mysterious, and we should approach it only by letting it be what it is in truth."[108]

In our study we've focused on entrepreneurial action as the efficient cause of the "wealth of persons." And we've seen how human decisions in the economic arena and resulting actions create new situations that move us beyond our "uneasiness" (which Mises spoke about) with the limits encountered. But when we think about it, it's the reality of human limitation that's actually the source and dynamic that gives rise to inventions, creativity, and changes of direction in economic action. So, we can actually hold on "to the slender thread of transcendence"[109] in human economic action by realizing "the superiority of what is not to what is."[110] This insight into the human being's "transcendent dimension" can recover for us the understanding that the "wealth of persons" so constituted is the bedrock of any "wealth of nations." As Pope Francis says, "We are convinced that 'man is the source, the focus and the aim of all economic and social life.'"[111]

106. Bellow, *Dangling Man*, 119.

107. Walsh, *Guarded by Mystery*, 114.

108. Derrida, *Gift of Death*, 38.

109. See Walsh, "Theory and Practice as Responsibility," 47–50.

110. Ibid.

111. *Laudato Si*, no. 127.

Bibliography

Aeschylus. *The Oresteia*. Translated by Robert Fagles. London: Penguin, 1977.

———. *Prometheus Bound; The Suppliants; Seven Against Thebes; The Persians*. Translated by Philip Vellacott. London: Penguin, 1973.

Alves, André Azevedo, and José Manuel Moreira. *The Salamanca School*. New York: Continuum, 2010.

Alvey, James E. *A Short History of Ethics and Economics: The Greeks*. Cheltenham, UK: Edward Elgar, 2011.

Amin, Samir. *The Liberal Virus: Permanent War and the Americanization of the World*. Translated by James Membrez. New York: Monthly Review Press, 2004.

Anderson, Bruce, and Philip McShane. *Beyond Establishment Economics: No Thank-You Mankiw*. Vancouver: Axial, 2002.

Applebaum, Anne. *Gulag: A History of the Soviet Camps*. London: Penguin, 2004.

———. *Iron Curtain: The Crushing of Eastern Europe, 1944–1956*. London: Penguin, 2012.

Aquinas, Thomas. *Selected Writings*. Edited and translated by Ralph McInerny. London: Penguin, 1998.

Aristotle. *The Ethics of Aristotle: The Nicomachean Ethics*. Translated by J. A. K. Thomson. Rev. ed. Harmondsworth, UK: Penguin, 1976.

———. *Metaphysics*. Translated by Hugh Lawson-Tancred. London: Penguin, 1999.

———. *Politics*. Translated by T. A. Sinclair. Revised and re-presented by Trevor J. Saunders. London: Penguin, 1992.

Aron, Raymond. *In Defense of Political Reason: Essays*. Edited by Daniel J. Mahoney. Lanham, MD: Rowman & Littlefield, 1994.

———. *The Opium of the Intellectuals*. New Brunswick, NJ: Transaction Publishers, 2001.

Arrow, Kenneth, and Gérard Debreu. "Existence of an Equilibrium for a Competitive Economy." *Econometrica* 22 (1954) 265–90.

Atkinson, Anthony B. *Inequality: What Can Be Done?* Cambridge, MA: Harvard University Press, 2015.

Auspitz, J. Lee, et al., eds. *Praxiologies and the Philosophy of Economics*. Praxiology 1. New Brunswick, NJ: Transaction Publishers, 1992.

Backhouse, Roger E., and Bradley W. Bateman. *Capitalist Revolutionary: John Maynard Keynes*. Cambridge, MA: Harvard University Press, 2011.

Baggio, Antonio María. *Etica ed economia: Verso un paradigma di fraternità*. Rome: Città Nuova, 2005.

Baggio, Antonio María, et al. *La crisi economica: Appello a una nouva responsibilità*. Rome: Città Nuova, 2009.

Baker, Bruce. "Entrepreneurship as a Sign of Common Grace." *Journal of Markets & Morality* 18 (2015) 81–98.

Bandow, Doug, and David L. Schindler, eds. *Wealth, Poverty, and Human Destiny.* Wilmington: ISI, 2003.

Bateman, Bradley W. *Keynes's Uncertain Revolution.* Ann Arbor: University of Michigan Press, 1996.

Baumol, William J. *The Free-Market Innovation Machine: Analyzing the Growth Miracle of Capitalism.* Princeton: Princeton University Press, 2002.

Beaubout, Gregory R., et al. *Beyond Self-Interest: A Personalist Approach to Human Action.* Lanham, MD: Lexington, 2002.

Becchetti, Leonardo. *Oltre l'homo oeconomicus: Felicità, responsibilità, economica delle relazioni.* Rome: Città Nuova, 2009.

Beckert, Jens. *Beyond the Market: The Social Foundations of Economic Efficiency.* Translated by Barbara Harshav. Princeton: Princeton University Press, 2002.

Bellow, Saul. *Dangling Man.* New York: Penguin, 2007.

Benedict XVI, Pope. *Caritas in Veritate: On Integral Human Development in Charity and Truth.* Vatican City: Libreria Editrice Vaticana, 2009.

Berger, Johannes. "Changing Crisis-Types in Western Societies." *Praxis International* 1 (1981) 230–39.

Berger, Peter L., and Thomas Luckmann. *The Social Construction of Reality: A Treatise in the Sociology of Knowledge.* New York: Anchor, 1967.

Berkeley, George. *The Querist.* Rockville, MD: Serenity, 2008.

Bhidé, Amar. *A Call for Judgment: Sensible Finance for a Dynamic Economy.* New York: Oxford University Press, 2010.

Blaug, Mark. *Economic Theory in Retrospect.* 5th ed. Cambridge: Cambridge University Press, 1997.

Boettke, Peter J., ed. *The Elgar Companion to Austrian Economics.* Cheltenham, UK: Edward Elgar, 1998.

Böhm-Bawerk, Eugen von. *Capital and Interest.* Translated by George D. Huncke and Hans F. Sennholz. 3 vols. Grove City, PA: Libertarian, 1959.

———. *Karl Marx and the Close of His System.* Edited by Paul M. Sweezy. New York: A. M. Kelley, 1949.

Bowles, Samuel, et al. *Understanding Capitalism: Competition, Command and Change.* 3rd ed. Oxford: Oxford University Press, 2005.

Brecht, Bertolt. *Die Dreigroschenoper: der Erstdruck 1928.* With a commentary by Joachim Lucchesi. Frankfurt am Main: Suhrkamp, 2004.

Bruni, Luigino. *Civil Happiness: Economics and Human Flourishing in Historical Perspective.* London: Routledge, 2006.

———. "Economic Crisis and the Eyes of the Resurrection." http://www.edc-online. org/en/publications/articles-by/luigino-bruni-s-articles/2368-crisi-economica-e-occhi-di-resurrezione.html.

———, ed. *The Economy of Communion: Toward a Multi-dimensional Economic Culture.* New York: New City, 2002.

———. *Reciprocity, Altruism and the Civil Society: In Praise of Heterogeneity.* New York: Routledge, 2008.

———. "Su imprenditori e concorrenza: Una guida alla lettura nei tempi di crisi." *Nuova Umanità* 34 (2012) 1–14.

———. *The Wound and the Blessing: Economics, Relationships and Happiness.* Hyde Park, NY: New City, 2012.

Bruni, Luigino, and Vittorio Pelligra, eds. *Economia come impegno civile: Relazionalità, ben-essere ed economia di comunione.* Rome: Città Nuova, 2002.

Bruni, Luigino, and Pier Luigi Porta, eds. *Economics and Happiness: Framing the Analysis.* Oxford: Oxford University Press, 2007.

Bruni, Luigino, and Amelia Uelmen. "Religious Values and Corporate Decision-Making: The Economy of Communion Project." *Fordham Journal of Corporate and Financial Law* 11 (2006) 645–80.

Bruni, Luigino, and Stefano Zamagni. *Civil Economy: Efficiency, Equity, Public Happiness.* Bern: Peter Lang, 2007.

Buchanan, James. "Economics in the Post-Socialist Century." *The Economic Journal* 101 (1991) 15–21.

Buffett, Warren E. *The Essays of Warren Buffett: Lessons for Investment Managers.* Edited by Lawrence A. Cunningham. Singapore: Wiley, 2009.

Burrough, Bryan, and John Helyar. *Barbarians at the Gate: The Fall of RJR Nabisco.* London: Arrow, 2004.

Caldwell, Bruce. *Hayek's Challenge: An Intellectual Biography.* Chicago: University of Chicago Press, 2004.

Cambón, Enrique. "Communione trinitaria e sviluppo sociale." *Gen's: Rivista di vita ecclesiale* 40 (2010) 7–13.

———. *Trinità modello sociale.* Rome: Città Nuova, 2009.

Cameron, Rondo E., and Larry Neal. *A Concise Economic History of the World: From Palaeolithic Times to the Present.* 4th ed. Oxford: Oxford University Press, 2003.

Campiglio, Luigi, and Stefano Zamagni. *Crisi economica, crisi antropologica: L'uomo al centro del lavoro e dell'impresa.* Rome: il Cerchio, 2010.

Camus, Albert. *The Outsider.* Translated by Joseph Laredo. London: Penguin, 2000.

Cantillon, Richard. *Essay on the Nature of Commerce in General.* Translated by Henry Higgs. New Brunswick, NJ: Transaction Publishers, 2006.

Casey, Gerard. *Murray Rothbard.* New York: Continuum, 2010.

———. "Scholastic Economics." In *Yearbook of the Irish Philosophical Society 2006,* 70–83. Maynooth: Irish Philosophical Society, 2006.

Casson, Mark, et al., eds. *The Oxford Handbook of Entrepreneurship.* Oxford: Oxford University Press, 2009.

Cervantes Saavedra, Miguel de. *The Ingenious Hidalgo Don Quixote de la Mancha.* Translated by John Rutherford. London: Penguin 2003.

Chafuen, Alejandro A. *Christians for Freedom: Late-Scholastic Economics.* San Francisco: Ignatius, 1986.

———. *Faith and Liberty: The Economic Thought of the Late Scholastics.* Lanham, MD: 2003.

Chesterton, G. K. *Utopia of Usurers.* London: IHS, 2002.

Clarke, Peter. *Keynes: The Twentieth Century's Most Influential Economist.* London: Bloomsbury, 2009.

Colander, David, ed. *Post-Walrasian Macroeconomics: Beyond the Dynamic Stochastic General Equilibrium Model.* Cambridge, MA: Cambridge University Press, 2006.

Coda, Piero. *Il negativo e la Trinità: Ipotesi su Hegel.* Rome: Città Nuova, 1987.

Coda, Piero, and Andreas Tapken, eds. *La Trinità e il pensare: Figure percorsi prospettive.* Rome: Città Nuova, 1997.

Coogan, Tim Pat. *The Famine Plot: England's Role in Ireland's Greatest Tragedy.* New York: Palgrave Macmillan, 2012.

Cooper, George. *The Origin of Financial Crises: Central Banks, Credit Bubbles and the Efficient Market Fallacy.* Petersfield, UK: Harriman House, 2008.

Coote, Tony, ed. *Colour on a Grey Canvas.* Dublin: University College Dublin, 2005.

Crosby, John F. *The Personalism of John Henry Newman.* Washington, DC: Catholic University of America Press, 2014.

———. *Personalist Papers.* Washington, DC: Catholic University of America Press, 2004.

———. *The Selfhood of the Human Person.* Washington, DC: Catholic University of America Press, 1996.

Crowley, John, et al., eds. *Atlas of the Great Irish Famine, 1845–52.* Cork: Cork University Press, 2012.

Cubeddu, Raimondo. *The Philosophy of the Austrian School.* Translated by Rachel M. Costa, née Barritt. London: Routledge, 1993.

Dahl, Robert A. *A Preface to Economic Democracy.* Berkeley: University of California Press, 1985.

Dahms, Harry. "The Entrepreneur in Western Capitalism: A Sociological Analysis of Schumpeter's Theory of Economic Development." PhD diss., New School for Social Research, 1993.

Danner, Peter L. *The Economic Person: Acting and Analyzing.* Lanham, MD: Rowman & Littlefield, 2002.

Dawson, Christopher. *The Age of the Gods: A Study in the Origins of Culture in Prehistoric Europe and the Ancient East.* London: John Murray, 1928.

Delaney, Enda. *The Curse of Reason: The Great Irish Famine.* Dublin: Gill & Macmillan, 2012.

Defoe, Daniel. *Robinson Crusoe.* New York: Bantam, 1981.

Dembinski, Paul H. *Finance: Servant or Deceiver? Financialization at the Crossroads.* Translated by Kevin Cook. London: Palgrave Macmillan, 2009.

Dembinski, Paul H., et al., eds. *Enron and World Finance: A Case Study in Ethics.* Basingstoke, UK: Palgrave McMillan, 2006.

Derrida, Jacques. *The Gift of Death & Literature in Secret.* Translated by David Wills. 2nd ed. Chicago: University of Chicago Press, 2008.

Desmond, John F. *Walker Percy's Search for Community.* Athens: University of Georgia Press, 2004.

Dickens, Charles. *A Tale of Two Cities.* Edited by Richard Maxwell. London: Penguin, 2000.

Donohue-White, Patricia, et al., eds. *Human Nature and the Discipline of Economics: Personalist Anthropology and Economic Methodology.* Lanham, MD: Lexington, 2002.

Dooley, Mark. *Roger Scruton: The Philosopher on Dover Beach.* New York: Continuum, 2009.

Drucker, Peter. *Innovation and Entrepreneurship: Practice and Principles.* Oxford: Elsevier, 2010.

Dulles, Avery. *John Henry Newman.* New York: Bloomsbury Academic, 2009.

Easterlin, Richard A. "Does Economic Growth Improve the Human Lot? Some Empirical Evidence." In *Nations and Households in Economic Growth: Essays in*

Honor of Moses Abramowitz, edited by Paul A. David and Melvin W. Reder, 89–125. New York: Academic Press, 1974.

Ebenstein, Alan. *Friedrich Hayek: A Biography.* New York: Palgrave, 2001.

Eliot, T. S. *The Complete Poems and Plays.* London: Faber & Faber, 1969.

Evans, Joseph W., and Leo R. Ward, eds. *The Social and Political Philosophy of Jacques Maritain: Selected Readings.* New York: Image, 1965.

Fanning, Bryan. *Evil, God, the Greater Good, and Rights: The Philosophical Origins of Social Problems.* Lewiston, NY: Edwin Mellen, 2007.

Federici, Michael P. *Eric Voegelin: The Restoration of Order.* Wilmington: ISI 2003.

Fergusson, Adam. *When Money Dies: The Nightmare of the Weimar Hyper-Inflation.* London: Old Street, 2010.

Finlay, T. A. *Foxford and the Providence Woollen Mills: Story of an Irish Industry.* Dublin: Fallon, 1932.

Finnis, John. *Aquinas: Moral, Political and Legal Theory.* Oxford: Oxford University Press, 1998.

Frey, Bruno S., and Alois Stutzer. *Happiness and Economics: How the Economy and Institutions Affect Human Well-Being.* Princeton: Princeton University Press, 2002.

Friedman, Milton. *Capitalism and Freedom.* 40th anniv. ed. Chicago: University of Chicago Press, 2002.

Friedman, Milton, and Rose Friedman. *Free to Choose: A Personal Statement.* New York: Harcourt Brace Jovanovich, 1979.

Frydman, Roman, and Michael D. Goldberg. *Imperfect Knowledge: Exchange Rates and Risks.* Princeton: Princeton University Press, 2007.

Fukuyama, Francis. *The End of History and the Last Man.* New York: Free Press, 2006.

Fullbrook, Edward, ed. *The Crisis in Economics: The Post-autistic Economics Movement; The First 600 Days.* London: Routledge, 2003.

———, ed. *A Guide to What's Wrong with Economics.* London: Anthem, 2004.

———, ed. *Intersubjectivity in Economics: Agents and Structures.* London: Routledge, 2002.

Gadamer, Hans-Georg. *Truth and Method.* 2nd rev. ed. Translation revised by Joel Weinsheimer and Donald G. Marshall. New York: Continuum, 2004.

Galbraith, John Kenneth. *The Great Crash, 1929.* London: Penguin, 1992.

———. *A History of Economics: The Past as the Present.* London: Penguin, 1987.

Gallagher, John, and Jeanne Buckeye. *Structures of Grace: The Business Practices of the Economy of Communion.* Hyde Park, NY: New City, 2014.

Gasparski, Wojciech W., and Timo Airaksinen, eds. *Praxiology and the Philosophy of Technology.* Praxiology 15. New Brunswick, NJ: Transaction Publishers, 2008.

Gasparski, Wojciech W., and Leo V. Ryan, eds. *Human Action in Business: Praxiological and Ethical Dimensions.* Praxiology 5. New Brunswick, NJ: Transaction Publishers, 1996.

Gildea, Denis J. *Mother Mary Arsenius of Foxford.* London: Burns, Oates & Washbourne, 1956.

Gloria-Palermo, Sandye. *The Evolution of Austrian Economics: From Menger to Lachmann.* London: Routledge, 1999.

Gold, Lorna. *New Financial Horizons: The Emergence of an Economy of Communion.* Hyde Park, NY: New City, 2010.

———. *The Sharing Economy: Solidarity Networks Transforming Globalisation.* Aldershot, UK: Ashgate, 2004.

Gordon, David. "The Fallacies of Voegelian Antiliberalism." *The Mises Review* 6.3 (Fall 2000). https://mises.org/library/collected-works-eric-voegelin-eric-voegelin.

——. *The Philosophical Origins of Austrian Economics*. Auburn, AL: Ludwig von Mises Institute, 1996.

Grassl, Wolfgang. "Integral Human Development in Analytical Perspective: A Trinitarian Perspective." *Journal of Markets & Morality* 16 (2013) 135–55.

——. "*Pluris Valere*: Towards Trinitarian Rationality in Social Life." In *The Whole Breadth of Reason: Rethinking Economics and Politics*, edited by Simona Beretta and Mario A. Maggioni, 313–48. Venice: Marcianum, 2012.

Grassl, Wolfgang, and Barry Smith, eds. *Austrian Economics: Historical and Philosophical Background*. London: Croom Helm, 1986.

Greaves, Bettina Bien, ed. *Austrian Economics: An Anthology*. New York: Foundation for Economic Education, 1996.

——. *Free Market Economics: A Basic Reader*. Auburn, AL: Ludwig von Mises Institute, 2007.

——. *Free Market Economics: A Syllabus*. Auburn, AL: Ludwig von Mises Institute, 2007.

Greenspan, Alan. *The Age of Turbulence: Adventures in a New World*. London: Penguin, 2007.

Gregg, Samuel. *The Commercial Society: Foundations and Challenges in a Global Age*. Lanham, MD: Lexington, 2007.

——. *Tea Party Catholic: The Catholic Case for Limited Government, a Free Economy and Human Flourishing*. New York: Crossroad, 2013.

Gregg, Samuel, and Harold James, eds. *Natural Law, Economics and the Common Good*. Exeter, UK: Imprint Academic, 2012.

Gregg, Samuel, and Gordan R. Preece. *Christianity and Entrepreneurship: Protestant and Catholic Thoughts*. CIS Policy Monographs 44. St. Leonards, NSW: Centre for Independent Studies, 1999.

Gregory, Brad S. *The Unintended Reformation: How a Religious Revolution Secularized Society*. Cambridge, MA: Belknap Press of Harvard University Press, 2012.

Grice-Hutchinson, Marjorie. *The School of Salamanca: Readings in Spanish Monetary Theory, 1544–1605*. Auburn, AL: Ludwig von Mises Institute, 2009.

Gronbacher, Gregory M. A. *Economic Personalism: A New Paradigm for a Humane Economy*. Grand Rapids: Acton Institute, 1998.

——. "The Humane Economy: Neither Right nor Left; A Response to Daniel Rush Finn." *Journal of Markets & Morality* 2 (1999) 247–70.

——. "The Need for Economic Personalism." *Journal of Markets & Morality* 1 (1998) 1–34.

——. "The Wedding of Three Philosophical Traditions toward a Refined Philosophy of Economics." *Religion & Liberty* 2.6 (November–December 1992). http://www.acton.org/pub/religion-liberty/volume-2-number-6/wedding-three-philosophical-traditions-toward-refi.

Habermas, Jürgen. *Legitimation Crisis*. Translated by Thomas McCarthy. Boston: Beacon, 1975.

——. *The Theory of Communicative Action*. Translated by Thomas McCarthy. 2 vols. Boston: Beacon, 1984–87.

Habermas, Jürgen, et al. *An Awareness of What Is Missing: Faith and Reason in a Post-secular Age*. Translated by Ciaran Cronin. Cambridge, UK: Polity, 2010.

Habisch, A.,and C. R. Loza Adaui. "Entrepreneurial Spirit and the Role of Gratuitousness for Innovation." In *Human Development in Business: Values and Humanistic Management in the Encyclical "Caritas in Veritate"*, edited by Domènec Melé and Claus Dierksmeier, 217–36. London: Palgrave Macmillan, 2012.

Hadas, Edward. *Human Goods, Economic Evils: A Moral Approach to the Dismal Science*. Wilmington: ISI, 2007.

Hancock, Ralph C. *The Responsibility of Reason: Theory and Pratcice in a Liberal-Democratic Age*. Lanham, MD: Rowman & Littlefield, 2011.

Havel, Václav. *Summer Meditations*. New York: Knopf, 1992.

Hayek, Friedrich A. von, ed. *Collectivist Economic Planning*. Auburn, AL: Ludwig von Mises Institute, 2009.

———. *The Constitution of Liberty*. Chicago: University of Chicago Press, 1978.

———. *The Counter-Revolution of Science: Studies on the Abuse of Reason*. 2nd ed. Indianapolis: Liberty Fund, 1979.

———. *The Fatal Conceit: The Errors of Socialism*. Edited by W. W. Bailey. Chicago: University of Chicago Press, 1988.

———. *Individualism and Economic Order*. Chicago: University of Chicago Press, 1992.

———. *Law, Legislation and Liberty*. Vol. 2, *The Mirage of Social Justice*. Chicago: University of Chicago Press, 1976.

———. *New Studies in Philosophy, Politics, Economics and the History of Ideas*. Chicago: University of Chicago Press, 1978.

———. *Prices and Production and Other Works: F. A. Hayek on Money, the Business Cycle, and the Gold Standard*. Edited by Joseph Salerno. Auburn, AL: Mises Institute, 2008.

Hazlitt, Henry. *The Failure of the "New Economics": An Analysis of the Keynesian Fallacies*. Auburn, AL: Ludwig von Mises Instiute, 2007.

Heathcote, Edwin. "The Moral Angle." *Financial Times*, May 17, 2003, 21.

Heilbroner, Robert, ed. *The Essential Adam Smith*. New York: Norton, 1987.

Heilbroner, Robert, and William Milberg. *The Crisis of Vision in Modern Economic Thought*. Cambridge, MA: Cambridge University Press, 1995.

Heilke, Thomas W. *Eric Voegelin: In Quest of Reality*. Lanham, MD: Rowman & Littlefield, 1999.

Hemmerle, Klaus. *Dreifaltigkeit: Schlüssel zum Menschen, Schlüssel zur Zeit; Beiträge zu Zeitfragen des Glaubens*. Munich: Neue Stadt, 1989.

———. *Partire dall'unità: La Trinità come stile di vita e forma di pensiero*. Rome: Città Nuova, 1998.

Heuser, Uwe Jean. *Humanomics: Die Entdeckung des Menschen in der Wirtschaft*. Frankfurt: Campus-Verlag, 2008.

Heyne, Paul. *The Economic Way of Thinking*. Upper Saddle River, NJ: Prentice Hall, 2006.

Hobbes, Thomas. *Leviathan*. Edited by C. B. Macpherson. London: Penguin, 1979.

Holcombe, Randall G., ed. *15 Great Austrian Economists*. Auburn, AL: Ludwig von Mises Institute, 1999.

Hülsmann, Jörg Guido. *Mises: The Last Knight of Liberalism*. Auburn, AL: Ludwig von Mises Institute, 2007.

Huntington, Samuel P. *The Clash of Civilizations and the Remaking of World Order*. New York: Simon & Schuster, 1998.

Hurwicz, Leonid, and Stanley Reiter. *Designing Economic Mechanisms.* Cambridge: Cambridge University Press, 2006.

Jisheng, Yang. *Tombstone: The Untold Story of Mao's Great Famine.* Translated by Stacy Mosher and Guo Jian. London: Penguin, 2012.

Joyce, Bernie. *Agnes Morrogh-Bernard, 1842–1932: Foundress of Foxford Woollen Mills.* Foxford: Foxford I.R.D., 1989.

Kauder, Emil. *A History of Marginal Utility.* Princeton: Princeton University Press, 1965.

Kay, John. *Culture and Prosperity: Why Some Nations Are Rich but Most Remain Poor.* New York: HarperCollins, 2005.

Keane, John. *Global Civil Society?* Cambridge: Cambridge University Press, 2003.

Keen, Steve. *Debunking Economics: The Naked Emperor of the Social Sciences.* London: Zed, 2004.

Kelly, Kel. *The Case for Legalizing Capitalism.* Auburn, AL: Ludwig von Mises Institute, 2010.

Kelly, Morgan. "How the Rich Got Richer: *Capital in the Twenty-First Century,* by Thomas Piketty." *Irish Times,* May 10, 2014. http://www.irishtimes.com/culture/ books/how-the-rich-got-richer-capital-in-the-twenty-first-century-by-thomas- piketty-1.1786787.

Kerr, Ian, and Terence Merrigan, eds. *The Cambridge Companion to John Henry Newman.* New York: Cambridge University Press, 2009.

Keynes, John Maynard. *The General Theory of Employment, Interest and Money.* London: Macmillan, 1936.

———. *A Tract on Monetary Reform.* London: Macmillan, 1923.

———. *A Treatise on Money.* New York: Harcourt, 1930.

Kierkegaard, Søren. *Purity of Heart Is to Will One Thing.* Translated by Douglas V. Steere. New York: Harper, 1956.

Kincaid, Harold, and Don Ross, eds. *The Oxford Handbook of Philosophy of Economics.* New York: Oxford University Press, 2009.

Kinealy, Christine. *The Great Calamity: The Irish Famine, 1845–52.* Dublin: Gill & Macmillan, 2006.

Kinsella, Ray, and John McNerney. "Corporate Sickness and Corporate Health." *Studies* 94 (2005) 375–84.

Kirman, Alan. *Complex Economics: Individual and Collective Rationality.* London: Routledge, 2010.

Kirzner, Israel M. *Competition and Entrepreneurship.* Chicago: University of Chicago Press, 1973.

———. *Discovery and the Capitalist Process.* Chicago: University of Chicago Press, 1985.

———. *The Driving Force of the Market: Essays in Austrian Economics.* London: Routledge, 2000.

———. *The Economic Point of View: An Essay in the History of Economic Thought.* Edited by Laurence S. Moss. Menlo Park, CA: Institute for Humane Studies, 1976.

———. *How Markets Work: Disequilibrium, Entrepreneurship and Discovery.* London: Institute of Economic Affairs, 2000.

———. *Ludwig von Mises: The Man and His Economics.* Wilmington: ISI, 2001.

———. *The Meaning of Market Process: Essays in the Development of Modern Austrian Economics.* London: Routledge, 1992.

Knight, Frank. *Freedom and Reform: Essays in Economics and Social Philosophy.* Indianapolis: Liberty Fund, 1982.

Kornai, János. *Anti-equilibrium: On Economic Systems Theory and the Tasks of Research.* Amsterdam: North-Holland, 1991.

———. *By Force of Thought: Irregular Memoirs of an Intellectual Journey.* Cambridge, MA: MIT Press, 2006.

———. *The Economics of Shortage.* Amsterdam: North-Holland, 1980.

———. *Overcentralization in Economic Administration: A Critical Analysis Based on Experience in Hungarian Light Industry.* Oxford: Oxford University Press, 1994.

———. *The Socialist System: The Political Economy of Communism.* Princeton: Princeton University Press, 1992.

———. "Some System-Specific Features of Capitalism." http://www.kornai-janos.hu/ Kornai2008%20Some%20system-specific%20features.pdf.

Kraut, Richard. *Aristotle: Political Philosophy.* New York: Oxford University Press, 2002.

Krugman, Paul. "Rich Getting Wealthier but Inequality Denial Persists." *Irish Times,* June 3, 2014. http://www.irishtimes.com/business/economy/rich-getting-wealthier-but-inequality-denial-persists-1.1817794.

Kurrild-Klitgaard, Peter. "The Viennese Connection: Alfred Schütz and the Austrian School." *Quarterly Journal of Austrian Economics* 6 (2003) 35–66.

Lachmann, Ludwig. "From Mises to Shackle: An Essay on Austrian Economics and the Kaleidic Society." *Journal of Economic Literature* 14 (1976) 54–62.

Landreth, Harry, and David C. Colander. *History of Economic Thought.* Boston: Houghton Mifflin, 2002.

Langholm, Odd Inge. *The Legacy of Scholasticism in Economic Thought: Antecedents of Choice and Power.* Cambridge: Cambridge University Press, 2006.

———. *Price and Value in the Aristotelian Tradition: A Study in Scholastic Economic Sources.* Bergen: Universitetsforlaget, 1979.

Langlois, Richard. "Risk and Uncertainty." In *The Elgar Companion to Austrian Economics,* edited by Peter J. Boettke, 118–22. Cheltenham, UK: Edward Elgar, 1998.

Lawson, Tony. *Reorienting Economics: Economics as Social Theory.* London: Routledge, 2003.

Leen, Auke R. "The Consumer in Austrian Economics and the Austrian Perspective on Consumer Policy." In *Modern Applications of Austrian Thought,* edited by Jürgen Backhaus, 41–75. London: Routledge, 2013.

Lévinas, Emmanuel. *Alterity and Transcendence.* Translated by Michael B. Smith. New York: Columbia University Press. 2000.

———. "Après Vous, Monsieur!" In *Is It Righteous to Be? Interviews with Emmanuel Levinas,* edited by Jill Robbins. Stanford: Stanford University Press, 2001.

———. *The Cambridge Companion to Levinas.* Edited by Simon Critchley and Robert Bernasconi. New York: Cambridge University Press, 2002.

———. *God, Death, and Time.* Translated by Bettina Bergo. Stanford: Stanford University Press, 2000.

———. *Totality and Infinity: An Essay on Exteriority.* Translated by Alphonso Lingis. Pittsburgh: Duquesne University Press, 1998.

———. *Unforeseen History.* Translated by Nidra Poller. Urbana: University of Illinois Press, 2004.

Lewis, Hunter. *Where Keynes Went Wrong: And Why World Governments Keep Creating Inflation, Bubbles and Busts*. Mount Jackson, VA: Axios, 2009.

Licht, Amir N., and Jordan I. Siegel. "The Social Dimensions of Entrepreneurship." In *The Oxford Handbook of Entrepreneurship*, edited by Mark Casson et al., 511–39. Oxford: Oxford University Press, 2009.

The Life and Work of Mary Aikenhead, Foundress of the Congregation of the Irish Sisters of Charity, 1787–1858, by a Member of the Congregation. London: Longmans, Green, 1925.

Locke, John. *An Essay Concerning Human Understanding*. Edited by Roger Woolhouse. London: Penguin, 1997.

Lonergan, Bernard J. F. "Analytic Concept of History." *METHOD: Journal of Lonergan Studies* 11 (1993) 5–35.

———. *Caring about Meaning: Patterns in the Life of Bernard Lonergan*. Edited by Pierrot Lambert et al. Montreal: Thomas More Institute, 1982.

———. *Collection*. Edited by Frederick E. Crowe. 2nd ed. Collected Works of Bernard Lonergan 4. Toronto: University of Toronto Press, 1988.

———. *For a New Political Economy*. Edited by Philip J. McShane. Collected Works of Bernard Lonergan 21. Toronto: University of Toronto Press, 1998.

———. *Insight: A Study in Human Understanding*. Edited by Frederick E. Crowe and Robert M. Doran. Collected Works of Bernard Lonergan 3. Toronto: University of Toronto Press, 1992.

———. *The Lonergan Reader*. Edited by Mark D. Morelli and Elizabeth A. Morelli. Toronto: Toronto University Press, 1997.

———. *Macroeconomic Dynamics: An Essay in Circulation Analysis*. Edited by Frederick G. Lawrence et al. Collected Works of Bernard Lonergan 15. Toronto: University of Toronto Press, 1999.

———. *Method in Theology*. London: Darton, Longman & Todd, 1972.

———. "*Pantôn Anakephalaiôsis*: Restoration of All Things." *METHOD: Journal of Lonergan Studies* 9 (1991) 139–72.

———. *Phenomenology and Logic: The Boston College Lectures on Mathematical Logic and Existentialism*. Edited by Philip J. McShane. Collected Works of Bernard Lonergan 18. Toronto: University of Toronto Press, 2001.

———. *Philosophical and Theological Papers, 1958–1964*. Edited by Robert C. Croken et al. Collected Works of Bernard Lonergan 6. Toronto: University of Toronto Press, 1996.

———. *Shorter Papers*. Edited by Robert C. Croken et al. Collected Works of Bernard Lonergan 20. Toronto: University of Toronto Press, 2007.

———. *The Subject*. The Aquinas Lecture, 1968. Milwaukee: Marquette University Press, 1982.

———. *A Third Collection: Papers*. Edited by Frederick E. Crowe. New York: Paulist, 1985.

———. *Understanding and Being*. Edited by Elizabeth A. Morelli and Mark D. Morelli. Collected Works of Bernard Lonergan 5. Toronto: University of Toronto Press, 1990.

Lowenstein, Roger. *Buffet: The Biography*. London: Duckworth, 2009.

Lubich, Chiara. *Essential Writings: Spirituality, Dialogue, Culture*. Compiled and edited by Michael Vandeleene. English-language editors Tom Masters and Callan Slipper. London: New City, 2007.

MacIntyre, Alasdair. *Edith Stein: A Philosophical Prologue, 1913–1922*. Oxford: Sheed & Ward, 2006.

Macmurray. John. *The Self as Agent*. London: Faber & Faber, 1956.

Macpherson, C. B. *The Political Theory of Possessive Individualism: Hobbes to Locke*. Oxford: Oxford University Press, 1970.

Madison, G. B. "Phenomenology and Economics." In *The Elgar Companion to Austrian Economics*, edited by Peter J. Boettke, 38–47. Cheltenham, UK: Edward Elgar, 1998.

Magro, Giacinto G. "Trinità e vita sociale." *Nuova Umanità* 192 (2010) 791–95.

Mankiw, Gregory. *Principles of Economics*. Mason, OH: South-Western, 2004.

———. "A Quick Refresher Course in Macroeconomics." *Journal of Economic Literature* 28 (1990) 1645–60.

Maritain, Jacques. *The Person and the Common Good*. Translated by John J. Fitzgerald. Notre Dame: University of Notre Dame Press, 1985.

Marx, Karl. *Capital*. Edited by David McLellan. Oxford: Oxford University Press, 2008.

———. *Selected Writings*. Edited by David McLellan. Oxford: Oxford University Press, 1977.

Marx, Karl, and Friedrich Engels. *The Communist Manifesto*. London: Penguin, 2002.

Mathews, William A. *Lonergan's Quest: A Study of Desire in the Authoring of* Insight. Toronto: University of Toronto Press, 2005.

McCarthy, Thomas. *The Critical Theory of Jürgen Habermas*. Cambridge, MA: MIT Press, 1979.

McCraw, Thomas K. *Prophet of Innovation: Joseph Schumpeter and Creative Destruction*. Cambridge, MA: Belknap Press of Harvard University Press, 2007.

McDonald, Lawrence G., and Patrick Robinson. *A Colossal Failure of Common Sense: The Inside Story of the Collapse of Lehman Brothers*. New York: Three Rivers, 2009.

McEvoy, James, and James Dunne, eds. *Thomas Aquinas: Approaches to Truth*. Dublin: Four Courts, 2002.

McNerney, John. *John Paul II: Poet and Philosopher*. New York: Continuum, 2004.

———, ed. *New Horizons: Faith to Life and Life to Faith*. Dublin: University College Dublin, 2005

———. "The Wealth of Persons: Re-capturing a Person-Centred Economic Perspective." In *Human Voyage of Self-Discovery: Essays in Honour of Brendan Purcell*, edited by Brendan Leahy and David Walsh, 70–88. Dublin: Veritas, 2014.

McShane, Philip. *Economics for Everyone: Das Jus Kapital*. Edmonton: Commonwealth Publications, 1996.

———. *Piketty's Plight and the Global Future: Economics for Dummies*. Vancouver: Axial, 2014.

Meadowcroft, John. *The Ethics of the Market*. London: Macmillan, 2005.

Medearis, John. *Joseph A. Schumpeter*. New York: Continuum, 2009.

Medema, Steven G., and Warren J. Samuels, eds. *The History of Economic Thought*. London: Routledge, 2003.

Menger, Carl. *Investigations into the Method of the Social Sciences*. Edited by Louis Schneider. Translated by Francis J. Nock. Grove City, PA: Libertarian Press, 1996.

———. *Principles of Economics*. Auburn, AL: Ludwig von Mises Institute, 2007.

Milanovic, Branko. *Worlds Apart: Measuring International and Global Inequality*. Princeton: Princeton University Press, 2005.

Milberg, William. "The Robert Heilbroner Problem." *Social Research* 71 (2004) 235–50.

Mises, Ludwig von. *Epistemological Problems of Economics*. Translated by George Reisman. Auburn, AL: Ludwig von Mises Institute, 2003.

―――. *Human Action: A Treatise on Economics*. San Francisco: Fox & Wilkes, 1996.

―――. *Marxism Unmasked: From Delusion to Destruction*. Irvington-on-Hudson, NY: Foundation for Economic Education, 2006.

―――. *Planning for Freedom: Let the Market System Work; A Collection of Essays and Addresses*. Indianapolis: Liberty Fund, 2008.

―――. *Socialism: An Economic and Sociological Analysis*. Translated by J. Kahane. Indianapolis: Liberty, 1981.

―――. *Theory and History: An Interpretation of Social and Economic Evolution*. New Haven: Yale University Press, 1957.

―――. *The Ultimate Foundation of Economic Science: An Essay on Method*. Edited by Bettina Bien Greaves. Indianapolis: Liberty Fund, 2006.

Mitchell, Mark T. *Michael Polanyi: The Art of Knowing*. Wilmington: ISI, 2006.

Moggridge, D. E. *John Maynard Keynes*. London: Penguin, 1976.

Mokyr, Joel. *The Lever of Riches: Technological Creativity and Economic Progress*. New York: Oxford University Press, 1990.

―――. *Why Ireland Starved: A Quantitative and Analytical History of the Irish Economy, 1800–1850*. London: Allen & Unwin, 1985.

Molloy, Margaret. *Agnes Morrogh-Bernard: Foundress of Foxford Woolen Mills*. Cork: Mercier, 2014.

Moramarco, Vito, and Luigino Bruni, eds. *L'economia di comunione: Verso un agire economico "a misura di persona"*. Milano: Vita e Pensiero, 2000.

Moran, Dermot. *Introduction to Phenomenology*. London: Routledge, 2000.

Morris, Tom. *If Aristotle Ran General Motors: The New Soul of Business*. New York: Holt, 1997.

Morrissey, Thomas J. *Thomas A. Finlay, SJ, 1848–1940: Educationalist, Editor, Social Reformer*. Dublin: Four Courts, 2004.

Moss, Laurence S., and Christopher K. Ryan, eds. *Economic Thought in Spain: Selected Essays of Marjorie Grice-Hutchinson*. Aldershot, UK: Edward Elgar, 1993.

Mueller, John D. *Redeeming Economics: Rediscovering the Missing Element*. Wilmington: ISI, 2010.

Murrell, Peter. *The Nature of Socialist Economies: Lessons from Eastern European Foreign Trade*. Princeton: Princeton University Press, 1990.

Musil, Robert. *The Man Without Qualities*. Translated by Sophie Wilkins. Editorial consultant, Burton Pike. 2 vols. London: Picador, 1995.

Nanini, Riccardo. "A Catholic Alternative to Globalization? The *Compagnia delle Opere* as a Mediator between Small and Medium Enterprises and Catholic Social Teaching." In *The Economics of Religion: Anthropological Approaches*, edited by Lionel Obadia and Donald C. Wood, 47–76. Bingley, UK: Emerald, 2011.

Neeve, Eileen de. *Decoding the Economy*. Montreal: Thomas More Institute, 2008.

Newman, John Henry. *The Idea of a University*. Edited by Teresa Iglesias. Dublin: UCD International Centre for Newman Studies, 2009.

Niehans, Jürg. *A History of Economic Theory: Classic Contributions, 1720–1980*. Baltimore: Johns Hopkins University Press, 1990.

Norman, Jesse. *Compassionate Economics: The Social Foundations of Economic Prosperity; A Personal View*. London: Policy Exchange, 2008.

Norman, Jesse, and Janan Ganesh. *Compassionate Conservatism: What It Is, Why We Need It*. London: Policy Exchange, 2006.

Norris, Thomas. *Living a Spirituality of Communion*. Dublin: Columba, 2008.

Novak, Michael. *Free Persons and the Common Good*. Lanham, MD: Madison, 1989.

———. "The Future of Democratic Capitalism: Why We Need to Renew Our Moral and Cultural System." *First Things*, June 2015. http://www.firstthings.com/article/2015/06/the-future-of-democratic-capitalism.

———. *The Spirit of Democratic Capitalism*. Lanham, MD: Madison, 1991.

———. *Three in One: Essays on Democratic Capitalism, 1976–2000*. Edited by Edward W. Younkins. Lanham, MD: Rowman & Littlefield, 2001.

Oakeshott, Michael. *Rationalism in Politics and Other Essays*. New and expanded ed. Indianapolis: Liberty Fund, 1991.

Offe, Claus. *Contradictions of the Welfare State*. Edited by John Keane. Cambridge, MA: MIT Press, 1984.

———. *Disorganized Capitalism: Contemporary Transformations of Work and Politics*. Edited by John Keane. Cambridge, MA: MIT Press, 1985.

Ó Gráda, Cormac. *Black '47 and Beyond: The Great Irish Famine in History, Economy and Memory*. Princeton: Princeton University Press, 2000.

———. *Eating People Is Wrong, and Other Essays on Famine, Its Past, and Its Future*. Princeton: Princeton University Press, 2015.

———. *Famine: A Short History*. Princeton: Princeton University Press, 2009.

———. *The Great Irish Famine*. Cambridge: Cambridge University Press, 1995.

Ó Grada, Cormac, et al. *Ireland's Great Famine: Interdisciplinary Perspectives*. Dublin: University College Dublin Press, 2006.

Ó Murchadha, Ciarán. *The Great Famine: Ireland's Agony, 1845–1852*. New York: Continuum, 2011.

Ormerod, Paul. *The Death of Economics*. New York: John Riley, 1997.

Otteson, James, R. *Adam Smith*. New York: Bloomsbury Academic, 2013.

Pareto, Vilfredo. *Manual of Political Economy: A Critical and Variorum Edition*. Edited by Aldo Montesano et al. New York: Oxford University Press, 2014.

Pavan, A. *Dire Persona: Luoghi critici e saggi di applicazione di un'idea*. Bologna: il Mulino, 2003.

Pearce, David W., ed. *The MIT Dictionary of Modern Economics*. 4th ed. Cambridge, MA: MIT Press, 1992.

Percy, Walker. *Love in the Ruins*. New York: Picador, 1971.

———. *Signposts in a Strange Land*. New York: Picador, 1991.

Phelps, Edmund S. "Economic Justice and the Spirit of Innovation." *First Things*, October 2009, 27–31.

———. *Mass Flourishing: How Grassroots Innovation Created Jobs, Challenge and Change*. Princeton: Princeton University Press, 2013.

Phillipson, Nicholas. *Adam Smith: An Enlightened Mind*. London: Penguin, 2010.

Pieper, Josef. *Scholasticism: Personalities and Problems of Medieval Philosophy*. Translated by Richard and Clara Winston. South Bend, IN: St. Augustine's, 2001.

Piereson, James. "Thomas Piketty's 'Le Capital.'" *The American Spectator*, June 2014. http://spectator.org/articles/59189/thomas-pikettys-%E2%80%98le-capital%E2%80%99.

Piketty, Thomas. *Capital in the Twenty-First Century*. Translated by Arthur Goldhammer. Cambridge, MA: Belknap Press of Harvard University Press, 2014.

————. *Economics of Inequality.* Translated by Arthur Goldhammer. Cambridge, MA: Belknap Press of Harvard University Press, 2015.

Plantin, Guillame, et al. "Fair Value Accounting and Financial Stability." *Banque de France: Financial Stability Review* 12 (October 2008) 86–94.

Plato. *The Republic.* Translated by Desmond Lee. 2nd ed. London: Penguin, 2003.

Plender, John. *Capitalism: Money, Morals and Markets.* London: Biteback, 2015.

————. *Going off the Rails: Global Capital and the Crisis of Legitimacy.* Hoboken, NJ: J. Wiley, 2003.

Polanyi, Michael. *The Logic of Liberty: Reflections and Rejoinders.* Indianapolis: Liberty Fund, 1998.

Pontuso, James F. "Free Markets and Civil Society: Citizen in the Global Economy." In *Václav Havel: Civic Responsibility in the Postmodern Age,* 123–51. Lanham, MD: Rowman & Littlefield, 2004.

Prychitko, David L. "Comparative Economic Systems." In *The Elgar Companion to Austrian Economics,* edited by Peter J. Boettke, 224–30. Cheltenham, UK: Edward Elgar, 1998.

Purcell, Brendan. "Towards a Trinitarian Humanism: Piero Coda's Development of a Heuristic of Radical Fraternity as a Lived Theology of History." *Sophia: Ricerche su i fondamenti e la correlazione dei saperi* (Rome) 4 (2012) 247–71.

Putnam, Robert D. *Our Kids: The American Dream in Crisis.* New York: Simon & Schuster, 2015.

Rajan, Raghuram G. *Fault Lines: How Hidden Fractures Still Threaten the World Economy.* Princeton: Princeton University Press, 2010.

Rand, Ayn. *The Virtue of Selfishness: A New Concept of Egoism.* New York: Signet, 1964.

Ranieri, John J. *Eric Voegelin and the Good Society.* Columbia: University of Missouri Press, 1995.

Ratzinger, Joseph Cardinal. *Introduction to Christianity.* Translated by J. R. Foster and Michael J. Miller. San Francisco: Ignatius, 2004.

Raybaut, Alain, and Franck Sosthé. "Schumpeter on Competition." In *The Contribution of Joseph Schumpeter to Economics: Economic Development and Institutional Change,* edited by Richard Arena and Cécile Dangel-Hagnauer, 184–200. London: Routledge, 2002.

Raymaker, John A. "The Theory-Praxis of Social Ethics: The Complementarity between Hermeneutical and Dialectical Foundations." In *Creativity and Method: Essays in Honor of Bernard Lonergan, SJ,* edited by Matthew L. Lamb, 339–52. Milwaukee: Marquette University Press, 1981.

Reisman, George. *Capitalism: A Treatise on Economics.* Ottawa, IL: Jameson, 1996.

Ricoeur, Paul. *The Course of Recognition.* Translated by David Pellauer. Cambridge, MA: Harvard University Press, 2005.

————. *The Just.* Translated by David Pellauer. Chicago: University of Chicago Press, 2000.

————. *Memory, History, Forgetting.* Translated by Kathleen Blamey and David Pellauer. Chicago: University of Chicago Press, 2004.

Rixon, Gordon. "Derrida and Lonergan on Human Development." *American Catholic Philosophical Quarterly* 76 (2002) 221–36.

Robbins, Lionel. *An Essay on the Nature and Significance of Economic Science.* London: Macmillan, 1932.

Roberts, Richard, and David Kynaston. *The Lion Wakes: A Modern History of HSBC*. London: Profile Books, 2015.

Roover, Raymond de. *The Rise and Decline of the Medici Bank, 1397–1494*. Cambridge, MA: Harvard University Press, 1963.

———. *San Bernardino of Siena and Sant'Antonio of Florence: Two Great Economic Thinkers of the Middle Ages*. Cambridge, MA: Harvard School of Graduate Business, 1967.

Röpke, Wilhelm. *Against the Tide*. Translated by Elizabeth Henderson. Chicago: Henry Regnery, 1969.

———. *Economics of the Free Society*. Translate by Patrick M. Boarman. Auburn, AL: Ludwig von Mises Institute, 2008.

———. *A Humane Economy: The Social Framework of the Free Market*. 3rd ed. Wilmington: ISI, 1998.

———. *The Social Crisis of Our Time*. New Brunswick, NJ: Transaction Publishers, 2009.

Rostow, W. W. *Theorists of Economic Growth from David Hume to the Present: With a Perspective on the Next Century*. New York: Oxford University Press, 1990.

Rothbard, Murray N. *An Austrian Perspective on the History of Economic Thought*. Vol. 1, *Economic Thought before Adam Smith*. Auburn, AL: Ludwig von Mises Institute, 1995.

———. *An Austrian Perspective on the History of Economic Thought*. Vol. 2, *Classical Economics*. Auburn, AL: Ludwig von Mises Institute, 2006.

———. *The Ethics of Liberty*. New York: New York University Press, 2002.

———. *The Logic of Action*. 2 vols. Cheltenham, UK: Edward Elgar, 1997.

———. *Ludwig von Mises: Scholar, Creator, Hero*. Auburn, AL: Ludwig von Mises Institute, 1988.

———. *Man, Economy, and State: A Treatise on Economic Principles*. Auburn, AL: Ludwig von Mises Institute, 2004.

Rousseau, Richard W. *Human Dignity and the Common Good: The Great Papal Social Encyclicals from Leo XIII to John Paul II*. Westport, CT: Greenwood, 2002.

Sacks, Jonathan. *The Dignity of Difference: How to Avoid the Clash of Civilizations*. London: Continuum, 2002.

Salter, Malcolm S. *Innovation Corrupted: The Origins and Legacy of Enron's Collapse*. Cambridge, MA: Harvard University Press, 2008.

Samuelson, Paul. *Foundations of Economic Analysis*. Enlarged ed. Cambridge, MA: Harvard University Press, 1983.

Sandelin, Bo, et al. *A Short History of Economic Thought*. 2nd ed. London: Routledge, 2008.

Sandoz, Ellis. *The Voegelinian Revolution: A Biographical Introduction*. New Brunswick, NJ: Transaction Publishers, 2000.

Schall, James V. *Jacques Maritain: The Philosopher in Society*. Lanham, MD: Rowan & Littlefield, 1998.

Schindler, David L., ed. *Hans Urs von Balthasar: His Life and Work*. San Francisco: Ignatius, 1991.

Schlitt, Dale M. *Hegel's Trinitarian Claim: A Critical Reflection*. Albany: State University of New York Press, 2012.

Schroeder, Alice. *The Snowball: Warren Buffett and the Business of Life*. London: Bloomsbury, 2008.

Schumpeter, Joseph A. *Business Cycles: A Theoretical, Historical, and Statistical Analysis of the Capitalist Process.* 2 vols. New York: McGraw-Hill, 2005.

———. *Capitalism, Socialism and Democracy.* New York: Harper & Row, 1976.

———. *The Economics and Sociology of Capitalism.* Edited by Richard Swedberg. Princeton: Princeton University Press, 1991.

———. *Essays on Entrepreneurs, Innovators, Business Cycles and the Evolution of Capitalism.* Edited by R. V. Clemence. New Brunswick, NJ: Transaction Publishers, 2006.

———. *History of Economic Analysis.* Edited by Elizabeth Booty Schumpeter. Oxford: Oxford University Press, 1994.

———. *Ten Great Economists: From Marx to Keynes.* New York: Oxford University Press, 1951.

———. *The Theory of Economic Development: An Inquiry into Profits, Capital, Credit, Interest, and the Business Cycle.* Translated by Redvers Opie. New Brunswick, NJ: Transaction Publishers, 2005.

Schutz, Alfred. *Collected Papers.* Vol. 1, *The Problem of Social Reality.* Edited by Maurice Natanson. The Hague: M. Nijhoff, 1964.

———. *On Phenomenology and Social Relations : Selected Writings.* Edited by Helmut R. Wagner. Chicago: University of Chicago Press, 1970.

———. *Phenomenology of the Social World.* Evanston: Northwestern University Press, 1967.

Screpanti, Ernesto, and Stefano Zamagni. *An Outline of the History of Economic Thought.* Translated by David Field and Lynn Kirby. 2nd ed. Oxford: Clarendon, 2004.

Shionoya, Yuichi. *Schumpeter and the Idea of Social Science: A Metatheoretical Study.* 2nd ed. Cambridge: Cambridge University Press, 1997.

Sirico, Robert A. *Defending the Free Market: The Moral Case for a Free Economy.* Washington, DC: Regnery, 2012.

Skidelsky, Robert. *John Maynard Keynes.* 3 vols. New York: Viking, 1986–2000.

———. *John Maynard Keynes, 1883–1946: Economist, Philosopher, Statesman.* London: Pan, 2003.

———. *Keynes: The Return of the Master.* London: Penguin, 2009.

———. "Winning a Gamble with Communism." *New York Review of Books*, May 31, 2007, 9, 31. http://www.nybooks.com/articles/archives/2007/may/31/winning-a-gamble-with-communism/.

Smart, William. *An Introduction to the Theory of Value: On the Lines of Menger, Wieser, and Böhm-Bawerk.* Auburn, AL: Ludwig von Mises Institute, 2007.

Smith, Adam. *The Theory of Moral Sentiments.* Edited by D. D. Raphael and A. L. Macfie. Indianapolis: Liberty Fund, 1982.

———. *Wealth of Nations.* Edited by Kathryn Sutherland. New York: Oxford University Press, 1998.

Smith, Barry. *Austrian Philosophy: The Legacy of Franz Brentano.* Chicago: Open Court, 1996.

Snyder, Timothy. *Bloodlands: Europe between Hitler and Stalin.* New York: Basic Books, 2013.

———. "Holocaust: The Ignored Reality." *New York Review of Books*, July 16, 2009. http://www.nybooks.com/articles/archives/2009/jul/16/holocaust-the-ignored-reality/?pagination=false.

Solzhenitsyn, Aleksandr. *Communism: A Legacy of Terror*. Flesherton, ON: Canadian League of Rights, 1976.

———. *From Under the Rubble*. Translated by A. M. Brock et al. London: Collins & Harvill, 1975.

———. *The Gulag Archipelago*. Translated by Thomas P. Whitney. London: Collins, 1974.

———. "Live Not by Lies." In *The Solzhenitsyn Reader: New and Essential Writings, 1947–2005*, edited by Edward E. Ericson Jr. and Daniel J. Mahoney, 556–60. Wilmington: ISI, 2006.

———. *The Nobel Lecture on Literature*. Translated by Thomas P. Whitney. New York: Harper & Row, 1972.

———. *The Solzhenitsyn Reader: New and Essential Writings, 1947–2005*. Edited by Edward E. Ericson Jr. and Daniel J. Mahoney. Wilmington: ISI, 2012.

Sophocles. *Antigone*. Translated by Elizabeth Wyckoff. In *Greek Tragedies I*. Edited by David Grene and Richmond Lattimore. Third edition edited by Mark Griffith and Glenn W. Most. Chicago: University of Chicago Press, 2013.

———. *The Theban Plays: King Oedipus; Oedipus at Colonus; Antigone*. Translated by E. F. Watling. London: Penguin, 1974.

Sorkin, Andrew Ross. *Too Big to Fail: Inside the Battle to Save Wall Street*. London: Penguin, 2009.

Soto, Hernando de. *The Mystery of Capital: Why Capitalism Triumphs in the West and Fails Everywhere Else*. New York: Basic Books, 2003.

Soto, Jesús Huerta de. *The Austrian School: Market Order and Entrepreneurial Creativity*. Cheltenham, UK: Edward Elgar, 2008.

Spiegel, Henry William. *The Growth of Economic Thought*. Durham: Duke University Press, 2004.

Sternberg, Elaine. *Just Business: Business Ethics in Action*. 2nd ed. Oxford: Oxford University Press, 2000.

Stiglitz, Joseph E. "Another Century of Economic Science." *The Economic Journal* 101 (1991) 134–41.

———. *Freefall: Free Markets and the Sinking of the Global Economy*. London: Penguin, 2010.

———. *Globalization and Its Discontents*. New York: Norton, 2002.

Tawney, R. H. *Religion and the Rise of Capitalism: A Historical Study*. Gloucester, MA: Peter Smith, 1962.

Tedeschi, Ettore Gotti. "John Paul II as Economist." *Wall Street Journal*, June 8, 2005. http://www.wsj.com/articles/SB111817680524053260.

Tett, Gillian. *Fool's Gold: The Inside Story of J. P. Morgan and How Wall Street Greed Corrupted Its Bold Dream and Created a Financial Catastrophe*. New York: Simon & Schuster, 2009.

Tismaneanu, Vladimir. *The Devil in History: Communism, Fascism, and Some Lessons of the Twentieth Century*. Berkeley: University of California Press, 2012.

Tocqueville, Alexis de. *Democracy in America; and Two Essays on America*. Translated by Gerald E. Bevan. London: Penguin, 2003.

———. *Memoir on Pauperism*. Translated by Seymour Drescher. Chicago: Ivan R. Dee, 1997.

Tomasi, John. *Free Market Fairness*. Princeton: Princeton University Press, 2013.

Tsoulfidis, Lefteris. *Competing Schools of Economic Thought*. Heidelberg: Springer, 2010.

Uhlaner, Carole Jean. "'Relational Goods' and Participation: Incorporating Sociability into a Theory of Rational Action." *Public Choice* 62 (1989) 253–85.

Vaggi, Gianni, and Peter Groenewegen. *A Concise History of Economic Thought: From Mercantilism to Monetarism*. New York: Palgrave Macmillan, 2006.

Vaughn, Karen I. *Austrian Economics in America*. Cambridge: Cambridge University Press, 1994.

Veatch, Henry B. *Rational Man: A Modern Interpretation of Aristotelian Ethics*. Bloomington: Indiana University Press, 1970.

―――. *Swimming Against the Current in Contemporary Philosophy: Occasional Essays and Papers*. Studies in Philosophy and the History of Philosophy 20. Washington, DC: Catholic University of America Press, 1990.

Voegelin, Eric. *Anamnesis: On the Theory of History and Politics*. Translated by M. J. Hanak. Edited by David Walsh. Collected Works of Eric Voegelin 6. Columbia: University of Missouri Press, 2002.

―――. *Autobiographical Reflections*. Edited by Ellis Sandoz. Baton Rouge: Louisiana State University Press, 1989.

―――. "Democracy and Industrial Society." In *Published Essays, 1953–1965*, edited by Ellis Sandoz, 207–23. Collected Works of Eric Voegelin 11. Columbia: University of Missouri Press, 2000.

―――. *The Drama of Humanity and Other Miscellaneous Papers, 1939–1985*. Edited by William Petropulos and Gilbert Weiss. Collected Works of Eric Voegelin 33. Columbia: University of Missouri Press, 2004.

―――. *The Ecumenic Age*. Order and History 4. Baton Rouge: Louisiana State University Press, 1974.

―――. *History of Political Ideas*. Vol. 8, *Crisis and the Apocalypse of Man*. Edited by David Walsh. Collected Works of Eric Voegelin 26. Columbia: University of Missouri Press, 1999.

―――. *Israel and Revelation*. Order and History 1. Baton Rouge: Louisiana State University Press, 1956.

―――. "Man in Society and History." In *Published Essays, 1953–1965*, edited by Ellis Sandoz, 191–206. Collected Works of Eric Voegelin 11. Columbia: University of Missouri Press, 2000.

―――. *The New Science of Politics*. In *Modernity Without Restraint*, edited by Manfred Henningsen, 75–241. Collected Works of Eric Voegelin 5. Columbia: University of Missouri Press, 2000.

―――. *Plato and Aristotle*. Order and History 3. Baton Rouge: Louisiana State University Press, 1957.

―――. *Published Essays, 1966–1985*. Edited by Ellis Sandoz. Collected Works of Eric Voegelin 12. Baton Rouge: Louisiana State University, 1990.

―――. *Science, Politics and Gnosticism*. In *Modernity Without Restraint*, edited by Manfred Henningsen, 251–313. Collected Works of Eric Voegelin 5. Columbia: University of Missouri Press, 2000.

―――. *What Is History? And Other Late Unpublished Writings*. Edited by Thomas A. Hollweck and Paul Caringella. Baton Rouge: Louisiana State University Press, 1990.

―――. *The World of the Polis*. Order and History 2. Baton Rouge: Louisiana State University Press, 1957.

Wallich, Henry. *The Cost of Freedom: A New Look at Capitalism*. New York: Harper, 1960.

Walsh, David. *After Ideology: Recovering the Spiritual Foundations of Freedom*. 1st ed. San Francisco: Harper & Row, 1990.

———. *The Growth of the Liberal Soul*. Columbia: University of Missouri Press, 1997.

———. *Guarded by Mystery: Meaning in a Postmodern Age*. Washington, DC: Catholic University of America Press, 1999.

———. *The Modern Philosophical Revolution: The Luminosity of Existence*. New York: Cambridge University Press, 2008.

———. "The Person as the Heart of Benedict's New Evangelization." Unpublished essay, 2013.

———. "Persons as Beyond Good and Evil." Unpublished essay, 2010, for future publication.

———. *Politics of the Person as the Politics of Being*. Notre Dame: University of Notre Dame Press, 2015.

———. "Theory and Practice as Responsibility." *Perspectives on Political Science* 42 (2013) 47–50.

Weber, Max. *The Protestant Ethic and the Spirit of Capitalism*. Translated and introduced by Stephen Kalberg. New York: Oxford University Press, 2010.

Weil, Simone. *Gravity and Grace*. Translated by Emma Craufurd. London: Routledge, 1987.

———. *La condizione operaia*. Milan: Mondadori, 1994.

———. *Oppression and Liberty*. Translated by Arthur Wills and John Petrie. New York: Ark, 1988.

White, Lawrence H. *The Clash of Economic Ideas: The Great Policy Debates and Experiments of the Last Hundred Years*. New York: Cambridge University Press, 2012.

White, Mark D. *Accepting the Invisible Hand: Market-Based Approaches to Social Economic Problems*. New York: Palgrave Macmillan, 2010.

Whitehead, Alfred North. *Introduction to Mathematics*. New York: Oxford University Press, 1958.

Wicksteed, Philip H. *The Common Sense of Political Economy, and Selected Papers and Reviews on Economic Theory*. Edited by Lionel Robbins. Vol. 1. London: Routledge, 2003.

Wittgenstein, Ludwig. *Tractatus Logico-Philosophicus*. Translated by D. F. Pears and B. F. McGuiness. London: Routledge & Keegan Paul, 2014.

Wojtyła, Karol. *The Acting Person*. Translated by Andrzej Potocki. Dordrecht: Reidel, 1979.

———. *Person and Community: Selected Essays*. Translated by Theresa Sandok. New York: Peter Lang, 1993.

Woodham-Smith, Cecil. *The Great Hunger: Ireland, 1845–1849*. New York: Harper & Row, 1962.

Woods, Thomas, E., Jr. *Meltdown: A Free-Market Look at Why the Stock Market Collapsed, the Economy Tanked, and Government Bailouts Will Make Things Worse*. Washington, DC: Regnery, 2009.

Yeats, W. B. *The Poems*. London: Everyman's Library, 1990.

Zamagni, Stefano. *L'economia del bene commune*. Rome: Città Nuova, 2007.

Zięba, Maciej. *Papal Economics: The Catholic Church on Democratic Capitalism, from Rerum Novarum to Caritas in Veritate.* Wilmington: ISI, 2013.

Zmirak, John. *Wilhelm Röpke: Swiss Localist, Global Economist.* Wilmington: ISI, 2001.

Zsolnai, László, and Wojciech W. Gasparski, eds. *Ethics and the Future of Capitalism.* Praxiology 9. New Brunswick, NJ: Transaction Publishers, 2002.

Index

ability, success achieved by, 235
abstractions, Keynes thinking in,
   182
accountability, lack of, 165
accounting
   adequacy of ,methods, 122n119
   need for, 123
acting, as selecting behavior, 220
acting man
   characteristics of, 250
   concerned both with "material"
     and "ideal" things, 261n85
   described, 237
   eager to substitute a more
     satisfactory state of affairs,
     272
   economic investigation dealing
     with, 238
acting person, 18, 19
   in economic action, 42
   "enlargement" of understanding
     of, 9
   functioning as "the
     entrepreneur," 112
   ontological absurdity of, 283
   qualities and capacities
     constitutive of, 252
   in the reality of the free market
     process, 255
   toward a more comprehensive
     vision of, 210–17
   transcendent and mysterious
     reality of, 294
   Trinitarian model illuminating,
     278
   truth of the reality of, 267
   within the economic horizon, 26

within the free market process,
   13
action. *See also* economic action;
   entrepreneurial action;
   human action(s); human
   economic action
   concept of wider, 220
   embedded in the flux of time,
     239
   as a full concrete activity of the
     self, 171
   grasping the meaning of, 273
   involving both taking and
     renunciation, 151n99, 250
   as purposive conduct, 164
"activistic basis," 164
actors
   in the economic drama, 132
   in the economic process, 222
   personality or individuality of,
     171
"acts of exchange," 261
"acts of man" (*actus hominis*), 249
"*actus personae*," 230
Aeschylus, 53, 53n113
"Age of High Imperialism," 1870-
   1914, 150n96
agents, activities of different kinds
   of, 146
aggregates, 48, 181, 182
"aggregative" economics, 182
Agnes. *See* Morrogh-Bernard, Agnes
alertness, 205
   of the entrepreneur, 211, 214,
     215, 260
alienation, 69–71
Allen, Paul, 213, 252

317

describing entrepreneurial
action, 201
engendering crises, 96
fundamentals of, 134
needing to expand as rapidly as
possible, 70
as "organized or state-regulated
capitalism," 50
"patrimonial, 3
power to create productive
capacity, 118
"sore thumb" of, 40
Capitalism (Reisman), 97
*Capitalism, Socialism and
Democracy* (Schumpeter),
118
Capitalism: A Treatise on Economics
(Reisman), 106
"Capitalismo e Impresa" (Capitalism
and Enterprise), 291
capitalist finance, 134
"The Capitalist Is in the Dock"
(Chesterton), 34
capitalist production, 119
capitalist system, technical advance
and continual innovation
as the central driving force
of, 196
Carey, Henry C., 118
Caring about Meaning (Lonergan),
39
Carney, Mark, 34–35
"catallactis," 261n85
"the category of gift or sharing," in
businesses, 279
"category of relation," 282, 290
Catholic-Thomistic pattern of
thought, 110
causes or fashions, identified by
Aristotelian method, 167
Centesimus Annus Foundation, 14,
14n43
Centesimus Annus (John Paul II),
14n43
central banking, requiring creativity,
192
central banks, 184, 184n95

central planning, inevitable failure
of, 192
centralism, rigid machinery of, 201
centrality of "trust," 98
centralized knowledge, limitations
of, 194
centrally planned economies, 32,
193
change
central to any economic theory,
127
explaining, 213
not just quantitative in nature,
149
character
failure of, 169
having value, 238
charismatic entrepreneurial
intuition, Agnes Morrogh-
Bernard emerging with, 230
"charismatic entrepreneurial spirit,"
221
Chesterton, G. K., 34
Chicago school of economics, 105
choice, between alternatives, 211
choosing, determines all human
decisions, 195
"Christian Chiliasm," 187
Christianity, rationalist
reinterpretation of, 187
chronic shortage economy, 201
Cicchese, Gennaro, 277
"circular flow," 126, 149, 151n97
City of God, Soviet bloc's efforts to
create, 31
civil society, composed of "real
communities of persons,"
270
class struggle, 135
classical economists
term invented by Marx, 113n74
on the theme of actors in the
economic process, 138–39
classical liberals, 5
classical socialist economy, 202, 204
classical theorists
actual "vision" or model of, 116

classical theorists (*continued*)
  general theory not "general" at
    all, 113
classical theory, postulates of, 114
Coda, Piero, 276, 289
cognitive frameworks, stepping
  outside existing, 203
cognitive function, of meaning,
  67–68
Colander, David, 11, 102n23
"collaborative creativity," xvi, xvii
Collectivist Economic Planning
  (Hayek), 263
A Colossal Failure of Common Sense
  (McDonald), 7
combinations, 142
commerce, as a natural opponent of
  all violent passions, 61
common meaning and community,
  75
common meanings, histories of, 78
common sense
  general bias of, 107
  incapable of analyzing itself, 218
  political specialization of, 176
  retreat of economics from the
    philosophy of, 29
*The Common Sense of Political
  Economy* (Wicksteed), 256,
  258
"common-sense" approach, to
  economic activity, 38
communicative role, of meaning, 78
Communism
  collapse of, 30, 55
  experience of, 12
  failure of, 229
  Kornai's faith in shaken, 194
communist "collectivism,"
  Mises's and the Austrian
    economists' critique of, 186
The Communist Manifesto (Marx
  and Engels), 120
"community," 78
community of being, primordial,
  164
"compact" accounts of reality, 139
"compactness," 139, 143

Compagnia delle Opere, 279n37
*Compassionate Conservatism:
  What It Is, Why We Need It*
  (Norman and Ganesh), 27
competition, 17, 201
Competition and Entrepreneurship
  (Kirzner), 205
competitive model, 77
"comprehensive reality," accounting
  for, 139
computer models, trading strategies
  created by, 163n4
Comte, Auguste, 187n104
"concrete individuality," of data, 246
Congested Districts Board, works
  of, 228
"conscious dishonesty," 115
consciousness, 211n95–12n95
The Constitution of Liberty (Hayek),
  26, 190–91
constitutive meaning, 71–78
consumers
  as entrepreneurs, 116n87, 132
  not choosing to save, 185
"content," of human value that is
  objective, 268
contentual sense, "happiness"
  considered in, 267
"contractions," 100
conversion, in the subject, 173
co-operative system members, 234
Copernicus, Nicolaus, 76, 80
"corporate governance," 33
"corporate social responsibility," 33
corruption, 100n17
*The Counter Revolution of Science:
  Studies on the Abuse of
  Reason* (Hayek), 25
"countercyclical ameliorative
  proposals," 120
Cournot, Augustin, 80
The Course of Recognition (Ricoeur),
  240
creation, activity of versus
  Kirznerian, 216
"creative collaboration," between
  scholars and practitioners,
  200

economic order (*continued*)
  of the free market, 177
  fundamental issues regarding,
    88
  of great importance, 92
  of the market economy, 178
  meaning of, 80
  philosophy of, 57–58, 60
economic "ordering," going beyond
    the local or domestic
    horizon, 81
economic paradigm or system, as
    critical, 28
"economic personalism," need for,
    15n46
economic planning, mass murder
    integrated with, 31
economic policy, undisclosed
    preferences in every
    proposal of, 84
economic process, adequacy and
    legitimacy of a particular, 60
economic progress, as a
    consequence of the "I act,"
    173
economic rationality, Morrogh-
    Bernard's concept of, 236
economic reality, context of the
    eclipse of, 104–12
economic recessions, 16
economic reflection
  after the Industrial Revolution,
    245
  Austrian approach to, 14
  missing link in, 224
economic relation, 261, 262
"economic relationship," 256
"economic slum," not seeing the
    "human person," 79
economic structures, grounding
    upon a philosophy of the
    human person, 49
economic system
  being representative of a "good
    of order," 86
  built upon anthropological
    principles, 36
  as a set of interrelations, 129–30

structuring incentives to
    mobilize knowledge, 264
economic textbooks
  "axial questions" not reflected
    on, 63
  some taking up Schumpeterian
    themes, 127
economic theorists, rarely referring
    to their anthropological
    model, 217
economic theory
  "anthropological lag" in, 181
  "embedded" into the
    philosophical and social
    fabric of a civilization, 49
  of innovation, 217
  "inward turn" of, 76
  measuring, 281
  never neutral from the
    anthropological perspective,
    xvi
  outside shell of a particular, 24
  presupposing a concept of the
    human person, 293
  presupposing an understanding
    of the human person, 242
  remapping of, 278
  returning to its roots, 80
  tendency of "occlusion" in, 106
economic thinking, based upon a
    philosophical anthropology,
    25
economic thought, schools of, 11
economic "vision"
  clarifying, 23–30
  importance of, 113
The Economic Way of Thinking, 151
economics
  as about men, 237–38
  "atomized" as a science, 254
  based upon a philosophical
    perspective, 208
  dealing with all human action,
    218
  dealing with society's
    fundamental problems, 64
  definition of, 206
  as democratic, 29

financial regulation, increased
suggested, 165
financier, role of, 36
Finlay, Thomas, 226, 233–34,
234n63, 238
Fisher, Irving, 71–72, 120, 120n108
"flash of self-transcendence," 230,
285
"flash of transcendence," 236, 242
flight from understanding, 28, 65
"flourishing," Aristotelian concept
of, 18–19
flux, humans experiencing a world
of, 63–64
Focolare Movement, 239n95, 278
Fool's Gold (Tett), 7
For a New Political Economy
(Lonergan), 40
For an Ontology of Morals (Veatch),
268
formal cause, 167
Fortini, Franco, 69
foundations, of the free market
economy, 134
Foxford, gathering waters from a
wide area, 227
*Foxford and the Providence Woolen
Mills* (Finley), 235
Foxford industry, as the story of a
prolonged struggle against
adverse conditions, 235
Foxford Woolen Mills and Visitor
Centre, 232n57
Foxford Woolen Mills
entrepreneurial project, 220,
247
confidential report on, 232–33
fractured relationship, between Wall
Street and Main Street, 97,
121
Frageverbot or restriction, 208
fragility, of the human person in
the free economy process,
185–92
fragmentation, of reality within
economics, 121
Francis (Pope), 6–7, 14, 241, 242,
277–78, 285, 293n101, 295

Francis of Assisi (Saint), 278
Franciscan movement, laid the
groundwork for a market
economy, 230
free economy
applying a philosopher's
understanding to, 11
based on the good of order, 62
based upon fundamental
anthropological principles,
132
as being a catalyst, 159–60
excision of the anthropological
reality presupposed by, 47
fragility of, 186
having a "human face," 223
as the human person "written
large," 177
as a human process of continual
discovery, 121–22
legitimacy of, 60
as person-centered, 61–62
person-centered roots of, 286
pertaining to an "order," 84
philosophical basis of, 26
philosophical understanding at
the kernel of, 61
as "polycentric" in nature, 205
presupposing actions of many
individual human purposive
agents, 263
as a "process" rather than a
"mechanism," 40
recapturing the creative human
perspective of, 122
retrieval of the human meaning
of, 64
seeking to adapt economic
principles to the human
person, 94
"sore thumb" of, 40
free exchange, 84
free market
central agents of, 96
compatible with the principle of
human creativity, 160
economic distortions, 47

intelligence
  human action full of, 276
  intervention of, 27, 176
  as irrelevant to practical living,
    65
intelligibility, pertaining to
    economic events, 176
intent to deceive, trumping
    compliance with arcane legal
    rules, 170
"intentionality"
  attention given to, 254
  derived from the Scholastic
    philosophers, 156n123
  described, 199n38
  reducing our understanding of,
    251
  theory of, 199
"interdependent" dimension, of
    human reality, 210
interest, theory of, 71
Interest and Prices (Wicksell), 72
interpersonal dimension, inherent
    to economic action, 281
"intersubjectivity"
  applying the perspective of
    economics, 282
  participating in the reality of,
    271
  renewed revival of, 289
  rethinking of, 277
"interventionism," 186, 187
intransitive human action, 74–75
"intrinsicality," 285, 293
Introduction to the Theory of Value
    (Smart), 257n60
"introversion," 107
investigation, in social science, 162
*Investigations into the Method of the
    Social Sciences* (Menger), 42
investors, 166
"invisible hand," 77, 208
"the invisible hand of the market,"
    replacing with one guided by
    the government, 263
Irish Agricultural Co-operative
    Movement, 233
Irish famine

literature on, 225n21
  ravages of, 224–25
  as supply and demand, 41
Irish Sisters of Charity, 221, 226
*Iron Curtain: The Crushing of
    Eastern Europe, 1944-1956*
    (Applebaum), 31
irreducible "anthropological
    projection," 265

Jacobite rebellion of 1745, 109
Jacobitism, 109n53
Jaspers, Karl, 63
Jevons, William Stanley, 245
John Paul II: Poet and Philosopher
    (McNerney), 66
John Paul II (Saint), 14n43, 229, 241
Jouvenel, Bertrand de, 91
judgment, along with "creativity," 22
The Just (Ricoeur), 239–40
*Just Business: Business Ethics in
    Action* (Sternberg), 269, 287
"Just the Person" framework, 287

Kant, 208, 276
*Karl Marx and the Close of His
    System* (Böhm-Bawerk), 196
Kay, John, 61, 88, 185
Kellaway, Lucy, 172n38
Kelly, Kel, 99
Kelsen, Hans, 103
Keynes, John Maynard, 15–16, 27,
    77, 113
  on classical economists, 117
  on the contribution of
    Scholasticism to economics,
    106
  literature on, 113n71
  perspective of the "aggregate,"
    182
  point of view of, 114
  Röpke's criticism of, 48, 131
  Schumpeter critical of, 120
"Keynesian consensus," unraveling
    of, 76
"Keynesian" school of economic
    thought, 15

not the sole motivation for most
people, 36
money economy, based on precious
metals, 81
monopoly position, 142
moral status of an act, 170
morality, based on reciprocity, 209
Moran, Dermot, 258n67
Morgenstern, Oskar, 175
Morris, Tom, 268
Morrogh-Bernard, Agnes, 20, 220,
221, 247, 284–85
as charismatic entrepreneur of
the human person, 231–43
charismatic entrepreneurial
intuition of, 230
described as unbolting the
prison, 233
distinctive approach in the face
of frightful poverty, 242
early years, 224
entered the Irish Sisters of
Charity, 226
entrepreneurial "creativity" of,
236
established a Woolen Mills at
Foxford, 228
realization of "human
capacities," 240
as a "social entrepreneur,"
236n79
unfolded and recaptured the
truth of the "creative" reality
of the human person, 243
mortality, motivating prosperity
by, 31
mother, as a person, not an
individual, 262
mother model, 262
"mother" of a family household, as
the economic agent, 257
mother's actions
mirroring the actions of others, 261
paradigm of, 280
motivation, for human actions, 156
motivational considerations, of the
economic act, 152–55
motivations, of agents, 265

Mounier, Emmanuel, 283
movement, from compactness to
differentiation, 82
Moy, utilizing the forces of, 228
Mueller, John, 261–62
"'multi-causal' methodology," 167
multidimensional nature, of human
reality, 56
"multidimensional" reality,
economic activity as, 265
multidisciplinary approach, need
for, 2
multidisciplinary collaboration, 200
Münchau, Wolfgang, 22
Mundell, John, 291
Murrell, Peter, 203n57
myself, losing something of, 284
Myserson, Roger, 263n93
mystery
applied to the acting person, 251
of the person, 295
*The Mystery of Capital: Why
Capitalism Triumphs in the
West and Fails Everywhere
Else* (Soto), 93–94

National Socialism in Europe,
experience of, 70
natural sciences
methods of, 145
studying certain areas of human
life, 248
*The Nature of Socialist Economies:
Lessons from Eastern
European Foreign Trade*
(Murrell), 203n57
Neal, Larry, 82
Neapolitan school of economics,
98–99
*Negation and the Trinity: A
Hypothesis Concerning Hegel*
(Coda), 277
neoclassical economics, as "one-
dimensional," 77
neoclassical economists,
Schumpeter on, 125–26
neoclassical theorists, 126n131

348   INDEX

value (*continued*)
  measurement of, 53
  of money, xv
  as "objective," 267
  Smith's theory of, 108
  "subjective" theory of, 42
  of "value," xvi
value co-creation, 273
value judgments, of individuals, 179
Vaughn, Karen, 251
Veatch, Henry, 268
Veenhoven, Ruut, 73
venture capital, form of investment
  of, 201–2
Verdross, Alfred von, 103
vertical dimension(command), 127
via negativa investigation, 214
viewpoints
  meaning of, 273
  need of successive higher, 9
virtues, among economic
  participants, 293
vision
  questioning in any economic
    analysis, 115
  Schumpeter on, 113
  of a theorist, 114
  within economic thought, 27
"vision" and "praxis," dichotomy
  between, 113
Voegelin, Eric, 16n54, 24n4, 57, 103
  on anamnesis, 140n48
  borrowed the symbol of
    Apperzeptionsverweigerung,
    166
  characterized human existence
    in terms of "participation,"
    164
  on compactness and
    differentiation, 82, 139n45
  on consciousness, 211n95
  contemporary with Mises, 175
  on dangers of "disease of
    contraction," 100
  on "different objects requiring
    different methods," 214

  distinction between
    "compactness" and
    "differentiation," 139
  on "eclipse of reality," 156
  elements constitutive of the
    meaning of science, 253
  on entrepreneurs, 97, 99
  on *Frageverbot* or restriction,
    208, 208n82
  on Gnostic attitude, 188
  on Gnosticism, 187
  on the good or bad nature of
    institutions, 91–92
  immigration visa for, 103
  on the meaning of theory, 198
  on new differentiation, 82–83
  on "participation," 164
  on Plato's parable of the cave,
    233n60
  on Plato's phrase "that a polis is
    man written large," 177
  on problem of deformation
    within reality, 136
  on science, 207
  useful reflection about science,
    144
"volitional beings," 170
von Hermann, Friedrich, 292
von Thünen, Heinrich, 292

Walker, William J. D., 232–33, 238
Wall Street: Money Never Sleeps,
  166n14
Wallich, Henry, 84
Walras, Léon, 126, 197, 245
Walrasian, Schumpeter regarded
  himself as, 126
Walrasian equiribrium model, 197
Walsh, David, 18n61, 21, 208,
  208n82, 222–23, 222n8, 229,
  239, 241, 285, 288
wealth
  of human persons, 19
  important for anthropological
    reasons, 5
  ultimate cause of, 18